# PALESTINE AND ISRAEL
# IN THE 19th AND 20th CENTURIES

# PALESTINE AND ISRAEL IN THE 19th AND 20th CENTURIES

Edited by
**ELIE KEDOURIE**
and
**SYLVIA G. HAIM**

**FRANK CASS**

*First published 1982 in Great Britain by*
FRANK CASS AND COMPANY LIMITED
Gainsborough House, Gainsborough Road,
London, E11 1RS, England

*and in the United States of America by*
FRANK CASS AND COMPANY LIMITED
c/o Biblio Distribution Centre
81 Adams Drive, P.O. Box 327, Totowa, N.J. 07511

ISBN 0 7146 3121 3

Printed in Great Britain by
Bourne Press Limited, 3-11 Spring Road, Bournemouth

# Contents

FOREWORD   vii

EUROPEAN JEWS IN MUSLIM PALESTINE   **Emile Marmorstein**   1

THE ZIONIST ATTITUDES TO THE ARABS 1908–1914   **Yaacov Ro'i**   15

THE BALFOUR DECLARATION AND ITS MAKERS   **Mayir Vereté**   60

NAZI GERMANY AND THE PALESTINE QUESTION   **R. Melka**   89

THE THIRD REICH AND PALESTINE   **David Yisraeli**   103

THE 'STERN GANG' 1940–1948   **Y. S. Brenner**   114

ARAB IMMIGRATION INTO PRE-STATE ISRAEL   **Fred M. Gottheil**   143

CROP-SHARING ECONOMICS IN MANDATORY PALESTINE   **Ya'akov Firestone**   153

CHANGES IN THE SETTLEMENT PATTERN OF JUDEA AND SAMARIA DURING JORDANIAN RULE   **Elisha Efrat**   195

RASHID HUSAIN: PORTRAIT OF AN ANGRY YOUNG ARAB   **Emile Marmorstein**   211

INTELLECTUALS IN ISRAELI DRUZE SOCIETY   **Gabriel Ben-Dor**   229

THE POLITICAL STATUS OF JERUSALEM IN THE HASHEMITE KINGDOM OF JORDAN 1948–1967   **Naim Sofer**   255

# Foreword

*Middle Eastern Studies* first appeared in 1964. The brief Editorial Note prefixed to the first number declared that the purpose of the Journal was the promotion of the study of the Middle East and North Africa since the end of the eighteenth century, and that it aimed to take within its ambit the political, economic, religious and legal history of the area, its literature, social geography, sociology and anthropology. That the Journal, now in its fourteenth volume, has been able to conform to this programme is due to its contributors who, over the years, have kept it supplied with a constant and abundant flow of articles on the various subjects here enumerated.

This selection of articles on Palestine and Israel in the nineteenth and twentieth centuries, drawn from its first thirteen volumes, illustrates the great variety of subjects which authors have thought worth investigating, and the diversity of approaches which they have adopted. This book also shows that an appreciable part of the Journal, in terms simply of volume, has been devoted throughout to Palestine and Israel. In retrospect, it seems indeed as though the first article in the first number of the first volume served to prefigure things to come. This article—reprinted in the present volume—was Emile Marmorstein's examination of the work of a young Arab Israeli writer, Rāshid Husain.

The pair of articles with which the book begins, Emile Marmorstein's 'European Jews in Muslim Palestine' and Yaacor Ro'i's 'Zionist Attitude to the Arabs 1908–1914' are both concerned with the first reactions of Jewish immigrants to Muslim Arab society in the midst of which they found themselves, and to the political conditions of a province in an Ottoman Empire shaken from its traditional moorings by administrative and legal 'reform', by a military coup d'état, and by the political agitations to which the abrupt disappearance of Hamidian autocracy opened the door.

The three articles which conclude the volume—Marmorstein's discussion of Rāshid Husayn, Gabriel Ben Dor's examination of the state of mind of Druze 'intellectuals' under Israeli rule and Naim Sofer's account of East Jerusalem under Jordanian rule—are, in a sense, the other side of the coin. They deal with some of the myriad effects and reactions within indigenous society which were the consequence of the Zionist-Arab conflict and the establishment of Israel.

Another group of four studies revolves around the history of Zionism and Palestine during the British connexion. These are Mayer Vereté's detailed scrutiny of the Balfour Declaration and its makers, Y. S, Brenner's account of the 'Stern Gang' in the last years of the Mandate, and the pair of studies by the late R. Melka and by David Yisraeli on National Socialist policies and attitudes towards Zionism and the Jewish settlement in Palestine.

The last group of studies included in this book concerns social and economic history. Perhaps by reason of their difficulty and of the paucity of material these subjects seem to attract fewer scholars than other topics, and the Editors of *Middle Eastern Studies* have tried to look out for and encourage the submission of articles on them. Of the many studies concerned with these subjects which over the years have appeared in the Journal, the Editors reprint here three which, it is hoped, will throw some light respectively on the historical demography of Palestine (by Fred. M. Gottlieb), on the economics of Arab agriculture (by Ya'akov Firestone), and on the pattern of settlement in the West Bank under Jordanian rule (by Elisha Efrat).

E.K.
S.G.H.

# European Jews in Muslim Palestine

## Emile Marmorstein

Since this study was prompted by reading three books in one another's company, I had better begin by introducing them and their authors. They all help, albeit indirectly, to show how the experience of living in the Holy Land during the last hundred years of Muslim rule impinged upon the minds of European Jews. *

A. R. Malachi (Engelsman) was born in Jerusalem of Eastern European parents in 1895, emigrated to New York shortly before the outbreak of the First World War and has been writing for Hebrew and Judaeo-German periodicals ever since. His native community provided him with a theme and a mission: well before the prosperity of a few of its sons turned their forbears' adventures into a minor academic industry, he was exhuming the literary relics of its factions and feuds. He became its champion, rebutting charges of mendicancy and sloth with evidence of the 'productive' aspirations of its worldlier members and their preparatory role in the process of Zionist colonization—a propaganda line started at about the time of his birth, Nevertheless, the fact that what his community professed, and was subsidized, to 'produce' was an accumulation of merit before the Throne of Glory emerges openly from his accounts of its experiences.

On the other hand, the late Galiyah Yardeni, who was responsible for this useful selection from Malachi's numerous and dispersed articles and used them extensively for background information in her own book, evidently regarded all Jewish settlement in the Holy Land as a forerunner of the Zionist state—such, at least, is the inference that makes her allocation of praise and blame so monotonously predictable. Somehow, perhaps owing to her prim approach to their frequent and intense quarrels, she brings out the worst in her picturesque characters. Naftali Herz Imber, for instance, who had published a Hebrew dirge in lament for Baron Edmond de Rothschild's mother, accused Eliezer Ben-Judah (Perlman) of palming-off his French rendering as the original and then pocketing the bereaved son's reward; and Ben-Judah replied with a denunciation of Imber's vulnerable character—he was the alcoholic of the group, which also included a morphine-addict (p. 197). Not that they were all rogues: many of Jerusalem's early journalists led austere and honourable lives, and the consistency with which defenders of the communal leadership upheld principles unpopular with the wealthiest of potential patrons points to a certain degree of courage on the part of a community whose sole economic asset was the Holy Land's appeal to charitable Jews. That appeal was, of course, the basis of Hebrew journalism in Jerusalem: the proprietors of primitive presses, around whom Hebrew journalists were grouped, relied less on their local than on their distant readers—indeed,

*Peraqim Betholedhoth Hayyishuv Hayyashan (Studies in the History of the Old Yishuv) by A. R. Malachi. Tel-Aviv University, 1971. Pp. 412.
Ha'itonuth Ha'ivrith Be'eres Yisra'el 1863-1904 (The Hebrew Press in Palestine 1863-1904) by Galiyah Yardeni. Tel-Aviv University, 1969. Pp. 419 + Catalogue of Hebrew periodicals, annuals, etc.
Pirqe Hayyay (Autobiography and Diaries) by Artur Ruppin. 'Am 'Oved. Tel-Aviv, 1968. Three Volumes. Pp. 238, 314, 393 (a shortened version of this book entitled Memoirs, Diaries and Letters was published by Weidenfeld and Nicolson in 1972).

they descended on them in person from time to time in order to cadge subscriptions and donations; and their slender and irregular periodicals, although inferior to the more substantial journals that were then distributing a Hebrew version of the Enlightenment in Eastern Europe, could attract readers by virtue of their direct news and views of the Holy Land. Some of these entrepreneurs, however, were far from content with the proceeds of their export trade; and in their attempts to take over the institutions, the sources of communal power, they used their papers to discredit the administrators and publicize rival projects originating within their own circles. Allegations that their schemes were solely designed to deflect the flow of alms into their purses, which derive largely from their own attacks on one another, are all too plausible.

Ben-Judah's arrival (1881) sharpened the tone of ideological argument. He was imported by Israel Dov Frumkin to deputize for him during his absence in Europe. It was a curious appointment: here was a staunch Pietist putting his paper in the charge of a writer whom he knew to be sceptical of essential belief and neglectful of compulsory practice. According to Ben-Judah's account, Frumkin accepted his promise to conform on nationalist grounds to Jerusalem's standards, i.e. he would hardly jeopardise his chances of winning over the whole community to the cause by allowing suspicions of his orthodoxy to arise: and, in fact, until he despaired of making headway, he conformed quite convincingly. Perhaps Frumkin, who was then at the peak of his own nationalist phase, did not need much persuasion. At any rate, their collaboration continued amicably for a year or so, with Frumkin, who had put off his European tour, concentrating on local affairs and leaving nationalism to his colleague's ardour. By the middle of the decade, however, each was openly returning to his basic allegiance. Their press war culminated in Ben-Judah pouring out his venom on the communal leadership and Frumkin dramatically acknowledging its foresight, confessing his own past errors and branding the nationalist movement as the enemy of the faith.

An impeccable reputation was by no means all that set Artur Ruppin apart from these communal politicians and their successors. Born and bred in a society in an advanced stage of secularization, he was indifferent both to their rhetoric and to their schemes. His arrival in Jaffa to take charge of the Palestine-Amt was the result of a decision taken at the cost of the more dignified and remunerative career which his legal qualifications and commercial experience should have ensured him. For him it was a matter of destiny: a chain of circumstances had made him available and willing at the very time (1907) when the Zionist Organization turned to 'practical activity' and needed someone fit to conduct it (I, p. 238). Had he not taken this opportunity, 'his life would have missed its mark' (II, p. 42). Accordingly, the rest of his working life was occupied with the development of the Zionist economy and with Jewish demography, his favourite academic pursuit. Within the movement, his prestige may ultimately have rested on his share in promoting organized labour's political and economic hegemony, but it was originally earned by his avowed aloofness from factional ties, his ability to get on with all kinds of useful people and his lucid presentation of facts and figures. He was unique among the Zionists of his generation in that he harmoniously combined the role of the dispassionate administrator of Western legend with that of the committed servant of a fervent nationalist organization.

His diary is a model of discretion: it revealed no secrets and criticized only those, such as Weizman, whom he had rebuked for unwarranted interference in tasks specifically allotted to him. It is one of those diaries kept in order to convince the diarist that he is achieving something of value and still continues a warm-hearted and cultivated human being. Unlike the politicians, he invariably wrote in his native tongue—at least until 'Sonnabend, 19 Juli 1941,' nearly eighteen months before his death, when he wrote: 'I think I should try to write this diary in English. If anybody should be interested in it, it would be probably one of my children, and I am doubtful if, 20 or 30 years hence, they would be able to understand my German in my hasty handwriting' (facsimile, III, p. 339). Why not in Hebrew, the language in which his children were reared? Did he then despair of Zionism's prospects? Not necessarily, despite the doubts occasionally confided to the balance-sheet for the outgoing year that he was in the habit of compiling on Sylvesternacht. On his arrival, he knew enough Hebrew to read a vocalized printed text 'and not always correctly' (II, p. 62); but he was soon persuaded that Hebrew had to be imposed on the polyglot Jewish population for the sake of national unity—'though from the point of view of practical advantage the adoption of a European language would have perhaps been far preferable' (II, p. 63). So he diligently studied Hebrew with Agnon as his teacher and became proficient enough not only to use it for business purposes but even to lecture in it (from a script), though constantly envying others whose fluency was less inhibited by grammatical mistakes more numerous and glaring than his own. It was probably his concern for precision that prevented him from expressing himself in it to his own satisfaction. 'I did not want to speak German in public so as not to set a bad example and worsen the state of affairs. The result was that I either tried to hold back from appearing in public or, though a special effort, I managed to force myself to speak Hebrew, however faulty it might be. It often appeared to me that by giving up the German language, I forfeited, as it were, a large part of my personality and of my influence on the public as well' (II, pp. 64–5).

Evidently Ruppin was no more attracted by the romance of the Hebrew revival than by the ideology of organized labour, although he firmly appreciated the value of both for the implementation of his plans. Race attracted him more, perhaps because he accepted it as a branch of science: at one time he thought of taking photographs and measurements of the Middle East's varied ethnic types as a means of demonstrating that Jews were included in its racial pattern; but he never succumbed to the mysticism that so often accompanies racial studies. It was from a practical standpoint that he came to regard relations with Palestinian Muslims as Zionism's gravest problem and founded an organization to study it. By that time, however, Palestine was no longer under Muslim rule.

Professor Kedourie's quip, 'The Ottoman Empire died of Europe', (*England and the Middle East*, p. 14), makes the history of European settlement in Jerusalem read like the Sick Man's temperature-chart. The Capitulations concluded with France (1536) and England (1583) when he was at his healthiest had made little difference there. Three French attempts to establish a consulate (in 1621, 1699 and 1713) were soon and easily thwarted—allegedly by the local elements with most to gain from helpless foreigners; and even in the eighteenth century when most of the remaining Capitulations were signed, the signatories' representatives resided only in the maritime cities with commercial interests to be protected. The change came with the conquest of Syria (1831) by Mehmet Ali's troops under the command of his son, Ibrahim Pasha, but was more conspicuous after their enforced withdrawal (1841). Britain, the first to appoint a consul in Jerusalem (1838), was followed by France, Prussia and Sardinia (1843), the United States (1844), Austria (1849), Spain (1854) and Russia (1858)—from 1839 Russia had entrusted a (Jewish) consular agent with the protection of Russian Jews. Britain also took the lead in promoting Christian prestige in as much as the Anglican Bishopric (1841) preceded the actual, if not the titular, presence of the Greek Patriarchate (1845) and the inauguration, under Pio Nono, of the Latin (1847). While European Christians were the main beneficiaries, European Jews were also offered hope for the future. Their past had been perilous.

In 1687, when they first organized a community of their own, Europeans constituted a small minority of the Jewish population of Jerusalem. Their numbers increased in 1700 with the arrival of survivors of the 'holy company' of Judah the Pious. So did their troubles; there were outbreaks of plague in the two following years; and a revolt in the third exposed them to pillage, as long as the city was under siege, and to the indiscriminate ferocity of suppression (1706). A more lasting threat was the burden of debt incurred in the hope of additional support from Europe. Their creditors were powerful Muslims, whose documents may have conformed to the Islamic prohibition of usury, but whose demands, reinforced by rough methods of exacting payment, swiftly mounted. The leaders of the older Jewish community who were better equipped to cope with such threats, managed through their connections in the imperial capital, to secure 'compromises', i.e. instructions freezing debts at current levels; and in Europe, where epistles and emissaries from the Holy Land had spread a sense of emergency, exceptionally large sums were raised. Why these efforts failed is not at all clear from the correspondence, from which the bulk of the evidence for this episode derives—there are, of course, the usual hints of mismanagement at both the collecting and receiving ends—but in 1720 a mob was let loose on the European Jewish quarter and set fire to its synagogue. Some of the inhabitants found shelter in the homes of their oriental brethren, others fled to Hebron or Galilee. Not until 1836, under Ibrahim Pasha, was the quarter redeemed from the creditors' heirs.

Between these dates, European Jews lived in Jerusalem clandestinely in oriental dress, although they continued to solicit alms separately and were even joined from time to time by newcomers from their native lands. However, Jerusalem was then altogether less hospitable than Galilee, which had long been the centre of Jewish life in the Holy Land. The fresh waves of European immigration at the turn of the century were almost entirely drawn there—and not only the Pietist groups, with their obvious affinity to the sites of Jewish mysticism. Even their staunch opponents who, apart from resenting the proximity, let alone the predominance, of Pietists, had set their hearts on Jerusalem, settled first in Tiberias and soon afterwards in Safed; and although they subsequently helped to revive the European Jewish community of Jerusalem on a much larger scale—it was on Safed's ruins. Indeed, the first of them to set foot in Jerusalem came as fugitives from the plague that raged in Safed in 1813—and the few who remained there after the plague had eased still looked to Safed for leadership.

It is with this group's preparations for settlement in the Holy Land that Malachi's sketches begin. He traces them from Shklov to Safed, where their peace was shattered by a series of calamities, the insurrection in the summer of 1834, the earthquake at the beginning of 1837 and the three-day occupation of the city by Druze rebels in July 1838. According to his sources, the fiercest fighting in the 1834 rising took place around Hebron where insurgents from Jerusalem and Nablus had gathered to make a last stand; and the Jews of Hebron were plundered and ill-treated both by them and by the Egyptian soldiers who were granted a free hand for six hours as a reward for their hard-won victory—'had not Ibrahim Pasha hastened to the aid of the Jews, none of the Jews of Hebron would have survived' (p. 73). As a result, Galilee was undefended; the Jews of Tiberias sold all their belongings to purchase their safety for a ransom of 'a hundred purses' (pp. 72–3); and the larger community of Safed endured thirty three days of terror. Malachi, who names many victims of murder, torture and rape, suggests that most of the atrocities were committed in cold blood for the sake of gain; and he also reports that large sums of money had to be paid to the Qadi of Safed and to the village elders of 'Ayn Zaytun for sheltering Jews. (Throughout this tale of cruelty and greed the solitary and heroic exception is a woman who rebuked her son and was stabbed to death by him when she tried to hinder him from joining the looters.) Again, the deliverer is Ibrahim Pasha, who is credited with a concern for justice and the will and capacity to administer it. When he was informed, through the consuls in Beirut, to whom a messenger had been sent, of the situation in Safed, he despatched a force under Amir Bashir to restore order and inflict punishment (pp. 67–72).

Scenes of pillage and torture were re-enacted four years later with the Druzes as the villains. This time 'a miracle occurred' (p. 76). The leader of the Pietists, Abraham Ber of Owrucz, who had already handed over 75,000 piastres out of his group's funds, lay fettered while a sword was being sharpened in front of him. A respite for prayers had been granted him, and his assailants sat down to a meal, intermittently mocking and menacing their unfortunate captives who had sought refuge in the Rabbi's house and were listening in awe to his fervent acceptance of Heaven's judgement. Suddenly an elderly man burst in to announce the arrival of Ibrahim Pasha's men, and the rebels fled leaving all their spoil behind them. So fierce was Ibrahim Pasha's revenge and so acute was the dread of his subsequent house-searches that much of the loot was abandoned in the open and eventually restored to the owners. Meanwhile many Jews were naked and penniless. 'Fortunately for them, an Arab friendly to Jews by the name of Muhammad Mustafa, who had tried to protect them during the troubles, lent them money and was concerned to procure food and clothing for them' (p. 77). He is one of the very few Palestinian Muslims to be identified by name in this book, which relies exclusively on Jewish material, i.e. chronicles, memoirs, letters, appeals, dirges and legends, for its fairly detailed accounts of Safed's tribulations.

Some of the following articles, and particularly the survey of the blood-libel's recurrences (pp. 79–89), reflect Jerusalem's rise in the estimation of World Powers, Christian Churches and the Ottoman Empire itself. They certainly testify to the value attached to consular intervention during the second half of the century when European Jews were rapidly increasing in numbers. On the Russian Consul's withdrawal at the start of the Russo-Turkish war of 1877, Russian Jews in Palestine were reported to have paid relatively large sums to consular officials for documents which they erroneously believed would entitle them to the protection of the U.S.A. The alternative, acceptance of Ottoman citizenship, was apparently regarded as exposure to robbery and outrage. Indeed, European Jews tended to register their institutions with their consulates and thus to embroil them in their own internal as well as external disputes— Malachi suggests that Jewish quarrels, grievances and anxieties saved consular staffs from utter boredom (p. 271). Muslims, on the other hand, were involved collectively and almost impersonally in Jewish affairs. To illustrate the interplay of factors, rapacious landlords exploiting the increase in immigration provided a motive for Jewish suburbs outside the Old City; the military posts set up to secure the completion of the Jaffa-Jerusalem road in readiness for the Emperor Franz Josef's visit (1869) made suburbs outside the walls habitable; and the impetus to buy land came from the influence of Christian romantics on Jewish philanthropists. Mrs Yardeni's study enables us to observe the different stages of such developments. For instance, the Gawlors, father and son, devised schemes for Jewish agricultural settlement in Palestine as a first step towards universal redemption and for some forty years pressed them on Sir Moses Montefiore. He passed the message on to other magnates more amenable to 'the spirit of the age' and less to rabbinic authority. It was discussed in the Jewish communal press of Europe (pp. 46–7). Thence it was conveyed to Jerusalem, where a few Jewish newspapers had correspondents. But the initial response of Jerusalem's European Jews was less enthusiastic.

An article in Jerusalem's first Hebrew newspaper (*Lebanon* Vol. 1, Nos. 5 and 6, 1863), referred to the interest shown by Christians over the previous twenty years in Palestine, to their declared belief 'that the Holy Land would be draped in mourning as long as the people which had once dwelt there did not return' and to their attempts to persuade their governments to help Jews 'to settle on their land, the land of the Lord'. This agitation has led 'several of our brethren abroad' to suppose that it was now possible to buy Palestine from the Turks. After ridiculing the delusion that Turkey would ever sell the land, which every child knew to be sacred to Muslims as well, the writer of the article turned to the desolate and lawless state of the country 'beset by robbers and murderers'. Even in the towns Jews were insulted by Muslims. 'All his spittle and vomit do not suffice him, when he passes a Jew walking in his direction, for spitting in his face' What would be their fate if they entered rural areas and tried to acquire large stretches of land? The article concluded with an emphatic warning, based on the previous British Consul's disastrous failure, of the folly of agricultural ventures. 'We will sit still and continue to wait for the Lord's salvation . . . We will not entertain the vain notion spreading to the ends of the earth that we should attempt in these days to acquire our land' (p. 22).

The Consul was James Finn, who, with the aid of his determined missionary wife, encouraged Jews to engage in agriculture. When his long service (1846–62) was abruptly terminated in consequence of his bankruptcy, two of his Jewish protégés were forced to abandon the land they had purchased in the vicinity of Jerusalem, and to appeal, in the next issue of *Lebanon*, to the philanthropists to obtain a decree confirming them in legal possession of it (*ibid.*, p. 23). Soon afterwards *Ḥavaṣṣeleth* published an article in favour of Jewish agriculture and reported an improvement in security following the Pasha's recent tours of intimidation (*ibid.*, pp. 31–2); but its motives would seem to have had little or nothing to do with either agriculture or security. Shortly before *Lebanon's* appearance, its publishers had started a printing-press in competition with Israel Bak's, which had been transferred from Berditchev to Safed in 1831, only to be wrecked in 1834 and re-established in Jerusalem in 1841 thanks to Sir Moses' munificence; and Bak's claim to a monopoly of Hebrew printing in the Holy City was rejected by the Rabbinical Court. Consequently, seeing that *Lebanon* tended to publicize the dominant faction, Bak accepted a subsidy from its opponents to publish *Ḥavaṣṣeleth* on their behalf. Their press war came to a sudden end in the following year (1864) when both were suppressed on the grounds that their publishers had neglected to apply for permission; and public discussion of Jewish factional strife in the Holy Land was once again confined to that section of the Jewish press of Europe whose readers had been—and, in later years, continued to be—the main target of Jerusalem's Jewish journalists.

It was not until 1870 that Israel Bak managed to obtain a license to publish *Ḥavaṣṣeleth*, which then continued, under the editorship of his son-in-law, Frumkin, until 1911. A new breed of Jewish philanthropist was now wielding the power of the purse in Europe; and their eagerness to wean young men from sacred study to manual toil was liable to tempt any writer with a grudge against the spiritual leaders of Jerusalem's ever growing European community and the administrators of its institutions. Frumkin was perhaps the most successful exploiter of the call for self-help. The slur that the poor were being provided with synagogues instead of chances to earn a livelihood began in his editorials and was repeated with topical variations in his appeals to the charitable in Western European cities and in the Eastern European towns which he (and his competitors) visited at intervals in order to retrieve their fortunes. Fund-raising, however, was not in itself a qualification for communal leadership. In addition to fomenting strife inside the community, one had to defend it against external foes. Most of the paper's allusions to Muslims came in the form of protests against outrages, e.g. assaults on Jews (and the customary arrest of the victims rather than the perpetrators) and the desecration of Jewish places of worship and burial. Indeed, an article on the plight of the Jews of Hebron resulted in the editor's appearance in court—which he, of course, attributed to his enemies' machinations. But he also published travelogues by Joshua Yellin, one of James Finn's protégés, who still cherished the prospect of Jewish agriculture and was then the warmest supporter of a plan for settlement near Jericho. Yellin was enthusiastic not merely about the landscape of the Holy Land but also about its inhabitants' uprightness and the extent of their hospitality which had enabled him to observe the commandments of the Torah during his extensive travels. He concluded his appeal to Jews to settle in the villages and support themselves by cultivation of the soil with the assurance 'that even the shadow of fear has departed from us on the other side of the Jordan as well as on this' (p. 75). Frumkin also maintained, despite reports to the contrary in his columns, that one could now travel safely throughout the length and breadth of the land.

More reliable testimony that fear was being gradually dispelled came from Joel Moses Salomon, the editor of *Judah and Jerusalem* and, like Yellin, a native of Jerusalem. In 1877, five years after Yellin's article, Salomon was sent by the Rabbis of the European community to investigate certain orchards with a view to discovering whether grafting was practised and, if so, forbidding the ritual use of their citrons during the Feast of Tabernacles. He described his friendly reception:

in the manner of the people of the Orient to whom flattering speech and a smooth tongue are a heritage from ages past. The faces of the proprietors of the orchards and the look in their eyes in this lonely plain cast terror and dread upon anyone unacquainted with them, for they resemble desert wolves in the mountains of prey and their glances pierce kidneys and heart (p. 100).

On closer acquaintance, he asserted, fear changed to contempt; and there was every reason for Jews to emulate the Wuertembergers who had proved that Europeans could farm in Palestine. Four years later (1881), Pethah Tiqwah, the first Jewish agricultural colony in the Holy Land, was founded by European Jews from Jerusalem.

The other colonies started during the eighties were inhabited by fugitives from the outbreak of violence that marked the end of the most promising reign in Russian history. Zionism (in the modest form that it assumed before Herzl came to it) gained a foothold in Palestine in 1882 when some hundreds of Russian Jewish families landed in Jaffa. No preparations had been made to feed and shelter them, opportunities of employment were few, and dismay at the prospect of watching their savings fruitlessly dwindle prompted some of them to leave, even more hastily than they had come, for other havens of refuge. The plight of the remainder was gradually relieved by the philanthropists, who now renewed their efforts to provide work for them, but not before the government imposed restrictions on immigration from Russia and Rumania. The decree, according to Mrs Yardeni, was greeted by a mixture of regret and relief in the press (p. 107). In addition to the burden of the immigrants' poverty on a far from prosperous community, they had attracted the unfavourable attention of the populace and the government. Even Ben-Judah, who was later to support the newcomers, felt that they were too conspicuous. His disciple, David Yudelovitz, claimed that their arrival had brought about two major misfortunes: 'the tumult that arose among the Arabs', who had doubled and trebled the prices of their lands, and immigration of 'a mob of people expecting to find in front of them a table laid with all the land's bounty'. The best of them, he added, left almost as soon as they had come, while the worst remained and were caught in the snares of the missionaries (pp. 123–4). Ben-Judah himself was privately troubled as to whether the official decree had been partly provoked by his writing, and the vehemence of Frumkin's editorial disclaimer suggests that at least a share of responsibility was popularly attributed to his paper. On parting from Frumkin soon afterwards, Ben-Judah formed a secret society. Its manifesto (September 1882) stated:

> We shall not succeed . . . If we proceed with storm and tempest and carry out our work with a loud noise, for the government will view us adversely, however far the thought of rebellion and disobedience may be from us, and the people of the land will be hostile to us, should they think that we have come to drive them from the land (p. 119).

To judge from a letter written in the following year, that was precisely what he wanted (pp. 320, 403).

During their collaboration Frumkin had ridiculed Ben-Judah's agitation in favour of Hebrew as the medium of instruction in schools. His own stubborn advocacy of secular education, in the teeth of the community's ban on it, was based largely on its capacity to relieve poverty, a purpose which Hebrew, unlike Arabic, Turkish and French, could hardly be expected to fulfil. To him, apart from its value as a path to employment for the bread-winners of needy families, the Arabic language had no special appeal. He was more interested in the manners and customs of those who spoke it, since folklore belonged to his general notion of enlightenment. In the seventies, for instance, *Ḥavaṣṣeleth* published a translation of a translation of an Arabic poem and two stories of Beduin life—which had all been received from Russia—the fact that they were outnumbered by articles on the exotic habits of more distant peoples may merely indicate the relative scarcity at that time of material pertaining to the life of the region in the European (mainly German) papers from which Frumkin, his contributors and competitors borrowed freely and often without acknowledgement of their sources. Admittedly, Ben-Judah displayed a keener interest in Arabic on the grounds of its power to enrich the Hebrew vocabulary and throw light on the mentality and condition of contenders for the ownership of the country. In respect of them, his paper, on its appearance in 1885, differed from Frumkin's in that it identified them by language instead of, as was more common at the time, by religion and that it regularly contained his versions of articles on their social and economic life by European writers.

By then Frumkin also tended to pay more attention to a subject of increasing relevance to his readers. The colonists were in daily contact with the villages around them—the satires composed by their critics picture the men as watching labourers at work on their land and the women as reading novels and leaving domestic work to servants—and the growth of trade and industry in the towns was introducing more European Jews to their Muslim and Christian counterparts. In the early nineties, the first crop of direct translation from Arabic into Hebrew was produced—a sparse crop derived for the most part from oral rather than written material and selected on grounds of resemblance to Jewish tradition rather than literary or historical merit. Mrs Yardeni's final chapter, ostensibly devoted to translation from the Arabic in the Hebrew press of the second half of the period under review, mentions only one Arabic author—al-Samaw'al, the famous Jewish poet of pre-Islamic Arabia. The Hebrew translator of extracts from his *diwan* was David Yellin (the son of Joshua Yellin by a Baghdadi mother). Though probably not the first Palestinian Jew to read or write Arabic as well as Hebrew characters, David Yellin was undoubtedly the mentor of a small band of writers grouped round a political myth more lasting than their literary and educational work. Three of them were his pupils and followed him into teaching at the secular schools founded under the aegis of European philan-thropists. (School-teaching, it must be stressed, was then a new profession in Palestine, and its pretensions to a higher status than was accorded to elementary instruction in traditional institutions were not yet generally accepted).

Since the schools, though banned by the European, were initially patronized by the Ottoman Rabbinate, a high proportion of their pupils came from Arabic-speaking homes. One of them was David Yellin, whose father, ex-communicated and deprived of his share in the monthly subsidy from Eastern Europe for sending him to school, was more or less affiliated to the Ottoman community. From youth onwards, Joshua Yellin had courted the friendship of the Muslims whom he encountered in the course of his commercial activities; and he now saw to it that his son was taught literary Arabic and instilled in him a partiality for the *milieu* in which it was cherished. David's feet, together with those of his emulators, were thus set on the path to Orientalism, for their secular education imbued them with a respect for current modes of European thought among which enthusiasm for Oriental studies was the most easily applicable to their circumstances. Not only was it likely to raise their status but it also helped to overcome a technical difficulty to their profit. As Hebrew teachers in secular schools, they envied their colleagues the text-books available for instruction in secular subjects: more specifically, they wanted compatible readers to supplement the sacred texts they were employed to expound. So they compiled their own, ransacking Arabic folklore to fill anthologies with legends, maxims, verses, anecdotes, witticisms, rites and ceremonies parallelled in biblical and rabbinic literature. Their quest inevitably exaggerated the extent to which the whole cultural zone had been permeated by Judaism before the rise of Islam. From there, under the secularizing pressure of linguistic nationalism, it was but one step towards emphasis on the unifying force of cultural ties as opposed to the divisive demands of religion. To quote Joseph Meyuhas, as assiduous collector of 'mass-literature' (*sifruth hamonith*):

> The two peoples are one people, and these two branches belong to one stock, and the more we explore the roots, disposition, language and literature of the Arab people, the more shall we reveal Israel and the secrets of its language (p. 323).

They found allies outside their circle. Indeed, Israel Belkind, who was also a teacher and an author of text-books but belonged to the first batch of Zionist immigrants, went a step further. While travelling on both sides of the Jordan in 1894, he came to the conclusion that 'the overwhelming majority' of the inhabi-tants were descended from Jews 'who had not left the land but had endured their political and spiritual exile in it'. This discovery impelled him to ask: 'Are we to go on distinguishing them as Arabs . . . only because they speak Arabic?' Evidently not. 'We are brothers, brothers in stock, brothers, sons of one people' (p. 320). He and the kindred spirits whose predilection for tribal and village traditions with scriptural connotations was amply reflected in the press of the period, were searching for ancestors whose prestige would redress their doubts of themselves and their future—naturally enough, since they had brought with them from Europe the new Jewish learning whose ancillary aim was to meet the challenge of emancipation by showing up Jewish self-esteem with historical scaffolding. In all traditional faiths, a shift from theology and sacred law to history has myth-forming propensities, and a myth involving the rediscovery of remote ancestors invariably issues from a family rift. Accordingly, the colonists, under constant attack from *Ḥavaṣṣeleth*, then virtually the organ of the European community of Jerusalem, were now being harassed by fellow-nationalists. Yet while both trends of criticism converged on the colonists' failure to adjust themselves to their new surroundings, the motives underlying them were very different. Frumkin, for example, resented their attachment to Russian headgear and other characteristics that led Muslims to identify them—to their pride and pleasure—with Islam's foremost enemy in the society of nations. He was actuated, as he stated more than once, by fear of the consequences for his own community and, particularly for those who wanted to join it for, in his final phase, he became more appreciative of his community's value as a shelter for devout pilgrims. Besides, he now subscribed more readily to the traditional concept of Exile: in this unredeemed world Jews had to pay for protection in the discharge of their sacred duties, and subservience and tact were part of the price exacted from them. (*Havaṣṣeleth* paid it with inordinately long and flowery eulogies on the 25th anniversary of the Sultan's accession, the German Emperor's visit and the death of Queen Victoria in addition to the respectful tone of its routine references to Ottoman personalities and occasions). Belkind, on the other hand, was not content to be a protected outsider: it was in order to renew their oriental roots that he urged the colonists to jettison their European outlook, enter into genuine partnership with the people of the country and learn from their ways and skills.

His blend of Russian populism and biblical romaticism became fashionable. By the turn of the century it was providing Hebrew fiction with fresh characters and the younger generation in the colonies with ideological support for their imitative inclinations. Zionist writers, residents and tourists alike, were soon to acclaim a new breed of Jew, at home in the saddle and a fair marksman, fluent in Arabic and crowned with the distinctive headgear of the countryside, as proof of the capacity of Eastern European Jews to take root in the land of their fathers; and for many years exotic modes of entertainment, e.g. the sword-dance performed on the occasion of the Baron's inspection of Kinnereth in 1912 (Ruppin, II, p. 130), were used to convince visiting philanthropists of the efficacy of their donations. But Joseph Klausner in Odessa, while welcoming signs that the exilic aura of timidity and helplessness was being dispelled, 'would have liked it to be a direct result of the new life itself, of the cultivator's and vine-grower's life in nature's bosom, of the life close to nature of an inhabitant of a land far from Europe's over-rated and artificial civilization; but I would not at all have liked —and all Zionists will surely agree with me here—Jews to imitate the Arabs and the Beduins, that is to say, that they should be influenced by a primitive civilization, which, despite its virtues, has ever so many grave defects.' He was quick to note the one-way direction of the cultural traffic and to contrast Hebrew's minimal influence on Arabic with Arabic's growing intrusion into Hebrew speech and writing. The colonists, he alleged, not only called their own settlements by their Arabic names instead of by the Hebrew names conferred on them, but had in certain instances failed to give them a Hebrew name at all—a dangerous omission, in Klausner's view, since the retention of an Arabic name sustained hopes of the land's ultimate reversion to Arab ownership. He was also indignant about the arrangement of facilities for immigrants to learn Arabic 'as if our fathers and mothers had not learned as much Polish, Russian and even Lithuanian as they needed for their business without evening-classes' (*Hash-shiloah*, 11, Nos. 5–6, 1907–8).

Ruppin, whose preliminary tour of Palestine preceded the publication of these criticisms by several months, may have disagreed: in his account of his impressions (which the Zionist Organization's paper, *Die Welt*, published in March 1908), he advocated the inclusion of Arabic 'since it is the dominant language in the land' in the primary school curriculum (II, p. 29); and throughout the second volume of his memoirs, which he compiled towards the end of his life, the settlements' original names (followed by the Hebrew in brackets) frequently occur. Yet he undoubtedly shared the implicit fear of a permanently dependent Jewish minority. All his own undertakings seemed to him (in 1908) insignificant in the light of the task he had set himself. 50,000 out of a total Jewish population of 70,000 were 'indifferent or hostile to the national movement'; of the remainder only about a thousand families were engaged in agriculture; 'and their situation was by no means satisfactory. It is a matter of urgency to extend this narrow base immediately, if colonization activity in the country is not to become a kind of children's game' (II, p. 96). To raise funds he travelled widely, wrote informatively and appealed earnestly. Much of the manpower had already been imported, from 1905 onwards, with the second wave of Zionist immigration, young men reared in the movement and eager to work on the land. Nevertheless, their absorption into Jewish agriculture presented difficulties. The colonists, far from affluent in the best of years and on the verge of ruin in the worst, were reluctant to employ labourers twice as expensive as, and less experienced, industrious and obedient than, neighbouring villagers; and the would-be labourers accused them of looking after their own material interests while posing as 'idealists' and soliciting aid from Zionists on that score. Ruppin characteristically tried to please both sides—and succeeded up to a point: in order to enable Jews to compete in the agricultural labour market, he encouraged immigration from the Yemen, provided cheap housing in the settlements and entrusted organized groups of workers with the development of some of the newly purchased areas. He was thus in a position to report to the eleventh Zionist Congress (1913) an increase in the number of Jewish agricultural workers from a few hundred to over a thousand (II, pp. 96–100).

Organized labour then started on its march to power under the influence of A. D. Gordon and J. H. Brenner, whose writings offered a more exacting alternative to the complacent romanticism of the time; and Ruppin was drawn to it by its consciousness of long-term Zionist aims and readiness for arduous toil and sacrifice in their service. Before he set foot in the country, Brenner had recognized the Arabs of Palestine as the enemy and foreseen his own death at their hands. An encounter with ruffians on his first evening in Haifa (1908) followed by observation of bullying and extortion on the part of minor officials and of the settlers' passivity in the face of highway-robbery and murder, led him to associate them not with rustic idylls of scriptural antiquity but with their Eastern European counterparts, whose victims were similarly inhabited by fears of vengeance from retaliating. He envied the Arabs only their assurance, despite poverty and disease, of their right to be there; and he derided the idealization of their lives by contemporary writers as an example of the debilitating pacifism engrained in Jews by their long depression. Ruffin was extremely reticent on the subject of violence and expressed his disapproval of it in the slightest of hints. He mentions Brenner, who translated his *Die Juden der Gegenwart* into Hebrew, only once—in a brief entry reporting his murder in the May-day massacre of 1921. His own allusions to insecurity are singularly brief and unemotional. Clashes over land, for instance, elicit a sober resolve to compensate tenants in all future land-deals, regardless of the additional burden on the movement's resources (II, p. 125). Like most Zionists at that time, he attributed hostility to economic grievances alone. It was in order to show 'tangible benefits' that the Baron gave large sums to the Jerusalem and Jaffa municipalities for the relief of the Muslim poor and offered to endow an Arabic *gymnasium* in Damascus (II, p. 137).

The military coup which forced the Sultan to restore the constitution (July 22, 1908) escaped the diarist's notice, despite the public displays of fraternization between members of all three faiths—David Yellin is reported to have addressed Arab nationalist meetings in those days. Ruppin's solitary reference to the

Committee of Union and Progress occurs in one of a series of articles on the situation in Asiatic Turkey, which he wrote for the *Berliner Tageblatt* in the summer of 1912. After noting that elections in the Arab provinces were being held later than in European Turkey and Asia Minor, he added: 'The Arabs have no love for the Young Turks and would willingly have voted for the opponents of the government. Yet when news of the Committee's victory arrived from the rest of the country, they preferred to support the victors, and in the event the Committee's candidates were elected with a decisive majority' (II, pp. 189–190). Apart from this paragraph, he concentrated on government projects and the need for the administration of public health, education and justice to match them; and his diary confirms that he really believed his cautiously optimistic forecast. In an entry dated January 1, 1914—his customary appraisal of the past year—he wrote that 'with the end of bloody quarrels between Turkey and its neighbours Asiatic Turkey is about to Europeanize itself, with the aid of the Turkish government or with the aid of Western powers; and in a Europeanized state it is seven times as hard to secure economic and cultural predominance. We must now surpass our previous efforts if we are to take advantage of the interlude' (II, p. 224).

His philosophy—'man can find comfort in his troubles only if he links them with history or destiny' (II, p. 188)—was to undergo a severe test. At the end of the year, during the expulsion of Russian Jews who declined to become Ottoman subjects, he could still write: 'Yet this expulsion by order of the Turkish authorities is no worse than the actions of all the European states now waging war; the Turkish authorities are even more lenient than they are and behave more decently; but they work clumsily and thereby cause many difficulties and great distress' (II, p. 235). Under Jamal Pasha, the Military Governor of Syria, the country reverted to a cruder and more capricious style of government. For instance, on January 16, 1915, thirty Jewish notables of Jerusalem, Jaffa and the colonies assembled before him only to be told brusquely that they were all to be deported to Constantinople: but after private conversation with Antebi, a favoured Turkish-speaking Jew, agreed that only fourteen of the thirty should be exiled and not to Constantinople but to Haifa, Tiberias or Damascus for a period of between ten to fourteen days (II, p. 237). Again, on March 2, 1915, towards evening, he unexpectedly arrived in Jaffa. 'He spent most of his time walking through the streets of Tel-Aviv and inspected the *Gymnasium*. Moreover, in a speech which he delivered, he declared that he was friendly to Jews and guaranteed their safety. He also ordered the distribution of printed leaflets to the effect that he absolved Jews from the charge of lack of patriotism that was being levelled at them and would punish anyone accusing them of anything of the kind' (II, p. 241). Ruppin hints that this gesture followed American diplomatic intervention, which, together with material aid, partially relieved the very grave plight of the Jewish population.

Zionists were in greater danger than other Jews of blackmail, denunciation, home-searches and arrests, since Jamal had openly condemned their movement as subversive. Ruppin tried repeatedly to explain his case but was not even admitted—indeed, as a result of the mediation of Jamal's German Chief-of-Staff, he incurred hatred. After a succession of threats had failed to move him, he and four of his colleagues were put on trial. The entry on the verdict reads as follows:

Jerusalem February 13, 1916. I have now tasted the pleasure of appearing before a Turkish military court. Five years ago they denounced me for selling Qeren Qayyemeth le-Yisrael stamps and thus offending against state sovereignty. For five years prosecution documents went to and fro between Constantinople and Jaffa. In January, 1916, a court investigator in Jaffa took evidence from me and when I returned from my journey to Transjordan and was getting off my horse, a policeman confronted me and handed me a summons to appear before the military court in Jerusalem. In addition to myself, Dr Thon, Ulitski, Feldman and Blumenfeld were prosecuted as accomplices. The trial lasted, with intervals, for three weeks (six sessions) and ended on February 9, with a declaration that, on the proposal of the government prosecutor, we were all acquitted, since nothing had been said about the distribution of forged stamps, which the prosecution had alleged, and even though collecting money for the benefit of foreign organizations was not allowed, it was neither prohibited nor punishable by a fine in any clause of the Constitution. The trial was conducted by the President of the Court (Major Ibrahim Bey) with extraordinary courtesy and friendliness. I was allowed to explain the nature of Zionism to the court and to read to the judges extracts from my book *Die Juden der Gegenwart*. Nevertheless, I think that my German citizenship and the energetic intercession of the German Embassy in Constantinople and the German Consul here contributed more than logical reasons towards my acquittal.

Indeed, the German Embassy refused to comply with Jamal's request for Ruppin's, at least temporary, recall from Palestine. (Although prepared for publication during 1941, the extracts from the diary and even the narrative covering the earlier war testify to the consistent and vigilant friendliness and humanity of German's representatives, military and civilian, towards Jews). Soon afterwards, however, Jamal let it be known that the colonies would suffer for Ruppin's obstinacy. In order to spare them, Ruppin sought and was granted an interview during which he offered to hand over his functions to his assistant, Dr Thon, who was ready to become an Ottoman subject, and withdraw to Jerusalem where he would write a book on Syria's economy. To his astonishment, Jamal immediately agreed; and Ruppin, armed with Jamal's letters of introduction, visited the main cities to collect material and then wrote it up in the American Archaeological Institute. As soon as the work was finished, a French translation was made and sent to Jamal, who naturally expected to find in it a tribute to his own contribution to Syria's economic progress. In his disappointment, he sent for Ruppin, gave him eight days in which to leave the country and swore that he would never return (II, pp. 256–8). So Ruppin spent the last two years of the war in Constantinople where, with the use of German facilities, he helped to keep open the movement's channels of information and aid.

The second volume ends with his second rendezvous with destiny. On July 2, 1920, he was engaged in amicable conversation with a Jewish High Commissioner in the very room where he had been irrevocably expelled by a ruler once all powerful and now a fugitive under sentence of death (II, p. 313). Two years later (July 22, 1922) Jamal was assassinated in Tiflis by two Armenians.

To summarize, the situation of European Jews in the Holy Land was unique during the period under review: nowhere else in the world did a Jewish community depend on charity from abroad for sustenance and on the consuls of foreign states for safety. Yet they still submitted to their immediate environment in traditional fashion: that is to say, they respected lawful authority, appeased lawless power and were circumspect in their dealings with their neighbours, whom they judged solely by their behaviour towards themselves. Indeed, their initial resentment of the first wave of Zionist Immigration was provoked by indiscretion rather than ideology.

The newcomers relied heavily not only on subsidies from Europe and consular protection but also, if they were to survive as farmers, on the experience, industry and low wages of the cultivators in nearby villages. They came to admire their qualities, to adopt some of their ways and even—in literature, at any rate—to assume an ethnic kinship with them and with the population as a whole. In their enthusiasm, which undoubtedly helped them to acclimatize, they were evidently ready to overlook the implication of permanent dependence; and it was left to the second wave of Zionist immigration to recall the movement's basic purpose and subordinate myths to it.

The final episode serves to remind us of the consular regime's merit in relieving the plight of victims of oppression and hardship. In its annals, the humanitarian endeavours of the representatives of the United States and Germany in Palestine during the First World War deserve a place of honour.

# The Zionist Attitude to the Arabs 1908-1914

## Yaacov Ro'i

### I

A good deal has been written about the beginnings of the Arab national movement, its cultural background and early teachings. A certain amount has been written about its political manifestations in the period before World War I, the different groups and societies and their various inclinations and aspirations. However, one aspect of this movement has received very little attention, namely its relations with the Zionist movement and Jewish activity in Palestine, one side of which will be discussed in this article.[1]

As early as 1905 a number of Arab nationalist and anti-Zionist manifestations drew the attention of the European press and of Zionists to the Arab national movement. In that year Negib Azoury published *Le Réveil de la Nation Arabe* which demanded the establishment of an independent Arab empire from the Nile to the Euphrates. He indicated the danger to the fulfilment of the project inherent in the Zionist movement, the ultimate aim of which, according to Azoury, was the revival of the ancient Jewish state at its most expansive.[2]

An article on the Arab movement devoted largely to an analysis of Azoury's book, was the first of three articles published on the subject in the Jewish nationalist periodical *Hashiloah*. The article discussed 'the Arab movement, that has just come to light and attracted the gaze of all the peoples of Europe'. The writer pointed out that while there was as yet no real Arab nationalist movement, and although the Arab was still living in a state of ignorance, serfdom and religious fanaticism 'in history it is the movements, not the

15

governments, that are victorious. And if the Arab movement
— if such a movement exists as yet — develops into a
movement that is simultaneously nationalist and popular,
it can be expected to prove dangerous to Zionism, for even
if they cannot say that Palestine is their country historically,
the Arabs are *in effect* the masters of the country in that they
comprise the majority of its population and, most important, of the tillers of the land'.[3]

At the Seventh Zionist Congress that took place in Basle
in July 1905, the President of the Congress, Max Nordau
referred to 'a movement' which 'has taken hold of a large
part of the Arab people' and 'can easily take on a direction
that will affect Palestine'.[4] On the occasion of the Congress,
a Palestinian then studying in Switzerland gave a detailed
account of the Arab problem as encountered by the new
Jewish settlers in Palestine, a lecture that was printed in 1907
under the caption: 'An Unapparent Question'.[5] A prominent Russian Zionist suggested to M. Ussishkin, who had
been appointed by the Seventh Congress to the Inner Zionist
Actions Committee (or Executive, as it was later known) that
the Actions Committee 'appoint a *political commission*....
This commission will decide concerning our attitude to the
movement of the Arabs so that everyone will not hold forth
according to his inclination'.[6]

It soon, however, became clear to the Zionists — as to
others — that the Arab awakening had not yet adopted
concrete form, and Zionist literature, official and otherwise,
seems to have made no further mention of the problem until
after the Young Turk Revolution of July 1908.

Before turning to the main theme of this article, it is
worth recording — notwithstanding the above-mentioned
essay — that the new Jewish Yishuv (or settlement) had not
been entirely oblivious to an inherent Arab question even
though it gave it relatively little attention. The Yishuv,
whose history begins about 1880, grew out of the 'Lovers
of Zion' movement and later, to an extent, out of political
Zionism and a number of the more observant and farseeing of
its members drew some important conclusions concerning
their new Arab neighbours, with whom they had daily
contact. It is not possible, within the scope of this article,
to discuss the attitude of the Jewish population of Palestine
to the Arabs before 1908 or even from 1908-1914 except

insofar as it is represented in the attitude of official Zionist institutions. Nevertheless it is necessary to make the point that a few people in the new Yishuv were aware of the fact that the expansion of the Yishuv could not be undertaken without taking into consideration in one way or another and on various levels the country's Arab population. This demand for a positive attitude to the Arabs was relevant to the commercial life of the towns, to the development of the country's agriculture, to co-existence within the framework of local administrative institutions and to the cultural and educational aspects of the Jewish national movement which were of great import in the Yishuv.

Finally, mention must be made of the few occasions on which Theodore Herzl, the creator of the Zionist Organization and its president from its founding in 1897 until his death in 1904, made allusion to the Arabs or an Arab problem. In 1899 Herzl wrote to the Arab Yusuf Ziya al-Khalidi that as far as the Arab population of Palestine was concerned, the Zionist has no intention of expropriating it; on the contrary, the non-Jews would only be enriched by the introduction of Jewish wealth into Palestine.[7] Herzl's diaries include only very sparse and unimportant reference to the Arabs, the last of which, entered four months before his death, mentions 'an Arab movement which intends to make a descendant of Mohammed Caliph. The Caliphate was stolen by Sultan Selim. Now it ought to be restored, as a sort of papacy with Mecca as Rome !'[8]

## II

Although the Zionist Organization was founded in 1897, it had no official representative in Palestine until 1908 when in accordance with a decision taken the previous year at the Eighth Zionist Congress, an official office was opened in Jaffa known as the Palestine Office (Palästina-amt).[9] The head of the office for the entire period under discussion was Dr. Arthur Ruppin, who came to Palestine specifically to fill the post. He was assited by Dr. Jacob Thon and a very small staff, among them Joshua Radler-Feldmann, who joined the office towards the end of 1909; Joshua Ḥankin, engaged in May 1910; and Nissim Malul whose task it was from January 1912 to read the Arab press, and report on, translate into Hebrew and reply to articles concerning the Jews and Zionism.[10]

The Palestine Office was responsible to the Zionist Inner Actions Committee, the seat of which was in Cologne from 1905 until August 1911, and in Berlin from that date until the end of our period. From September 1911, the Inner Actions Committee (which was, in effect, as already mentioned, the executive body of the Zionist Organization) had a representative in Istanbul, Dr. Victor Jacobson, whose functions included the supervision of all that occurred in Palestine. Jacobson had been in the Turkish capital since September 1908, at which time he was placed at the head of the Anglo-Levantine Banking Company, then created to provide official camouflage for an office of the Zionist Organization that could not be otherwise established in the Turkish capital.

We shall try to show the attitude to the Arabs and the Arab national movement of the various Zionist institutions: the Congress held biannually in the years under discussion; the Zionist Greater and Inner Actions Committee; the Zionist office in Istanbul and the Palestine Office.

This article cannot feasibly deal with the land purchase policy of the Zionist Organization as a whole or of the Palestine Office, nor with the labour question, except insofar as they reflect the attitude of these institutions to the Arabs. Both of these subjects were, however, of primary significance in the development of the Yishuv, and had important repercussions on relations with the Arabs. Suffice it to say at this point that Dr. Ruppin as well as many of the Russian Zionists looked upon the purchase of every available tract of land as the foremost, immediate objective upon which every effort must be concentrated. At the same time the socialist element in the Zionist movement in general, and in the Palestine Yishuv in particular, placed special stress on the need for Jewish labour. The motives in both instances were internal, emanating from considerations of the inherent needs of the Jewish revival; but the local Arab fellaheen occasionally reacted — from the earliest days of the new Yishuv — by perpetrating physical violence. These outbreaks were not the results of the actual purchase by Jews of land in Palestine — since most of the fellaheen themselves were not landowners — but of its implementation. Hitherto the proprietors had been chiefly absentee landowners to whom a percentage of the crops had to be paid but who did not interfere with the traditional rights of pasture, or with other aspects of everyday life that gave rise to bad feeling and sometimes conflict when the Jewish colonists came to settle on the land they purchased. In the course of time the neighbouring Arabs of each village or colony also manifested their dissatisfaction with the attempts to introduce Jewish labour.

These disputes and the resulting incidents had become an important feature of Palestinian life in the last year before the First World War. Yet at this time Jews possessed little more than 100,000 acres, or 2 per cent of the land of Palestine, while the number of Jewish agricultural labourers was approximately 2000, or 10 per cent of the total hired labour employed in Jewish farms and villages.[11]

The meagre results of over thirty years of endeavour and a good deal of suffering were certainly not the outcome of lack of trying or vision as far as the Palestine Office, for example, was concerned. The constant setbacks and slowness of achievement reflected a number of phenomena which were the bane of the Yishuv. The first was internal dissension and strife: only in the last two or three years of the entire period 1880-1914 was there any more or less recognized concerted action and leadership, personified in the Palestine Office. The second factor was the extreme poverty of the Zionist Organization as a whole and the paucity of means at the disposal of the actual Palestine effort, in view of which the myth of international Jewish influence and high finance stands out in tragi-comic contrast. The third obstacle was external: the corruption and intricacies of Ottoman rule and the virtually constant, though not always open, hostility of the Ottoman government to the Yishuv and to its expansion in which the Arabs played no small role, though not always a direct one.

This article will try to show the beginnings of an official or semi-official policy towards the Arabs of Palestine, both per se and within the framework of Zionist Turkish policy. It will also try to indicate the first moves towards contact with the incipient Arab national movement.

## III

The Arab-Jewish incidents in which settlers or labourers were attacked and sometimes killed, and their farms and livestock pillaged, increased in number and intensity after the Young Turk Revolution of 1908, or more specifically from April 1909 onwards. Such mention as was made of the Arabs or an Arab problem at Zionist congresses or in the Zionist press was mostly in connection with those incidents, of which official Zionist opinion was inclined to make light. Conflicts with local Arab villagers or cases of infiltration on the part of desert tribes who came to pasture their flocks on land now in Jewish possession, were considered simply examples of the Arab nomads' tendency to plunder wherever the opportunity presented itself. Alternatively, they were described as manifestations of deliberate provocation on the part of unrepresentative Arab elements, who, for the sake of their own vested interests, wished to cause bad feeling between the Arab population and the Jewish Yishuv.

A Poalei Zion delegate at the Tenth Zionist Congress, S. Kaplansky, thus took pains to stress the animosity of the Christian Arabs and the Arab landowners as distinct from the community of interests of the Jews and the Arab population as a whole. The latter reaped great economic benefit from the coming of the Jews to Palestine and from the expansion of the Yishuv. The speaker was convinced of the feasibility of achieving an understanding with the local populace ('mit der arabischen Demokratie').[12] This essential identity of interest was a major theme in the ideology of the Palestine Social-Democratic Poalei Zion party which thus countered the charges of other Russian Jewish socialist elements that Zionism meant the depopulation and disfranchisement of the Palestine Arabs. The Poalei Zion theoretician Y. Ben-Zvi indicated the benefit to the Arabs of the introduction into Palestine of modern mechanized and intensive agriculture.[13]

At the same Tenth Zionist Congress, Dr. J. Thon of the Jaffa Palestine Office, likewise referring to the frequent outbreaks of violence in Palestine between Arabs and Jews, said that they must not be exaggerated in that they did not reflect popular Arab opinion. The disturbances were caused, according to Thon, by individual local officials and journalists. Like Kaplansky he was convinced that there was no discrepancy between the basic interests of Arabs and Jews, and the time would come when the Arab population would appreciate the benefits brought to them by the Jews as a cultural element and as the only group in Turkey which was free of the stigma of dissolution and disintegration. This was quite apart from the profit accruing to the country from the very existence of the Yishuv, a profit reaped for the most part by Palestine's Arab inhabitants.[14]

The Tenth Congress Palestine Committee dealt inter alia with the relations of the Zionist Organization and the Yishuv on the one hand with Turkey and the Arabs, on the other. As far as the Arabs were concerned Dr. A. Hausmann's report in the Congress plenum mentioned the committee's anxiety concerning 'the Arab question' in view of the friction caused both by incitement and by inevitable resentment created by change in landownership and economic regrouping. 'The committee considers it of utmost importance that both the Palestine Office and the party leadership [i.e. the Zionist Inner Actions Committee] follow the position in Galilee [which had been the scene of the severest and most frequent incidents] with constancy and with close attention, and take the necessary steps'. While the committee made no specific suggestions as to the nature of the steps to be taken, it indicated two general directions for action. Firstly, the establishment of 'contact and a friendly neighbourly relationship with the Arabs and, secondly, the countering of instigations and promptings on the part of our opponents by informing the Arabs concerning our intentions and especially concerning the intentions of those who from outside incite the Arabs against us'.[15]

At the last pre-World War I Zionist Congress, the eleventh, which was held in Vienna in September 1913, Dr. Chaim Weizmann mentioned the need to enlighten the Arab population. Both he and the Chairman of the Actions Committee, O. Warburg, expressed their optimism concerning future relations between Jews and Arabs on the basis both of kinship between the races and their cultures, and of the advantages derived by the Arabs from Jewish activity in Palestine.[16]

Ruppin, who appeared for the first time at a Zionist Congress since the opening of the Palestine Office, surveyed the activities of Zionist work in Palestine in the past years and explained and justified the policies adopted by his office. Ruppin pointed out that in the early days of the Zionist movement, the opinion had been prevalent that Palestine was an unpopulated country. He even suggested that this incorrect assumption might have guided the movement's entire policy in its first stages. It was true that Palestine was populated very sparsely; yet the Yishuv had been forced to learn that an indigenous population did exist. One of the Jews' most urgent objectives must be to make their relationship with the local Arabs one of peace and friendship. On this score there was a great deal to be retrieved, for the matter had been neglected — very few efforts had been made by either Jews or Arabs. Although attempts were now being made by the Yishuv to correct the position, this could only be achieved by deeds and not by words, and particularly, by tact and thoughtfulness in the purchase of land — there was sufficient land to be bought that was of no use to the Arabs on account of their different systems of farming — and by the establishment of personal contact with that small stratum of Arab society which controlled the Arab press and influenced the ideas of the Arab masses.[17]

As far as relations with the Arabs were concerned, a number of important points were thus made at the Zionist congresses of the period under discussion, notably at those of 1911 and 1913. At the same time, there was no discussion on this issue and virtually no sign of any positive, clearly defined attitude towards the Arabs, apart from the generally expressed hope for the establishment of friendly relations. Arab attacks on individual Jews in the towns and villages or on the roads, the violation of Jewish fields and plantations and the molestation of livestock, and a number of vehement articles in the Arab press, and speeches in the Ottoman parliament could not help but make Zionists everywhere conscious of the need to come to terms with the local Arab population. However, the delegates at the Zionist congresses were sufficiently far away from the scene of trouble not to feel the need for a debate on the problem or to demand that it be grappled with, while the movement's leadership clearly did not want a spontaneous public discussion of the 'difficult political situation' in Palestine.[18]

## IV

The Zionist leadership was made more acutely aware than the rank and file of the gravity of Arab-Jewish relations by constant reports from Palestine, particularly from the Palestine Office in Jaffa. Mention has already been made of the fact that the incidents increased in frequency and severity from April 1909, a phenomenon to be attributed to the general unrest prevalent in the Ottoman Empire and the deterioration in local government. Yet there had been several serious incidents even prior to the Young Turk Revolution. Already in December, 1907, Z. Levontin had written to D. Wolffsohn that the hostility to the Yishuv was growing daily, under the aegis of the Mutasarrif in Jerusalem and the Kaymakam of Jaffa. 'The local Christian Arabs... have formed an Anti-Semitic gang under the leadership of one Anton Cassar and they make every effort to harm the Jews at every turn'.[19] Tension reached its peak in March 1908 in the form of a fairly large-scale incident in Jaffa which gave cause to a great deal of excitement and comment in the European Jewish and Zionist press. Three months after this incident, in a circular to the members of the Greater Actions Committee, Wolffsohn wrote that 'our original opinion that undue significance must not be attributed' to this incident had been confirmed by Ruppin who had meanwhile arrived in Jaffa. Ruppin claimed that the situation was now absolutely quiet; 'It is completely incorrect to compare the disturbances [in Jaffa] with the pogroms in Russia. In my view it was an accidental brawl such as occurs daily in countries, the population of which speaks different languages, and is culturally or religiously heterogeneous. Instead of being surprised that disturbances had occurred in Jaffa, one should rather be surprised that the relations between Jews and Arabs here in Palestine are so peaceful notwithstanding all differences'.[20]

The virulence of the Arab press on the subject of the Yishuv and the Zionist movement was a further cause of concern. The freedom of the press granted by the Ottoman constitution of 1908 had an instant effect on the Arab and other press, and attacks on the Yishuv appeared already that year in the Arabic *al-Aṣmaʿi*. In the following year *al-Karmal* began to appear in Haifa and it at once became, and remained throughout the years under discussion, one of the chief and most unrestricted Arab antagonists of Jewish Palestine activity. A number of other newspapers followed suit, particularly *Falasṭin* and *al-Munadi* that were printed in Palestine, and *al-Muqtabas* edited in Damascus by Muḥammad Kurd 'Ali.[21]

The Palestine Office decided to take effective action by trying to influence the Arab press in various ways, in particular by inspiring replies to anti-Zionist and anti-Jewish articles. After a number of sporadic efforts to have the main Arab newspapers read, a special press office was finally established. From January 1912 until the outbreak of World War I, this office was responsible for the systematic monitoring of the Arab press, the translation into German and Hebrew, or the preparation of resumes, of articles concerning Zionism and the Yishuv and the publishing in the Arab press of replies to the above-mentioned attacks and of other articles calculated to induce a more favourable opinion in Arab circles of the Zionist movement and its aims. These articles did not necessarily touch directly on the subject of the Yishuv or Zionism, but were supposed to attain the requisite ends by indirect means precisely because they were not obviously Zionist-inspired.

The German versions were more or less regularly dispatched to the Zionist Head Office in Berlin, to Jacobson in Istanbul and to several other Zionist leaders who required to be *au courant* of Arab opinion and contributed to the upkeep of the press office. A considerable proportion of the circulars sent by the Zionist Head Office to the various local organizations and to members of the Greater Actions Committee contained references to the Arab press and often even extracts from articles that had appeared in the Arab press on the subject of Zionism and Zionist work in Palestine.[22]

Further opportunities for gauging Arab opinion were provided by the elections to the Ottoman Parliament that took place in October 1908, April 1912 and April 1914. These elections necessitated concerted action with non-Jewish elements, since the Jewish voters in Palestine, i.e. those Jews who were Ottoman subjects, were not sufficiently numerous to elect even one representative to the Parliament in Istanbul. Already in 1908 Ruppin wrote to the President of the Zionist Actions Committee: 'We share completely your opinion that any Jewish attempt to influence the elections must first of all bear in mind the relation of the Jews to the Arab population of Palestine'.[23] The Jewish elections committee decided to combine efforts with two Muslim candidates who were considered to have good chances and to be favourably inclined towards the Jews; but events quickly showed that neither Christians nor Muslims would give their votes to Jewish candidates.[24]

The Jews were slightly more successful at the elections of 1912 than at those of 1908, yet the final outcome was virtually the same: the success of opponents of the Yishuv. For, although the members elected were all Union and Progress candidates — according to expectations the more nationalist Entente Libérale had good chances — the central party made considerable concessions to local Arab feeling in appointing these candidates. Ruppin's appraisal of the Young Turks' tactics was as follows: 'The Arabs are in fact no friends of the Young Turks and would undoubtedly have preferred to give their votes to the opposition party. When, however, news came from European Turkey and Asia Minor of the Young Turk [Union and Progress] victory, the Arabs considered it better to join the victors. The Young Turk party, with clever foresight and knowing the Arab character, had arranged the date of the elections in such a way that those in Palestine took place two weeks later than in the other provinces. At the elections the local voters were thus under the impact of the news of the Union and Progress committee victory'.[25]

The policy of the Zionist leadership was clearly orientated towards Istanbul and the Ottoman government, not only before but also in the years immediately after 1908. Within this framework, however, it gradually became clear that special efforts had to be made towards gaining the goodwill of Palestine's Arab population as an important factor in negotiations with the Ottoman government. As long as the Arabs demonstrated their antagonism to the Zionist effort in Palestine there was little chance that the Ottoman authorities would alleviate restrictions on Jewish immigration and the purchase of land. Concurrently government legislation directed against Jewish immigration and land purchase had a perverse effect on Arab-Jewish relations insofar as it undermined Jewish prestige, so that a vicious circle was created.[26]

Jacobson's report to the Greater Actions Committee in April 1911 showed the complexity of this triangular situation in the light of the recent attacks on the part of Arab deputies in the Ottoman parliament. 'Arab agitation against us had recently become increasingly strong both in and outside Palestine. This agitation manifested itself in an endless series of telegrams from the Arab deputies and in the incitement of extensive circles against Zionism'. Jacobson explains this opposition as the antagonism of the great landowners to any innovation and to every new element. He claimed that the fellaheen favoured the Jewish Yishuv but were powerless against the feudal landowners who feared Jewish competition and their own consequential decline. Account had also to be taken of the fact that the Young Turk committee of Union and Progress would stop at nothing to compromise the Yishuv, were an Arab revolution to break out. In order to disprove the charges of the opposition, Jacobson demanded a fundamental change in Zionist Ottoman policy, more specifically in the principle of *do ut des*, since Zionist promises of financial advantage to the Ottoman government in exchange for services enabled enemies to talk of bribes. Furthermore, the Arab question must be thoroughly studied for the Arabs constituted an important factor in Ottoman policy and in Parliament whose 75 Arab members had a purely nationalist programme.[27]

The Zionist Head Office in Berlin and the movement's leaders in the various countries were already aware of the existant disparity, if not friction, between the Union and Progress Committee and the Arabs. At an Inner Actions Committee meeting on 11 October, 1911, the dubiousness of the Arabs' patriotism was brought up.[28]

A circular letter sent to the members of the Greater Actions Committee in March 1912, explained that the majority of the Arabs tended to the opposition party, the Entente Libérale. Consequently, 'we can come to no binding agreement with the Committee in Palestine, as not only the disposition of the Turkish government circles is of importance to us, but above all that of the Arab population'.[29] This standpoint was taken even farther in the following circular which referred to letters received from the Palestine Office to the effect that 'the Jews in Palestine must, whatever happens, steer clear of being in opposition to the Arab population of Palestine in the parliamentary elections [which were to take place in April]. The governing party in Constantinople comes and goes, but the Arab population of Palestine stays where it is and it must be our first axiom to live in peace with the population. We are even more dependent on concord with the Arab population of Palestine than on the goodwill of the central government'.[30] It is worthy of mention that Wolffsohn had written very shortly after the Young Turk Revolution in a similar vein, warning the leaders of the Yishuv against alliance with any one particular political party. 'Now this party is on top, but it may be, when times change and circumstances alter, that those with the upper hand fall, etc. This possibility must always be borne in mind and in particular attention must be paid to the *Arab dignitaries* for they are in the final reckoning the masters of the country. It may be that they have not yet been able to organize but there is no doubt that they too will organize and heaven forbid that we make a permanent alliance with the other groups, for we shall thus arouse their jealousy'.[31] There does not, however, seem to have been any follow-up to this letter which remained, therefore, a solitary piece of advice and apparently merely a passing thought on the part of the President of the Zionist Organization.

The basic policy having thus been determined in the spring of 1912, there remained the very problematic issue of how in fact to achieve friendship with the Arabs in Palestine. Ruppin's report of the activity of the Palestine Office, which was circulated among the members of the Greater Actions Committee on 28 July, 1912, stressed the need for dealing with the hitherto neglected issue of good relations with the Arabs, and suggested methods of implementing this policy.[32]

The Inner Actions Committee meeting that confirmed the importance of directing 'our efforts to gaining the sympathy of Palestine's Arab population' determined that this was to be effected 'especially through a cultural policy in the economic and cultural sphere'.[33]

The political situation, however, became increasingly intricate and it gradually became apparent that only political and cultural compromise and concessions would satisfy the Arabs. At the end of 1912, the Arabs began to express intentions of autonomous rule within the Ottoman empire or even of complete secession from it. 'Arabs of both higher and lower classes can now be heard discussing the idea of the secession of the Arab provinces from the Empire, of the union of all Arab peoples and the founding of an Arab Caliphate. It is inconceivable that the Arab population, which is completely unorganized really, rise in a successful political rebellion. Occupation by a foreign power would, however, probably not meet at this moment with any real resistance on the part of the population'.[34] The idea 'of a possible annexation of Syria and Palestine by one of the great powers' was much discussed in the Arab press in December 1912-January 1913[35] and a number of Arab nationalists put out feelers in this direction in the period before the outbreak of World War I.[36]

The immediate factor, however, which complicated the political situation was not that of relations with the Great Powers, but the growth of the Arab national movement. 'As yet the Arabs are unorganized, and are not sufficiently strong that they need be feared as a threat for our colonization activity. When the Turkish crisis ends, however, [the reference is to the First Balkan War] the Arabs will presumably emerge strengthened. After the conclusion of peace, the autonomous Arab movement may well be stronger than hitherto and the enlightenment and organization of the population by the Arab "intelligentsia" will probably proceed at a quicker tempo than previously. This makes it all the more urgent that we try immediately with all our might to strengthen our position in Palestine. If we exploit the opportunity given us today of purchasing really large tracts of land and cultivating them, if by doing so we are able to bring to Palestine several thousand Yemenites and at least a few hundred European labourers, that would mean a respectable strengthening of our position which would be of significance for the future'.[37]

The memorandum sent to the members of the Greater Actions Committee on 20.2.13 gave considerable attention to the Arab movement and was even more explicit. The Arabs were indeed neither organized nor strong but it was clear that in the near future the Zionist movement and the

Yishuv would be faced with an enemy that would have to be taken seriously. 'If the national consciousness of the Arabs grows stronger, we shall come up against resistance, that it will perhaps be no longer possible to overcome with the help of money. If, in fact, the Arabs reach the stage where they feel it a national disgrace and betrayal to sell their land to Jews, the situation will become a truly difficult one for us'.[38]

Jacobson wrote to Berlin demanding an Actions Committee Conference at which the agenda would include the item: '*Arabs* ! ! ! A trip of inquiry to Syria and Egypt must be undertaken *at once*'.[39]

In the winter of 1912-13, two new nationalist Arab groups were formed, the Decentralization Party and the Beirut Reform Committee. The activities of the latter were soon prohibited by the Ottoman authorities, while the Decentralization Party with its headquarters in Cairo, continued to function until after the end of the period under discussion. The overtures of the Decentralization committee in Cairo to the Zionists in Istanbul have already been described elsewhere.[40] Both committees were also reported to have negotiated with members of the Yishuv: 'Two secret committees have been formed in Palestine among the Arabs: the one for the unification of Palestine with the Lebanon, and thus with France, while the other stands for unification with Egypt and thus with England. These committees have turned to the Jews of Palestine with the demand that they join them'.[41]

The Syrian Arab nationalists, according to the Palestine Office, were to be taken more seriously than the Cairo Decentralizationists. Thon, returning from Egypt, claimed that very little could be reported concerning an Arab movement. 'There is indeed a committee that is active in the cause of decentralization, and which has recently disseminated a pamphlet, but the committee seems to have neither connection with the masses nor an organization throughout the Empire.

'The Arab movement in Beirut and Damascus seems to be more serious. The Arab Christians of Beirut and the Arab Muslims of Damascus are indeed far apart in their positive aims, yet they concur in their enmity towards foreigners, among whom the Jews who settle in Palestine are more or less included. Details you can see from the extracts from the Arab press that we send every week to Dr. Jacobson'.[42]

The feelers that were put out by the Arabs provided an ideal opportunity to send a Zionist representative to Egypt and Syria for the dual purpose of appraising the situation and creating personal relationships with outstanding Arabs. 'As you know, we have been thinking for a long time of establishing relations with Arabs. I have been planning for a long time to send someone to Egypt and Syria'.[43] Jacobson asked the Actions Committee's consent and promised that his envoy would not conclude any agreement with the Arabs, but would merely find out the position and try to impress upon these people the importance of friendly relations. 'At first, I wanted to go myself, but that is out of the question, it would be too official'.[44]

The spring of 1913 was thus a time for optimism as it seemed that both Arabs and Turks appreciated the utility of establishing good relations with Zionists and the Yishuv. 'The Turks are now beginning to understand that they are *dependent* to a high degree on the Jews. It will likewise be explained to the Arabs that it is to their advantage to walk hand in hand with the Jews. There seems to be no reason to anticipate any difficulties or unpleasantness for the future Jewish immigrant'.[45]

Jacobson wrote to Lichtheim, on the latter's initiation as his assistant in Constantinople, that the government, Union and Progress, circles were favourably inclined towards Zionism, but feared the Arabs: 'In a confidential talk between Oberarm [the codeword for the Hakham-Bashi Ḥaim Naḥum] and Vogeljagd [the codeword for the Grand Vizier Talaat Bey] the latter said: 'You must first of all come to an understanding with the Arabs, we shall do the rest. We have in fact already begun negotiations with several Arab leaders, who say they too are in favour of concord with us. Yet it all seems to me to be still very vague and doubtful'.[46]

Reports from Istanbul described the mood of different Arab groups in the capital with special stress on the young, more extreme nationalists with whom the Palestinian Asher Saphir was in constant contact. They intended, according to Lichtheim, to provide the Arabs with a systematic education so as 'to make them mature for an Arab political movement... These circles propose collaboration with the Jews. According to them, the Jews must become Ottoman subjects and "good Syrians". They consider this primarily to be a sort of Jewish assimilation with the Arabs'. Saphir thought it would not be difficult to explain to these Arab nationalists the need for 'Jewish national and cultural autonomy'. It seemed to the Zionists in Istanbul that as these Arabs required Jewish help 'in educating the people through schools and the press' and not financial assistance, it might be feasible to implement some of their wishes.

Yet Lichtheim was very sceptical, first and foremost concerning the Jewish-Arab 'brotherhood theory'; at the same time he considered that advantage could be had, given 'the prevalent mood and situation', through constant contact with the Arabs in that the government might then be prevented from 'rejecting our wishes out of fear of the Arabs'.[47] Lichtheim was also doubtful, already in October 1913, as to the likelihood of a successful outcome of any negotiations both because the Jews were not in his view in a position to offer anything practical to the Arabs and because he was uncertain as to the reliability of some of the Arabs with whom the Zionists were in contact in Istanbul.[48] He nevertheless agreed that every effort must be made to win the goodwill of the Arab nationalists — for as long as possible — and asked for a letter from Jacobson to the effect that 'our colonization must be organized in such a way as would also serve Arab interests, that the development of Palestine is the identical task of Jews and Arabs'. This alone could provide a basis for continued negotiations with the Arab leaders.[49]

Thus, while considering good relations with the Arabs of primary importance, Lichtheim was not very hopeful that they could be permanently established. 'The Arabs are and will remain our natural opponents. They do not care a straw for the "joint Semitic spirit", just as they do not care a straw for Muslim solidarity. I can only warn urgently against a historical or cultural chimera that can cause us severe damage. The Arabs do not require a Semitic revival. They want orderly government, just taxes and political independence. The East of today aspires to no marvels other than American machinery and the Paris toilet. Of course, the Arabs want to preserve their nation and cultivate their culture. What they need for this, however, is specifically European: money, organization, machinery. The Jew for them is a competitor who threatens their predominance in Palestine...

'In such a situation, we must naturally make every effort to hold back Arab animosity'. Among other ways of doing this, Lichtheim urged that 'our young people here, in Beirut and in Cairo penetrate the [Arab nationalist] clubs and thus create the most favourable atmosphere possible'.[50]

A 'highly confidential' memorandum of the Inner Actions Committee summed up the situation as it stood in November 1913. 'The national-autonomist efforts of the *Arab population* of Syria and Palestine have recently acquired a much more explicit character. At the same time, Turkey's weakness compels her to be much more accommodating to the Arabs, as we can verify in the latest resolutions of the government. It is not possible to ascertain exactly how organized and strong the Arab movement is yet. Even if it does not seem strong at present, its future development cannot be anticipated. We must, of course, take this movement into account much more than do the Turks. One of our most immediate tasks must therefore be to try to form an agreement with it. The means at our disposal are personal relations with influential circles, the exertion of influence on the press, public institutions which are accessible to the Arabs (as for example our Banks and Health Bureau),[51] specific agreements with the spokesmen of the Arabs. As you know we have already been working in this direction. Now this work has to be conducted systematically and on a larger scale. It seems that we can reckon on the understanding of Baron [Edmond de] Rothschild and on his cooperation in this direction.[52] In our opinion an agreement with the Arabs on the lines indicated above can be achieved. As you know the resolution that we wished for concerning Jewish immigration was in fact passed at the congress of the Arab leaders held in Paris in June of this year, at which Mr. Hochberg was present.[53] A number of contracts which Mr. Jacobson has made with individual leaders in Istanbul, as well as reports we have recently received, confirm our hypothesis [concerning the feasibility of agreement with the Arabs]. Dr. Jacobson will have to travel from Istanbul to

Palestine and Beirut [in this connection]. Sokolow, who will be visiting Palestine in the course of the winter, will be paying special attention to this issue'.[54] Sokolow was already well aware of the problem and of the importance of showing the compatibility of interest between Jews and Arabs. He knew of the efforts being made to prove that the Jews were not coming to Palestine 'to expel or eliminate the Arab population' but that by introducing new agricultural methods 'we are enabling the fellah to exist on a smaller holding' which 'would clearly allow the *co-habitation* of the two elements'.[55]

Even at this stage, however, the Inner Actions Committee, which discussed the Arab press at a meeting held on 28 November 1913, postponed a decision as to the way in which influence was to be exerted on the Arab press, pending the reports of Jacobson and Sokolow. The same meeting simply decided that a special doctor should be active among Arabs who suffered from trachoma in order to further good Jewish-Arab relations.[56]

Sokolow finally went to Palestine only in the spring of 1914 as a member of a commission of Zionists sent for purposes of Comptrol ('*Zwecks-Revision*'). The commission had a considerable agenda of which the fourth item was 'political-organizational questions'. This included the following: relations with the Arab intelligentsia and population; Arab labourers in the Jewish colonies; relations with the Arab press; admittance of Arab children to Jewish schools; public institutions (hospitals, Health Bureau, etc.); Ottomanization.[57]

In February, 1914, the Inner Actions Committee was still unable to achieve any specific progress. 'Our efforts to sustain *good relations with the Arabs* are being continued. [i.e. apparently, despite increased tension in Palestine where there had recently been a number of serious incidents]. For lack of a concrete basis these efforts are at the moment of a general character and only events of secondary importance can be noted. Yet these are essential points which can be acted upon'.[58]

In June, the members of the Greater Actions Committee received a report of Sokolow's findings: 'the question of settling *our relations with the Arab population has become acute*. We wish to emphasize at this point that it would be incorrect to speak of antisemitism in the sense in which we usually use the term. I am of course not taking individuals into account. The reasonable Arabs, according to whom the present situation is not a normal one, stress our common semitic origin, are well aware of our importance in Palestine as a stimulating and instructive element, and appreciate the advantages of Jewish cultural activity as against Christian, of which they were always afraid. At the same time they do not conceal the fact that a *force* has now appeared in Palestine which, while being from the point of numbers of very little account, in proportion to the [local] Arab population, from the point of view of quality has already acquired such dimensions that they [the reasonable Arabs] do not feel themselves capable of opposing them. They demand from us that we steer and organize our colonization work in such a way that the Arab population will be advanced as a result of it. True, our colonization activity even now — and these gentlemen know it very well — leads automatically to an improvement of the economic position of the Arab population: in the colonies by the enrichment of the surrounding fellaheen, and in the towns through the credit of our banks. However, further steps in this direction are now involved. They want our schools to be put at the disposal of their children, that Arabic be taught intensely in them, that we care for the fellaheen, that Jewish, and not Christian, capital implement the large concessions, etc.

'There can be no question, but that these wishes absolutely correspond with our own interests. Were we able to conduct colonization activity like a Great Power with the means at her disposal, we would in our interests proceed in precisely this fashion'.[59]

Sokolow gave an interview to N. Malul who, as well as being a Jewish member of the Decentralization Party and employee of the Palestine Office, was a frequent and long-standing contributor to the Arab press. In this interview, published in the Cairo daily *al-Muqaṭṭam*, Sokolow explained that the Jewish immigrants to Palestine were coming not as a foreign colonizing power, but as people returning to their own homeland. There were only two possibilities for Palestine in the future: 'Either she remains barren, in which case there will be as little for the Arabs as for the Jews, or the Jews remain in which case the Arabs will also remain'.

Sokolow hoped the Jews would draw near to Arab culture in every respect, and that they would learn Arabic and Arabic literature in their schools. 'I also hope that we build up together with united forces, a great Palestinian culture to replace that of ancient times... But this we can do only if we revive our Semitic tongue [i.e. Hebrew] and open our schools. In this way we also draw closer to the Arabs'.

In reply to this article, the secretary of the Decentralization Party, Ḥakki Bey al-ʿAzm said that the words of the Zionist leader in no way corresponded to reality: 'Quite the contrary, we see the Jews excluding themselves completely from the Arabs in language, school, commerce, customs, in their entire economic life. They cut themselves off in the same way from the indigenous government, whose protection they enjoy, so that the population considers them a foreign race. This is the reason for the grievance of the Arabs of Syria and Palestine against Jewish immigration. 'The Arabs have as yet made no steps on the road to their national renaissance... they, therefore, see their very existence threatened by the Jews. Many also see a political danger in that the Jews retain foreign nationality and in this way conquer the country for foreign states... The youth of Palestine is already inspired with the idea of assembling in order to take up the struggle against the Zionist movement. We do not think that the educated Jews and Zionists will mock at the defence movement of the Arab youth and intelligentsia'.[60]

Notwithstanding this threat of violence as the major or only effective way of opposing the Yishuv — a threat that had already been used by Arab leaders — the Zionist Actions Committee was still unable in the summer of 1914, on the eve of the outbreak of World War I, to determine on any clear-cut Arab policy or on any specific way of dealing with the Arab question. Such a decision was postponed until the convention of the projected conference with Arab notables which was being planned, but was postponed several times until it finally fell into oblivion due to the outbreak of war.[61]

The Zionist leadership, centred in Europe, was sufficiently removed from the scene of action to allow itself to vacillate and procrastinate insofar as efficacious steps in the field of relations with the Arabs were concerned. Moreover, the Zionist Organization was in effect so weak that it was content not to have to face up to such problems as could be put off, nor is there any evidence that any of the members of the Greater Actions Committee or of the leaders of the Zionist federations made any attempt to force upon the executive a more deterministic and activist policy as regards the Palestine Arab question, although all of them had been made aware of extensive Arab antagonism to Zionism and the Yishuv through the circulars received from Berlin.

Only Jacobson and his assistants in Istanbul were sufficiently close to the Arabs, with many of whose leaders they established personal contact, to be determined in their efforts to establish friendly relations with as many Arab leaders and groups as possible. The Zionist representatives in Istanbul were well aware of the harm that could be, and was in fact, done to the Zionist cause and the Yishuv by the Arabs, particularly in the sphere of Ottoman relations: immigrant and land purchase regulations, parliamentary and other institutional representation, and so on and so forth. But here, too, the Zionists were frustrated and thwarted by a number of factors. Firstly, by the insignificant means that stood at their disposal, comprising a striking contrast to Arab demands; secondly, by the intricacies and duplicity of Turkish politics; and, thirdly, by the complexity of Arab groups which were neither united on a single clearly-defined policy as far as Palestine and the Zionists were concerned, nor represented a homogeneous front on the implementation of their own nationalist aspirations. As Jacobson himself wrote in May 1914 after five and a half years of personal contact with different Arab leaders: 'We here are in contact with several gentlemen who call themselves the chiefs and leaders of the different Arab groups. Each one claims that it is he who is the real, the only real, the important one... There is no way of knowing what truth there is in what they say, what is behind them. They do not have *a single* organization'.[62]

But this was only a secondary aspect of the dilemma; the main obstacle was clearly the total inability of the Zionists to fulfil Arab demands both in the cultural and financial fields. The only solution lay in procrastination, 'to promise to give all their demands serious consideration; to talk constantly of the necessity for both sides of a lasting agreement; to demand that everything that might prejudice this future agreement be avoided: the polemic in the press, attacks in parliament, mass petitions...'.[63]

The Zionist office in Istanbul also suggested the following train of thought to the Arabs: 'The Arab question is much more extensive than the Palestine question. If the Arabs allow us to buy land in Palestine and to colonize (in the process of which the fellaheen must somehow be cared for), they will be able to win through our agency the goodwill of the European press and eventually of Jewish financial circles for the development of Arabism'.

The long-term Arab 'national aspirations', both cultural and political, 'the creation of a great Arab empire', would not, of course, be satisfied for the dual reason of irreconcilability with Jewish Palestine aspirations and of lack of means — but 'our discussions are moving in this direction'. The Arabs knew this full well, but each side declared itself in favour of a joint study of the question in order to reach an understanding of the other's demands and to work towards an accord. Both sides were clearly in favour of delaying tactics, the Zionists in order to stall Arab attacks in parliament and in the press, the Arabs in order to gain as much benefit as possible from the Jews before their paths irretrievably parted. The Zionist officials is Istanbul concluded from their talks with the Arabs that the latter 'considered us a future dangerous power whom they feared would dispossess Arabism', whereas they themselves realized the growing strength of Arab nationalism and dismissed as unduly optimistic the verdict of the Vali of Beirut, Sami Bekir Bey, who told them that the Arabs were all purchasable, and the Arab movement consisted of 'unimportant leaders without an army'.[64]

## V

We have seen the attitude of the Zionist Congress and of the Zionist Actions Committee to the Arabs and the dilemma of leaders in Berlin who lacked personal contact with conditions in Palestine and who had no acquaintance with Arabs and their mentality and aspirations. These disadvantages as well as the shortage of qualified manpower, the absence of a satisfactory political organization and, especially, the requisite financial means virtually prevented the Zionist Head Office and executive from appreciating the real issues at stake and therefore from making, or even accepting, concrete suggestions as to the way in which to achieve the sought after friendship with the Arabs of Palestine.

As already mentioned, most of the information which comprised the basis for discussions at Actions Committee meetings and for the official reports to local Zionist federations and leaders, emanated from Jacobson in Istanbul — whose attitude and that of his assistants to the Arabs has been included in the discussion of the attitude of the Zionist leadership — and, even more so, from Ruppin or Thon in Jaffa, whose letters were often quoted verbatim. In this way the description of the Zionist leadership's attitude to the Arabs represents also that of the organization's official representatives on the spot. Nevertheless, a number of aspects of the attitude and policy of the latter warrant additional elaboration.

Less than one month after the Young Turk Revolution, Ruppin commented on the inherent consequences of the change of regime as far as Zionism was concerned. The position had 'completely changed. It was conceivable that under an autocratic sovereign the Jews in Palestine not only receive special privileges on paper (for land purchase, organization etc.) but that these privileges be defended with the State's entire power — should the Sultan wish it — against the possible opposition of Arabs and Christians. In a constitutional regime it must be considered out of the question that the Jews be granted any privileges that might comprise special rights for Jews as against other inhabitants '.[65] 'As long as the Jews in Palestine constitute a *quantité negligeable* from the point of view of numbers and economic influence, even the best will of the central government in Constantinople cannot help the Jews to procure political power in the country. Arabs and Christians would soon make any Jewish privilege illusory. It holds true in a parliamentary, even more than in an absolutist, Turkey, that the government's goodwill can clinch the predominancy already attained by a certain group of the population, but it cannot *create* this predominance... '[66]

Ruppin expressed the desire to foster in the Arab po-

pulation a more mature and favourable view of the aims
and purposes of Zionism. He suggested that this be done
by various means: by starting an Arabic newspaper in
Jerusalem, by influencing the existing press, by disseminating
broadsheets among the Palestinian Arabs, etc.[67]

Yet, as we have seen, the rapprochement to the Arabs, as
understood by Ruppin, involved not only political action
and propaganda but also, and perhaps chiefly, the establishment of friendly relations and understanding in everyday
life. Ruppin stressed, as in his speech at the Eleventh Zionist
Congress, the need for tactfulness in the purchase of land
and he refused to accept the theory that only Jewish labour
be employed in Jewish enterprises and villages.

Ruppin wrote to the representative of a Russian Zionist
group who proposed the purchase of land on the east bank
of the Jordan: 'if, furthermore, we write you that the land
cannot be colonized immediately by East European Jews
because it is far away from the Jewish colonies, we are trying
to tell you that the Arabs in the Zarqa area have as yet had
no acquaintance with Jewish settlement and that therefore
it is necessary to be especially careful in the first years in
intercourse with these Arabs. Unpleasant incidents between Arabs and Jews in Palestine keep occurring simply
because the Jew understands neither the language nor the
customs of the Arab and the Arab views with animosity
what has in reality to be ascribed to the Jew's ignorance'.
In order to avoid 'misunderstandings and hostilities'
Ruppin suggested that for the first years the land be settled
by 'such Jewish labourers as have already learnt Arabic and
Arab customs. In a few years the Arabs will have become
accustomed to Jewish neighbours and then other Jews can
also gradually settle'.[68] Ruppin wrote in a similar vein to
representatives of workers' groups: 'We need labourers who
know Arabic for they must live in peace with Beduin neighbours...', or again in connection with the first settlement
established in the Negev (Ruḥama): 'We need a group of
6-10 labourers. In view of local conditions we are looking
for labourers who know Arabic, the Arab's way of life and
traits and how to live peacefully with their neighbours.
The development of the agricultural settlement of the Negev
depends on the good relations of these pioneers and their
neighbours. They must, therefore, be temperate and un-

derstanding, capable of refraining from quarrels and of controlling themselves in unpleasant circumstances. It is known that the Arabs there are quiet people and if they [the Jews] know how to behave towards them, we can hope for satisfactory development'.[69]

The implementation in everyday reality of lessons learnt from earlier mistakes in land purchase which had caused friction with neighbouring Arabs and the emphasis of the need for cultivating land purchased by Jews with Jewish labour, insofar as such labour was available, were among the most important axioms of the Palestine Office's policy. Dr. Ruppin, therefore, used for purposes of land purchase the services of a number of men who had long experience and intimate knowledge of local conditions (such as Joshua Ḥankin and Albert Antébi), whereas all efforts to achieve closer relations with the Arabs in other realms failed, according to Ruppin, because no person fitted for such activity was to be found.[70]

The Palestine Office likewise initiated and encouraged the immigration of Yemenite Jews to Palestine as they were considered potentially satisfactory agricultural labourers. The European labourers, mostly Russian Jews, on the other hand, often could not endure the combination of physical labour and climate nor could they subsist on the accepted local wage.

These Russian Jewish labourers, together with the principle of exclusive Jewish labour, were considered by a number of Zionists and members of the Yishuv to constitute a major factor in arousing the hostility of the Palestinian Arabs. Levontin wrote in this vein to Herzl as early as 1903[71] and the charge was brought against the Russian Jewish labourers and their political party, Poalei Zion, that they were largely responsible for the aforementioned tension and disturbances in the spring of 1908, as well as for later incidents and bad feeling between Jews and Arabs.[72] Dr. Ruppin appreciated the main arguments of both sides in this internal controversy and adopted an intermediate position: 'although in all our enterprises we must, of course, think first of all of giving work and bread to our own poorer brethren, we must avoid anything that may resemble an exclusion of Arabs. If many, particularly among the workers, advocate the principle that Jewish land must be cultivated solely by Jews, it is an understandable reaction to the fact that hitherto in several Jewish colonies, Jewish labourers have been to an extent excluded and only Arabs employed. In its own right, however, this principle cannot be approved. Insofar as Jewish labourers seek employment in our farms we shall give them preference, but it would be very dangerous to reverse the axiom and for us to give employment only to Jews '.[73]

It was widely accepted in Jewish circles, and examples have been given above, that the Christian Arabs were the source of animosity to the Yishuv and to Jewish activity in Palestine in general. A number of Christian schools and other institutions, particularly those connected with the Jesuits, had for many decades educated young Arabs to hate the Jews. Originally, the motivation had been religious, but in many instances the lesson remained while its raison d'être had become irrelevant. Writing about *al-Karmal*, already mentioned as the most virulent of the Palestinian Arab anti-Jewish papers and the source of inspiration of many Arab organs outside Palestine, Ruppin said: '...its hostile attitude does not indeed originate in any anti-semitic tendency among the Muslims but in the hate of several Haifa Christians...'[74] Shortly afterwards he wrote on the same theme: '...there are many indications that we shall come up against strong resistance to the progress of our colonization activity from the Christian Arabs of Haifa and Nazareth, while the Muslim population is less to be feared.

'It is our opinion that we must adapt ourselves to this situation and explain to the government and the Muslim Arabs that from every point of view the Jewish colonization is far less dangerous than the strengthening of the position of the Christian Arabs who are under the sway of Russia, and comprise the best starting-point for Russia's advance into Palestine. We know that the member for Acre (a Muslim Arab) is of a similar opinion...'[75]

We have already mentioned the fact that Arab nationalists were thinking some two years later in terms of a foreign, specifically a British or French annexation or mandate, and Paris was already in 1905 and again in 1909 the centre of Arab nationalist activity. The Russians, however, as the Ottomans' traditional enemy, were a different matter and their growing influence was widely feared in the Middle East where their schools and other cultural institutions were multiplying rapidly and attracting not only the largest Christian sect, the Orthodox, but also many Muslims.

There seems to be no doubt that Ruppin was sincerely convinced of the benefit to be derived by the local Arab population as well as the Ottoman government from the Yishuv and its expansion. In a memorandum which he composed together with Levontin, stress was laid on the high wages paid by Jews to Arab labourers, on the value of Jewish agricultural methods as an example for the fellaheen and on the fact that the Jews purchased the worst land from the Arabs. 'The one and only source of hatred of the Jews that raises its voice against Jewish immigration is the Christian establishment, the rich Christians in Palestine and those who were educated in the Jesuit schools — these are the arch-enemies of the Jews and likewise of the Ottoman government. The rich Christians who stand on a culturally higher level than the Muslims, always lend money in the villages at exorbitant rates of interest, they exploit the fellaheen to their last penny and have appropriated their property for nothing. Since the Jews came to Palestine, however, the economic position of the country's population has improved; the Arab, although occasionally still compelled to sell his property, is no longer dependent on the rich effendi who deprives him of his land at a ridiculously low price. The Arab prefers to sell to a Jew at a higher price — and thus no more fields remain for the usurious activity of the wealthy Christian Arabs'.

Ruppin and Levontin proceeded to make an important exception to their own rule by claiming that 'a number of Muslim effendis' who, like their Christian counterparts, strove to enrich themselves at the expense of the population, also wanted to keep the Jews out of Palestine for they comprised 'the sole intrusion in their work of suppression'.[76]

The most virulent speakers in the attacks on Zionism and Jewish immigration to Palestine that took place in the Turkish Parliament in March and April 1911, were in fact Muslim Arabs. '... all the Arab members from Jerusalem and one from Damascus are Muslims and our bitterest and most dangerous enemies who are evolving the keenest propaganda against us'.[77] This propaganda directed against Jewish immigration and land purchase was not restricted to Parliament, but included protests sent from Palestine to

Istanbul and, as already mentioned, in increasingly frequent and often very exaggerated opposition in the Arab press.[78]

The Palestine Office went to great pains to demonstrate that Jewish land purchase was not only inconsiderable but also beneficial to the local population. It thus prepared a detailed analysis of the various tracts of land purchased since 1880.[79] Ruppin and Thon also interpreted the recurrent manifestations of antagonism that took the form of assaults on colonists and watchmen, or of pillage of the colonies, as demonstrations of Arab nature and custom and examples of inter-village strife and conflict that were the lot of every colony in its initial stages.[80]

Ruppin specifically attributed 'the deterioration of the political situation, i.e. the hostility which our work in Palestine is encountering' to 'a strong dislike' secretly harboured by 'leading Arab circles, especially the Christian Arabs'. These elements dared not express their true feelings nor their principal demand, which was for an Arab autonomy. They, therefore, 'vented their anger' on the Yishuv which constituted good material for agitation among the easily incitable masses and against which the rich landowners already had economic grudges. 'The Turkish government is, in my opinion, not unfavourably inclined towards the Jewish colonization in Palestine, even considering it a barrier against the growing Arab danger. Yet it does not dare to come out openly against the Arabs who comprise almost one third of all the members of parliament, and actually makes small concessions to them at the expense of the Jews in order to appease them...

'Voices can be heard here demanding that the Jews side either with the Arabs or with the Turks. In my opinion it is impossible at the present embryonic stage of party relationships in Turkey to determine a certain role for the Jews. They must not fall out with the Arab population in whose midst they live and whose animosity could be extraordinarily harmful to our activity'.[81]

Representatives of the various organizations and villages of the Jewish Yishuv had been called together in Jaffa under the auspices of the Palestine Office on 6 February 1911 to discuss 'the present situation of the Jews in Palestine and especially measures against the increasing hostility on the part of the non-Jews'.[82] A provisional committee was duly appointed to deal with current political questions and from time to time the plenum or council reassembled. On 4 August 1911, Ḥaim Cohen (from Petaḥ Tikvah) stressed that all defence measures intended to consolidate the organizational strength of the Yishuv must be secondary to a healthy attitude of basic friendship to the Arabs. 'The cause of many of the recent incidents is apparently a lack of knowledge of how to behave towards our neighbours. It must be seen to that at least in every village a few people will pay attention to this factor'. David Yellin, a native of Palestine, expressed his complete agreement: 'Here it is not the government but the local population which persecutes us. Fifteen years ago the Muslims hated the Christians, while their attitude to the Jews was one of contempt. Now their attitude to the Christians has changed for the better and to the Jews for the worse'.[83] On the previous day a discussion of the political situation with stress on the north, took place in Haifa and Aaron Aaronson and Drs. W. Bruenn and E. Auerbach, none of them alarmists by nature, wrote to Ruppin: 'Those who are sufficiently involved with the native population to comprehend their mentality are alarmed to see with what speed the poison sown by our enemies is spreading among all layers of the population.

'We must fear all possible calamities. It would be criminal to continue preserving the attitude of placid onlookers'.[84]

While chary of undue pessimism and any tendency to panic — we have already seen how Ruppin assuaged the fear of the Actions Committee in September 1911 — Ruppin was fully aware of the seriousness of the situation. He was insistent that consideration must be taken of the effect on the Arab population of any step taken vis-à-vis the Ottoman government, which was of no greater importance to Zionism and the Yishuv than the local Arabs: 'We must not purchase the goodwill of the one by incurring the enmity of the other'.[85]

Early in 1912, the Palestine Office was forced to admit, as a result of a number of surveys of the Arab press (as Yellin and others had indeed already claimed) that there were new forces at work among the Muslim Arabs. As we have seen, these — in contradistinction to the Christian Arabs — had hitherto been generally considered friendly to the Yishuv, with the exception of a number of powerful effendis. 'The opinion which we had advocated so strongly, that our only opponents are the Christians, while the Muslims are our friends — at least as far as the press is concerned — is erroneous. On the contrary, it seems that Christian, Young Turk and pro-Jewish papers or those neutral in Jewish questions, are almost identical, while all Muslim papers are opposed to the Young Turks and also the Jews, Christians and foreigners in general. We do not as yet want to pronounce conclusive judgment on the basis of this evidence but it will in any case be of interest to follow up this issue and to submit to reexamination our views concerning the attitude of the Muslims and Christians to our efforts'.[86] This was written almost a year before the Palestine Office began to draw the attention of the Head Office in Berlin to an incipient Arab national movement.

A number of further surveys of the Arab press were made in these years, the most comprehensive of which, that of N. Malul, carried out under the auspices of the Palestine Office,[87] demonstrated explicitly that the Arab press could not be divided, as far as its attitude to the Yishuv was concerned, according to religion or even according to party. There were neutral, friendly and antagonistic Christian and Muslim papers.[88]

While many of the Arab notables of Palestine were openly hostile to the Yishuv, there were a few important exceptions. One of these was the member of parliament for Acre, As'ad Shuqayr who, appreciating the benefit to the country intrinsic in the expansion of the Yishuv, expressed his willingness to intervene in Constantinople in favour of land purchase in a number of protracted cases. When As'ad asked Ḥankin for a loan for his friend Tawfiq 'Abdullah, the President of the local Young Turk committee (who suggested mortgaging his property as guarantee for the loan), 'Ḥankin pleaded strongly not to let slip by this opportunity of obligating two such influential people by doing them a service. He sees in this the beginning of an "Arab policy" which we have hitherto unfortunately completely neglected and which appears to be absolutely essential if we wish to continue our work in Palestine. This will not only be a matter of attaining good relations with the influential families through favours but we shall have to demonstrate to the common people by gratuitous medical help, etc, that we are coming to Palestine not as enemies but as friends. This can, however, wait till later'.[89]

In November 1913, in a general survey sent to the Actions Committee, Thon wrote of the importance he attached to the fact that 'we are finding increasing opportunity in our work to make influential Arab leaders indebted and obliged... The Arab population is still dependent on the views of the effendis who are respected for their wealth, learning, office or extraction'.[90]

In the meantime the Palestine Office, while stressing the importance of good relations with the Arab population as a whole, continued to attribute such political influence as was exerted on Turkish government circles to a few leading Arab individuals and groups.[91]

It was only in the course of 1913 with the appearance of Arab nationalist groups or committees with representatives in various parts of the Arab world (in Cairo, Beirut, Damascus) as well as in Palestine and Istanbul, that the Palestine Office came to appreciate the need for specific efforts to reach concrete agreements with wide Arab circles and particularly the intelligentsia and various ideological groups. At the same time, notwithstanding the publicity given to the Arab movement and its growth and consolidation throughout the year 1913, the Palestine Office continued to insist that there was no place for alarmism. Thon tried to collect as much material as possible concerning the Arab Congress held in June 1913 in Paris 'so that we can pacify all those who try to raise cries of alarm'.[92]

The Palestine Office was adamant in its view, which it held from the beginning, that there was no place for panic or undue concern. Yet the Yishuv must show no signs of weakness but rather prove its strength at every opportunity. This standpoint was demonstrated by the office's attitude to the newspaper *Haherut*, on the one hand, which laid considerable emphasis on the Arab 'danger' whenever the opportunity arose, and to the defence organization Hashomer, on the other. *Haherut*, the editors and correspondents of which were for the most part Palestinian-born Jews, had the specific intention of making the Yishuv aware of what the Arabs thought and wrote about the Jews. It thus published many translations or resumés of articles concerning the Jews and the Yishuv that had appeared in the Arab press and accompanied them by alarmist editorials on the imminence of the Arab 'danger' which were far removed from the methods adopted by Ruppin and his associates. *Haḥerut* likewise tended to exaggerate Jewish-Arab incidents which specifically aroused the antagonism of the Palestine Office. At the same time, Ruppin and Thon made every effort to strengthen Hashomer and to avail themselves of its services. This group, whose principal idea derived from the self-defence organizations that had been founded in Russia after the Kishinev programme of 1903, strove to introduce Jewish watchmen into Jewish villages and town quarters, just as the Poale Zion party, to which most of the members belonged, endeavoured to extend the use of labour. The Arab watchmen were notorious for their collaboration with pilferers and thieves.

In September 1913, Thon wrote to Ruppin, who was then in Vienna: 'The opposition of the Arab population will likewise increase considerably as soon as it is certain that the Jews have possession of the state domains. On the other hand, our prestige will also mount in the eyes of the population if we can point to such an important success and if we have the government on our side'.[93] In the same way the Palestine Office, commenting on the proposal — discussed in one of the reports on the Arab press — to hold an 'anti-Zionist Arab Congress', said that it was obvious that this idea was 'still in the stage of preparation', whereas the alarmists were already discussing the organization of Arab opposition.[94] In one of its reports on the Arab press, the Palestine Office viewed very favourably an article published by J. Eisenstadt (Barzilai) in *Haḥerut* criticizing the undue emphasis laid by the paper on the Arab press. The translations it published from the Arabic press were decidedly injurious in that they frightened the Jews 'who should now be devoting all their strength to furthering large-scale activity'.[95]

Thon wrote to the Zionist Actions Committee that the most effective way of creating a favourable attitude to the Jews among Arab public opinion was to consolidate the activity of the Yishuv. Large-scale enterprises 'cause, it is true, jealousy and fear, but first and foremost, they infuse respect, which significantly tempers hostility. Thus Tel

Aviv arouses a certain amount of apprehension about our strength, yet the recognition of Jewish talent for such cultural feats is preponderant'.[96]

As part and parcel of its attempt to moderate Arab anti-Jewish incitement, the Palestine Office made numerous attempts to encourage the Ottomanization of the Yishuv — to persuade the Jews to relinquish their foreign citizenship. This was necessary for other purposes as well, notably to enable the Jews to make themselves felt in parliamentary elections and in the institutions of local government, but Arab attacks on the Yishuv in 1914 constantly harped on the foreign attachments and connections of the Jews of Palestine.[97]

The Palestine Office also strove for the establishment of direct contact with influential Arabs. In the spring and summer of 1914 when the Office was well aware of the existence of nationalist elements among the Arabs, Ruppin and Thon continued to press for an Arab-Jewish meeting or conference in which the different groups and opinions might be represented. In May, Ruppin wrote to Jacobson that the latter's plan for creating a Jewish-Arab committee had so far miscarried for lack of people in the Yishuv who were both willing and competent to work judiciously in such a committee.[98] Dr. I. Levy also had plans for talks with the Arabs in which he, Yellin and Thon were to participate; the idea was apparently mooted by an Arab friend who had told Levy that the talk of the day in Arab Palestine and in Syria centred around the Zionist question: 'in the most remote places, day and night, in cafés, clubs, societies and even in the mosques this burning question was being discussed'. He also said that there were a number of important Arabs who were in favour of Arab-Jewish talks, while the extremists on both sides must be left out of the picture.[99] Thon and Yellin did, in fact, meet Levy's Arab acquaintance who proceeded to establish a purely Muslim 'benevolent society' in which he worked for an Arab-Jewish rapprochement.[100]

As for Sokolow's talks with Arab leading personalities who declared themselves in favour of Arab-Jewish talks, Thon wrote that the 'elaboration of a concrete programme for an agreement cannot but face great obstacles. The Arabs will not let themselves be played off with simple phrases, while we can hardly consent to such concessions as they would in fact demand from us: restriction of land purchase, the partial restriction of Hebrew in favour of Arabic in the schools and in public life, and living together with them in the exclusive Jewish quarters. Furthermore, we must first of all ascertain that the Arabs are not seeking our friendship in order to have us as allies in the struggle against the central government. It seems that such a tendency exists, which compels us to a certain reserve from the start'.[101]

The preparations for the projected Jewish-Arab conference were considerable. Ruppin wrote to one of the prospective participants that the exact agenda was not yet known but the conference would discuss 'methods to be employed to reconcile the differences that exist between the Arabs and the Jews and to establish more friendly relations between the two sides'.[102] Two weeks later, Ruppin wrote to another suggested participant that he prepare a blueprint concerning the nature of Zionism: 'The Arab members of the conference still have in fact quite primitive views concerning Zionism and they have expressed the wish that at this conference the question be answered what Zionism in fact is, the answer to be given in the form of documentary evidence. Of course, this answer cannot be given ex improviso'.[103]

In the end the conference was postponed, as already mentioned, for external reasons, and although it was decided in no way to permit a sharp breach with the Arabs, Ruppin felt a certain relief for he was convinced that the conference agenda and composition as planned could only have led to a worsening of the situation.

## VI

The attitude of the Zionist Organization and its representatives in Palestine to the Arabs was thus very complex. It is impossible to speak of an inherent Zionist policy to the Arabs: as we have seen, in the early stages the Zionist movement and organization showed few signs of appreciation of the need for any such policy and even in the years under discussion (1908-14) the majority — both rank and file Zionists and leaders — gave little consideration to the problem. It seems that this was less the result of a conscious contempt for natives of the Orient — then common to most

Europeans, and which might perhaps have prevented any serious thought in this direction — than to the topographical and mental remoteness from Palestine. Most European and American Zionists before World War I seem to have been primarily concerned with aspects of the movement that had impact on their own local organizations and federations. Insofar as their considerations were political, they did not include the Arabs.

Among the exceptions, among such Zionists as developed a specific attitude or policy to the Arabs, there was general agreement that their friendship had to be attained, whether for ideological reasons or for practical purposes. Among the ideologists there were socialist groups that could not on the one hand accept the idea that a Jewish colonization of Palestine must necessarily lead to the disenfranchisement of the local Arab population. Yet, on the other hand, the Poalei Zion, who made every effort to prove the community of interest between the Yishuv and the indigenous population, were prepared for an inevitable conflict — though admittedly only as an intermediary step — between the Jewish and Arab proletariat. They preached that the international brotherhood of workers applied only to workers who were already secure in their employment; it did not apply to a potential proletariat that had to struggle to find employment and could not refrain from conflict with those workers whose places of work they must take for themselves.

There were other idealists notably Aḥad Ha'am and his followers who sought friendship with the Arabs. This group, which included a number of leading personalities in the Yishuv (such as M. Smilansky, J. Lurie) refused to accept the idea that the Jewish national revival could be built on a basis of animosity and conflict. The Jewish cultural tradition, and the Jewish message to mankind were those of the prophets who taught peace and goodwill, and any deviation meant that the national rebirth was being conducted along false lines.

There was yet a further line of thought that held that the Jews were essentially orientals — semites — who in returning to their ancient homeland must assimilate to the Eastern way of life, and would in fact assimilate without difficulty. This idea, as indeed the above mentioned theories, had a number of very interesting manifestations in the years 1908-14 that cannot be dealt with in the framework of this article. Suffice it to say that the obvious conclusion was a stress on common semitic origin and cultural similarities, an increased rapprochement to the Arabs, a profound study of their language and customs, and to an extent even an imitation of their way of life.

A combination of the two above-mentioned theories was expounded by Radler-Feldmann, according to whom a political, economic and general amalgamation of the two nations in Palestine was a 'sine qua non', which — while it could not be accomplished overnight — must be one of the Yishuv's main objectives. Radler-Feldmann was convinced that the Jews had a special task to fulfil in the Arab national revival for the implementation of which the Arabs lacked sufficient 'moral strength' and in which the Jews must be interested as they would be adversely affected by the presence of 'an inferior Arab group in our midst'. The problem was, then, one of 'conviction and ethics', though 'the conviction must also receive expression by action'.[104]

Concurrently, there were realists who strove to achieve good relations with the Arabs for the very practical purpose of enabling the uninterrupted progress of the Jewish colonization of Palestine and of facilitating the implementation of the Jewish national revival. In this way both Jacobson and Ruppin constantly stressed the need for friendship with the Arabs. The former was concerned with the point of view of Zionist activities in Istanbul where the Zionists were incessantly encountering Arab opposition both in the form of outspoken attacks and in the more indirect form of Turkish obstructionism that emanated from the fear of displeasing the Arabs. Ruppin's motives were more specifically Palestinian.

In the same way the nationalistically conscious Sephardic Jews (a number of whom edited *Haḥerut*) warned the leaders of the Yishuv of the danger of Arab opposition and tried to demonstrate that as long as the Jewish colonization was conducted by European Zionists there was little chance of any real understanding of and with the local Arabs and thus little hope for the success of the Yishuv. (There was an Ashkenazi Yishuv of old standing in Palestine that was also closely acquainted with the Arab way of life, but it was basically non-nationalist and thus for the most part irrelevant to our topic). All the above-mentioned groups agreed on the existence of an 'Arab question' which had to be solved as a preliminary to successful Jewish nationalist activity in Palestine. Radler-Feldmann summed up the position in a memorandum which was significantly entitled 'Concerning our Arab question', and a copy of which was sent to the Zionist Head Office in Berlin in March 1913: 'In Palestine we can hear two contradictory opinions: the one underrating the Arab question, the other perhaps exaggerating it... The fact is that approximately 30 years ago our leading thinkers felt themselves attracted (in the first instance platonically) by the Arabs as a related race and by Islam as a religion close to Judaism. In practice, however, the Jews who came here within the last 30 years (those who came earlier adopted a different attitude) were unable — for reasons which I cannot explain here — to establish friendly relations with the Arabs. At the moment their hatred against us is being fanned by the press and animosity is becoming more frequent. Altogether, it must be accepted that two nations such as the Jews and the Arabs can only live side by side either in friendship or in enmity. A third relationship, one of indifference, does not exist'.[105]

The appearance of Arab nationalist groups and aspirations to which no-one who was in the centre of Turkish and/or Palestinian politics could be oblivious from the spring of 1911, introduced a new element into Zionist-Arab relations. The Arab nationalist movement was not organized within a single framework, with a generally recognized leader or unanimously accepted policy and the official active members of the various groups have been shown to have been very small. Yet it gradually became clear in the last five, and in particular in the three, years preceding World War I, that the Zionists had no longer to deal with the Arabs of Palestine alone but with an Arab national movement, that dreamt of an extensive Arab unity — even if under a European protectorate — of which Palestine was only a small but apparently important part.[106]

The realization of a political Arab national revival introduced a note of frustration into Zionist attempts to reach a modus vivendi with the Arabs. Various feelers had indeed been put out both by Zionists and by various Arab nationalist leaders and groups especially in the course of 1913 when each side was in dire need of the other for purposes of its Ottoman policy. But it became increasingly clear that there was no common ground for negotiation between the two nationalist revivals. The Zionists were neither sufficiently strong and wealthy to be able to help the Arabs substantially nor were they willing on grounds of principle to make all the concessions requested of them. Furthermore, the Ottoman authorities who had hitherto advocated Zionist-Arab negotiations discouraged in July 1914 the continuation of attempts at an entente.[107] All this became evident in the course of preparations for the Jewish-Arab Conference in the summer of 1914 which was constantly postponed by both sides until finally put aside by the confusion and difficulties that were the lot of both the Yishuv and the Arab nationalists within the Ottoman Empire after the outbreak of World War I.

It was still agreed by the men most actively connected with the problem of relations with the Arabs both in Istanbul and in Palestine, that the Arab population of Palestine did, in fact, and could not but benefit from Jewish colonization activity in the country, and that no effort might be spared to achieve good relations with the local Arabs and their leaders. Yet it had become apparent to them that neither economic and cultural advantage on the one hand nor Zionist initiative and attempts to establish friendly relations on the other were relevant to the position as it stood in 1914. The vociferous demands of the more extremist Arab nationalists had a popular appeal and drowned the voices of those Arabs who sought cooperation with the Zionists. These extremists, putting an end to theories of racial brotherhood and mutual advantage, made it abundantly clear that their plans left no room for both an Arab and a Jewish nationalist revival in one and the same place and they were prepared to use every means at their disposal to bring home their point. In the face of this the weakness and vacillations of the European Zionist leadership and its Ottoman policy merely served to contrast its inefficacy, remoteness from reality and failure to understand the issues at stake. The Zionist office in Istanbul and the Palestine Office on the other hand, which had stressed from 1908 the importance of the Arab population as a permanent element

which must be taken into consideration in all spheres and
on all levels of activity (in contradistinction to the Turkish
government or any of the parties in the Ottoman political
arena) and had believed, at least until the latter half of
1913, in the possibility of coming to terms with the Palestinian Arabs and with the incipient Arab national movement,
came gradually and reluctantly to the conclusion in the last
months of our period that there was no practical ground for
any long-term agreement between the two national movements. But whereas Lichtheim in Istanbul decided that
an eventual conflict between Arabs and Jews was inevitable
and that the most that could be hoped for was to delay the
struggle for as long as possible, Ruppin and Thon continued
to believe in the possibility of ignoring the extremist nationalists whose demands they knew they could not satisfy,
while explaining to the more moderate Arabs by means of
written and oral propaganda, that there was an essential
community of interests between both sides and convincing
them that the implementation of Zionism need not be
achieved at the expense of the Arabs and their specific
interests and requirements.

[1] The material used has been entirely Zionist, chiefly that preserved in the
Central Zionist Archives (henceforth CZA) in Jerusalem. The correspondence of the Zionist Central Bureau, both in Cologne (Z2) and in Berlin
(Z3), and that of the Palestine Office in Jaffa as also the latter's copybooks
(L2) have enabled a thorough and uninterrupted study of the attitude of
the Zionist Organization and its representatives in Palestine to the Arabs and
the Arab national movement. The subject has in fact already been touched
upon by P. A. Alsberg, 'The Arab question in the policy of the Zionist
Executive before the First World War', *Shivat Zion*, 1955, pp. 161-209,
Heb, henceforth Alsberg, *op. cit.*, and by N. J. Mandel, 'Attempts at an
Arab-Zionist Entente, 1913-1914, *Middle Eastern Studies*, 1965, pp. 238-267,
henceforth Mandel, *op. cit.* N. Mandel also published an article in *St. Antony's Papers*, Number 17 (pp. 77-108), 'Turks, Arabs and Jewish Immigration
into Palestine, 1882-1914'.
[2] In other words, a territory virtually identical with that of the projected
Arab empire. For Negib Azoury and his book; for the *Ligue de la Patrie Arabe*
which published two manifestos, one addressed to the powers, the other to
the Arabs; and for Eugène Jung, formerly a French official in Indo-China,
who published in 1906 *Les puissances devant la révolte arabe, la crise mondiale de
demain*, see A. Hourani, *Arabic Thought in the Liberal Age*, Oxford, 1962,
pp. 277-9; *Arab Nationalism - an anthology* edited by Sylvia G. Haim, California,
1962, pp. 29-30.
[3] A. Ḥermoni, 'The Arab Movement and its Purpose' *Hashiloaḥ*, XV, pp.
377-390.
[4] *Stenographisches Protokoll der Verhandlungen des 7 Zionisten-Kongresses*, henceforth

SPVZK 7 etc., p. 25. For further mention of the question at the same Congress see *ibid.*, pp. 100-.1

[5] The author was Y. Epstein. (*Hashiloah*, XVII, pp. 193-206).

[6] M. Shenkin to M. Ussishkin 12.9.05, CZA, A24/111.

[7] Yusuf al-Khalidi, in a letter to the Chief Rabbi of France Zadok Kahn mentioned the possibility of a popular movement directed against the implementation of Zionism. Zadok Kahn passed the letter on to Herzl who replied directly to Khalidi on 19.3.99, *Herzl's Letters*, Jerusalem, 1957, pp. 309-10, Heb. Cf. also Herzl's novel *Altneuland*, Book 3, p. 245, 1925 ed., German.

[8] *The Complete Diaries of Theodore Herzl*, New York and London, 1960. The date of the entry is 5.3.04. As for its content cf. Azoury's demands v.s. For the other entries mentioning the Arabs see *ibid.*, 20.2.97, 9.10.98, 29.3.03.

[9] The Zionist Organization had a semi-official representative in Palestine from July 1903 when Z.D. Levontin opened in Jaffa a filial company of the Zionist Organization's bank, the Jewish Colonial Trust. Branches of this filial bank, the Anglo-Palestine Company, were opened within 3 years in Jerusalem, Beirut, Haifa and Hebron. Levontin's reports to Herzl and his successor D. Wolffsohn touched on all aspects of the Palestine situation.

[10] Radler-Feldmann had already, in 1905, expressed his views on the Arab question of the acuteness of which he was well aware, while both Hankin and Malul had a good deal of previous experience with Arabs with whom they had both been in constant close contact for many years.

[11] The Jewish population of Palestine comprised in 1914 approximately 85,000 souls out of a total population of some 700,000. The great majority of the Jews belonged to the old religious, rather than to the new nationalist Yishuv. The latter comprised 12,000 souls scattered over 43 villages or colonies and perhaps another 20,000 souls in the towns, of which the most important concentration was in Jaffa. Cf. also Mandel, *op. cit.*

[12] SPVZK 10, pp. 81-2.

[13] Y. Ben-Zvi, *Poalei Zion in the Second Aliyah*, Tel Aviv, 1950, Heb., pp. 98-103.

[14] SPVZK 10, pp. 90-1.

[15] *Ibid.*, p. 258.

[16] SPVZK 11, pp. 10, 159. The projected Hebrew University would also play its role by admitting Arab students (*ibid.*, p. 305).

[17] *Ibid.*, pp. 213 ff.

[18] See protocol of the Zionist Greater Actions Committee meeting of 7-9.8.11 (CZA, Z2: 237). Zionist Congresses were open to the public and given wide publicity in the non-Jewish as well as in the Jewish press, not only in Europe but in the Middle East as well.

[19] Z. Levontin to D. Wolffsohn, 18.12.07, CZA, W 125/3.

[20] 15.6.08, CZA, Z2: 251.

[21] The anti-Zionist press in Syria and Egypt copied a great deal of material, almost verbatim, from the Palestinian Arab papers and particularly from *al-Karmal*.

[22] The first monthly circular 'an die Landes — und Sondesverbaende der Zionistischen Organisation' was written on 24.1.12 (CZA, Z3: 425) while the first circular to members of the Greater Actions Committee (henceforth A.C.) and of the Zionist annual conferences bore the date 2.9.08 (for those circulars for the period 1908-14 see CZA, L2: 24 I-VI).

[23] A. Ruppin to D. Wolffsohn, 24.9.08, CZA, L2.: 437, cf. Alsberg, *op. cit.*

[24] A. Ruppin to D. Wolffsohn, 6.10.08, 19.10.08, CZA, L2: 437.

[25] A. Ruppin to the Zionist Inner Actions Committee 18.2.12, CZA, Z3: 1447, and to J. L. Magnes, 23.5.12, CZA, L2: 466. (All further mention of the Zionist A. C. refers to the Inner, as distinct from the Greater, Actions Committee).

26 V. Jacobson to Reshid Bey, 27.12.12, CZA, Z3: 45. A. Ruppin to V. Jacobson, 3.7.11 (in. orig. 3.6.11), CZA, Z2: 635.

27 Minutes of the Greater A.C. meeting of 27.4.11, CZA, Z2: 247.

28 Minutes, CZA, Z3: 363. The source of information was Thon.

29 Circular dated 1.3.12, CZA, L2: 24 III.

30 Circular dated 8.3.12 *ibid*. Ruppin's letter to the Zionist A.C. which was the origin of this statement and which was reproduced almost verbatim was written on 18.2.12, CZA, Z3: 1447.

31 D. Wolffsohn to A. Ruppin, 12.9.08, CZA, W126/1. Cf. p. 207 above.

32 CZA, L2: 24 IV. This report was almost identical, on this topic, with his aforementioned speech delivered a year later at the Eleventh Zionist Congress.

33 In original, 'und zwar vorwiegend durch eine auf wirtschaftlichem und kulturellem Gebiet liegende Kulturpolitik'. Minutes 24.11.12, CZA, Z3: 355.

34 Circular letter to members of the Greater A.C., 9.12.12, CZA, L2: 24 IV. The source of information was Thon's letter to the Zionist A.C., 19.11.12, CZA, L2: 479.

35 Circular as above, 28.1.13, CZA, L2: 24 V.

36 The growing influence of France in Palestine and Syria led the Zionist A.C. to stress the need for Zionist political activity in French government and official circles. (A certain amount of Zionist activity was already being conducted — in a somewhat dilettante and haphazard fashion — in London and Berlin). See memorandum of the Inner A. C. to members of the Greater A. C., Nov. 1913 (CZA, Z3: 341).

37 Circular No. 12 to the Zionist Federations, Feb. 1913, CZA, Z3: 425. The circular was based on Thon's letter to the A.C. of 29.1.13, CZA, L2: 482.

38 CZA, L2: 24 V. A great deal of Thon's letter of 20.1.13 was quoted verbatim.

39 V. Jacobson to the Inner A. C., 4.2.13, CZA, Z3: 45.

40 N. Mandel, *op. cit.*

41 I. Neufach to V. Jacobson, 6.3.13, CZA, Z3: 45. His source of information was a letter from A. Eisenberg, a colonist of Reḥovoth, to his son-in-law G. Frumkin, who was then studying in Constantinople.

42 A. Ruppin to I. Neufach, 1.4.13, CZA, L2: 486. The letter was a reply to Neufach's inquiry after receiving the above information given him by Frumkin. Thon enumerated the Palestine members of the Decentralization Party in a letter to the Zionist A. C., 8.4.13 (*ibid.*). It is worth noting that the party's leaders were chiefly Syrian Arabs who were in exile in Egypt.

43 V. Jacobson to R. Lichtheim, then secretary of the Zionist Central Office in Berlin, 10.4.14, CZA, Z3: 45. As to Jacobson's intentions cf. above.

44 *Ibid.* Jacobson therefore sent S. Hochberg; see P. Alsberg, *op. cit.*, M. Mandel, *op. cit.*

45 V. Jacobson to R. Lichtheim, 17.4.13, CZA, L5: 1/3. On the same day S. Hochberg left for Cairo for his talks with 'influential people in the Arab movement'. I. Neufach to A. Ruppin, 17.4.13, *ibid*.

46 As above, 25.9.13, CZA, Z3: 47.

47 R. Lichtheim to the Zionist A.C., 9.10.13, *ibid*.

48 As above, 14.10.13, *ibid*.

49 As above, 28.10.13, *ibid*.

50 As above, 20.11.13, *ibid*. Thus Malul for example, as mentioned elsewhere, was a member of the Decentralization Party.

51 One of the most controversial issues, which caused a good deal of internal Zionist discussion, was whether it was permissible to let non-Jews avail themselves of such institutions as the Anglo-Palestine Bank, the purpose of which was specifically to help Palestinian-Jewish agriculture and commercial and industrial enterprises.

52 'The Baron' had always striven towards friendly relations with the Arabs

and had given generously to the non-Jewish, as well as the Jewish, local population; as he did again on his visit to Palestine in 1914 (A. Ruppin to the A. C., 2.3.14, CZA, L2: 515). His contacts and cooperation and those of the Jewish Colonization Association with the Zionist Organization, and particularly with Jacobson and Ruppin were of recent standing. Rothschild now offered 15,000 francs for the favourable influencing of the Arab press and agreed to cooperation with the Zionists in purchasing land in Palestine. Cf. A. Ruppin to V. Jacobson, 8.8.13, CZA, L5: 15; [V. Jacobson ?] to H. Frank, 7.7.14, *ibid.*

[53] See N. Mandel, *op. cit.*, and 'Turks, Arabs and Jewish immigration into Palestine', cf. Note 1 above.

[54] CZA, Z3:341 (also L2: 24 V). For meetings conducted or initiated by Jacobson in Istanbul see eg. the report of a gathering held at the office of the Zionist-controlled paper *Le Jeune Turc*, sent to the Zionist Central Office together with Jacobson's letter of 27.3.11, CZA, Z2: 11. Naḥum Sokolow was a member of the Inner A.C.

[55] N. Sokolow to M. Nordau, 5.10.13, CZA, Z3: 32.

[56] CZA, Z3: 356. The Arab nationalist reaction to this irrelevant suggestion can be found in Ḥakki Bey al-'Azm's article, cf. n. below.

[57] CZA, L2: 24 VI.

[58] Confidential report to members of the Greater A.C., 27.2.14, *ibid.*

[59] Report of the Inner A. C., 5.6.14, *ibid.* As for the items mentioned in the quotation it is worth noting: a) it was already known that Arab leaders in Istanbul had specifically expressed a desire for agreement with the Zionists for they saw in this an advantage to their movement, thus R. Lichtheim to A. Ruppin, 24.4.14, CZA, Z3: 65; b) a few Arab pupils did in fact study at Jewish schools in Jerusalem, in Mikveh Israel, etc.; c) a number of people in the Yishuv, notably E. Sapir, had for over ten years been demanding the study of Arabic in Jewish schools etc.; d) the acuteness of the Arab problem had already been noted at the Inner A. C. meeting held on 21.5.14, CZA, Z3: 357.

[60] Both articles, published in *al-Muqattam* on 10th and 14th April respectively, were included in 'Anlage I aus der Arabischen Presse' sent by the Palestine Office Press Bureau to the Zionist Head Office in Berlin (CZA, L2: 24 VI). That Ḥakki Bey al-'Azm's threat of violence against the Yishuv was not a novel phenomenon can be seen from similar threats made by Shukri al-'Asali in 1911, cf. also A. S. Yehuda to O. Warburg 31.8.11, CZA, L2: 24 III, etc. In connection with these articles see: Ḥakki Bey al-'Azm to N. Malul 29.4.14, and N. Malul to A. Ruppin and N. Sokolow, CZA, A18/14/6.

[61] The history of the projected conference has been discussed by N. Mandel, *op. cit.* and there is, therefore, no point in recovering the same ground except insofar as is absolutely essential to the understanding of our subject. Sokolow explained to Ruppin while still in Palestine that the Jewish participants at the Conference were in no way to commit either themselves or the Zionist Organization. It was merely to be 'the first attempt at a personal agreement'. N. Sokolow to Y. Tchlenov, 5.7.14, CZA, Z3: 389. Tchlenov was adamant concerning the need not to make any commitments. (Y. Tchlenov to V. Jacobson, 6.7.14, CZA, Z3: 49) cf. also p. 214 above.

[62] V. Jacobson to A. Ruppin, 3.5.14, CZA, L2: 34 II. Cf. also Lichtheim's doubts, p. 214 above.

[63] R. Lichtheim to the Zionist Central Office, 28.4.14, CZA, Z3: 48, and to the Zionist A. C. 28.5.14, (CZA, Z3: 49; L3: 31 II; also R. Lichtheim to V. Jacobson, 7.6.14, CZA L3: 49.

[64] R. Lichtheim to Zionist A. C. 28.5.14 (see previous note).

[65] A. Ruppin to D. Wolffsohn, 18.8.08, CZA, L2: 436.

[66] A. Ruppin to V. Jacobson, 29.9.08, CZA, L2: 437.

[67] As above, 24.8.08, *ibid.*; cf. also A. Ruppin to J. L. Magnes, 23.5.12, CZA,

L 2: 466, etc. It is worth noting that E. Ben Yehuda's Hebrew paper *Ha'or* began to put out an Arabic edition at the end of August. This was, however, very short-lived.

68 A. Ruppin to M. Menassewitsch, 29.4.10, CZA, L2: 445.

69 A. Ruppin to M. Krigser and M. Shaḥar in Merḥavia 15.9.11, CZA, L2: 458, and to the Workers' Committee at Ein Ganim, 6.9.11, *ibid.*

70 A. Ruppin to the Inner A. C., 30.5.13, Z3: 1445; L2: 24 V, cf. p. 223 below. Albert Antébi, director of all Palestinian institutions of the Alliance Israélite Universelle since 1898 and official representative of the Jewish Colonization Association in Palestine, began early in 1912 to work in close cooperation with the Palestine Office for which he acted as mediator in the offices of the local administration in Jerusalem.

71 The subject of the letter was the so-called Palestinian Congress convened by M. Ussishkin in Zichron Yaacov in August 1903. 'The worst of all is the fact that it was considered necessary to thunder forth from the Zichron platform against the use of Arab labourers in the [Jewish] colonies, which talk was repeated in the press... This had the sole result of discrediting the Jewish population in the eyes of the Arabs, whereas in reality everything is as before' (i.e. as far as the employment of Arabs was concerned). CZA, H. VIII: 496; W 124/1.

72 On 24.4.08, Levontin wrote to Wolffsohn that the politicians of the Yishuv were more dangerous than beneficial 'in that they increase the class struggle and preach verbally and in their organs against giving work to Arabs. They thus sow hatred against us in the heart of the local population'. CZA; W 126/1.

73 A. Ruppin to Zionist Central Office, 28.7.12, CZA; L2: 24 IV.

74 A. Ruppin to D. Wolffsohn, 9.11.10, CZA; Z2: 125.

75 A. Ruppin to V. Jacobson, 25.1.11, *ibid.* The reference is to the member of Parliament for Acre, As'ad Shuqayr (see below).

76 A. Ruppin and Z. D. Levontin to the Zionist Central Office, 16.2.11, *ibid.*

77 V. Jacobson to the Zionist Central Office, 14.3.11, CZA; Z2: 11.

78 Cf. A. Ruppin to the Zionist Central Office, 31.3.11, CZA; Z2: 135. There had been at least one important earlier protest in which Muslim Arabs had taken part, namely in 1891, which was apparently no longer remembered.

79 Also: J. Thon to V. Jacobson, 5.5.11, CZA; L 5: 15. (There are copies in Z2: 631 and L2: 453). Representatives of the Yishuv would thus invite the Kaymakam of Jaffa or the Mutasarrif to tour the Jewish colonies to see for themselves that there was no valid ground for the attacks on the Yishuv, which were motivated by a desire to cause strife, e.g. J. Thon to the Zionist A. C., 30.5.11, CZA; Z2: 635.

80 E.g. J. Thon to the Zionist Central Office, 28.5.11, CZA; Z2: 635. Cf. pp. 203 and 204 above.

81 A. Ruppin to D. Wolffsohn, 15.7.11, *ibid.* It was generally accepted in Zionist circles at this time that the Turks were essentially sympathetic to their activities, notwithstanding restrictive legislation (cf. p. 208). For an analysis of the Turkish attitude see N. Mandel, 'Turks, Arabs and Jewish Immigration into Palestine, 1882-1914'. (see n. 1 above).

82 As above, 17.2.11, *ibid.* The various measures decided upon were similar to those discussed on previous occasions. The novelty was the fact that the entire Yishuv was represented.

83 From the minutes, CZA; L2: 457.

84 3.8.11, CZA; L2: 363.

85 A. Ruppin to the Zionist A. C., 23.10.11, CZA; L2: 459.

86 J. Thon to the Zionist A. C. 19.3.12, CZA; L2: 167; L2: 466. The particular survey that provoked these conclusions was one of the Beirut Arab press submitted on the same date to Berlin. For a report on press appearing in Damascus see J. Thon to the Zionist A. C., 24.6.12, CZA; Z3: 1448; L2: 472.

[87] A. Ruppin to J. Feldman, 5.6.14, CZA; L2: 94 I.

[88] Malul's survey was published in *Hashiloaḥ*, XXXI, July-December, 1914, (pp. 364-374; 439-450.)

[89] A. Ruppin to the Zionist A. C., 21.5.12, CZA; Z3: 1448; L2: 470. Ruppin sent a copy of this letter to J. L. Magnes, 23.5.12, CZA: L2: 416 stressing the 'unpleasantnesses' that might have been avoided had an 'energetic Arab policy' been conducted. For one at least of Asʿad motives see above (p. 224).

[90] J. Thon to the Zionist A.C., 15.11.13, CZA; L2: 500.

[91] Cf. J. Thon to Zionist A. C., 19.11.12, CZA; L2: 479 where the writer discusses a recent ruling of the Mutasarrif limiting Jewish immigration.

[92] J. Thon to A. Many, 25.8.13, CZA; L2: 496.

[93] J. Thon to A. Ruppin, 3.9.13, *ibid.*

[94] The report was sent to Berlin, Istanbul etc. on 21.9.13, L2: 497; pp. 170-5. For the converse argument see p. 208 above.

[95] Arabic press report, 1.4.14, CZA; L2: 509.

[96] J. Thon to the Zionist A. C., 15.11.13, CZA; L2: 500.

[97] Cf. J. Thon to the Zionist A. C., 3.3.14, CZA; Z3: 341; L2: 509. Cf. also pp. 213 and 216 above.

[98] 21.5.14, CZA; L2: 34 II; L2: 513 cf. p. 223 above.

[99] Thon sent Jacobson a copy of Dr. Levy's letter to Ruppin, 15.5.14, CZA; Z3: 65; L2: 513.

[100] Dr. I. Levy to A. Ruppin, 28.6.14, CZA, Z3: 1456.

[101] J. Thon to V. Jacobson, 3.6.14, CZA; Z3: 65; L2: 34 II; L2: 514.

[102] A. Ruppin to M. Meirovich, 22.6.14, CZA; L2: 517.

[103] A. Ruppin to Dr. Moscovitz, 30.6.14, *ibid.*

[104] Memorandum, March 1913, CZA; Z3: 1449.

[105] *Ibid.*

[106] The various Arab national groups — their names, composition and aspirations — have been described elsewhere and this article cannot possibly cover this ground: cf. particularly C. Dawn, 'The Rise of Arabism', *Middle East Journal*, XVI, pp. 145-168.

[107] V. Jacobson to R. Lichtheim, 10.10.15, CZA; Z3: 55 cf. also N. J. Madel, *op. cit.*

# The Balfour Declaration and Its Makers

## Mayir Vereté

Today, fifty years after the Balfour Declaration, there are few people
who know what it exactly was about. Those who know more than the
average student have imbibed a fair dose of the various versions and interpretations that, over the years, have gained acceptance among the public
about the nature of the Declaration, its origins, the circumstances under
which it was made and issued and the factors and personalities that
brought it into being. The Declaration was a great event. It was, when
published, generally understood as a promise by the British government
to restore Palestine to the Jews and to assist them in setting up a Jewish
state—stirring tidings which excited or disturbed, as the case might be,
millions of Jewish and Gentile hearts. As many an outstanding event in
history, it soon became embellished with tales and legends. In the then
prevailing atmosphere of political idealism, when hopes and expectations
of international morality and justice to small nations were running high,
people were prone to believe that the Declaration was made in order to
settle a huge debt which 'Christian Civilization' owed to the Jewish people,
whom it had persecuted for centuries in almost every country of Europe—
and who to that very day were, in some of those countries, still subject to
oppression and discrimination. Undoubtedly the Declaration can be seen
in this light. But was this the motive that prompted the British government?

People versed in politics were inclined to be sceptical. Many of them,
seeing that the Declaration was tied up with an Arab question in Palestine
as well as with Britain's relations with the 'Arab world' and the entire
'Moslem world', were unable to comprehend why the government should
get involved in such a political entanglement. A few of them also felt that
there was no need to deal out justice to the Jews in the manner the Declaration meant to do. Some of them considered that Palestine was not quite
essential to the interests of Britain, at least not to the extent of her becoming involved in all the complications of a Zionist policy. For one reason
or another, those clever men came to the conclusion that it was the Jews,
and the Zionists in particular, who drew the British government into
Palestine. The Zionist leaders, for their part, seem to have believed that,
after all the exertions by the movement since the days of Herzl to win over
the active sympathy of the governments of the Powers for the Zionist idea,
it was they who finally succeeded in convincing the mightiest of them to
lend support to the righteousness of their ideal and claim.

In the opinion of all, protagonists and antagonists alike, the Declaration
was a great achievement. In historic achievements, which are ever dramatic
be they political or military, people are wont to look for a hero or a villain,
as the case may be. And for the Declaration likewise a hero had been
found, namely Chaim Weizmann. It was Chaim Weizmann, so they said,
who obtained the Declaration from Balfour, one of the righteous among

the Gentiles; or Chaim Weizmann who won the Declaration from Lloyd George in return for his important chemical discovery, so vital to Britain's war industry; or it was Chaim Weizmann who by his intelligence and charm influenced both Balfour and Lloyd George, and it was he who brought the Declaration to the people of Israel. Perhaps over the years all these versions proved useful to the Yishuv and to the Zionist cause in general. Weizmann himself was aware of the legendary element in his activities. Once, in a private conversation, not connected with the Declaration, he said, with that peculiar Jewish humour and charm which captivated the hearts of many: 'People say I am a great chemist; nonsense; but if this helps Zionism, so be it'. With regard to the Declaration, too, it would seem, he allowed legends to be woven around his political activity. Perhaps he thought this would help Zionism, not only himself. To history it was of no assistance, however, except maybe in the sense that it roused the scholar to inquire how things really happened.

(2)

What, in fact, is remarkable is, indeed, not that such a portentous deed as the Declaration should have become wrapped in layers of tales and legends, but rather that to some extent it remains so to this day. Historical research has not gone far enough yet to expose the core of the affair and lay it bare, so that whoever wishes to do so can see it in its naked reality. It is true, something had already been done in this direction over thirty years ago by Sir (as then he was) Herbert Samuel, the first High Commissioner in British Mandatory Palestine. Samuel was not a historian, but he read a paper to the Jewish Historical Society of England on his share in bringing the question of Palestine's future before the British government at the beginning of the war. In his Memoirs he enlarged upon this with notes and memoranda which he had written at the time. The late Dr N. M. Gelber, who wrote (in Hebrew) on *The Balfour Declaration and its History*, swallowed the words of Samuel but did not digest them. His book contained a lot of material, most of it new at the time, but there were defects in his presentation which were by no means negligible; and the resulting picture changed little of what had been carried in the mind of the public until then. *The Balfour Declaration* by Leonard Stein is a completely different book: here is an excellent work of historical research. The author makes a thorough analysis of the evidence furnished by all the material available to him, a subtle, as well as a thorough and minute analysis, and sets out the process and findings of his researches in a language which is both rich and at the same time restrained and cautious to the highest degree. In the excellence of the work are perhaps inherent some of its shortcomings. Stein does not, as a rule, reach conclusions, and even his talent for presentation is not always sufficiently compelling to make the reader draw the one and only conclusion that follows from his words. Stein removed many layers in order to get to the core of the matter; still a few remain. Quite possibly, in spite of much labour in investigation and writing, he himself does not yet see the core completely exposed.

Here I wish to add a small, interim contribution to the subject, making use of the material contained in Stein's book as well as in documents, official and private, from archives in Israel and in England, which I have examined during the last few years, before the publication of his book and after.* On this occasion I would like to try to show, along general lines only, that the British wanted Palestine—and very much so—for their own interests, and that it was not the Zionists who drew them to the country. Nor were the Zionists the first to bring the question of Palestine and her future before the British government during the war; neither was it the Zionists who initiated the negotiations with the government, but the government that opened up negotiations with them. And it was not Chaim Weizmann who brought the Declaration to the Jewish people, or Arthur James Balfour. Indeed, it seems to me that Balfour's share in the Declaration was rather small. What part Weizmann played we shall presently try to examine. For years I have been saying to my students on this subject that had there been no Zionists in those days the British would have had to invent them. I have recently been told that a similar statement was made by Max Nordau about the time of the Declaration. So I am in good company. Nordau spoke but did not clarify: I would like also to expound.

(3)

Let us, first of all, look at the position of Palestine within the complex of British imperial interests. Since, at least, the time of the occupation of Egypt (1882), the strip of territory between the Bay of Acre and the Egyptian frontier was increasingly becoming of interest to Britain's imperial system. This found expression, at first, in the Anglo-Ottoman dispute over Egypt's eastern boundary (1892–1906) which only ended when the London government forced the Sultan into withdrawing his frontier from the Canal to the Rafa-Aqaba line. It was now feared that the Ottoman Empire might seek an opportunity for revenging herself by an attack on Egypt. The hinterland of Sinai, western and eastern Palestine at least up to the Acre-Dar'a line, therefore assumed strategic importance. Military surveys of the Peninsula and 'the country round Haifa' were accordingly made for the General Staff. So that when, in 1913, the French government was considering the construction of a railway in southern Palestine down to El-Arish, Sir Edward Grey, after consulting Kitchener, objected, and the plan was dropped. In the following year all western Palestine, as well as a considerable part of Transjordania, were recognized by the German government as being within the British sphere of interest.[1]

Then, several months after the Ottomans had entered the war, Asquith appointed a committee of senior officials of the Foreign Office, the India Office, the Admiralty, the War Office and the Board of Trade, under the chairmanship of Sir Maurice de Bunsen, to consider Britain's desiderata in the Asiatic possessions of the Ottoman Empire. By the secret Constantinople Agreement, Russia had recently been allotted a considerable slice of Turkey; Italy and Greece had their demands in Asia Minor; and France, in pursuance of her well-known policy of gaining control over Syria down to Egypt and northern Arabia, claimed for herself 'la Syrie intégrale'—or, as Le Matin put it, La France du Levant—which included Palestine. It seemed rather obvious that in the event of an allied victory

---

* The interested reader will find in Stein's book most of the facts mentioned below. The references to sources indicated there will not be included in this article (originally written in 1967)—which is, on the occasion of the fiftieth anniversary of the Declaration, an essay in interpretation and an attempt at summing up my researches and lectures on the subject. The few footnotes which follow contain some references in support of the interpretation offered here.

the Ottoman Empire would be dismembered. What were the special interests that Britain should strive to secure for herself? After long deliberations the Report was practically ready by the end of May 1915. The committee accepted the view, mainly propounded by Sir Mark Sykes (one of its members, 'appointed at the personal request of Lord Kitchener'), that both western and eastern Palestine, from the line Acre-Dar'a, approximately, in the north down to the Egyptian frontier and Aqaba in the south, lay within the sphere of British interests. For two fundamental reasons: first, Britain needed the intervening area between the Mediterranean and Mesopotamia chiefly for convenient communication with the Persian Gulf and for meeting the danger of a possible attack on that country from Russia in the north, when it would be necessary to bring military reinforcements with all speed from England; second, the British 'could scarcely tolerate'—to quote the report—that the French should have the border of their sphere of interest along the Canal, the Arabian Peninsula and the Persian Gulf. The Committee, it is true, was very much aware of France's claim to Palestine, an obstacle likely to prevent the inclusion of the country within the British sphere. But they understood that action to attain the desiderata suggested in the Report was the affair of statesmen. It was Mark Sykes who consistently did his very best to guide the government towards the attainment of those desiderata. He seems to have throughout been supported at least by Kitchener and, later, by Lloyd George and, on the whole, not opposed by any member of the war-time Cabinets.

With the draft Report in his pocket, Sykes was sent out, in June, by Kitchener 'to go right round the Middle East'; and during the next six months he stayed three times in Cairo where the desiderata and their possible implementation were fully discussed with the leading British representatives. Then, in October, with the help of his experienced advisers, McMahon wrote—on the basis of general and rather vague instructions of the Foreign Secretary—the well-known letter to the Emir of Mecca. Disassociating himself from part of Hussain's claim in the name of 'the Arab nation' to the entire area between the Taurus and the Indian Ocean, he intimated that Palestine too could not be included within the limits of territories regarding which H.M.G. were prepared to recognize and support the independence of the Arabs. The wording of the reservation was rather intricate and not too lucid. Sharif Hussain may not—who could really say?—have grasped its meaning completely; or, in case he did, he may not have agreed. Documents which have recently come to hand, however, confirm the earlier assumption that the British negotiators in Cairo intended in that crucial passage of the letter *not* to promise Palestine to the Emir. The argument advanced as an excuse was the interests of Britain's French ally—not of England herself. How they viewed the possibility of France being a neighbour on the Canal, in the Red Sea and Arabia we have just seen from the report of the de Bunsen committee.*

* 'Independence of the Arabs' in Syria and Mesopotamia was, by the way, not exactly within Scheme D for settling the future of Turkey in Asia, which was favoured by the Committee. It was the first departure from the Scheme and the first actual proof that it could hardly be considered a practical proposition in the then existing political situation. The 1916 Agreement with France and Russia was the second. One wonders how seriously the members themselves regarded their own recommendations. Sykes was in favour of a clear, clean partition of Asiatic Turkey between the interested Powers, Arabia proper always excepted.

Arab claims to Palestine, western Syria, and part of Mesopotamia having been rebuffed, Sykes, back from his travels, offered to the War Committee of the Cabinet the reasons why in negotiations with the French he would demand Palestine, western and eastern. 'It is most important', he said, *inter alia*, 'that we should have a belt of English controlled country between the Sherif of Mecca and the French' [in Syria]. Kitchener, in supporting him, explained that this territory was necessary for safeguarding British 'control over the south'. This was on the eve of Sykes' talks with Picot. Some sixteen months later, when his contacts with the Zionist leaders were well advanced (and he could already see how the government was in the process of assuming control over Palestine), Sykes disclosed in a conversation with a distinguished military commentator how much of Palestine he already had got out of the French. England, he explained, did not want a European Power or an Arab state alongside Egypt. It must not be inferred that he wanted the Zionists right on the Egyptian border. He did not. The Zionist leaders seem to have been unaware of this. It is a fact, nevertheless, and we shall return to it later.

### (4)

It follows then that British statesmen were well aware of Palestine's importance to British interests. The de Bunsen Committee's Minutes and Report (as well as the schemes of Kitchener and Sykes) generally reflect what had been taking shape in the minds and memoranda of statesmen, experts and departments before its deliberations took place—and, in fact, what had been the basic British policy in the Middle East for some three generations.[2] Hence it was not the Zionist leaders who taught the English how much they needed Palestine and not they who pulled them into the country. Nor, most probably, Herbert Samuel's conversations with his colleagues on this subject, nor his memoranda on Palestine to the Cabinet. Samuel had not been a Zionist, neither had he any contact with Weizmann when he had begun his pro-Zionist activity in November 1914. His proposal to set up in Palestine, as a safeguard to Egypt, a Jewish state, or a British Protectorate which would allow extensive Jewish immigration and settlement and which might develop into an autonomous colony, must have been received by the Foreign Office (if it ever got there) with the same degree of scepticism accorded to a private memorandum on this subject submitted, at the beginning of 1915, by a young British Zionist.[3] Nahum Sokolow, a member of the executive of the World Zionist Organisation, was not even accorded then the privilege of an interview at the Foreign Office in order to put forward the Zionist case. It seems evident that the Foreign office evinced at the beginning of the war no interest in Zionism and in contacts with the Zionists. In the de Bunsen Report there is no mention of Zionists or Zionism or of any Jewish interest in Palestine. It goes without saying that this matter was not even hinted at in the correspondence between Cairo and the Emir of Mecca. Nor were the Zionists involved in the long-drawn-out negotiations at the end of 1915 and the beginning of 1916 between Mark Sykes and F. Georges Picot concerning the partition of the Ottoman Empire in which the future of Palestine was a hard bone of contention. Not that the Zionists tactfully refrained from intervening and waited patiently for the negotiations to end. They simply never knew what was going on. The fate of Palestine in the Sykes–Picot Agreement was decided without them and without any mention of Zionists or Jews.[4] Samuel may have had an inkling of what was afoot and perhaps he was on the alert. It is not clear. In any case, he breathed no word to the Zionists. And some two months after talking to Samuel and reading his memorandum, Sir Mark did not approach Weizmann and Sokolow but discussed Zionism with Dr Moses Gaster. About half a year later he met Aharon Aaronson, who had turned up in England at the end of October 1916 to gain backing in Army circles for his politico-military scheme (according to his diary, he too did not meet the Zionist leaders). It was only at the beginning of 1917 that contact between Sykes and Weizmann and Sokolow was established.

Possibly the Zionist leaders themselves were to blame for the fact that official circles knew nothing about them or ignored them. Weizmann clearly perceived the political opportunities that the War had opened up for the Zionist movement, and right from the beginning had initiated political activity in England. But this work seems to have been regarded by him as preparatory for the Peace Conference: he would not try to find a way to negotiate about a political programme before the end of hostilities was in sight, but rather prepare the ground to meet such a situation through public relations: conversations with leading personalities, publication of pamphlets on Zionist subjects, and so on. It was also necessary to unite the divided Jewish nationalist camp—Zionists belonging to various factions and the Territorialists—and also to try to bring together the Zionists, non-Zionists and anti-Zionists in a single Jewish front. All this important operation was begun by Weizmann. When Sokolow arrived in England, at the very end of 1914, he concerned himself chiefly with the 'internal front' while Weizmann continued to occupy himself principally with contacts, or the search for contacts, with statesmen and important public figures. He met Balfour, who, at the time, was not a member of the government. In the course of a lengthy and most interesting conversation they spoke of Zionism in general, and Balfour was moved. When at the end of the visit Balfour asked, as polite Englishmen habitually ask, whether he could do anything for him, Weizmann replied that he would come and talk again when the guns had ceased to fire—a nice turn of phrase showing, however, his disinclination to talk business. Also, he did not use the opportunity to ask Balfour to introduce him to other statesmen. It was without Balfour's help that Weizmann met Lloyd George, then Chancellor of the Exchequer. Nothing is known from Zionist sources of the content of their conversation—perhaps because it was not sufficiently important. But we do know that Lloyd George had been generally acquainted with Zionism before that meeting and had said on several occasions that he was in sympathy with Zionism. Weizmann also held conversations with Herbert Samuel, both on his own and together with Gaster and Sokolow. It appears, however, that after those first meetings with Balfour and Lloyd George he maintained no regular contact and discussion with them during the years 1915 and 1916. Nor did he ever meet the Foreign Secretary or the Prime Minister, or any other of the influential members of the Asquith governments. It is not quite certain whether he tried to meet them. If he did try and did not succeed, this would prove once again that those statesmen had no interest in Zionism or Zionists. Throughout those first twenty-eight months of the War, moreover, not only did Weizmann have no contact, on the whole, with those engaged in formulating foreign policy (Lord Robert Cecil could possibly be mentioned as the only exception), but the Zionist leaders did not submit or send a single memorandum to the Foreign Office. Even when they were informed in the spring of 1916 that the government was beginning to show interest in the Zionist question and it was finally decided to prepare a political memorandum, the work was done in a rather leisurely fashion and it was not ready until the end of the year.

(5)

About that time the initative was taken to establish contact between the government and the Zionist leaders. It came, however, not from the leaders but from Mark Sykes. The first time that Sykes wanted to get in touch with the Zionists was in the early spring of 1916, and his interest in Zionism sprang from his notorious Agreement with Picot, the negotiations for which were practically concluded in January 1916. The government seem to have derived little satisfaction from the Agreement on account of the many concessions made to France, respecting Palestine, among others. In the negotiations both sides seem to have claimed the country, and the British were prepared to make substantial concessions. As the French government made no concessions in return, a compromise was indicated: international administration for a part of western Palestine, with a British enclave in the Haifa-Acre Bay; as well as British influence in the territory south of the line Rafa—north end of the Dead Sea and down to the Gulf of Aqaba, and in the whole of Transjordania. The situation on the Western Front and the failure of the British attack in the Dardanelles compelled the government to tie up closer with her French ally than would probably have been the case had the Gallipoli campaign turned out sucessfully—and a compromise was unavoidable. As it was, the government was not happy about this and other concessions. Knowing his firm wish that Palestine should pass to England, we can safely assume that Sykes himself must have been unhappy.

The Memorandum Picot and he had prepared embodying the heads of a proposal for an Agreement came in for serious criticism from several government experts, mainly on the ground that Sykes was yielding to the French too much of their claims and sacrificing considerable British interests. The Director of Naval Intelligence, Reginald Hall, who passed the severest comments, doubted whether an agreement with France on spheres of influence in Syria and Mesopotamia was necessary at all at that juncture. If the government were, however, to decide that it was, and were prepared 'to abandon any claim to Alexandretta and the northern cultivable area' [of Syria and Mesopotamia], it should be borne in mind, he protested, that 'France's claim to Palestine cannot be justified'. 'South of Tyre she has not so good a claim . . . as . . . ourselves', he went on, indicating the vital interests England had in the country. He then pointed out that the Jews throughout the world had not only 'a conscientious and sentimental interest' (as mentioned in the Memorandum) but 'a strong *material* and a very strong *political* interest' in the future of Palestine, and were likely to oppose 'Arab preponderance in the southern Near East'; and he suggested that 'In the Brown area the question of Zionism . . . be considered'*[5]. It is safe to assume that Sykes looked into this criticism

* The 'Brown area' in the S.-P. Agreement comprises, with the exception of the Haifa–Acre zone, western Palestine between (the lines), approximately, Ras Nakura—Tiberias and Rafa—northern part of the Dead Sea. The status earmarked in the Agreement for this area was international administration.

and may even have discussed with Hall the points he had raised, including 'the question of Zionism'; and Hall may have referred him to Samuel's memorandum—if indeed Sykes did not know of it before—where it is clearly stated that Zionists and non-Zionists alike wish for a British Protectorate over Palestine. Sykes was not a Zionist and appears not to have liked Jews generally; the Jewish question did not bother him even to the extent that it did Balfour, withal a grain of anti-semitism tinged his opinions. Still, even without Hall's referring him to Samuel's memorandum, both of them must have understood that by encouraging Zionism the government could improve their position in the territory designated in the Agreement for international control. The idea of rejecting in effect the French claim to Palestine with the help of the Zionists may not yet have ripened in Sykes' mind. He may have thought at the time—in case, indeed, this had not occurred to him even earlier—that if his government supported Jewish immigration to, and settlement in Palestine, this would afford Britain a considerable measure of influence sufficient to balance, within the framework of the international administration, the measure of respective French and Russian influence on the Catholic and Greek Orthodox sectors of the population; while furthermore the Acre–Haifa enclave would be under direct British rule (according to the Agreement) and the Negev and Transjordania subject to her influence.

It is just possible—there seems to be a veiled hint in the records—that Sykes took up the point with Picot, who was probably unhelpful. But Sykes, habitually sanguine, must have remained hopeful. A few days later the Picot–Sykes Memorandum and the criticisms passed on it were discussed by an interdepartmental committee, and it was concluded that 'no insurmountable difficulty to the scheme [of the Memorandum] was put forward by any of them'. It is not inconceivable that the question of Zionism in the Brown Area, if brought up at all, was also thought as of 'no insurmountable difficulty'. It is of interest to note that in the Proposals for an Agreement and in the draft Agreement, both drawn up at the end of January, no mention is made of any Jewish interest in the future of Palestine—not even of the 'conscientious and sentimental interest' of world Jewry or of 'the conscientious desires . . . of Judaism . . . in regard to the status of Jerusalem' pointed out in the Picot–Sykes Memorandum. 'The question of the Holy Land [sic]' Grey informed the ambassador at Petrograd, 'was left over for further discussion between the Powers'.* Sykes, and perhaps Grey too, may have thought that this 'further discussion' as well as the 'form of international administration' in the Brown Area, which was also still to be discussed with Russia and other Allies, might yet afford the occasion for calling attention to 'the question of Zionism'.[6]

Just then another Jewish matter came up at the Foreign Office which fitted in with such a possibility. The British and French governments who were trying to draw the United States into the war on their side, were gravely exercised about the fact that the American Jews not only sided with their country's neutrality but even evinced an antagonistic attitude towards the Allies, particularly on account of their Russian partner, which attitude influenced the general public opinion. Someone in Wisconsin

* 'Places' instead of 'Land' should have probably been written, but it is an interesting slip. Nicolson changed the typed 'whole land' to 'Holy Land', and Grey, who revised and initialled the draft, let it pass.

privately broached the idea, which was passed on to the Foreign Office, of remedying this situation by 'a statement on behalf of the Allies favouring Jewish rights in every country . . . and a very veiled suggestion concerning nationalization [sic] in Palestine'. Lucien Wolf, who used to be in touch with the government on some specific Jewish affairs, was called to the Foreign Office to give an opinion on this important problem. Wolf was a good English patriot and wished to be as helpful as possible. But he, an assimilated Jew who refused to acknowledge Jewish nationalism, was discovering to his horror that highly placed people in the Foreign Office were inclined to believe that all Jews were answerable for one another, and feared lest the government's anger be vented on the Jews of England as well. It was, perhaps, chiefly this consideration that made him, the bitter anti-Zionist, admit in the course of a long letter (16.12.1915) to Lord Robert Cecil that the Zionist idea was more and more conquering the hearts of the Jewish masses and that Zionism was becoming a weighty factor among the American Jewish public. Therefore it would be possible, he agreed, to rally the sympathy of Jews in America and all over the world to the Anglo-French side by means of a 'public declaration' of a Zionist character. Cecil seems to have brought this and other suggestions of Wolf to the notice of Grey and also wrote to the ambassador in Washington for his opinion; but it does not look as if the matter passed through the department which dealt with Levant affairs, and Sykes may not have known of it. However, a similar suggestion, conveyed to the Office several weeks later, made a great stir.

It was received, in a dispatch of McMahon, on the very day (23.2.1916) that Grey's cable informing Buchanan that 'the question of the Holy Land was left for further discussion between the Powers' was sent out. Edgar Suares, the head of the Jewish community of Alexandria, presented as an Italian and anti-Zionist, was pretty certain—the dispatch goes on to record —that 'with a stroke of a pen, almost, England could assume to herself the active support of the Jews all over the neutral world if only the Jews knew that British policy accorded with their aspirations for Palestine'. Now the Office became immediately interested. Precisely what passed between the people who took council is impossible to establish, but it is certain that Sykes spoke to Samuel and read (again?) his memorandum. A scheme of what may be called a Zionist policy was quickly emerging. Grey it would appear had been consulted, before the matter was left to a senior official, Hugh O'Beirne, to be embodied in a minute for the Office, Sykes being about to leave for Russia—to continue the negotiations respecting those parts of the Agreement still pending.

In his minute O'Beirne put forward the suggestion that offering the Jews 'an arrangement completely satisfactory to Jewish aspirations in regard to Palestine' would have 'tremendous political consequences'; and he gave a few details of a Zionist scheme which bear some resemblance to what is said on this point in Samuel's Memorandum. Grey, in an effort to win over the French ambassador, instructed Nicolson to 'tell M. Cambon that Jewish feeling which is now hostile [to the Allies] and favours a German protectorate over Palestine might be entirely changed if an American protectorate was favoured with the object of restoring Jews to Palestine'. Cecil, believing that it was 'not . . . easy to exaggerate the international power of the Jews', evinced his support for the 'arrangement'. So did Crewe, who commented that it 'embraces remarkable possibilities'.

Cambon would, however, not listen to Nicolson's explanations. 'It was to be expected', noted O'Beirne; but he would not give in. He urged his chiefs in another minute to pursue the matter, pointing out that 'the Palestine scheme has in it the most far reaching political possibilities'. Crewe, who was now replacing Grey, did not accept Nicolson's advice to 'leav[e] it [the matter] alone'. He offered to talk to Cambon himself; and later observed: 'I am quite clear that this matter ought not to be put aside and I think Sir E. G[rey] is of the same opinion. . . . We ought to pursue the subject, since the advantage of securing Jewish goodwill in the Levant and in America can hardly be overestimated, both at present and at the conclusion of the war.'

About the same time Lucien Wolf wrote again, this time enclosing a draft of what in his view could pass for a Zionist public declaration. The idea itself appealed to the Office. Not so the suggested formula. It was deemed insufficient. An improvement was proposed to make it more substantial, 'far more attractive to the majority of the Jews'. Sir Edward Grey and the Office who, before the final stages of the negotiations with France and the arrival of Suares' suggestion, had displayed no real interest in Zionism and the Zionists, were now prepared to bring before the French and Russian governments a proposition for a declaration from which the Jews would undoubtedly understand that, with the support of the Allies, Palestine might eventually become something like an autonomous Jewish commonwealth.*[7]

(6)

Sykes may have spoken to Grey about the proposal in regard to Zionsim made by Hall; and, as Grey wanted to see him in order to instruct him on his Russian mission, they may have discussed the Suares' suggestion and the emerging Palestine scheme. Be this as it may, both men must have hoped that an arrangement with the Jews respecting Palestine with a propaganda value might stand a better chance of being acceptable to the French than the apparently altruistic proposition to do something for Zionism in the Brown Area. If accepted, it might of course, as suggested, sway world Jewry to the side of the Allies. The arrangement could, besides, achieve more than that, they must have thought. With the pro-British Zionists increasingly established in Palestine the position of England, if the country came under an international régime, would be greatly fortified. But the Zionists and the Jews generally with their 'international power' and more especially in America—where it was believed they wielded considerable influence—might be strongly opposed to an international administration and clamour for a British protection or trusteeship. Even if an American protectorate (as suggested to O'Beirne and by Grey), or a Belgian trusteeship (as Sykes wrote to Samuel), were sincerely thought of, this too was better for Britain than an international régime, especially with the French as partners. It is therefore not unlikely that it was just these considerations that prompted the Office to improve on Wolf's formula and offer in a declaration to the Jews a Palestine scheme that stood the best chance of being acceptable to the Zionists.

The idea of winning over world Jewry to the side of the Allies by means

---

* The Office (following Grey's comment), thought that Jerusalem and the Holy Places should be excluded. It may, however, be doubted whether this was likely to be mentioned in a declaration.

of a generous Zionist declaration and the Hall's notion of encouraging Zionism both manifested themselves to the Foreign Office almost simultaneously, just when the government began to feel dissatisfied with the Agreement they were concluding with France for a division of rule in Palestine.[8] Hall's notion appears to be the earlier chronologically; and in its nature, by fortifying England's standing in Palestine by means of backing the cause of Zionism, it carried the possibility of ousting France altogether from her share in the control over the country. This notion, both in its first stage and in its eventual development, makes the British government dependent to no small degree upon the assistance of the Zionists, and continues to do so incessantly for several years, at least until the Treaty of San Remo. It may be considered as the main and determining motive in the approach of the British government to Zionism and the Zionists.

The other idea, of a Zionist declaration for securing 'the active support of the Jews all over the neutral world', was chronologically second by the time it was adopted by the Foreign Office. In so far as it was meant to be of help to the Alliance as a whole, it can be regarded as a war measure, of immediate value indeed, but of limited duration. It handily gave, however, a new dimension to the former notion, and herein lay in part its attraction. The propaganda value of 'the Palestine scheme' could now become a forceful argument in trying to convince the French and Russian governments. It could thus, in addition, neatly help in eventually securing Palestine for Britain, the aim Sykes, Samuel, Kitchener and Lloyd George (as well as Hall and a few other men of influence), though for not altogether identical reasons, had in mind and sought to achieve. In this sense, from the British point of view, besides being a war measure, the idea comprised a long-range interest. More than one such interest could be read into the frank marginal comments (already quoted) made by Crewe. The thought that with the help of the Zionists backed by 'the international power of the Jews', Britain might possibly overcome the French claim to Palestine cannot be excluded. It would have taken someone far less intelligent, perceptive and adept at politics than Grey, Crewe and Cecil not to perceive this. The governments of France and Russia were offered a device which on the surface was intended to serve the Allied cause as a whole while in the long run was designed to be of value to Britain alone. In this respect (as well as in some others)—if an additional reflection may be allowed—there is an interesting similarity between England's diplomacy in the Zionist question and in her alliance with the Sharif Husain: his refusal to join in the Jehad and his revolt against the Sultan were supposed to be serving the interests of the Allied cause in general, but from her alliance with him Britain alone meant to profit in the long run.

However, because of those two main British interests, (the short- and the long-range ones) the Foreign Secretary was willing and prepared in March 1916 to befriend the Zionists and to draw the Jews to Palestine. Grey was not a Zionist and was not pro-Zionist; he had, it would seem, a conventional, decent sympathy for Zionism of sorts. In the matter of the declaration he—or Crewe—must have consulted Asquith, since the proposal was about to be sent to the French and Russian governments and, in the event of their agreement, it would become binding on the London government. As for Asquith, he did not have even that scant sympathy for Zionism which Grey had. All the same, they were both prepared to perform an act of Zionist policy. Here is the root and the source of the pro-Zionist policy of British governments until the Balfour Declaration and 'the National Home' and the Mandate. The policy and the motivation for it exist already in embryo in March 1916. During the next year the features emerge more clearly simply because the future of Palestine was then in the process of being decided by a very large British army and there was a resolute and forceful Prime Minister to carry out what he thought was advantageous and right for Britain to do. But in their Zionist policy Lloyd George and Balfour are in fact the followers of Grey and of those of his assistants and colleagues who had a hand in formulating it or acquiesced in it; while Mark Sykes seems to be the man who engineered the policy and formed a bridge between the two governments.

One ironical side to the Grey attempt is that the most cogent suggestions for an act of a pro-Zionist policy were offered by two anti-Zionists; and especially the recommendation for, and the draft of a Zionist declaration which came from Wolf, an 'Englishman of the Mosaic persuasion', who loathed both Zionism and the Zionists. Another ironical side is that the Zionist leaders, who were so desirous of some political achievement, who so wished for talks with the British statesmen and aspired to a partnership with the British government, had no knowledge whatsoever of what was being done on behalf of Zionism and Zionists. Nobody asked them and nobody consulted them; as though they did not exist. When Sykes took up the matter after his return from Russia he went to look for them.[9]

### (7)

For the Russian government was apparently inclined 'to view the proposed settlement of Jews in Palestine with sympathy'; and the task which seems now to have faced Sykes was not exactly to find out whether the Zionists would agree in principle to a Zionist policy by the Allied governments, but first and foremost to draw them to the side of his government and to British allegiance. (Information in the Foreign Office papers on the attitude of the Jews of the U.S.A. seems to suggest that the French representatives there might have been trying to get close to the Zionists.) From Dr Gaster Sykes learned that the Zionists were opposed to a condominium with France in Palestine and that they were not putting forward a claim for a Jewish state. He must have learned more, but what exactly we do not know yet. However, the contacts did not last, for the Paris government refused to entertain the proposed declaration and, somewhat later, Sharif Hussain raised the banner of revolt; and Sykes saw no sense in continuing the talks, preferring to wait and see how things were going to turn out.[10] Several months passed and Sykes did not look for Zionists and they did not look for him. About the turn of the year he was roused to seek them out once again.

Precisely why he chose to do so is uncertain. His talks, in November, with Aharon Aaronson, from whom he learned of his plans of a pro-British Jewish underground in Palestine and the disposition of the War Office to favour them, must have strengthened his wish to bring the Zionists into the Palestine question. The main reason for his strenuous search for the Zionist leaders in January 1917 seems, however, to be closely related to the situation on the Sinai front. By the end of the previous November the peninsula was practically cleared of the Turks; the British army was now standing on the threshold of Palestine; and it was decided, a few weeks later, that a vigorous offensive should be undertaken with the occupation of the country as its objective. This was a line of policy respecting the future of Palestine which had been envisaged by Sykes, Kitchener and Lloyd George and decided upon by the Cabinet War Committee a year earlier, when the negotiations with France had just begun. Now, in late December 1916, the French were persuaded to agree to a British thrust across the Palestine frontier. It was also agreed that, when the British troops entered Palestine 'a French political officer should be attached to the British Commander-in-Chief'; and on January 1, 1917 the Foreign Office was notified that Picot would 'represent the government of France in the future administration of Palestine'. The Palestine issue was plainly becoming a reality. It was high time for Sykes to act and bring in the Zionists. He wanted them to share in the administration right from the very beginning.[11]

By then the government had changed, Lloyd George had become Prime Minister and meant, as we know, to take into his hands not only the conduct of the war but also the making of foreign policy. Sykes had joined the Cabinet Secretariat, and on the Palestine question seems on the whole to have been, at least for the next few months, in touch with the Prime Minister and not particularly with the Foreign Secretary, Balfour.* Lloyd George was an 'Easterner'. He was, besides, not satisfied with the Sykes–Picot Agreement, nor did he want the French to have a foothold in Palestine. 'He does not care a damn for the Jews or their past or their future'—so wrote Asquith in March 1915 apropos Lloyd George's support for Samuel's memorandum—'but thinks it will be an outrage to let the Holy Places pass into the possession or under the protectorate of "agnostic, atheistic France".' Asquith seems to do some injustice to his Welsh colleague. Lloyd George had genuine sympathy for the Zionist cause, he wished the Jews to return to their Palestine. He came of those Fundamentalist Protestants who not only regarded themselves as the true Christians and felt hostile to the Catholics, but held to the belief that the Return of Israel was 'nigh at hand' and that England was destined to help them. However, Lloyd George wanted Britain to gain some material benefit while assisting God's purpose. He wanted, at least as early as the beginning of 1915, Palestine to be within the sphere of Britain's exclusive influence, from reasons of imperial interests and international prestige and because of his own religious sentiments. He wished and expected the British army to occupy the country, believing this would constitute a strong claim for its possession. The occupation coupled with support of the Zionist cause was the neatest, most convenient and becoming way of making France abandon her share in Palestine. This was almost exactly Sykes' approach. The Catholic Conservative Mark Sykes found an enthusiastic supporter for his subtle policy in the Protestant Radical Lloyd George. Both of them were great British patriots and pronounced imperialists, with a fertile mind and, sometimes, devious ways, which a ready and smooth tongue abounding in oratory together with plenty of personal charm enabled them to conceal.

By force of these circumstances and against this background, Sykes once again turned to the Zionists. This time he found Weizmann and

* He may have kept in touch with the P.M. through Hankey (Secretary of the Cabinet), who was also close to Balfour—even as he had kept in touch with Kitchener through Fitzgerald.

Sokolow and the group of British Zionists who were helping them in their work. The contacts between the Zionists and the authorities for all practical purposes began, then, not when the guns ceased to thunder, but when they were about to roar in full force on Palestine's frontiers; not as a direct result of the political activity of the Zionist leaders, but when Sykes and the Prime Minister thought it right to initiate talks. Lloyd George may perhaps not have known in advance of Sykes' approach to Weizmann. Once the talks got under way he seems to have been kept informed.

## (8)

This is not the place to recount in detail the contacts and talks and discussions, so I shall indicate only the more salient facts. Sykes wanted to know what the Zionists were seeking to attain. Lord Rothschild spoke about a Jewish state, and Harry Sacher—of the group of young British Zionists who were helping Weizmann, of an independent and sharp mind —spoke in the same vein. The leaders themselves did not mention a state. For the meeting with Sykes they submitted a memorandum in the composition of which many participated, but its main author was Sokolow and its reviser and editor was Herbert Samuel. The memorandum spoke of Palestine as a Jewish National Home (a term coined by Sokolow, apparently) and equal rights for all citizens of the country, and autonomy for the Jewish population in all matters of religion and education; and of a charter that the Zionists would receive from England for the settlement of the country and its development. However, the Zionists made it clear to Sykes that they wanted British rule in the country, not international rule and not French rule. Sykes replied that his government could not raise this point with the government of France; perhaps the Zionists would choose to do so on their own; he was prepared to arrange a meeting with her representative in London. Sokolow was detailed to fulfil the mission. Now there emerged a sort of triangle in the negotiations: Sokolow–Weizmann with Sykes, Sokolow with Weizmann at one meeting with Picot, Sykes with Picot. Sokolow explained at length to Georges Picot the Zionist ideal, its mainspring and its aims, and the admiration and gratitude that the Jews felt towards the French nation, as well as the apprehensions of the Zionists because of the tendency manifest in French Colonial history to impose her culture on the natives. For this reason, he said, the Zionists preferred that Britain should be the Power under whose protection the Jewish population would live and develop in Palestine. Picot understood, of course, where this was leading to, but he was impressed with Sokolow's diplomacy. Sykes continued to press. In a long letter, which seemed frank on the surface (but was rather cunning below) he explained to Picot what the Zionists wanted; how Sokolow had explained to him (to Sykes) their settlement programmes and the extent of these plans and how it seemed to Sykes that, since France and Britain wished to gain the support of world Jewry and to encourage the Zionists, it was essential to meet their demands; and that, finally, it might perhaps be possible to find some government, not France and not England, that would be prepared to undertake the protection of Palestine.[12]

After this, Sykes advised the Zionists to continue negotiations with the French government, and Sokolow was sent to Paris. By then it was believed in London that the British army would very soon be in occupation of at least a small part of Palestine; the preliminary negotiations with the

F

Zionists were concluded for all practical purposes; Sykes was going out to Egypt to serve as Political Officer attached to the Commander-in-Chief, and Weizmann was about to join him there. The Prime Minister now felt it was high time to come into the open with his policy on Palestine. At a Cabinet meeting of April 3 he instructed Sykes that it was important to secure 'the addition of Palestine to the British area [in the Sykes–Picot Agreement]' and to ensure the development of the Zionist movement 'under British auspices'. And no sooner did Sykes see Picot than he impressed on him 'the importance of meeting Jewish demands' and of preparing 'the French mind for the idea of British suzerainty in Palestine by international consent'.[13]

The Zionist leaders may not have known of the instructions, but the military and diplomatic background which the French government confronted eased, to some extent, matters for Sokolow. Nevertheless, during the numerous and protracted conversations Sokolow had with ministers and high officials, the French stood on their rights in Palestine and proved very difficult. In the end he managed to obtain an assurance of French 'sympathy for your cause'.[14] On the advice of the French and of Sykes, Sokolow went to Rome as well. Italy was a partner of Britain and France in the division of the Ottoman Empire and it would be correct, of course, to inform her of what was going on in regard to Palestine. There were, however, other reasons apart from the niceties of behaviour. The French reasons are not yet sufficiently clear; whereas Sykes, the Catholic, it seems, intended to draw to the British side of England both Italy and the Vatican, who were not satisfied with the very influential position of France in respect of everything connected with the Holy Places. The support of the Italian government and the Vatican for the Zionists who favoured England, he must have thought, would gain Britain an important ally against France in the Palestine question; and, in return for this, Italy could depend on England to encourage Italian, at the expense of French influence in the Catholic institutions in Palestine and with regard to the Holy Places generally.* In his conversations with ministers and the Holy See, Sykes paved the way for Sokolow, who spoke about Zionism with the Pope, the Prime Minister and senior officials, until finally he was assured of the goodwill and sympathetic interests of the Italian government.

After Sokolow had laboured and achieved so much also in behalf of British interests, it was the turn of the British government to make public its attitude towards the Zionists. Sokolow (Weizmann being away on his mission to Gibraltar) and the political committee appointed by the leaders sat down to work on the wording of a draft that would be submitted as a proposal to the Cabinet. As against the drafts of some of his colleagues that tried to secure Jewish rule in an integral Palestine, Sokolow argued that such demands would not be acceptable to the government. Sokolow's formula was adopted; he must have previously discussed it along general

* It may be apposite to quote the following sentence of Balfour's which discloses a thought similar to the conjecture made here respecting Sykes' intention in consulting the Italians on Palestine. Discussing at a meeting (11.7.1918) of the War Cabinet's Eastern Committee the S.-P. Agreement and the complaints of the Italian government at not having been consulted or even informed about it, Balfour said: '. . . if we invariably kept the Italians informed, we could almost certainly rely on their support where we were in diplomatic difficulties with the French'.

lines with a senior official in the Foreign Office. About the middle of July it was submitted as a proposal for confirmation by the Cabinet.[15]

Balfour, who was a Zionist both at heart and by outlook, appears to have been prepared to accept, on the whole, Sokolow's formula, which spoke of Palestine as the reconstituted National Home of the Jewish people, without any reservations of importance—all of which were added later.[16] But opposition was forthcoming from other quarters. In particular, strong protest and criticism was raised by the Secretary of State for India, Edwin Samuel Montagu, a violently anti-Zionist Jew. Possibly Sykes, as well as others, considered that it was only fair to secure in the declaration the rights of the non-Jewish communities in Palestine. Anyhow, the work on revision was started, and ministers as well as officials of the Cabinet Secretariat and the Foreign Office all tried their hands at probing and examining and altering. The fruit of this group-labour is the text of the Declaration as known to us, which Balfour brought before Cabinet meetings during October. In fact, already at the very beginning of September, Cecil urged the Cabinet to decide on a definite policy in favour of the Zionist movement, stressing that 'it would be of most substantial assistance to the Allies' to have the Zionists 'on our side'. Now in October, in presenting the subject to his colleagues, Balfour expressed the apprehension lest the German government might 'capture the sympathy of the Zionist movement'. Then, at another Cabinet meeting, he explained that a declaration favourable to the ideals of Zionism would be an instrument of 'extremely useful propaganda both in Russia and America'. For it was thought by one or two people in the Foreign Office that under the beneficent influence of the declaration the Jewish public in Russia would bring pressure on their government to continue in the war and to oppose a separate peace with Germany. Nothing was said at the meetings about the justice of the Zionist cause as such, or the right of the Jews, as that of any other nation, to have a National Home of their own. There was, of course, no mention of the intention to diddle France out of Palestine. Of such matters the English are not in the habit of speaking openly, especially in public. Still, it must, for some time, have been known or understood by Cabinet members and acceptable to them, or at least to most of them. The Cabinet's last discussion, of October 31, conveys the impression of mere formality: since Montagu was abroad and the rest of the participants were known to be supporters of the measure, with the possible exception of one, Lord Curzon, who displayed rather a lack of sympathy. But although he was invariably critical, his colleagues knew it was not his habit to oppose.[17]

(9)

We have seen, then, the great strides made by the Zionists and the British, one towards the other and both of them together; and it seems to me that, in so far as the Declaration is considered, it is of no significance how many times Weizmann or Sokolow visited the Foreign Office and Sykes, and how many times they met with ministers, officials, journalists and personages in England, France and Italy, or who visited or met or conversed the more. One may perhaps dare to go farther and say that for the purpose of a government's Zionist policy in itself, it was not very important what the Zionists did, nor was there any need for Weizmann and Sokolow in particular; just as the Zionism of Balfour, Lloyd George, Milner and Smuts or of the War Cabinet which approved of the Declaration, was of no great consequence either. Asquith, Grey, Lloyd George and Churchill—by way of example—had no previous sympathy for the Arab National Movement; at least, no one has yet heard of this. Nevertheless, Asquith's government agreed to the famous scheme to contact the Arabs and negotiate and conclude an alliance of sorts with them, and the British even found those very men whom they, to some degree, transformed into leaders of the Movement. In the case of the Declaration, the compelling and decisive motives were those which drove England towards Palestine and the Zionists, and the special circumstances in which the motives were activated. If Lloyd George's government wanted Palestine for Britain alone and strove to get rid of the French partner in Palestine, and wished to gain the support of the Jewish masses of the United States as well as of other belligerent and neutral countries, in order to sway the governments and people to the British side, then sympathy or otherwise for the Zionist idea would be of small account as far as the Declaration is concerned, and the presence of this Zionist leader or that would make little difference. We have already seen that the initiative for a declaration originated with men who in their attitude to Zionism differed from Balfour and Lloyd George; that the subject was pursued without the knowledge of the Zionist leaders; and that the formula roughly suggested for such a declaration was more specific and promising, from the Zionist standpoint, than the text of Lloyd George's 'Zionist Cabinet'. (One cannot say, of course, what would have happened to that formula had an agreement in principle been forthcoming from the government of France.) One may also say, I suppose, with a considerable measure of certainty, that the sympathy alone of Balfour and Lloyd George for the Zionist cause would not have convinced the Cabinet to accept the Declaration. And had there been on their part sympathy alone without interests, or (as in the case of Balfour) without an argumentation pointing to material interest, it is nearly certain that the Zionist question would not have been raised by them at all in the Cabinet. Without Britain's interest both in Palestine and in the Zionists, or granting her interest in Palestine but not in the Zionists, it is not difficult to conclude what the Zionist leaders could have achieved at the Peace Conference. It would be fitting to use for the purpose of examination the parallel of the Armenian question and the proposal for an Armenian state at that same Conference.

Therefore, it was sheer interest in all its aspects that was the decisive motive in making the government resolve on viewing with favour, and lending support to Zionist aspirations. One must, however, admit that it was nice and convenient and agreeable that Balfour, Lloyd George, Smuts, as well as some important personages in the highest reaches in general, were sympathetic to the Zionist cause. This attitude was of considerable importance mainly *after* the Declaration. On the other hand, it was nice and useful that the Zionists—who indeed had thought that negotiations with the government were possible or desirable only at the termination of the war—nevertheless made some preparations in advance, at first on the initiative of Weizmann and, later, under his and Sokolow's guidance and control. It was, besides, convenient that they knew more or less what they wanted, or rather what they did not want to demand from the government (although it looks as if there was no proper planning in the preparatory work for the reconstruction of the country and its upbuilding, nor for any of the important political problems).

Nevertheless, a measure of passivity was displayed on the Zionist side: not only in that all of a sudden, without any provocation on the part of the leaders, the government started to court them, but also after the contacts had been made. Admittedly, there never is absolute passivity in contacts, even on the side of the passive party. The passive character of the Zionist side is evident, however, mainly from the fact that it did not succeed in forcing the other party into accepting the programme which it had prepared. In one matter Sokolow was successful: in thwarting what appears to be the intention of Sykes to attempt to limit Jewish settlement to specific regions, keep the Zionists away from Jerusalem, and fix the centre of Zionist operation in the neighbourhood of Haifa. On the other hand, the parties never reached the stage of a binding discussion regarding the boundaries of that same National Home about which they had been talking so much. Lloyd George seems possibly to have hinted, in the course of a chance and hurried meeting with Weizmann, that the Zionists would have to restrict themselves to western Palestine. But how far in the north and how far in the south? Someone—it is not clear whether Sokolow or Lloyd George— let fall the phrase 'from Dan to Beersheba'. The Zionists understood this to signify at least all of western Palestine, from the Litany to Wadi el-Arish. But the British apparently meant 'to Beersheba' and no more. The Zionist leaders were not aware of this. (Neither can they be credited with the restoration of the Negev to the boundaries of the National Home. This was bestowed on the Zionists by the revolt in Egypt in the spring of 1919 when it was decided by the British that it was not worth while annexing the Negev to the Sinai Peninsula and Egypt or to any territory to the east. The leaders seem not to have known about this either.) In short, on the question of boundaries as on every important question that directly affected the future of the Yishuv and of settlement, no agreement was reached, and the British did not commit themselves on anything concrete. The Zionist leaders agreed, perhaps on Sykes' advice, to postpone negotiations on all practical matters, believing these would be settled satisfactorily at the next stage. They were ready to be satisfied, for the time being, with 'a declaration'—something which had apparently not been thought of by them earlier. A declaration which—as Sokolow pointed out when the wording of the draft was discussed—would be 'a general approval of the Zionist aims, very short and as pregnant as possible'.[18]

(10)

In point of fact, the Declaration—as Weizmann wrote after its publication—is in the nature of a principle. That is to say, the government acknowledged in principle Jewish nationalism as well as the right of the Jews to re-establish their own political centre in Palestine, and promised in principle to help in the realization of this object. All these aspects of the Declaration were given fuller, broader and more binding expression in the formula suggested by Sokolow. Nevertheless, the leaders thought that the principle remained in force also in the text approved by the Cabinet. More than this it was perhaps impossible to get from the British. If this is correct, it is to the great credit of Weizmann and Sokolow that they grasped this and relied upon the principle itself. On the basis of this principle, they believed, it would be possible to reach an agreement with the government which would bind it to carry into effect the practical demands of the

Zionists. It is still not clear whether, during those months of discussion with Sykes and the Foreign Office, the leaders understood that the British needed them and why exactly. Seemingly, over and above their comprehending this and being sure about it, they placed their faith in Balfour and Lloyd George and in the group of Englishmen with whom they worked, and perhaps also in the British generally; and they relied on the Declaration as a pronouncement in the nature of a gentleman's agreement: in exchange for that measure of promise by the government to help them establish a National Home, they would do whatever they could to ensure that Britain alone would be the ruler of Palestine. For just as in the Declaration itself there was no guarantee yet that H.M.G. was bound to help in establishing a viable national home within the historic boundaries of Palestine, as envisaged in the Zionist programme, so there was no guarantee in it that Great Britain alone would acquire control over the country. The Zionists and the British continued to need one another after the Declaration. Then came Weizmann's great hour.

In the policy of this principle—we would do well to bear in mind when summing up—it was the government that took the initiative: on the basis of Samuel's memorandum, as well as on the basis of proposals from Lucien Wolf, Suares and others regarding the expediency of a Zionist declaration—a proposal that earned the approval of Lord Robert Cecil, who sympathized with Zionism, of Lord Crewe and of Sir Edward Grey, as well as of several of the officials in the Foreign Office. The architect of the government's Zionist policy was Mark Sykes, with Reginald Hall, and possibly also Fitzmaurice and O'Beirne of the Foreign Office coming forward with suggestive notions. And by way of emphasis and slight exaggeration one may perhaps speak of the 'Sykes Declaration'—though the turn the policy was taking during 1917 was apparently not what he had originally envisaged. Weizmann and Sokolow were, so to speak, the big contractors of that policy. Its builders were all those who lent a hand in its making, some more, some less. Much of the construction work was done by Harry Sacher, Leon Simon, Lord Rothschild, Shmuël Tolkovsky, Herbert Sidebotham, Israel Sieff and Aqiva Ettinger. Above all, by Herbert Samuel, who guided, directed and advised whenever he was asked and assisted greatly even when he was not requested by the Zionists; and by C. P. Scott, who put Weizmann in touch with important personalities and commended the Zionist case to Lloyd George and other personages and served Weizmann and Zionism faithfully and tirelessly; and by Achad Ha'am, whose great caution sometimes held up the building progress but whose profound wisdom helped it on the whole. Balfour's share does not seem to be large. That of Lloyd George was greater; he appears indeed to have been more forward with his Zionist policy than Sykes, who seems to have been a trifle hesitant. While Sokolow was also a great builder. His part in the talks and negotiations with Sykes was considerable. The discussions and negotiations with the French and the Italians were far more difficult to handle than those with the British; and in these he acted without Weizmann. He was, in addition, the chief author of the memorandum of Zionist 'Demands' submitted to Sykes, and of the formula for the Declaration submitted to Balfour. Weizmann's share in the work of construction and in the incessant activity for its execution and completion was certainly very great. Particularly his initiative in sounding out ministers and important British public figures, Jews and non-Jews, and establishing relations with them, as well as in talks with Sykes, Balfour, Lloyd George, Cecil, Smuts, and many lesser figures of the Foreign Office, War Office and Cabinet Secretariat; and in pushing on with the Declaration. But it is not easy to decide whether his share was greater than that of Sokolow. The question of 'Weizmann the Leader' does not directly affect the subject. Here we are speaking first and foremost about the nature of his activities up to the Declaration. Regarding his part and its value one may perhaps resort to the words of Smuts: We were persuaded, he said, that the policy embodied in the Declaration should be approved, but it was Weizmann who persuaded us. I do not know exactly what Smuts meant to say. To my mind it calls the story of the lady who—as the saying goes—was willing, and only wanted to be seduced. Britain likewise willed Palestine, wanted the Zionists and courted them. Weizmann happened to come her way, talked to her to have the Zionists and go with them to Palestine, as only her they desired and to her they would be faithful. Britain was seduced. She was ready to be seduced by any Zionist of stature.

## NOTES

1. Public Record Office, CAB 16/4: Report and Minutes of Evidence of a Sub-committee of the Committee of Imperial Defence . . . [1907–1909], 1909, pp. 101–02, App. II, § 7, App. VIII, p. 187, App. X; The Report, pp. I–II; CAB 16/12: C.I.D. paper 115 B, 1910, p. 13, § 18; W.O. 106/43, CL$_3$(C$_3$)29: General scheme for invasion of Syria [1908], and C338: Military report on Sinai, 1912. Sir E. Grey sat on the above mentioned [Morley's] sub-committee. F.O. 371/1813, nos. 18858, 22533, F.O. 371/1823/25533; Die Grosse Politik, XXXVII, no. 14833 and App. IB. It is of interest to note that in his letter to Grey of 30.10.1914 (F.O. 800/111), Sykes, before being employed by the War Office, was proposing a plan of action against a Turkish threat to Egypt very similar to that suggested by the General Staff in 1907 and included in the Morley sub-committee Report. So is the plan put forward in a memorandum of 3.1.1915 by Gilbert Clayton (F.O. 371/2480/5189). Quotations from Crown copyright papers by kind permission of the Controller of Her Majesty's Stationery Office.

2. CAB 27/1: Minutes and Report of the Committee on Asiatic Turkey, June 1915, especially pp. 48–50, App. VI (Note by Gen. E. Barrow) and §§23, 32, 35 of the Report. It is hardly possible to exaggerate the importance of the Report for the formulation of British policy in Asiatic Turkey during the war and the Peace Conference.

As to Sykes' stay in Cairo, see Sykes' letters to Gen. Callwell in F.O. 882/14 and The Sudan Archives, Durham, box 469/10: Wingate to Clayton, 21.8.1915. While in Cairo, Sykes spoke, in July, to the French minister about the partition of the Middle East expounding frankly British desiderata and explaining in detail why his government wanted Palestine up to Haifa—the scheme he had in fact put forward before the de Bunsen Committee. A[rchives] du Ministère des A[ffaires] E[trangères], Paris, Guerre 1914–1918, Turquie (Syrie-Palestine) vols. III, pp. 132–8, IV, 43–52.

For letting me consult these and other French filmed documents bearing on the subject under discussion in this paper I am indebted to my former student Mr Edie Kaufman, now working under Professor Durosselle on a thesis on French policy in Syria and Palestine.

As to the reservations in regard to the boundaries demanded by Sharif Hussain, see general instructions of Grey to McMahon, 20.10.1915, in F.O. 371/2486/155203. These instructions were sent out after the receipt of McMahon's cable (18.10) in which he wrote that it had been understood from talks with Al-Farouki that in 'the north-west limits of Arabia' the Arabs would accept modifications where French interests were concerned, 'leaving in Arabia purely Arab districts of Aleppo, Damascus, Hama and Homs' (ib. 153045). 'Arabia' here denotes for some reason the Arabian Peninsula as well as Iraq, Syria, Lebanon and Palestine; and on a map comprising the whole area, the Syrian-Palestinian littoral is of course the 'north west limits of Arabia'. As to the position of France in this area, see the apposite observations of 19.10 by George Clerk (who had been a member of the de Bunsen Committee): 'France has secured her position by acquiring special interests in the north western portion of Arabia as now defined by the Arabs' (ib. 152901). The 'special interests', economic and religious, of France in Palestine and her claim to 'La Syrie intégrale' were well known at the time (see Minutes, Appendices and Report of de Bunsen Committee); and they are too well known to historians to require elaboration. McMahon's own explanation as to the wording of the modifications actually employed in his letter to Hussain of 24.10 is given in his secret dispatch of 26.10 to Grey (ib. 163832): 'I have been definite . . . in excluding . . . those districts on the northern coast of Syria which cannot be said to be Arab, and where I understand that French interests have been recognized. I am not aware of the extent of French claims in Syria, nor of how far HMG have agreed to recognize them. Hence, while recognizing the towns of Damascus, Hama, Homs and Aleppo as being within in the circle of Arab territories, I have endeavoured to provide for possible French pretensions to those places by a general modification, to the effect [that] HMG can only give assurances in regard to those territories in which she can act without detriment to the interests of her ally France.'

Sir Reginald Wingate, who received from Cairo copies of McMahon's letters to Hussain (24.10) and to Grey (26.10), wrote back on 1.11.15 of his talks with the Sudanese religious leader Sayed ʿAli Al-Mirghani—himself in correspondence with the Emir of Mecca: 'I have of course discussed with him the frontier questions and pointed out the necessity for the reservations which we have made in Syria, Palestine and Mesopotamia' (to G. Clayton, Sudan Archives box 135/5; this letter has already been mentioned in note 33 of Elie Kedourie's article in *The Historical Journal*, 1964). That McMahon thought of Palestine's eastern frontier as being somewhere in Transjordania (as mentioned by him in a letter of a later date) appears to be borne out by a cable of Sykes from Cairo, 20.11.1915 (F.O. 371/2767/23579). He ascertained from talks with Al-Farouki that 'Arabs would agree to convention with France granting her monopoly of all concessionary enterprise in Syria and Palestine, Syria being defined as bounded by Euphrates as far South as Deir Zor, and from thence to Deraa and along Hedjaz Railway to Maan' (this accords to a great extent with a map of Palestine attached to the de Bunsen Report and with a map attached to Tyrrell's memo of October 1917 in F.O. 800/214).

The possibility of Palestine becoming a British possession after the war must have already been discussed at the end of 1914 in London and Cairo. Ronald Storrs, who appears to be referring to what Fitzgerald (Kitchener's right-hand man) had written to him on the subject, wrote that a Jewish state as a buffer between Egypt and 'the inevitable French protectorate over the Lebanon' was 'an attractive idea' but impracticable, owing to the big numerical preponderance of the Arab population. To his mind—and his letter was meant for Kitchener's eye—'the inclusion of a part of Palestine in the Egyptian Protectorate' with Jerusalem as a free city could be 'a possible solution'. This would make 'Jewish infiltration into Palestine . . . less obvious and annoying to the susceptibilities of the Moslem and even certain elements in the Christian world' (P.R.O. 30/57/45—the Kitchener Papers—Storrs to Fitzgerald, 28.12.1914).

For Sykes' evidence before the Cabinet's War Committee—CAB 42/6, G. 46. For his conversation with the military commentator—H. Sidebotham's memorandum, 9.3.1917, in the Weizmann Archives (Rehovoth). For the roots of the formulation of British Foreign Policy in the Levant, see my article in the *Journal of Modern History*, 1952.

3. This refers to a memorandum on 'England and the Jewish Settlement in Palestine' drawn up by Norman Bentwich and submitted privately in January 1915 to an acquaintance in the Foreign Office following a chance conversation between them in the previous autumn about the rights of small nations (see covering letter of 8.1.1915). In the Foreign Office the memo was endorsed 'The Zionist Movement in Palestine' (F.O. 371/2482/8366). A clerk, Lancelot Oliphant, a nephew of Laurence Oliphant, observed (24.1.) that he feared Bentwich had 'no greater justification for his hopes of the future of Zionism than had my 'wayward and brilliant' namesake and relative'. But there is no indication whether at the time the memo was also read by higher officials. At the beginning of March 1916 it appears, however, to have been perused by N. [Lord Newton?]—an Assistant under-secretary in charge of the foreign propaganda department. Professor Bentwich remembers that his acquaintance (F. D. Acland, parliamentary under-secretary 1911–15) suggested he should write a memo on the subject, but he cannot recall whether he consulted the Zionist leaders on the matter (the memo was sent from Cairo where B. served at the time). Herbert Samuel's memorandum of March 1915 is not among the Foreign Office documents; it was circulated to the Cabinet and can be found in CAB 37/126.

4. In a Memorandum by Picot and Sykes (January 5, 1916—written apparently by

Sykes) embodying the desiderata of England and France and the various interests involved in the negotiations between them, mention is made in one place of the need for an 'arrangement satisfactory to the conscientious desires of Christianity, Judaism and Mahommedanism in regard to the status of Jerusalem and the neighbouring shrines'. In another section of the memorandum, dealing with Jerusalem and the Holy Places, it is pointed out 'that members of the Jewish community throughout the world have a conscientious and sentimental interest in the future of the country' (F.O. 371/2767/2522). In the Agreement itself, as we know, there is no reference or allusion to Jews and Judaism and their interest in Palestine or even in Jerusalem.

5. Comments of Captain W. Reginald Hall, January 12, 1916 (op. cit., No. 8116). Hall is not sure whether 'French support in dealing with the Arabs is necessary'. He thinks that 'France's claim to Palestine cannot be justified'; and it is an error to ascribe to the Arabs 'a general desire for unity. . . . They will never be united.' England should secure for herself, for the assurance of her position in Egypt', at least 'the exclusive control of all the railways in South Palestine'; the annexation of Southern Palestine and of Transjordania to Egypt; and 'the right of possession and fortification of a naval base on the Syrian coast'. Another series of Hall's observations read: 'Opposition must be expected from the *Jewish interest* throughout the world to any scheme recognising Arab independence and foreshadowing Arab preponderance in the Southern Near East. . . . Jewish opposition may be partly placated by the status proposed for the *Brown area*, but it may not wholly or, indeed, very largely be placated. The Jews have a strong *material*, and a very strong *political* interest in the future of the country' [i.e. Palestine—and not only 'conscientious and sentimental interest', as mentioned in the Picot–Sykes Memorandum; see note 4]. 'In the Brown area the question of Zionism, and also of British control of all Palestinian railways, in the interest of Egypt, . . . have to be considered.' Hall concludes his paper by saying that 'The First Sea Lord [Adm. Jackson] has read my memo, with which, he directs me to say, he concurs'. It is of interest to note that he does not mention the First Lord of the Admiralty, A. J. Balfour. Jackson sat on the de Bunsen Committee.

It is most puzzling to know where Hall got the idea of world Jewry's opposition to any scheme of Arab Independence in the Southern Near-East—something which is completely unknown from any Zionist or general Jewish source—and of the strong political interest that it shows and is liable to show in the future of Palestine. One possible source for his views regarding the future of Palestine could be Samuel's memorandum of March 1915. In the Samuel Papers (Israel State Archives) there is a letter (of April 1915) by Lord Fisher, expressing admiration for the memorandum, also hinting that it might be brought before the de Bunsen Committee. One may assume that from Fisher the memorandum was passed on to the Director of Naval Intelligence. It may also be just possible that Hall was already in possession of some information respecting the attempted contacts between Naval Intelligence in Egypt and Aaronson's 'Nili' organization in Palestine, although these were only in the initial stage. Apparently there was also in those days a generally accepted belief in the magnitude and importance of the influence of world Jewry. On one occasion when the Foreign Office was engaged on the draft of a declaration regarding Palestine (beginning of March 1916, see note 7 below), Lord Robert Cecil observed: 'I do not think it is easy to exaggerate the international power of the Jews.'

One should also bear in mind that many of the top people in the Admiralty and the War Office were strongly opposed to most of France's claims in the Levant. Hall's colleague on the interdepartmental committee for the negotiations with France was the Director of Military Intelligence, General MacDonogh, who seems to have favoured Aaronson's plans and became a staunch supporter of Zionism and the Zionist leaders. He too may have read Samuel's memorandum, and there can be little doubt that he read Hall's above-mentioned comments on the Picot–Sykes Memo. Direct evidence for the dissatisfaction with the proposed agreement of at least one Cabinet member comes from Curzon—'private' to Grey, 3 and 20.2.1916, F.O. 800/106.

6. If Samuel's memorandum was in fact brought before the De Bunsen Committee it is quite possible that Sykes, who was a member, read it for the first time as far back as the spring of 1915. If so, Hall's observations made him aware of the matter once again.

For the deliberations of the interdepartmental committee and the proposals— F.O. 371/2767, nos. 14106, 23579; for Grey's cable of 23.2.1916—ib. no. 35529.

In connection with the British giving in to the French over Palestine it is of interest to note Grey's memorandum on 'The position of Great Britain with regard to her Allies' of 18.2.1916. There Grey argues that Britain is extremely dependent on her Allies for bringing the war to a successful conclusion and should therefore not exert too much pressure if she cannot make her 'views prevail by argument and influence' (CAB 22 /8).

7. The idea of winning over the Jewish public—particularly in the United States, but also in the Levant and in the enemy and neutral countries—to the side of the Allies by means of a declaration of a Zionist character, is faintly suggested in Foreign Office documents for what seems to be the first time in November 1915. A private letter from H. M. Kallen—an American Jewish Zionist—(to Alfred Zimmern?), came into the hands of Lord Eustace Percy; and he on his part passed it on to Lord Robert Cecil, parliamentary under-secretary at the time (F.O. 371/2579/187779; see also Eustace Percy's letter to Cecil, 11.2.1916 in F.O. 371/2835/66227). Cecil's conversations with Wolf and Wolf's first letter to Cecil, who seems to favour the idea, are of December (ib. no. 193902). Edgar Suares' views on the subject were received at the F.O. on 23.2.— F.O. 371/2671/35433: dispatch and enclosure. It should be mentioned that a few thousand Palestinian Jews came to Alexandria for the duration of the war, and it was there that the idea of a Jewish Legion to fight alongside Britain in the East was ardently discussed and the Zion Mule Corps formed. It is conceivable that this lively crowd of of Zionists, with their many long political discussions and the contacts some of them had with Alexandria Jewry, had some effect upon the views of the non-Zionist Suares. It may also be of interest to point out that Sir Ronald Graham, who later gave much help to the Zionist leaders in London, served at the time in Egypt and had some connection with the formation of the Zion Mule Corps.

Sykes' letter to Samuel, after an evident earlier contact, is of 26.2 (Israel State Archives). O'Beirne's first minute is of 28.2. It is in typeprint, which may suggest the possibility that there had been an earlier handwritten version which had been seen and commented upon by one or two persons. But even before the supposed handwritten version, the subject seems to have been discussed at the Office, and it appears from the minute that O'Beirne was advancing ideas which had not originated with him. An American Protectorate is one such idea. The other is the 'arrangement' as a line of policy which might bring about the collapse of the Turkish government. G. H. Fitzmaurice, the former Dragoman of the British embassy in Constantinople and a recognized authority on Turkey, is mentioned by O'Beirne as the man to be consulted on Jewish colonization and other conditions in Palestine. While in Constantinople, Fitzmaurice was of the opinion that the Jews of the Levant and world Jewry generally were staunch supporters of the Young Turk régime as well as pro-German. So it may well have been F. who suggested the 'arrangement' to O'Beirne. F. was a Catholic and did not like Jews generally; but from a somewhat later period there is evidence in the Zionist Archives of rather close contact between him and the Zionists.

The possibility of Sykes too having a hand in the scheme for an 'arrangement' must not be overlooked. Not just because he was a friend of Fitzmaurice, but because he must have been consulted on every proposal of importance concerning the future of Palestine. His contact with Samuel two or three days after the receipt of Suares' proposition is very suggestive. Before leaving for Russia he probably talked to O'Beirne, who had recently returned from Petrograd, and the 'arrangement' may also have been brought up. He had also to see Grey (Grey's comment of 18.2 on Nicolson's letter in F.O. 371/2767/35529), and it is not improbable that he saw him shortly before leaving London, when he already knew of Suares' proposition. It should be noted that O'Beirne's minute advances the idea of 'an arrangement', 'a deal' with the Jews or the Zionists, not of a declaration.

Wolf's draft formula was received at the F.O. on 4.3. O'Beirne's second minute is of 8.3. The draft cable to be sent out (11.3) in Grey's name to the ambassadors in France and Russia was also written by him; it was corrected and endorsed by Crewe. O'Beirne's note to Drummond (of 8 or 9.3?) as well as Drummond's letter to Crewe of 11.3 (F.O. 800/96) go to indicate that Grey must have been consulted, through his private secretary, on important matters during his absence from the Office in March. He, besides Crewe, may have therefore encouraged the Office 'to pursue the matter' and possibly also to draft the cable (F.O. 371 vol. 2671/35433, vol. 2817/nos. 42608, 43766).

In his letter to Samuel Sykes mentions the possibility that 'Belgium should assume the administration [of Palestine] as the trustee of the Entente Powers'. It is of some interest to note that Churchill had made a similar suggestion about a year earlier in a comment on Buchanan's cable of 18.3.1915, where Grey was informed that the Russian government do not agree with France's definition of Syria as comprising Palestine (F.O. 800/88).

Nicolson thought that the Zionist idea was not attractive to the majority of the Jews and that the Zionists constituted a tiny minority. He besides appears not to have had a sympathetic attitude to Jews generally. And Cecil thought (to John Simon, 22.12.1915, in F.O. 371/2579/200406) Nicolson 'really does not know or care anything about news or propaganda in a general way'.

Nothing of substance is yet known of any connection between O'Beirne and Jews in general, or Zionists in England or Russia. (In June he perished together with Kitchener.) The Marquis of Crewe seems to have been in sympathy with Zionism, but it is not yet known for what reasons in addition to those arising out of British advantage. Nothing is known of any contacts between him and the Zionist leaders in those years. His wife, whose mother was a Rothschild, became a Zionist, apparently through the influence of Mrs James de Rothschild, the daughter-in-law of the well-known philanthropist Baron Edmond of Paris. His wife's brother, Neil Primrose, was considered a Zionist. Lord Cecil first met Weizmann in August 1915 (his memorandum on the meeting, 18.8.1915— F.O. 800/95), but declared himself to have been pro-Zionist even before then. Crewe and Cecil evince in several of their observations a lack of sympathy for Lucien Wolf's anti-Zionism (their feelings in this respect, particularly Cecil's, could be described in even stronger terms). The same is true of Cecil's feelings towards Edwin Montagu. Drummond appears not to have trusted Wolf, and in a comment on one of the many letters Wolf used to send to the F.O. he and the Conjoint Committee, in whose name he wrote, are referred to as 'Mr. Wolf and his gang' (F.O. 371/2817/54791).

The activity of Jabotinsky in the matter of the Jewish battalions also became linked at that time with the attempts to win over Jewish public opinion. At the end of 1915 and the beginning of 1916 he raised the idea of a Jewish legion in letters to the War Office and to Lord Cecil, maintaining that Britain's support for a Jewish legion for 'service in the East' would arouse sympathy for England among the Jews of the United States in the belief that an Allied victory would serve Zionist ends (letter dated January 26, 1916). Col. Patterson, who had commanded in Gallipoli the Zion Mule Corps, in a private letter to Cecil (January 19), also stressed the propaganda value of British support for a Jewish legion to serve in Egypt and Palestine. (F.O. 371/2835/17981. Cecil thought that 'from a Foreign Office point of view there is a good deal to be said for Patterson's proposal'.) The correspondence between Jabotinsky and Cecil began in December 1915. C. P. Scott, the editor of the *Manchester Guardian*, introduced Jabotinsky in a letter to Cecil. It is not clear whether Jabotinsky knew Scott personally; if he did not, possibly Weizmann asked Scott to help J. In any case this correspondence of Jabotinsky's with the War Office and Lord Cecil (November 1915—January 1916) is apparently the first official war-time contact between a Zionist leader and a British government department.

Approximately in the middle of February, the attitude of American Jewry was the subject of discussion and correspondence also between Lord Cecil and L. Greenberg, the editor of the *Jewish Chronicle* and Herzl's assistant in his negotiations with the British Government (ib., nos 31219, 37215).

8. A direct link between Samuel's memorandum and the proposal for 'an arrange-ment' and a Zionist declaration can be clearly discerned. The most explicit evidence comes from Sykes himself, as well as from Grey. In a cable from Russia connected with the proposed arrangement Sykes specifically refers to Samuel's memo of March 1915; and Grey too refers to 'Samuel's Cabinet memorandum' in an observation on that same cable. (There seems also to be one or two similarities of expression in Samuel's memo and O'Beirne's draft dispatch of 11.3.) In another cable from Petrograd, Sykes mentions that he had brought up the Zionist subject in his talks with Picot in London (371/2767/49669, 52384). In this connection it should be mentioned that, when in Cairo in summer and autumn 1915, Sykes seems to have sounded Arab leaders on the Zionist question (371/ 2767/49669). This too may have been the effect of Samuel's memo. But, if Sykes had not read Samuel's memo before 1916, he could have done this as a result of discussions between him and the chief British representatives in Cairo as to the future of Palestine when various possibilities must have been brought up, among them the scheme Storrs thought of which also envisaged 'Jewish infiltration' (see note 2). Sykes may also have heard about the Zion Mule Corps.

As to the future of Palestine, see the memoranda sent by McMahon in February, 1915—F.O. 371/2480/23865 and Clayton's enclosure in a letter to Wingate of 27.7.1915— Box 135/1 in the Sudan Archives. The awareness by the Syrian leaders of the strategic importance of 'southern Palestine' (i.e. the country up to Haifa) for Britain comes out in the Clayton enclosure. The recognition by the leaders of the Arab Movement of its vital imperial importance is clearly brought out in a statement by El Farouki, probably drawn up by Clayton in early October, 1915: '. . . England could hardly be expected to regard with equanimity the establishment of a powerful and united Arab Empire, marching with Egypt and on the flank of the highway to India' (ib. Box 135/4, enclosed

Note A, undated, in Clayton's memorandum of 11.10.1915). This may not have been exactly what El Farouki thought, but it undoubtedly reflects what he believed the British view was.

It should be noted that O'Beirne was aware of the difficulty of the Arab question in Palestine as well as of the opposition Arab leaders were likely to raise to 'the Palestine scheme' when made public. He pointed out, however, that although Sharif Husain was given enough money there was no sign of an Arab revolt, and that the value of the 'military co-operation which the Arabs are likely to give us in the war . . . must be placed very low' (F.O. 371 vols. 2671/35433, 2767 nos. 49669, 51288, 2817/54791). Sykes, of course, also saw the difficulty. His view, however, was: 'I deem problem soluble and think there is room for compromise' (371/2767/49669: private and secret of Buchanan, 14.3).

This entire stage (end 1915—autumn 1916) in the evolution of matters leading to the Declaration calls for further research and elaboration. I hope to publish a paper on the subject in the near future. But I should mention here that I am very much aware that part of what I am saying in the body of the article as to what took place, beginning with Hall's suggestion to consider the question of Zionism up to O'Beirne's first minute, is conjectural. There are, however, certain bare facts (which have been mentioned) that call for an explanation, and I have tried to see a connection between them and re-construct what I tend to believe must approximately have taken place. In doing so, I have been guided by the assumption that the government (I am using the term loosely) and Sykes wanted Palestine for Britain and were dissatisfied either with an international administration or with the French partner. If this is correct, it would I think follow that any reasonable scheme holding out the possibility of achieving their object to a consider-able degree must have been welcomed by them. Hence the suggested arrangement and the deal they contemplated with the Zionists.

Another assumption of mine is that Sykes, who in the negotiations with Picot naturally made it his business to get out of the French as much as possible, must have been in-formed by the Office, until his departure to Russia at the very end of February, about everything of importance which had any bearing on those negotiations. Hence the assumed connection between the Suares' suggestion and Sykes' talk with Samuel; as well as his share in the 'arrangement', although the turn it took after his departure may not have been to his liking. If Sykes did not know of Suares' suggestion, it must be concluded that his contact with Samuel just at that very time was sheer coincidence. This, of course, is not impossible; but with the evidence at my disposal at present I am not inclined to entertain it. More evidence may, in future, throw stronger light either way.

9. Yet another striking feature of the affair is the eager part taken in the pro-Zionist scheme by Sykes and Fitzmaurice—two true Catholics, not burdened by notions of the Restoration of Israel, or of Christian duty to do political justice to the Jews in compen-sation for persecution in the past, and known to be far from philo-Semites.

It might be of some value to round off the story of Wolf's attempts to have his sug-gestion formally adopted by the government (and thus become the messenger of good tidings to the Jews all over the world, discomfiting at the same time the Zionist leaders). At the end of June he reminded Oliphant that he had had no reply to his proposal respecting a public declaration based on his formula. In considering the answer to be given, several observations were made at the Office (F.O. 371/2817/130062). One was that, since the Arab revolt had just started 'it would be unwise to commit ourselves at present' (Oliphant; George Clerk had commented in the same vein). Another was that 'we cannot regard him [Wolf] as speaking for all Jews' (Oliphant—who had happened to talk to Dr Gaster and had found him most bitter against Wolf). Cecil too thought the moment was not propitious; and having pointed out during March that Wolf could not be regarded as speaking for the Zionists now also doubted whether 'the Wolf formula would be acceptable to Zionists', and suggested consulting Samuel 'on this point' (it could perhaps be deduced from this remark that for the F.O. Samuel must have been, at the time, the Jew who represented the Zionist cause). Hardinge observed, *inter alia*, that 'in principle I am opposed to the publication of all formulae as they invariably create embarrassment' (in the light of this comment it is interesting to reflect on his attitude to the question of the publication of the Balfour Declaration, respecting which little, I believe, is known so far). Grey agreed that the time was not opportune for a declaration and thought that 'privately and verbally' Wolf might be told (as indeed he must later have been told by Oliphant) 'that we did consult the French Government, who pointed out certain difficulties, one being that the Jews are not themselves agreed about it. (As a matter of fact Mr Samuel and Mr Montagu, I believe, do not agree.)'

The mention of Montagu here should be coupled with a note on document 54791 (ib.) of the end of March connected with the subject: 'Copy sent to Mr E. S. Montagu.' This would indicate not only that Montagu must have known of the proposed pro-Zionist declaration but that he also objected to it. The possibility that the subject may have briefly been brought up in the Cabinet, although not unlikely, seems to be remote. But if it was, it will go to show that the Cabinet, of which Balfour, Cecil, Crewe, Curzon, Lloyd George, Kitchener and Samuel were members, was prepared to sanction the attempted pro-Zionist policy of Grey. If it was not, Montagu may have come to know of the matter through Asquith. In that case, Grey or Crewe must have discussed the 'arrangement' with the Prime Minister—a conjecture I have already made in the text. But Montagu may of course have come to know about the matter in some other way. He had made his anti-Zionist attitude forcibly clear as early as 16.3.1915 in a 'confidential' memorandum, which can be found in the Asquith Papers, Vol. 27 (The Bodleian Library). This was in answer to Samuel's memo of the same month, but it may not have been circulated. I am indebted to Mr D. S. Porter of the Bodleian for mentioning to me the existence of this paper.

10. At the time when Sykes, after his return from Russia, began his contacts with Samuel and Gaster, a brief attempt was made on the part of the Foreign Office to sound out Sokolow privately. In the middle of March, after the proposal regarding 'the arrangement' took final shape, Oliphant suggested that 'useful information from the local point of view' could be obtained from Cumberbatch, former British Consul-General in Beirut. More than a fortnight passed before C. drew up a brief memorandum. He wrote that just before the war he had made the acquaintance of Sokolow when the latter came to Beirut for talks with Arab leaders [it transpires from the memo that C. was not aware of Sokolow's status in the Zionist Organization]; and that in talks he, C., used to have with 'leading Jews' in Beirut and other places in Syria and Palestine 'it has always been made clear to me . . . that in the event of the collapse of the Ottoman Empire the Jewish inhabitants of Palestine would welcome a British Protectorate in preference to that of France or Russia; and that 'interesting information as to anything that may be going on in Jewish circles' might be furnished by Sokolow. Oliphant suggested that perhaps C. 'could induce him [S.] to let us have a memo' on this matter. Nicolson agreed; and although it was not mentioned, there is no doubt that the department had in mind a private approach. It is not clear how C. had come to know about Sokolow's being in London, but he evidently saw him at least once and received from him two memoranda. One (handwritten and undated) about Palestine's Jewish population, its composition, numbers etc.; S. writes specifically that the new Yishuv desires a Jewish commonwealth under British protection. In the second (typewritten and dated April 12), S. explains at length why the Zionists of Palestine prefer Britain as the protecting Power as well as the benefits of such a protectorate to Britain. After this Nicolson informed C. that 'circumstances render it inadvisable to pursue matters with Mr Sokolow' (F.O. 371 vols. 2767/49669, 2817/63314).

It may also be mentioned in this connection that Lord Bryce was in favour of a Zionist scheme in a British protected Palestine (to Grey, 6.4.1916—F.O. 800/105).

Sykes does not appear to have been generally dependent on Nicolson, but it is not clear whether he made the contacts with Gaster of his own accord.

11. For the policy envisaged in December 1915—CAB 42/6, G. 46; CAB 22/3, War Committee of 16.12. For policy in December 1916 and January 1917—CAB 23/1, meeting of 15.12 (Sykes present): decision to carry on the war into Palestine and to ask the French to co-operate in the administration; CAB 28/2: I.C. 13 and I.C. 13(d), 26–28.12: Anglo-French Conference (Sykes attended the discussion of the Palestine question on 28.12); CAB 23/1, meeting of 2.1.1917: the 'Note [of 29.12.1916] on a proposal to undertake a campaign in Palestine during the winter with the object of capturing Jerusalem' [by Gen. Robertson—W.O. 106/310] accepted in principle; F.O. 371/3045/2087: French Embassy's notification, 1.1.1917 of Picot's appointment; CAB 23/1, meeting of 31.1.1917: decision to attach a Political Officer to the C.-in-C., Egypt to act in co-operation with the French P.O. The instructions for the P.O. should be settled by arrangement between the F.O., G.S. and Sykes. See also 371/3045/45320. I could find nothing, until 21.2.1917, to show conclusively that it had been decided to appoint Sykes Political Officer; but this must have seriously been thought of much earlier.

It is of interest to note (1) that the information about Picot's appointment was conveyed to Sykes—on 3.2.1917 (371/3045/2087); (2) that Sykes' first renewed initiative, after an interval of over seven months, for meeting Gaster, was made on January 4 or 5. (Gaster to Sykes, 5.1.1917: 'I shall be glad to see you . . .', from a letter quoted by Stein, 361.)

12. Minutes of talks with Sykes and Picot in the second week of February 1917—in the Central Zionist Archives. Sykes' letter to Picot, February 28—in the Sykes Papers (filmed), St Antony's, Oxford.

Mr Jon Kimche in *The Unromantics* (1968), pp. 26–27, quotes from Israel Sieff's letters to Weizmann of February 4 and 19, 1916, from which the uninitiated reader might understand that the Zionists met Sykes, or knew of the Sykes–Picot Agreement and the government's project of an Arab state as early as that. Such is not the case, however. The '1916' is an obvious error, and '1917' should have been written by Sieff instead—as Mr Kimche could have deduced from the beginning of the first-mentioned letter. But even in February 1917 the Zionists did not know of the S.–P. Agreement (Weizmann came to know of it, mainly through C. P. Scott, only at the beginning of the second half of April); and it is not yet sufficiently clear whether they really knew at the time of an Arab state in the making, or only suspected something from what Sykes had let intentionally and cautiously fall in one of his meetings with the Zionists.

13. The clear, definite and unequivocal stand taken by Lloyd George regarding the future of Palestine emerges from the oral instructions given to Sykes on the eve of his departure, *through Paris*, for Egypt: (1) 'the importance, if possible, of securing the addition of Palestine to the British area'; (2) 'the importance of not prejudicing the Zionist movement and the possibility of its development under British auspices'; (3) 'not to enter into any political pledges to the Arabs, and particularly none in regard to Palestine'. Curzon was present, and joined the Prime Minister in impressing on Sykes (No. (2)). (CAB 24/9, G.T. 372). See also the minute of Graham for Lord Hardinge (Permanent under-Secretary) of April 21, (F.O. 371/3052/78324): '... the Prime Minister insists that we must obtain Palestine and ... Sir Mark Sykes proceeded on his mission with these instructions'. '... His Majesty's Government are now committed [!] to support Zionist aspirations. Sir Mark Sykes has received instructions on the subject from the Prime Minister and Mr Balfour and has been taking action both in Paris and in Rome.'

Milner too (in spite of what he had said to C. P. Scott, Stein, 316) must have held at the time a similar view, and possibly on, in the main, similar grounds to that of Lloyd George. He appears never to have met Weizmann or Sokolow before the Declaration.

The instructions of Lloyd George to Sykes were given at the time when it was believed that a successful attack on Gaza would be the prelude to a quick advance northwards. They were the conclusive formal indication that, for his part, the policy on the future of Palestine as a British possession comprising a Zionist scheme was settled, Declaration or no Declaration. Other indications, though neither as formal nor as decisive, were evinced earlier. Curzon's attitude should be noted; and his subsequent criticism of the Declaration must not be taken for an opposition to a Zionist scheme developing under Britain's protection. The ground for those instructions had been laid by the preparations the British army had been making for an advance into Palestine and by the discussions Sykes had been conducting with the Zionists. The idea that he was conducting them without the Prime Minister's knowledge and countenance is too silly for words. It is, besides, not borne out by the available evidence, scanty and imperfect though it is.

After such a pronounced lead from the Prime Minister on a British Palestine, it is not surprising to read in the War Cabinet Minutes that 'the proposed internationalization of Palestine [in the S.–P. Agreement] was felt to be impossible' (CAB 23/2, meeting of 25.4). The minutes of the Imperial War Cabinet sub-committee on territorial desiderata in the terms of peace are more explicit. At a meeting of April 19 (CAB 21/77), Curzon maintained that 'Palestine should be included in a British protectorate'. In elaborating the point, he mentioned that 'the Zionists in particular would be very much opposed' to any other solution. The sub-committee agreed to recommend to the Cabinet that 'it was of great importance that ... Palestine ... should be under British control'. Smuts was all for securing the country, explaining that this was necessary in order to protect Egypt and ensure safe communications with the East; and that any other Power in Palestine would constitute a 'serious menace' to British imperial communications (arguments voiced in the de Bunsen Report).

It is of interest to note that Smuts had apparently not met Weizmann before June 1917 at the earliest (Stein, 480).

It might be mentioned that, when in Paris and at the Allied conference of St Jean de Maurienne, Lloyd George also spoke about a future British Palestine (Bertie to Hardinge, 21.4., F.O. 800/176; CAB 23/2, 25.4).

The commotion in regard to Lloyd George's 'British Palestine' and Zionist policy which appears to have arisen at the F.O. towards the end of April sprung first of all from the simple fact that the Office—with the exception of Balfour, possibly Cecil and, later, Ronald Graham—was not in the secret. The confusion seems to have lasted as long as the French government refused to recognize Zionist claims. Once Sokolow got the Cambon letter (next note) and returned to England, the Office too began to make out the sense of the Prime Minister's policy and to see its way. The commotion with its comically dramatic effect has its interest, but as far as the 'Zionist policy' goes had little importance. Lloyd George's Palestine policy may have been for the F.O. the first instance of the Prime Minister's attempt at making his own foreign policy. By the time of the Peace Conference the Office began to be accustomed to this experience.

14. In recommending to Jules Cambon a letter of sympathy with Zionism, de Margerie wrote (22.5.1917): . . . étant donné les rapports étroits de M. Sokolof avec le Foreign Office et la réception qui lui a été faite en Italie par le chef du Gouvernement, il serait *utile à notre* cause en Palestine et *plus encore* à l'action que pourra exercer M. Sokolof sur ses coreligionnaires de Russie, que Monsieur Ribot [the Prime Minister] voulût bien le recevoir et autoriser par exemple sous le signature de M. Jules Cambon l'envoi à M. Sokolof d'une lettre où seraient exprimées les sympathies du Gouvernement français pour la colonisation juive en Palestine (A.A.E., Guerre 1914–8, Question Juive, II, p. 1173).

Sokolow got from Cambon the French 'declaration' on June 4, after his return to Paris from Rome.

15. Exchange of letters between Sokolow, Sacher, Tolkowsky and Ettinger, and the drafts of the declaration, as well as discussion in the Political Committee—in Central Zionist Archives.

16. A draft of Balfour's reply to Rothschild containing the text of the Declaration, which is in the main as the proposed formula by Sokolow, is of the beginning of August —CAB 24/24, G.T. 1803; and Minute, 19.8.17, of Sir Ronald Graham in F.O. 371/3053/ 162458: 'The proposed letter to Lord Rothschild has been before the War Cabinet for a fortnight, but no decision has been taken in spite of reminders.'

One reason for not bringing up the subject of the Declaration for discussion in the Cabinet during that fortnight may have been the exchange of views in the F.O. on the possibility of a separate peace with Turkey. Balfour himself appears to have been doubtful (or, perhaps, unwilling at all) about such a possibility, but was instructed by the War Cabinet 'to keep the door open for a continuance of these negotiations' (see the relevant memoranda in F.O. 800/214; and CAB 23/13, meeting of 31.7). On August 23 Ormsby-Gore wrote that Milner wanted the subject to be brought up in the Cabinet as soon as possible (CAB 21/58). It appears to have been put on the agenda for the meeting of August 24. But other matters took up the time of the meeting; and then, because of Montagu, who wished to be present and could not attend for the next few days, the discussion on the subject was postponed again (ib. file 18/OA/5, notes 5–8).

It is of interest to observe that as late as mid-November the subject of a separate peace appears still to have been under discussion. Curzon, objecting to it, pointed out, *inter alia*, as one of the reasons: 'We have pledged ourselves, if successful, to secure *Palestine as a national home* for the Jewish people' (F.O. 800/214, Memorandum of November 16; my italics).

It is, besides, interesting to note the extensive frontiers of Palestine in a map attached to Tyrrell's memo on the subject (ib.).

17. On September 3, Cecil, in the absence of Balfour, urged the Cabinet to reach a decision on the question of the Declaration (by then there was already an alternative formula—without the well-known reservations—by Milner. CAB 21/58: Ormsby-Gore's letter of 23.8.1917). 'There was—he said—a very strong and enthusiastic organisation, more particularly in the United States, who were zealous in the matter, and his belief was that it would be of most substantial assistance to the Allies to have the earnestness and enthusiasm of these people enlisted on our side. To do nothing was to risk a breach with them. . . .'

On October 4, Balfour, bringing up the subject for decision, explained that 'the German Government were making great efforts to capture the sympathy of the Zionist movement'.

On October 25 Hankey reminded the War Cabinet that 'he was being pressed by the F.O. [he probably had in mind R. Graham's memo for Balfour of October 24—F.O. 371/3054] to bring forward the question of Zionism, an early settlement of which was regarded as of great importance'.

On October 31 Balfour, *opening* the discussion, said that 'he gathered that *everyone was now agreed* [my italics] that from a purely diplomatic and political point of view it was desirable that some declaration favourable to the aspiration of the Jewish nationalists should be made'. Pointing out that the great majority of Jews all over the world were in sympathy with Zionism, he explained: 'If we could make a declaration favourable to such an ideal, we should be able to carry on extremely useful propaganda both in Russia and America.' Curzon, after circulating a critical memorandum on Zionism and voicing again at the meeting a few sceptical remarks, agreed that there was value in the diplomatic and propaganda arguments. (CAB 23/4. The importance of propaganda in Russia was dealt with in the Graham memo.)

An additional item of information in regard to Balfour's support of Zionism early in 1917 comes from a private letter of Ormsby-Gore to Balfour. Writing on 29.3, he refers to a Cabinet meeting 'the other day' when Balfour expressed himself openly in favour of Zionism. (F.O. 800/204. I have however been unable to find the relevant Cabinet Minute.)

The letter of Ormsby-Gore is in respect of the Jewish Regiment. And it is interesting to observe from Cabinet Minutes of 3.9. the connection between the question of allowing a special badge for the Jewish Regiment and the question of adopting a definite policy towards the Zionist movement.

18. A Declaration seems not to have been an item of the Zionist plan of diplomatic campaign, and the origin of the idea at this stage is not clear. In case Sykes suggested it at a meeting with Weizmann (something which I doubt he did, if he did at all, seriously) then he must have had in mind the Grey attempt of March 1916. But it could well have been Weizmann's idea, and it appears to have sprung up in the following circumstances. When in March 1917, after the strenuous activity during February, meetings with Sykes had become less frequent, the Zionists seem to have begun worrying; especially after the publication of the 'Baghdad Declaration' where no hint was given—as they for some reason thought it should have—of the British government's sympathy with Jewish aspirations. Being apparently prodded about it, Weizmann made up his mind that the time had now arrived when 'our negotiations with the Government should have a more definite character', should 'be placed on a more definite basis'. In explaining in a letter (20.3.1917) what he meant by this, he does not mention a declaration, however. He seems not to have brought this point up when talking to Balfour and Lloyd George a few days later. But the mention of 'a declaration' is made in a letter written after an interview with Sykes on April 4. Exactly how the subject cropped up it is impossible to say, and with the scanty evidence at my disposal at present it would be idle to speculate who it was who mentioned it first. It is, however, clear that they talked about 'a declaration to be issued when the time arrives'—possibly when the British army entered Jerusalem, after the fashion of the 'Baghdad Declaration'; and that Sykes did not commit himself in any way. 'Please', Weizmann wrote to Sokolow, 'don't forget to talk the question of ['a' or 'the'?] declaration with Sir Mark and try to come to some definite conclusion.'

At this stage Weizmann thought he would soon be going out to Palestine; and may possibly have thought to be present when the British army entered Jerusalem, when the declaration would be read out by the Commander-in-Chief, as had been done on the capture of Baghdad. Since the plan of his going out had miscarried, he brought up the subject of the declaration in an interview he and Lord Rothschild had with Balfour *after* the Jules Cambon letter to Sokolow. Sykes' real sentiments on the subject of a declaration are not clear. He may not have held it in favour. He may have preferred, as he appears to have done in February–March 1916, 'quiet diplomacy'.

# Nazi Germany and the Palestine Question

## R. Melka

Nazi views on Palestine had their roots in Adolf Hitler's pathological fear of 'International Jewry'. In *Mein Kampf* he wrote:

> ... while Zionism tries to make the other part of the world believe that the national self-consciousness of the Jew finds satisfaction in the creation of a Palestinian State, the Jews again most slyly dupe the stupid *goiim*. They have no thought of building up a Jewish State in Palestine, so that they might perhaps inhabit it, but they only want a central organization of their international world cheating, endowed with prerogatives, withdrawn from the seizure of others: a refuge for convicted rascals and a high school for future rogues.[1]

This passage, however, is the only reference to Palestine in page after turgid page denouncing the wickedness of German Jewry. It is not too surprising, therefore, to discover that the Nazi government which came to power in Germany a decade after Hitler had penned these words concentrated its attention on getting rid of German Jews, even if this involved co-operation with Zionism.

In 1933 the Reich Ministry of Economics and Zionist groups concluded the Haavara agreements, which permitted German Jews emigrating to Palestine to deposit their assets in a special account in Germany. This account would then be used to pay for German exports to Palestine, the Jewish emigrant being reimbursed by the importer. It was hoped that this arrangement would nullify the effects of an anticipated Jewish boycott of German goods in Palestine.[2] Ernst Marcus, a Zionist who dealt with German officials in connection with these agreements, believes that they received Hitler's blessing.[3] Marcus is probably referring to a speech of October 24, 1933, in which Hitler, without naming the Haavara Agreements, noted that Germany, in contrast to Britain, was aiding Jewish emigration.[4]

Not until 1937 did the leadership of the Third Reich show any concern over Palestine. In January of that year Grobba, German Minister to Iraq, reported that a delegation of Palestine Arabs had told him that continued Jewish immigration would in five years create a Jewish majority and, eventually, a Jewish and therefore Germanophobe state. The Arabs sought German help against the Jews and the British. Grobba replied that although Germany understood the plight of the Arabs, she also desired good relations with Britain, and could therefore not intervene in Palestine.[5] The Arabs' warning to Grobba was confirmed by a German source when in late March, Döhle, the German Consul in Jerusalem, told Berlin that if Germany persisted in the policy of supporting Jewish emigration by the Haavara agreements she would not only lose the good will which she had theretofore enjoyed among the Arabs, but might very well be confronted

89

with a Jewish State which would become a centre of Germanophobia, would boycott German goods, and would seal the fate of German institutions and settlements in the Holy Land.[6]

On June 1, 1937, in response to these and similar reports, Foreign Minister von Neurath formulated German policy on Palestine. He began by dutifully paraphrasing *Mein Kampf*:

> The formation of a Jewish State or a Jewish-led political structure under British mandate is not in Germany's interest, since a Palestinian State would not absorb world Jewry but would create an additional position of power under international law for international Jewry, somewhat like the Vatican State for political Catholicism or Moscow for the Comintern.

This being the case, Neurath continued, it was in Germany's interest to strengthen the Arabs. For the moment, however, Grobba was simply to put more emphasis on German sympathy for the Arabs, without making any promises. Döhle was informed that his proposals for modifying the Haavara Agreements were 'reserved for later decision'. Neurath also instructed his ambassador in London to inform the British government that Germany's support of Jewish emigration to Palestine was not to be construed as German approval of a Jewish State there. Germany, on the contrary, did not feel that such a development would help 'tranquilize the international situation. . . .'[7]

Three weeks later, the Foreign Ministry, having learned that the Peel Commission would propose partition of Palestine and the creation of a Jewish State[8] which 'might have fateful results for German foreign policy', asked German diplomats to inform Berlin if Jewry was attempting to influence the governments to which they were accredited in favour of such a settlement.[9]

Despite all this ominous talk of a 'Jewish Vatican' and its 'fateful results', the actions of the German government during the next few years indicate that such fears were not taken very seriously, even by those who first voiced them. Nowhere is this more clearly seen than in the question of the Haavara agreements, by which Germany herself was co-operating in the building of Zion. In January 1938 Döhle reminded Berlin that this matter was still pending, warning that Arab opinion, once overwhelmingly pro-German, was showing signs of souring, and might turn completely if Germany's role in the Haavara system became known.[10]

The Haavara agreements had in fact become a bone of contention within the German government, where in June 1937 the brash and meddling *Auslandsorganisation*,[11] the Nazi Party branch for Germans outside the Reich, told the Foreign Ministry of its long opposition to Haavara and its present support of 'Party Comrade Döhle' because:

> Haavara transfers amount economically to draining off goods without an economic *quid pro quo* either in foreign exchange or in the form of goods. Politically it means valuable support for the formation of a Jewish national State with the help of German capital.[12]

In March 1938 *Referat Deutschland*, the Foreign Ministry office concerned with German internal affairs, added its warning that the Jewish State which the Haavara agreements were helping build in Palestine would, as Hitler and Neurath had said, become a centre of 'International

Jewry', while at the same time it would not absorb even German Jewry, which in 1937 had contributed only 1,500 immigrants to Palestine.[13]

The Haavara agreements also had their champions in the German government. In December 1937 the Foreign Exchange Control Office presented a report showing that in terms of foreign exchange this system provided the least costly method of encouraging the emigration of the greatest number of Jews. This report claimed that of the approximately 120,000 Jews who had left Germany since 1933, 40,000 had gone to Palestine, and held out the hope that in the future the Haavara system might enable 20,000–25,000 Jews to emigrate to Palestine annually. These facts, the report concluded, 'not only justify but demand the continuation of the activities of Haavara'.[14]

In the Foreign Ministry the Haavara system was strongly supported by von Hentig, head of Political Department VII (Middle East affairs) and one of the 'old school' diplomats opposed, albeit not very actively, to much of Nazism's programme.[15] Hentig advanced an argument which affirmed Nazi fantasies about the malevolence of 'International Jewry', but turned them in a pro-Zionist direction. Dispersing Germanophobe Jews to many countries, he wrote in late 1937, was more harmful to Germany than concentrating them in Palestine, where the emergence of a Jewish State would enable Germany 'when . . . attacked by Jewry, to deal with official representatives and not, as heretofore, with anonymous and therefore irresponsible elements'. What is more, Hentig claimed that the current rate of emigration to Palestine was 30,000–40,000 per annum,[16] meaning that in ten years Germany would be rid of her Jews.[17]

This conflict over Haavara meant that the question would have to be decided by Hitler himself, whose anti-Semitism was, after all, the root of the entire problem. Marcus says Hentig told him that at the time of the Peel Commission report, Hitler, seconded by Goebbels, had expressed his fears of a 'second Vatican' and criticized the policy of encouraging Jewish emigration to Palestine. Since the rumour of these remarks had interfered with emigration, Hentig had Marcus prepare a report for Hitler showing the relative unimportance of German Jews in Palestine.[18]

For whatever reasons, Hitler would seem to have changed his mind almost immediately and swung around to Hentig's position. In July 1937 a representative of the Ministry of the Interior reported that Hitler had decided that Jewish emigration should be concentrated on Palestine, because this would create '. . . only *one* centre of Jewish trouble in the world', a centre which would be weakened by internal strife, would be easier for Germany to influence, and which could be opposed by concerted German counter-measures.[19] Six months later, in January 1938, an official of the Foreign Ministry's Economic Policy Department reported that the Führer had 'recently decided again' that Jewish emigration was to be 'promoted by all available means'.[20] Although the official concluded that this meant directing much of the emigration to Palestine, Hitler's opinion was not given in writing, and also did not deal with the Haavara system. Therefore the dispute continued, and as late as November 1938 the *Auslandsorganisation* was still talking about '. . . once more . . . vigorously urging upon the authorities concerned the long-overdue abolition of the Haavara Agreement'.[21]

November 1938 was also the month of the *Kristallnacht* pogrom and increased pressure for emigration. A 'Central Reich Office for Jewish

Emigration' was established under Reinhold Heydrich, who at a conference on November 12, 1938, had told an incredulous Göring how his office in Vienna had, in the eight months since the *Anschluss*, sent 50,000 Jews out of Austria, while only 19,000 had left the old Reich.[22] Although there were still some in the German government, like the author of a Foreign Ministry circular of January 1939, who felt that Palestine was 'out of the question' as a target for Jewish emigration—because it could not absorb German Jewry and because of the old fear of a 'Jewish Vatican'—they did not include Heydrich, who in February told representatives of the agencies concerned that in order to get around quotas recently imposed by the British even illegal emigration to Palestine should be utilized.[23] In fact, the Gestapo and S.S. had been doing just that since the previous summer. Adolf Eichmann had even provided training farms and special trains for the 'illegals', who, according to one source, were by the end of 1938 arriving in Palestine at the rate of one thousand a month.[24]

Since the Heydrich–Eichmann system stripped a Jewish emigrant of his property, it could not be accused, as the Haavara system had been, of building a Jewish State with German capital.[25] It continued, however, to concentrate emigration on Palestine, and therefore followed the policy which, despite all objections, obtained in practice during the entire pre-war period: to get rid of German Jewry as quickly and cheaply as possible, without regard for the danger of a 'Jewish Vatican' in Palestine.

Nor does this spectre of a nefarious Jewish State, which Neurath had raised in his message of June 1, 1937, appear to have counted for much in German foreign policy. Neurath, it is true, had instructed his ambassador in London to make German fears known there. But less than two months later he said that a statement from a responsible German leader against a Jewish State in Palestine, which the government of Iraq had requested, was '. . . out of the question. We wish to keep aloof from this controversy'.[26] By October 1937 Neurath would seem to have accepted partition, and simply warned the British that the security of German settlers in the proposed Jewish area would have to be guaranteed.[27]

Neurath's message had also talked of strengthening the Arabs, but in this connection mentioned specifically only more definite expressions of German sympathy, with no strings attached in the form of promises. Accordingly, the Foreign Ministry did not respond to proposals from Haj Amin el-Husseini, the Mufti of Jerusalem and leader of the Palestine Arabs, for Arab–German collaboration in Palestine and elsewhere.[28] In August 1937 von Weizsäcker, head of the Political Department, wrote, in response to a suggestion of direct German support for the Palestine Arab revolt in the form of arms or money: 'As soon as we become visibly active, the effect will be the *opposite from the one desired by us*.'[29]

But this question, like that of Jewish emigration, was not entirely in the hands of the Foreign Ministry. In the summer of 1938 the *Aussenpolitisches Amt* of the Nazi Party, as part of its inept meddling in foreign affairs,[30] seems to have persuaded the *Abwehr* to smuggle arms to the Palestine Arabs via Saudi Arabia and also through Iraq. This scheme collapsed when it was discovered, just as the arms were about to sail, that King Saud's representative was in British pay.[31]

The attitude and role of the *Abwehr* in this question is not entirely clear. Canaris's biographer says that in 1938 the Admiral personally made an incognito trip to the Middle East, where he made the acquaintance of the

Mufti in Jerusalem.[32] In the same year Colonel Grosscurth, a member of anti-Nazi circles within the *Abwehr*, flew to Bagdad with counsels of restraint for Arab leaders like Fawzi al-Qawuqchi, the military leader of the Palestine rebellion.[33] Finally, there exists an *Abwehr* agent's report indicating that the German intelligence organization did give the Mufti money, thanks to which, the Arab said, it had been possible to carry on the Palestine revolt.[34]

This seems to have been the only material support which Germany extended to the Arabs. The German arms captured from the guerrillas, given the nature of the international arms trade, are no proof that they were supplied by the German government.[35] That German policy towards the Arab rebels was very cautious can also be seen from the fact that until 1939 German Nazi Party members in Palestine were forbidden to have anything to do with the Arab movement.[36]

Nor was Berlin ready to support interested Arab governments in their struggle against a Jewish State in Palestine. Iraq and Saudi Arabia several times solicited German diplomatic support, but were told that Germany first wanted to see proof of a united Arab front on Palestine. German diplomats feared that Britain could apply sufficient pressure to force any Arab State to yield on Palestine.[37] Thus the only diplomatic collaboration took place in Geneva, where the Foreign Ministry agreed that the German Consul might, provided his role remain concealed, advise the Iraqi delegation to the League of Nations on opposition to the planned partition of Palestine.[38]

Common opposition to a Jewish State in Palestine, even if it did not lead to active collaboration, did work in a general way to strengthen ties between Nazi Germany and the Arab States. Such was the case with Saudi Arabia, which in 1937 had no diplomatic ties with Germany. In November of that year Grobba met with King Ibn Saud's representative, Sheikh Yusuf Yasin, in Bagdad. After an exchange of views on the Palestine question, during which the Arabian assured Grobba that all Arabs, including his king, were united in their opposition to partition, Yasin said that Saud would welcome a German diplomatic representative: 'The Palestine case showed that it would be advantageous for both Governments if they had an opportunity of consulting with each other on questions in which both countries were interested.' After long negotiations—complicated by the meddling of the *Aussenpolitisches Amt*, which maintained its own contacts with Saudi Arabia—in early 1939 Grobba was accredited as a sort of part-time representative to Jidda.[39]

Concerning the subsequent history of German–Saudi Arabian relations, which centred around an Arabian request for German arms, we need only note that common opposition to 'International Jewry' was a frequent theme. Ibn Saud, in the audience which he gave Grobba on February 13, 1939, said that the Jewish question 'was as much a question of life and death for Germany as it is for the entire Arab world. . . .' The Arabian monarch praised Nazi opposition to Jewry, and declared that he '. . . always thought it a disgrace that the real Germans should have to struggle through an impoverished life while Jews and their families are putting on airs in the big hotels along Unter den Linden'.[40] In June 1939 Khalid Beg al-Qarqani, Ibn Saud's personal representative, had an interview with Hitler. The German dictator praised the Arab struggle in Palestine, and announced his own intention of driving every Jew from Germany. Al-

Qarqani, who might have wondered just how many of these Jews would eventually end up in Palestine, approvingly noted that this had been the Prophet's policy in Arabia.[41]

This theme of common opposition to Jewry also figured heavily in Nazi propaganda for Arab consumption, and whereas the reaction of the German government to developments in Palestine, on the level of official policy, had been quite restrained, such was not the case with propaganda. German Arabic radio services, which began broadcasting in 1938, found Palestine an inexhaustible source of stories—true, half-true, or false— illustrating Jewish and British wickedness, and permitting lavish expressions of German sympathy for the Arab cause. All observers agree that this propaganda enjoyed great popularity with the Arab masses.[42]

Palestine also figured in Nazi domestic propaganda. In July 1937 Rosenberg wrote that the Palestine problem was the fruit of British double-dealing and Jewish intrigue. Germans, although not directly involved, 'have every reason to follow carefully the development of this matter'.[43] Germans who followed it in their press got a picture distorted almost out of recognition. The Arab guerrillas were described as conducting 'retaliatory measures' against 'Jewish terrorism', and by October 1938 Nazi propagandists were trumpeting the news that the Arab rebels controlled most of Palestine. When, a month later, it became obvious that Britain was putting down the insurrection, the theme became the 'inhuman repressive methods' of Britain's 'rule of blood'.[44]

Nazi writers always underscored the conclusions which they wanted their readers to draw from this version of events in Palestine: (1) British and Jewish actions there gave them no right to criticize German treatment of Jews (thus, for example, atrocity stories from Palestine were given a big play in the month following the *Kristallnacht*); (2) Britain's mishandling of minority problems in Palestine showed that she was unqualified to interfere with Germany's settlement of such problems on her eastern frontier; (3) Britain's decadence and weakness were manifest in Palestine, and Germany need have no fear that Britain would or could seriously oppose her in Eastern Europe.

While the rest of the world probably took little note of the German press, it paid greater attention to Hitler's speeches, in which he referred with increasing frequency and acerbity to Palestine, always in order to impart one or more of these lessons. Thus in his Reichstag address of February 20, 1938, Hitler suggested that 'certain members of the House of Commons concern themselves with sentences passed by the British Courts Martial in Jerusalem, and not with the sentences passed in the German People's Court'.[45] In September, at the height of the Sudeten crisis, Hitler told the Nuremberg rally that he was:

> . . . in no way willing that here in the heart of Germany through the dexterity of other statesmen a second Palestine should be permitted to arise. The poor Arabs are defenceless and perhaps deserted. The Germans in Czechoslovakia are neither defenceless nor are they deserted. . . .[46]

On November 8 he scornfully told Churchill, Eden, and other critics of appeasement that they should apply their 'prodigious knowledge' and 'infallible wisdom' to Palestine, where things had 'a damnably strong smell of violence and precious little of democracy'. But, he added, he was merely using Palestine as an example, for he spoke only for Germany, and unlike his British enemies, was not 'an advocate for the cause of others'.[47]

However, Hitler's use of Palestine to justify his *Drang nach Osten* soon made him sound very much like a champion of the Arab cause. On April 1, 1939, he said

> We do not seek anything in Palestine, precisely so-little has England anything to seek in our German living space . . . what right has England to shoot down Arabs in Palestine solely because they support the cause of their homeland? Who gives England the right? In Central Europe at least we have not slaughtered thousands, but we have settled our problems in calm and order.[48]

Four weeks later, in his sarcastic answer to President Roosevelt's request that he guarantee the security of a number of countries, Hitler waxed even more indignant over Palestine:

> . . . the fact has obviously escaped Mr Roosevelt's notice that Palestine is at present occupied not by German troops but by the English; and that the country is having its liberty restricted by the most brutal resort to force, is being robbed of its independence and is suffering the cruellest maltreatment for the benefit of Jewish interlopers. The Arabs living in that country will therefore certainly not have complained to Mr Roosevelt of German aggression, but they do voice a continuous appeal to the world, deploring the barbarous methods with which England is attempting to suppress a people which loves its freedom and is but defending it.[49]

The Führer's words, which were probably intended for Europe, seem to have had their greatest impact on the Arabs, who could not know that as Hitler was delivering these self-righteous strictures his underlings Heydrich and Eichmann were working to push as many 'Jewish interlopers' as possible towards Palestine. Grobba several times reported the overwhelmingly favourable response in Iraq,[50] and in his war-time dealings with Hitler the Mufti of Jerusalem never failed to thank him for these 'ringing speeches'.[51]

As one might expect, German use of the Palestine club, and Hitler's gibes in particular, were very poorly received in Britain. But protests to Berlin brought little beyond the absurd lie that in this matter the German government had no control over the press.[52] Even Dirksen, the German ambassador in London, felt obliged to warn that mention of Palestine in Hitler's speeches 'touched on a sensitive spot'.[53] Hitler no doubt wanted to probe just this spot. But if he also wanted, as he always claimed, an understanding with Britain, then he might have pondered Dirksen's survey of Anglo-German relations in 1938, where he named German Palestine propaganda as one of the major factors in their deterioration. This propaganda, he wrote, was 'universally resented as intentionally insulting the British Army', and had cost Germany the valuable friendship of the ex-servicemen.[54]

By 1939 events forced Chamberlain's government to admit the truth of one conclusion of the Nazi propagandists: 'The key to friendship between British imperialism and Arab nationalism can be found only in Palestine.'[55] In the White Paper of May 1939 His Majesty's government abandoned partition, restricted Jewish immigration and land ownership, and envisioned the eventual establishment of an Arab Palestine tied to Britain by a special treaty.[56]

Nazi Germany had been a prime mover in the abandonment of the Peel Commission's proposals. Although Arab–German collaboration on Palestine was, as we have seen, very limited, the threat was there, and it was used by the Arabs. Pan-Arab conferences in 1937 and in 1938 bluntly told Britain that if she continued to give preference to Zionist aims, the Arabs would seek friends among Britain's enemies.[57]

The White Paper, as Zionists have always said, was Chamberlain's appeasement of the Arabs. It was also part of the long and painful process by which the British government abandoned appeasement of Hitler. As one recent study puts it:

> The concern of the Arab-speaking world with Palestine was not a chimera imagined by orientalists and Arabophils. It was a real fact and an extremely dangerous one. It tended to make the Arab world friendly disposed to Nazi Germany, and a large part of the oil resources of Britain were situated in the Arab world. To have opened a major quarrel with the Arab States when Europe was moving toward war would have been an act of folly by Great Britain without precedent.[58]

While Chamberlain's government was retreating in Palestine, it was preparing to resist, now by force if necessary, Hitler's insatiable demands in Eastern Europe. In these circumstances the Nazi government, even though its never very real fears of a 'Jewish Vatican' should have been laid to rest by the White Paper, was hardly ready to give up such an easy road to Arab friendship or so convenient a stick with which to belabour the British as the Palestine question provided. Not only did the Nazi press dismiss British concessions to the Arabs as 'deceit', 'British hypocrisy', and 'England's latest Palestine bluff',[59] but now in 1939 all restraints on the activities of the Palestine Nazi Party were lifted, and it was ordered to go underground and to incite the Arabs.[60]

When the collision came over Poland the German government could not resist a final self-justifying jab at Palestine. In its last official message to London the German régime said that it did not intend '. . . on account of any sort of British obligations in the East, to tolerate conditions which are similar to those conditions which we observe in Palestine, which is under British protection'.[61]

While these gibes would not defeat Britain, the rancours created by the Palestine question could be enlisted on one side or the other and might conceivably influence the final outcome. The Jews had no choice of sides in World War II. Those Arabs, like the Mufti of Jerusalem, who rejected the White Paper, turned to the Axis—that is, to Germany, for they feared Mussolini's ambitions in the Middle East. The story of why and how the German government failed to turn offers of Arab collaboration to any good advantage is beyond the scope of this paper.[62]

Here we are concerned only with Palestine, where the Mufti promised that with German support he could rekindle the Arab revolt, and this time carry it, as part of a general Arab uprising, to a successful conclusion. He assured the Germans that once the British, and with them the possibility of a Jewish State, had been driven out of Palestine, world Jewry, especially in America, would abandon the British. The Axis, for their part, were asked to issue a declaration promising, among other things, that after their victory the Palestine question would be settled in accordance with Arab wishes.[63]

Although, because of Italian objections and for other reasons, such a declaration was never issued, the Axis always emphasized in their propaganda and in contacts with Arab representatives their undying opposition to a Jewish State in Palestine.[64] The Germans were aware that for the moment Palestine had been pacified, but believed that the Arabs could again embarrass the British there. In early 1941 therefore the *Abwehr* attempted to run arms to the Palestine Arabs, but was thwarted by problems of transportation. Germany was unable to provide anything but money. This subsidy went to the Mufti, who, despite assurances that the Palestine uprising was 'in full swing', seems to have been unable to produce any significant disturbance in Palestine, even during Rashid Ali's struggle with the British in Iraq in May 1941.[65]

After the Iraq affair the Mufti and many of his followers fled to Axis Europe, where they continued to importune particularly the Germans for a promise to eliminate the Jewish national home in Palestine.[66] Although the Axis still refused a public declaration, Hitler, in his interview with the Mufti on November 30, 1941, said:

> Germany stood for uncompromising war against Jews. That naturally included active opposition to the Jewish national home in Palestine, which was nothing other than a centre, in the form of a State, for the exercise of destructive influence by Jewish interests.[67]

Here, as in other things, Hitler seems never to have lost the *idées fixes* of *Mein Kampf*. In April 1942 Ribbentrop and Ciano confidentially promised in writing that the Jewish settlement in Palestine would be abolished.[68]

During his stay in Axis Europe the Mufti also revived the question of Jewish emigration to Palestine with the Germans and with the governments of Bulgaria, Hungary and Rumania. He warned of the adverse effect such emigration, if permitted, would have on Arab opinion.[69] The Mufti's warnings may have reached Hitler, who in late May 1942 remarked that since the Arabs did not want the Jews in Palestine, it would be better to send them to Africa.[70] This observation, as we now know, was just more of Hitler's idle talk, and not the ultimate horror of his 'Final Solution'. It is in connection with the Nazi extermination machine that the Mufti, who seems to have had a part in closing off escape routes, has been called a war criminal and linked with Eichmann.[71]

According to Kastner, who dealt with him in his infamous 'sale' of Hungarian Jews, Eichmann absolutely refused to permit a group of Jews to go to Istanbul, that is, in the direction of Palestine. Such a move, Eichmann said, would turn the Arab world against Germany, and would also break a promise to his personal friend, the Mufti. On the other hand, Eichmann was prepared to let the Jews proceed to Lisbon and from there to West Africa: 'What happened to the group thereafter was no concern of his.'[72]

In any case, the *sine qua non* of the Mufti and his friends' plans for Palestine was Axis victory. To this end they made full use of the Axis propaganda machines to win the Arab and Moslem world, which naturally involved labouring the Palestine question, as, for example, at a well-publicized protest meeting on the anniversary of the Balfour declaration.[73] The Arab exiles also participated in unsuccessful *Abwehr* attempts to introduce agents and sabotage material into Palestine. The Mufti had to be told that his more dramatic proposals, like bombing Tel Aviv during a Zionist congress, were beyond the capabilities of the German war machine.[74] So, as it turned out, was victory.

Nazi Germany's Palestine policies evolved out of the contradictions of Nazi anti-Semitism, which dictated the persecution and expulsion of German Jewry, and therefore made it certain that, to the extent to which 'International Jewry' existed, it would be Germanophobe—a self-fulfilling prophecy. In Palestine this would mean both increased Jewish immigration from Germany, and the likelihood of a Jewish boycott against German goods. The Haavara agreements were designed to meet this situation.

That the Haavara agreements were concluded with Zionists, who thereby of course hoped to advance their own cause, was of little importance so long as a Jewish State in Palestine—which according to Hitler would be a centre for the nefarious schemes of the international Jew—was just a distant spectre. But suddenly in 1937 the possibility of this 'Jewish Vatican'—which, again by the mechanism of the self-fulfilling prophecy, would be Germanophobe—seemed no longer remote. Although those who professed anxiety over developments in Palestine had little influence on emigration policies—these were formed in response to the increasing ferocity of anti-Semitism within Germany—they did show the Nazi leadership how useful the Palestine question could be as a propaganda weapon in the increasingly acute confrontation with Britain. World War II simply brought an intensification of this propaganda, now accompanied by limited action, aimed mainly at winning the Arabs as allies by supporting their goals in Palestine.

After the collapse of the Third Reich the pre-war stream of refugees from Nazism became a flood of one-hundred thousand survivors of Hitler's holocaust. Because of what they and their co-religionists had suffered, these survivors found widespread sympathy and support for their plea to be permitted to go to Palestine and there build Zion.[75] Nazi Germany had ultimately proven a disaster for the Arab cause, which in the critical years after 1945 was further weakened by the Mufti and his friends' wartime collaboration with the Axis Powers.[76] Just as political Zionism had been fostered by the Dreyfus affair and the pogroms of Tsarist Russia, the creation of the State of Israel can be understood only in the light of the Nazi experience.

COUNTRIES CONTRIBUTING THE LARGEST NUMBERS OF JEWISH
IMMIGRANTS TO PALESTINE*

| Year | 1932 | 1933 | 1934 | 1935 | 1936 | 1937 | 1938 | Totals: 1932–38 |
|---|---|---|---|---|---|---|---|---|
| Germany | 352 | 5,392 | 6,941 | 8,630 | 8,180 | 3,611 | 6,733† | 39,839 |
| Poland | 3,156 | 13,125 | 18,028 | 27,843 | 11,596 | 3,636 | 6,269 | 80,653 |
| Rumania | 504 | 1,411 | 2,031 | 3,890 | 1,444 | 314 | 519 | 10,113 |
| Total: all countries | 9,553 | 30,327 | 42,356 | 61,854 | 29,727 | 10,536 | 12,868 | 197,221 |
| Per cent of total from Germany | 3·6 | 17 | 16 | 11 | 27 | 34 | 52† | 20 |

* Compiled from *Reports by His Majesty's Government in the United Kingdom of Great Britain and Northern Ireland to the Council of the League of Nations on the Administration of Palestine and Trans-Jordan 1932–1938*, Colonial Numbers 82, 94, 104, 112, 129, 146, 166 (London: His Majesty's Stationery Office, 1933–1939).
† Including Austria.

1. Adolf Hitler, *Mein Kampf* (New York: Reynal and Hitchcock, 1939), pp. 447–48.

2. *Documents on German Foreign Policy: 1918–1945* (hereafter: D.G.F.P.), (Washington: United States Government Printing Office), Series C, I, 661–62, 732–36.

3. Ernst Marcus, 'The German Foreign Office and the Palestine Question in the Period 1933–1939', *Yad Washem Studies on the European Jewish Catastrophe and Resistance*, II (1958), 190.

4. Norman H. Baynes (ed.), *The Speeches of Adolf Hitler: April 1922–August 1939* (London: Oxford University Press, 1942), I, 730.

5. German Foreign Office Political Archives, Bonn (hereafter: G.F.O.P.A.), Politische Abteilung VII (hereafter: P.A. VII), 'Politische Beziehungen Palästinas zu Deutschland, 15.7.1936 bis Januar 1939'.

6. G.F.O.P.A., Buero Reichsaussenminister (hereafter: Buero R.A.M.), 'Palästina'.

7. D.G.F.P., Series D, V, 746–47.

8. Great Britain, Palestine Royal Commission Report, *Parliamentary Papers*, Vol. XIV, Cmd. 5479, July 1937.

9. D.G.F.P., Series D, V, 750–53.

10. Ibid., 780–81.

11. On the *Auslandsorganisation* see Gordon A. Craig, 'The German Foreign Office from Neurath to Ribbentrop', *The Diplomats: 1919–1939*, ed. Gordon A. Graig and Felix Gilbert (Princeton: Princeton University Press, 1953), pp. 427–34.

12. D.G.F.P., Series D, V, 747–48.

13. Ibid., 785–87. The official British figure is 3,611 (see Table).

14. Ibid., 772–77. The British figures (see Table) indicate that the total number of German Jews entering Palestine in the years 1933–37 was 32,754.

15. Werner Otto von Hentig, *Mein Leben: Eine Dienstreise* (Göttingen: Vanderhock & Ruprecht, 1962), *passim*. Marcus, *Yad Washem Studies*, II (1958), *passim*.

16. An incredibly exaggerated estimate (see Table).

17. D.G.F.P., Series D, V, 762–65.

18. Marcus, *Yad Washem Studies*, II (1958), 190–93.

19. G.F.O.P.A., P.A. VII, 'Beziehungen Palästinas zu Deutschland'.

20. D.G.F.P., Series D, V, 784.

21. Ibid., 798.

22. Ibid., 904–05. *Trial of the Major War Criminals before the International Military Tribunal, Nuernberg, 14 November 1945–October 1946* (Nuernberg: International Military Tribunal, 1947), XXVIII, 499–540.

23. D.G.F.P., Series D, V, 926–36.

24. Jon and David Kimche, *The Secret Roads: The 'Illegal' Migration of a People, 1938–1948* (London: Secker and Warburg, 1954), pp. 15–44. Cf. Table, which of course reflects only legal immigration.

25. Marcus, *Yad Washem Studies*, II (1958), 196–201.

26. D.G.F.P., Series D, V, 756–57.

27. Ibid., 768–69.

28. Ibid., 755–57, 778–79.

29. Ibid., 764. Weizsäcker's italics.

30. On the *Aussenpolitisches Amt* see Paul Seabury, *The Wilhelmstrasse: A Study of German Diplomats Under the Nazi Régime* (Berkeley: University of California Press, 1954), pp. 33–37.

31. D.G.F.P., Series D, V, 810–11. Hentig, pp. 318–19.

32. Karl Heinz Abshagen, *Canaris*, trans. Alan Houghton Brodrick (London: Hutchinson, 1956), p. 208. Cf. Oscar Reile, *Geheime Ostfront: Die deutsche Abwehr im Osten, 1921–1945* (München: Verlag Welsermuhl, 1963), p. 174.

33. Unpublished MMS. of Friedrich Wilhelm Heinz (late nineteen-forties), p. 52. The writer is grateful to Professor Harold Deutsch for this information.

34. Institut für Zeitgeschichte, Munich, Nuremberg Document PS-792. This report, one of the few *Abwehr* documents available, is undated, but internal evidence indicates that it was written in the spring of 1939.

35. Even Italy, which did actively support the Palestine revolt, found it more expedient to give the Arabs money, with which, Ciano told Göring, they had no trouble purchasing arms from Greek suppliers. D.G.F.P., Series D, VI, 262.

36. H. D. Schmidt, 'The Nazi Party in Palestine and the Levant: 1932–1939', *International Affairs*, XXVIII (October 1952), 460–69.

37. D.G.F.P., Series D, V, 756–57, 766–72, 787–89, 793–97.

38. G.F.O.P.A., P.A. VII, 'Plan für Aufteilung Palästinas und Stellungnahme der fremden Länder dazu'.

39. D.G.F.P., Series D, V, 769–72, 781–82, 791–93, 798–800; Hans-Guenther Seraphim (ed.), *Das politische Tagebuch Alfred Rosenbergs aus den Jahren 1934/35 und 1939–1940* ('Quellensammlung zur Kulturgeschichte', ed. Wilhelm Treue, Vol. VIII; Gottingen: Musterschmidt-Verlag, 1956), pp. 67 and 191.

40. D.G.F.P., Series D, V, 807–10.

41. Ibid., VI, 743–44.

42. Robert L. Baker, *Oil, Blood and Sand* (New York: D. Appleton-Century Company, 1942), pp. 102–07; Seth Arsenian, 'Wartime Propaganda in the Middle East', *The Middle East Journal*, II (October 1948), 419–21; Nevill Barbour, 'Broadcasting to the Arab World: Arabic Transmissions from the B.B.C. and other Non-Arab Stations', *The Middle Eastern Journal*, V (Winter, 1951), 63–65.

43. *Völkischer Beobachter* (Berlin), July 9, 1937.

44. Ibid., July 8–13, 26, August 2, 9, 21, September 15, October 12, 19–23, November 15–23, 1938; February 26, 1939.

45. Baynes, II, 1402–03.

46. Ibid., 1497.

47. Ibid., 1558.

48. Ibid., 1595–96.

49. Ibid., 1648.

50. G.F.O.P.A., PA VII, 'Bezeihungen Palästinas zu Deutschland'.

51. D.G.F.P., Series D, XI, 1154, XIII, 881.

52. *Documents on British Foreign Policy: 1919–1945* (London: Her Majesty's Stationery Office), Third Series, III, 449–50, 551–52.

53. D.G.F.P., Series D, IV, 304.

54. Ibid., 361.

55. *Völkischer Beobachter* (Berlin), August 2, 1938.

56. Great Britain, *Palestine: Statement of Policy*. Parliamentary Papers, Vol. XXVII, Cmd. 6019, May 1939.

57. John Marlowe, *The Seat of Pilate: an Account of the Palestine Mandate* (London: The Cresset Press, 1959), pp. 145–46, 151–52.

58. Christopher Sykes, *Crossroads to Israel* (Cleveland: The World Publishing Company, 1965), p. 198.

59. *Völkischer Beobachter* (Berlin), March 18, May 18, 19, 1939.

60. Schmidt, *International Affairs*, XXVIII (October 1952), 460–69.

61. D.G.F.P., Series D, VII, 531.

62. For a detailed account see Lukasz Hirszowicz, *The Third Reich and the Arab East* (London: Routledge & Kegan Paul, 1966).

63. D.G.F.P., Series D, X, 415–16, 556–60, XI, 586–87, 1153–55; Uthman Kemal Haddad, *Harakat Rashid Ali al-Kilani sanat 1941* (Sidon: The Modern Library, 1950), pp. 29–40, 50–54. The writer wishes to thank Professor Belkacem Saadallah, University of Algiers, for translating these passages.

64. Hirszowicz, *passim*.

65. G.F.O.P.A., Buero R.A.M. 'Irak', Buero Unterstatssekretär 'Irak'; D.G.F.P., Series D, XI, 826–29, XII, 234–43, 323–25, 496–99, 775, 890; Institut für Zeitsgeschichte, Munich, *Dienstagebuch der Abwehr Abteilung II*, II, 115–19, 142–47.

66. D.G.F.P., Series D, XIII, 743.

67. Ibid., 882–83. The Mufti's record of this conversation in: The Nation Associates, *The Arab Higher Committee: Its Origins, Personnel and Purposes* (New York: 1947), pages unnumbered, records Hitler's words as: 'Primarily, I am fighting the Jews without respite, and this fight includes the fight against the so-called "Jewish National Home" in Palestine because the Jews want to establish there a central government for their own pernicious purposes, and to undertake a devastating and ruinous expansion at the expense of the governments of the world and of other peoples.' The Mufti mistakenly wrote the Christian date as 21 November.

68. Institut für Zeitsgeschichte, Munich, Eichmann Trial Documents Number 1302, 1303.

69. *The Arab Higher Committee*.

70. Henry Picker (ed.), *Hitlers Tischgespräche im Führerhauptquartier: 1941–1942* (Stuttgart: Seewald Verlag, 1963), p. 378.

71. Robert W. M. Kempner, *Eichmann und Komplizen* (Zürich: Europe Verlag, 1961), pp. 400–05. Hannah Arendt, *Eichmann in Jerusalem: A Report on the Banality of Evil* (New York: The Viking Press, 1963), p. 10, too readily accepts Eichmann's explanation that he had only met the Mufti during an official reception attended by a number of people. A more complete discussion is to be found in Joseph B. Schechtman,

*The Mufti and the Fuehrer* (New York: Thomas Yoseloff, 1965), pp. 159–63, which, however, probably goes too far in the other direction.

72. I. R. Kastner, *Der Kastner-Bericht über Eichmanns Menschenhandel in Ungarn* (München: Kindler Verlag, 1961), p. 115.

73. Bundesarchiv, Koblenz, Document NS-19/187, 'Persönlicher Stab Reichsführer SS'; *The Arab Higher Committee.*

74. *Kriegstagebuch der Abwehr Abteilung II*, II, *passim*: American Christian Palestine Committee, *The Arab War Effort: A Documented Account* (New York, 1947), pp. 43–47; The Nation Associates, *The Record of Collaboration of King Farouk of Egypt with the Nazis and their Ally, the Mufti* (New York), 1948; Reile, pp. 416–22.

75. This attitude was to be of particular significance in the case of leaders like President Truman. Harry S. Truman, *Years of Trial and Hope*, Vol. II, *Memoirs* (Garden City: Doubleday & Co., 1956), pp. 132–69.

76. Hitler and Nazi Germany, however, continue to enjoy widespread popularity in the Arab world. Even so presumably responsible a person as the Deputy Foreign Minister of Egypt has sought to paint Hitler as the victim of Zionists who 'compelled him to perpetrate crimes that would eventually enable them to achieve their aim—the creation of the State of Israel'! Quoted in Arendt, p. 17.

# The Third Reich and Palestine*

## David Yisraeli

The Third Reich introduced a new factor into German foreign policy—ideology. It created a climate in which it was sometimes difficult to distinguish where ideology ended and diplomacy began. This trend particularly was visible in the relations between the Third Reich and Palestine.

The Middle East in general, and Palestine in particular, never had special interest for Nazi diplomacy, formed but a marginal area in Hitler's strategy and diplomacy which was basically Europe-centred. The Middle East was seen at the most as a minor field for German economic, cultural and propagandist activity, the latter in the sense of spreading of Judaeophobia among the peoples of the region. Propaganda activities stemming from party rather than diplomatic sources were not solely 'missionary' in character, but also served to incite Moslem populations against Britain and France with the purpose of distracting some of these powers from their pre-occupation with European problems.

The Third Reich had some minor interest in Middle Eastern oil concessions, though Hitler was not particularly keen in developing them.[1] There were also plans to develop German airlines to central and west Africa through Palestine, although the area was basically considered to be a potential sphere for Italian rather than German political and economic penetration.[2]

Until the Munich crisis and the darkening of the international horizons, official German policy in the Middle East actually tended to follow the lines laid down under the Weimar Republic. The German Foreign Ministry concentrated on economic and trade relations. As far as possible it refrained from any activity that could be interpreted as hostile to Great Britain, whose friendship appeared vital for the diplomacy of the Nazis if the latter wished to achieve their aims in Europe.

With this background one can understand Germany's refusal to grant repeated Arab requests for arms in the 1936–39 disturbances in Palestine and the insistence of the German Foreign Ministry not to get involved *officially* in the Jewish–Arab struggle.[3]

It is interesting to note that at one stage (in 1936) even the Gestapo agent in Palestine, Dr Reichert (officially the representative of the German News Agency (D.N.B.) in Palestine) expressed his opinion against German involvement in the Jewish–Arab struggle from quite a different angle. In his report to his superiors, he referred to rumours that the German consul-general in Jerusalem, Doehle, had offered arms to the Arabs. Dr Reichert stated that such action 'would be dangerous, as it would strain the relations between Germany and Palestine Jewry'. His suggestion was to use the Jewish community in Palestine as a means against the economic boycott of Germany by world Jewry.[4] Even the Nazi *Landes-*

* This paper is part of a Ph.D. thesis, 'The Palestine Problem in German Politics, 1889–1945', prepared under the supervision of Prof. Meir Vereté and accepted by the University in Jerusalem.

*gruppenleiter* (head of the Nazi party) in Palestine, Cornelius Schwarz in 1936 ordered the local Nazis to keep strict neutrality in the Arab–Jewish conflict. The *Landesgruppenleiter* was not concerned with the diplomatic or ideological aspect of the problem, his interest was mainly directed towards the fate of the German colonies in Palestine. He motivated his stand as follows: '. . . we are here in the Jewish land . . . and should refrain from everything which could pour oil on the fire . . .'[5] On the other hand, there is some evidence that the *Auslandsorganisation* (A.O.), the organization of German Citizens Abroad (under the leadership of Gauleiter Bohle) tried to strengthen the Arab hand in the riots of the 'thirties, while Heydrich, Himmler's lieutenant, advised to refrain from this, as it would harm the emigration of German Jews to Palestine.[6] At the same time Admiral Canaris, head of the Army Intelligence, was granting financial aid to the Mufti of Jerusalem, Haj Amin al-Husseini.[7]

There was a certain inner contradiction in the attitude of the Third Reich towards Palestine. True, it was not opposed to the emigration of Jews from Germany to that country, but the attitude of Nazi ideology towards Zionism and Jewish statehood in Palestine was entirely negative. The political independence of the Jews and the Jewish race had to be opposed, from their viewpoint. The Aryan race alone was entitled to independent statehood, while the inferior Jews were incapable of maintaining a State at all, for they lacked the necessary qualities. In Hitler's opinion the Jews among themselves, in the absence of any external danger to their existence, would be transformed into a pack of rats fighting one another to the death. 'If the Jews were alone in the world', said he, 'they would choke in filth.' Statehood, he held, calls for an idealistic approach on the part of the race that constitutes the state; and particularly for a correct understanding of the concept of work. And since the Jews lacked this approach, and understanding, any attempt on their part to establish and maintain a state would be doomed to failure.[8]

Hitler was followed in this respect by Alfred Rosenberg, the ideologist of the Nazi Party. He also completely rejected Zionism and Jewish statehood. As far as he was concerned 'Zionism is in the best of cases . . . an ineffective attempt by an untalented people to make a productive effort . . . This is a step taken by speculators to ensure for themselves a new field of activities in order to exploit the world. . . .'[9]

Rosenberg's rage at Zionism also derived from another source. He believed that during the First World War Zionism had collaborated with the enemies of Germany in mobilizing the capital resources of the U.S.A. against the Reich. Rosenberg also held that statehood did not suit the Jewish spirit. This anti-Zionist approach also found subsequent expression in German publications, during the period of the Third Reich.[10]

In spite of the negative attitude of the Nazis towards the resurgence of the Jewish people in their homeland, the fact remains that until 1937 Nazi policy was directed towards the encouragement of the departure of the Jews from Germany to Palestine. *De facto* it also accepted their immigration to Palestine without drawing the logical conclusion that increased immigration to Palestine must inevitably strengthen the nucleus from which a Jewish state would emerge in due course. This contradiction between Nazi theory and practice is in no way surprising. It can also be observed in the relations between Germany and U.S.S.R., and was tactical in origin.

This combination of ideology and diplomacy also found expression in the technical field. The inter-departmental consultations dealing with the problems of Palestine were not confined to the realm of the Foreign Ministry alone. The Foreign Ministry was but one of many agencies determining policy towards Palestine. And even Foreign Ministry opinions regarding the Palestine question were not unanimous. Its Near Eastern Division advocated an affirmative stand towards the Transfer agreement, while the *Referat Deutschland* of the Foreign Ministry took a completely different stand.

In discussions on the Palestine problem party institutions also participated and for some of them it was the ideological rather than the diplomatic aspect which rated first importance. Besides the Foreign Ministry, the *A.O.* (*Auslandsorganisation*), the party organization for German citizens abroad, took part in conferences on Palestine. Other participants were the *A.P.A.* (*Aussenpolitisches Amt*) the Party Bureau for external affairs, headed by Alfred Rosenberg, the Ministry of Internal Affairs, the Gestapo, the Chancellery of the Führer, the Ministry of Economics, the Propaganda Ministry, the Bureau of the Führer's Deputy and the *Rassenpolitisches Amt*—the Office for Racial Matters. These various party and governmental agencies reflected the different schools of thought that existed in Nazi Germany concerning the Jewish problem at this period. No doubt the Nazi camp was of one mind in its general hatred towards the Jews, in its desire to wipe out their influence in Germany and, if possible, in the whole world. 'Out with the Jews' was a basic tenet of all streams of Nazi thought. The translation of this tenet into policy terms, however, was not a matter of unanimity. According to Winifried Martini, correspondent of the *Deutsche Allgemeine Zeitung* in Palestine in the 'thirties and representative of the *Völkischer Beobochter* at various Zionist congresses during the same period, there was no united official Nazi line on the implementation of the anti-Jewish policy until about 1938. According to W. Martini,[11] one trend among the Nazis, headed by Julius Streicher, editor of the *Stürmer* and Joachim von Leers, one of the main Nazi propagandists, advocated physical liquidation of the Jews from the very beginning of the Nazi movement. A second trend put the emphasis on Judaism as a revolutionary international power whose aim was world domination. World Jewry, according to this school, directed history and had already gained control of the Christian churches. The outstanding representatives of this trend were Alfred Rosenberg, Ludendorff and his wife, who even left the Nazi movement in 1933 because they suspected Hitler of not being extreme enough in his war on the Jews. These two above-mentioned trends based their attitudes on eschatological considerations. To their mind, World Jewry was the main obstacle to the realization of Germany's new 'Nazi era'. The men of this latter school of thought advocated the creation of closed 'reservations' for the Jews somewhere overseas, though not in Palestine. They also considered the holding of German Jews as hostages. A third trend in the Nazi camp, the 'pro-Zionist' one, as it were, was interested mainly in the exodus of the Jews from Germany. The men of this trend did not care where to, as long as Germany would become 'Judenrein' (free of Jews). More paradoxical still, this trend had adherents even in the Gestapo and the *S.D.* (*Sicherheitsdienst*—the party's intelligence service). Adolph Eichmann's predecessor in the Jewish department of the of the *S.D.*, Baron von Mildenstein, even published in the *Angriff* a series of favourable articles on the Jewish settlements after his tour of Palestine in 1934.[12] This faction also included economic circles, men of the *Deutschnationale*.[13] Their sympathy for Zionism though rooted in anti-semitism was nevertheless a factor of help in the framing of the Transfer Agreement.[14] A fourth trend also appeared in the Nazi movement, from the ranks of the *Völkische* (a nationalistic group which was formed after World War I on an anti-Jewish and anti-Catholic platform).[15] Its main interest lay in the de-assimilation of the Jews. The representatives of this trend were Professor Gross of the *Rassenpolitisches Amt* (of the party office for racial problems) and Dr Loesener of the Jewish department of the Ministry of Interior.

Nazi party members might have their various opinions—and even express them—on the various ways of executing the anti-Jewish policy, so long as the Führer had not decided the issue one way or another. Once he decided, however, the Führer's word was law.

The different shades of opinion in the Nazi field concerning the 'solution' of the Jewish problem found their expression in German policy towards Palestine. Under the pressure of circumstances—international Jewish boycott, German isolation in the international arena, unemployment, etc.—Hitler agreed in 1933 to the Transfer Agreement and until at least around 1937 the Nazi authorities did not put any obstacle in the way of emigration to Palestine. However, even while removing the Jews from Germany, Hitler did not relinquish his heart's desire of decimating the Jews and robbing them of all their possessions. The Jews who transferred their capital to Palestine by means of the Transfer Agreement were obliged to suffer a loss of 60 per cent to 75 per cent of their fortune, and as if this were not sufficient, they were to become, by Nazi manipulation, the distributors of German products in the Middle East. The Transfer Agreement was connected with the policy of encouraging German exports. Evidence of the connection between the export of Jews and German goods is to be found in a letter from Martin Bormann to the Reich's Ministry of Economics.[16] The Jews who emigrated from Germany to Palestine were obliged to cover the bonuses granted to exporters of German products from their own fortunes in order to equalize high German prices with those which prevailed on the world market.

Jewish immigration into Palestine aroused Arab enmity towards Britain, a fact most pleasing to Hitler, who wished to cause inconvenience to her in areas outside Europe, to weaken her attention in areas that were of German interest on the European continent. The Propaganda Ministry formed the Arab animosity towards England and the Jews, financing Arab newspapers out of secret funds (mainly the *Difaʿ* in Jaffa whose editor, Shanti, was also a Gestapo informer).[17] The editor of the *Angriff*, Schwarz van Berk, on his tour of Palestine in 1937, summarized his innermost feelings about Jewish immigration to Palestine in his letter to Dr von Hentig, head of the Near Eastern Division of the Foreign Ministry in this way: '. . . it is good that the Jews from Germany came to Palestine and spent their fortune here. . . . Palestine is a suitable place for German-Jewish immigration, they will not take root there, their fortunes will be spent and the Arabs will liquidate them . . . the Jews in Palestine are doomed, their end will be to leap from the frying pan into the fire. . . .'[18]

The ideological consideration—the Judeophobia—was of such importance in Nazi policy towards Palestine that sometimes it over-shadowed political considerations. Up to the publication of the report of the Peel Commission in 1937, which initiated the plan for establishing the Jewish nation in a part of Palestine, the Nazis overlooked Arab interests and even those of the Templars, the German settlers in Palestine.[19] The Nazi policy aimed at encouraging Jewish emigration from Germany was not seen favourably either by Arabs or by the Templars. The Transfer Agreement, too, can be used to prove the partial ignoring of political interests in deference to ideological considerations in relation to Palestine. If the Nazi leadership gave its blessing to this, it was to a great extent moved by ideological motives, by the desire to get rid of the Jews. At an interdepartmental conference on December 17, 1935, the representative of the Führer's Chancellery announced that the Führer had decided to encourage Jewish emigration, 'to open possibilities for them that will encourage voluntary emigration . . .'.[20]

This ideological motive was so important in the eyes of the Nazis in the period 1933–37 that, according to Consul Doehle (the German Consul-General in Jerusalem) they were ready to ignore the danger of the Transfer causing the loss of Arab sympathy to the Third Reich.

The question arises: Which were the agencies in the Third Reich placing emphasis on ideological factors in Palestine policy and which were those that preferred diplomatic considerations? In other words, which of them saw in relations with Palestine a function of Jewish policy alone and which of them wanted to base their relations on common foreign policy considerations? Did a certain criterion exist according to which the different agencies took their stand on questions concerning Palestine?

At first sight we might assume that the party agencies would have been inclined to put emphasis on the ideological considerations while Government agencies would have inclined rather towards diplomatic and political factors. However, as far as we can observe and analyse the problem from German documents, there existed no clear institutional dichotomy. The *A.O.*, the *Auslandsorganisation*, strictly party agency, did in fact stand at the head of the fight against the agreement to transfer Jewish capital to Palestine, and at one time even had a hand in the 1937 disturbances,[21] while the Foreign Ministry favoured neutrality and took a positive stand on the Transfer Agreement.[22] However, another party body, the *S.D.*, *Sicherheitsdienst*, the intelligence service of the party, encouraged Jewish emigration in the 'thirties and the Gestapo—also a party-controlled state institution—did not interfere with Zionist activities until at least 1937, and did encourage Jewish emigration to Palestine until the outbreak of the war.[23]

Mr P. Ginzburg of the Kibbutz Ramat Ha-Kovesh, a one-time emmissary of the Histradut, Kibbutz Meuhad and 'Mossad Le-Aliya', has told me that as late as 1939 the Gestapo helped him in organizing *Aliya B* (Jewish immigration without certificates from the Mandatory Authorities) from Germany. (This was known officially as *Sonderhachshara* or 'special training'.) On September 15, 1939, three ships with 5,000 Jews were due to leave the Port of Emden with the aid of the Gestapo, but nothing came of this because of the outbreak of the war. It should be noted that the official Zionist Institutions displayed a lukewarm if not hostile attitude to *Aliya B*. Mr Ginzburg told me that when engaged in his activities for *Aliya B*. he met with a reserved attitude on the part of the official Zionist representatives. In so far as the latter provided financial assistance, it was only after he on his own initiative had succeeded in organizing the immigrant groups.

Dr Friedenthal, now Director of the Zahalon Hospital in Jaffa, at one time Director of the Central Committee of German Zionists and Liaison Officer between the German Zionist Organization, the Gestapo and the London Zionist Executive, told me the following in a conversation on December 5, 1966: After the 'Crystal Night', when the distress of the German Jews increased sharply, Captain Folley of the British Embassy in Berlin hinted to him that it was necessary for Jews to leave Germany, even by unconventional means. Dr Friedenthal went to London to discuss this with Professor Weizmann and D. Ben Gurion, each of whom separately expressed his disapproval of *Aliya B*. 'We shall not be able to fight both the Arabs and the English,' was Ben Gurion's opinion. The Zionist Executive, as Dr Friedenthal informed me, held at the time that all efforts must be concentrated on increasing the official schedule of immigration certificates. It is against this background that he explains the lukewarm or at best very reserved attitude of the German Zionist Organization towards *Aliya B*. According to him the Organization was acting in accordance with instructions received from the Executive of the Zionist Movement.

On the one hand it was the representative of the Ministry of Interior, Dr Stuckart, who preferred to direct emigration to Palestine in 1935, rather than to South America; *not* for its own sake, of course, but for fear that Jewish settlers in South America would gain control over a continent which held great financial potentialities for Germany. In 1937, on the other hand, the representative of the *Deutschland* department in the Foreign Ministry wished to reduce the Transfer in order to avoid a concentration of too many Jews in Palestine, proposing to disperse them to the four corners of the earth instead and thus spread the 'germ' of anti-semitism in the world.[24]

Even the reasons given by the different agencies that worked on the Palestine problem as justification of their stand were not uniform. It is strange to note that the *Auslandsorganization (A.O.)*—the organization of the Party for German citizens abroad—gave as reason for its opposition to the Transfer economic considerations—export without foreign currency. Yet the general government offices, the Ministry for Economic Affairs, the Treasury, the Economic Department of the Foreign Ministry, were against the motivation of the *A.O.* at least in their official arguments, basing their stand on the desire of the Führer to get rid of the Jews.[25]

It is, therefore, impossible to find a uniform criterion regarding the position of the various party and government agencies of the Third Reich to the problems concerning Palestine in the pre-war period. The inter-departmental conferences always centred around the question: What does the Führer want? All the participants then tried to the best of their ability to interpret the Führer's will and to frame their policies according to their interpretation. Yet the Führer's policy may not have been clear for many months. Nazi documents reveal no clear instructions by Hitler concerning the Palestine problem. If he did decide, it was orally only, through those near to him at the moment. Against this background we can understand that at one of these meetings concerning the fate of the Transfer in 1935, the representative of the Ministry of Interior came forward with an announcement that the Führer had decided to stop Jewish emigration altogether and to use them instead as hostages, whereas the representative of the Führer's deputy informed the meeting that Hitler had decided to encourage voluntary Jewish emigration, and lacking voluntary submission to this line, would resort to the use of force.[26] The representatives of the different agencies, in so far as they took a stand concerning the Jews and Palestine, wanted (it seems) to prove their political reliability. Thus we witness many paradoxes. While the deputy of the Führer would not needlessly intensify anti-Jewish legislation, for fear of adverse reaction abroad, it was Baron von Neurath, the Foreign Minister, who was not considered a Nazi, who opposed any compromise with the Jews, as it might be interpreted as a German surrender to World Jewry.[27]

The ideological consideration that was noticeable in the years 1933–37 was along the 'pro-Zionist' line. Germany foreign policy towards Palestine underwent a volte-face in 1937, when the plan for a Jewish State was brought up. Nazi opposition to the possibility of a Jewish State in part of Palestine was motivated not only by its concern for Italian interests in the area but also by ideological considerations. The existence of such a state would fundamentally refute the truth of Nazi ideology concerning the Jews. The Jews were regarded as an inferior race, incapable of creative activity and statehood. The very possibility of a Jewish state negated the essence of this conception. Only aryans were considered to be worthy of statehood.

This ideological factor must be noted in understanding the role of the *Referat Deutschland*, the Nazi Department of the Foreign Ministry, in initiating German opposition to the planned Jewish State. Buelow-Schwante, the head of this department at that time, sent a circular on June 22nd, 1937, to all the German consulates and embassies abroad, expressing opposition to the plan for a Jewish State.[28] It is interesting that the same Buelow-Schwante, who in 1937 opposed the planned Jewish State and the Transfer Agreement, is the same man who in 1934 sent a memorandum to German representatives abroad in which he pointed to the similarity of view between the Zionist movement, which encourages emigration of the Jews from Germany and those of the Reich's government. This fact shows to some extent the fluctuations of policy in the Nazi camp concerning implementation of anti-Jewish policy and Nazi policy towards Palestine.

At first sight one might suppose that the opposition to the planned Jewish State would have caused a closer relationship with the Arabs, who categorically opposed the plan of dividing the country. One would assume that the Germans would increase their support of the Arabs in Palestine not only financially (as Admiral Canaris had already done during the disturbances of 1936), but also with arms. However, these assumptions cannot be proved by the documents available. Indeed, von Neurath, the Foreign Minister, on January 1, 1937, advised Dr F. Grobba, the German envoy in Baghdad to express to the Iraqi Foreign Minister: 'more sympathy to the aspirations of the Arabs in Palestine',[29] yet at the same time he refrained from concrete support. The request for arms from the Arabs remained unfulfilled. Even the financial aid of Admiral Canaris did not become regular according to Dr Fritz Grobba's testimony. It was stopped, according to Dr Grobba, after the Arab gangs showed no real achievement in their struggle. The German embassy in London, too, received an order in 1937 to raise the question of the Jewish state informally in conversation with the Foreign Ministry and to express German opposition to this plan. German policy, however, refrained from official action.[30]

The justification for this stand (in Baghdad as well as in London) lies perhaps in the fact that besides the ideological considerations that necessitated the opposition to the planned Jewish state, there were diplomatic considerations that played an important role in determining the German stand. These considerations obliged the Third Reich to refrain from public actions that might irritate Britain.

While relations to the Jews in Palestine were dictated by both ideological and policy considerations, attitudes towards the Mandatory were on a correct and formal basis, despite the Nazi theoretical opposition to the mandatory concept which was based on the Versailles system, built as it were on Germany's defeat in the First World War. Rightist circles considered Mandatory rule and the Balfour Declaration to be completely anti-German acts on the part of Germany's enemies, and therefore claimed that the Mandate, as well as everything connected with it, did not bind Germany.[31]

The Nazis were even more opposed to the Mandate in Palestine because it was based on the intention to form a national home for the Jewish people. Even though theoretically there existed a denial of the mandatory rule, Nazi policy in reality was reconciled to the idea. It undertook no official action aimed at weakening the Mandate or questioning its legality. Moreover, Nazi Germany actually continued in the footsteps of the Weimar Republic in the 'thirties as regards the Mandatory Government in Palestine. It saw the British administration in Palestine as a safeguard of the Templar settlements and the German welfare and cultural institutions in Palestine. The open door policy in the economic field to which the Mandatory power was bound was also of assistance. At the time of the conferences on the partition plan in 1937–38, the German Foreign Ministry even supported the demand of the Templars that their settlements should remain within the boundaries of the Mandatory area.[32] To German diplomacy a British Mandate for the Templar settlements seemed to be the least of all evils. If the stand regarding Jewish Palestine was to a great extent the result of general Nazi policy towards the Jews, the attitude towards the Mandatory power was largely dictated by German policy towards Britain in general. Until after the occupation of Czechoslovakia, when relations with England deteriorated, Hitler refrained from openly provoking Britain.

Ideological considerations are clearly apparent in the relations of the Third Reich with the Arab movement in Palestine. However, they are not a decisive factor. Nazi Germany's position in regard to the Arab national movement in Palestine openly showed its realism. Theoretically Judeophobia should have thrown Germany and the Arabs into close alliance. The Mufti of Jerusalem Haj Amin al-Husseini, in his many appeals to German agencies after Hitler's rise to power[33] and up to the last days of the Third Reich, repeatedly emphasized this basic fact in the relations between Germany and the Arabs. On the basis of Judeophobia, he felt, a friendship should be built between the Third Reich and the Arabs. However, here the ideological sentiment—the common enmity to the Jew—did not work as expected. Official German diplomacy, as far as it is expressed in the documents of the Foreign Ministry, refrained until the outbreak of the war from identifying itself publicly with the demands of the Arabs. 'Germany truly feels sympathy for the Arabs,' stated Dr F. Grobba, the German envoy in Baghdad, to an Arab delegation, '. . . but Germany neither can nor wants to support them with arms.'[34]

Moreover, even until the final stages of the war the Third Reich refrained from identifying itself fully and officially with the Pan-Arab aspirations of the Mufti, although his movement promised to abolish the Balfour Declaration and destroy the Jewish National Home. This stand towards the Arab National Movement in Palestine had its origins in a number of political factors:

(a) Until the period of European tension in 1938 Germany refrained from active politics in the Arab area out of consideration for the interests of Britain, whose friendship she desired. At the most, Nazi Germany was ready to cause minor irritation to Britain in the Middle East by means of limited assistance to the Arab movement, as long as this could remain secret.

(b) In Palestine, as well as in the Middle East, the Third Reich had no territorial interests. According to the original Nazi foreign policy the whole area was destined to be under Italian influence.

(c) After the defeat of France in 1940 and the establishment of the Vichy Government, the Third Reich was forced by circumstances to consider the interests of the Vichy Government in the Middle East for fear of strengthening De Gaulle's 'Free French' Movement. The Vichy Government disassociated itself from the Arab propaganda of the Mufti out of fear for their position in the Levant.[35] Besides Italy, German diplomacy during the war was forced to take the additional factor of Turkey into account. Turkey made it repeatedly clear to von Papen, the Reich's ambassador in Ankara, that the Pan-Arab aspirations of the Mufti were not in accordance with her interests. Too close a connection with the Mufti of Jerusalem was liable to affect Turkey's neutrality in the War.[36] (It is possible that the basis of the precautions and hesitancy of the Third Reich towards a national Arab movement was also motivated by ideological considerations, although no evidence of this exists in the German documents. The Nazi movement as a pan-movement could not, by its very nature, live hand-in-glove with another pan-movement.)

In conclusion: we can state that Judaeophobic ideology and diplomacy played a confused role in the relations of Nazi Germany with Palestine, i.e. with the three factors involved: the Jews, the Arabs and the British. It seems that the ideological factor was more prominent regarding the Jews, while relations with the Arab movement and the mandatory power were guided primarily by diplomatic considerations. The combination of ideology and diplomacy characteristic of the totalitarian countries of the twentieth century contributed to the fact that there was no consecutively uniform policy on the part of the Third Reich towards Palestine. There was an encouragement of Jewish emigration to Palestine on the one hand, and opposition to the establishment of a Jewish State on the other. Opposition to the Mandatory System in general did not affect correct relations with Britain in Palestine. As regards the Arabs, public German sympathy with their cause against the Jews was not backed by any serious military or political assistance.

## NOTES

1. Statement by Dr Fritz Grobba, ex-German envoy in Iraq, to the writer on June 26, 1964, in Bad Godesberg. On the partnership of German companies in the Middle East Oil, see S. H. Longrigg's *Oil in the Middle East* O.U.P. (1961).

2. Chef der Sicherheitspolizei, Bestand R 58/954, Bundesarchiv Koblenz. Concerning Italy's sphere of influence see also: *Ciano's Diplomatic Papers*, pp. 50–60; Wiskemann, A. E. *The Rome–Berlin Axis* (London 1949), pp. 20, 21, 29, 134, 150, 217; and Handakten Ettel, Politisches Archiv, Auswartiges Amt, Bonn.

3. D.G.F.P., series D. Vol. V, p. 761, note of Dr von Hentig, Head of the Near Eastern Division at the German F.M. to the German Consul in Beirut (1936), files of the Near Eastern Division Pol. VII, V 151, Political Archive, A.A. Bonn.

4. Files of the Near Eastern Division, Pol. VII, doc. No. 12 (1936), Political Archive, A.A. Bonn.

5. Mitteilungsblatt No. 278/34, Folge 15 (30, 4. 1936), Nazi files in Central Zionist Archives, Jerusalem.

6. *H*. Memo to *C* (Chef), apparently *Heydrich* to *Himmler*, R 58/956 (1937), R.S.H.A. files, Bundesarchiv Koblenz.

7. Statement by Dr Fritz Grobba, ex-envoy of Germany in Iraq, to the writer on June 26, 1964, in Bad Godesberg.

8. A. Hitler, *Mein Kampf*, 1935 edition, p. 331.

9. A. Rosenberg, *Der Staatsfeindliche Zionismus*, 1922, 'Judentum und Zionismus', *Volkischer Beobochter*, 11.7.1931.

10. G. Wirsing, *Englander, Arabern, Juden in Palaestina* (1937), Schneefuss W., *Gefahrenzonen des Britischen Weltreiches* (1938).

11. In his personal interview with the writer, July 1964, followed by letters dated August 13, 1966, and September 3, 1964.

12. Under the pseudonym Lim, 'Ein Nazi faehrt nach Palaestina' in *Der Angriff*, September 26, 1934; comments in *Die juedische Rundschau* No. 78/79, September 28, 1934.

13. Deutschnationale Volkspartei—German Nationalist Peoples Party—a rightist Monarchist and Antisemitic party, headed by Hugenberg.

14. Information by Mr Sam Cohen, co-director in the 'thirties of the Hanotea Citrus Company, Tel-Aviv. Mr Cohen was one of the main architects of the Transfer Agreement. The information was given by Mr Cohen to the writer on August 8, 1965.

15. See Martin Brossat, *Der Nationalsozialismus*, Deutsche Verlagsanstalt Stuttgart p. 21.

16. Files of the Reich Ministry of Economics, doc. 14069, Bundesarchiv Koblenz.

17. See R.S.H.A. files on the visit of Eichmann and Hagen to Cairo, 1937, Bundesarchiv Koblenz.

18. Files of Pol. VII (Near Eastern Division), Schwarz von Berk's personal letter to Dr von Hentig, dated July 9, 1937.

19. The Templars, a German Protestant sect, came to Palestine in the nineteenth century to await the coming of the Redeemer. One of their leaders, Consul Wurst of Jaffa, suggested to the F.M. in 1937 that the immigration of Jews to Palestine should be stopped.

20. Files of R.Wi.M. (Reichswirtschaftministerium) December 17, 1935, Bundesarchiv Koblenz.

21. Files of the R.S.H.A. (Reichssicherheitshauptamt) R 58/956, 1937.

22. Statement by Dr von Hentig, former Head of the Near Eastern Division, to the writer in July 1964 in Seibersbach, and D.G.F.P., series D, Vol. V, pp. 783–85.

23. Statement by Mr P. Ginzburg, delegate of the Hechalutz and Histradut in Germany from November 1938 till the outbreak of the War, to the writer in August 1966.

24. D.G.F.P., series D, Vol. V, doc. No. 564.

25. Memorandum by Clodius, D.G.F.P., series D, Vol. V, pp. 783–85.

26. Files of the Ministry of Economics, doc. No. 14069 (1935), Bundersarchiv Koblenz.

27. Files of Referat Deutschland, doc. No. 2487, 6, October 30, 1934, Politisches Archiv, A.A. Bonn.

28. D.G.F.P., series D, Vol. V, doc. No. 564, p. 752.

29. D.G.F.P., series D, Vol. V, doc. No. 564.

30. D.G.F.P., series D, Vol. V, p. 750, F.O., instruction of June 22, 1937.

31. See essay by Europaeus—'Die Balfour-deklaration', *Preussische Jahrbuecher*,

Band CCXXI, Heft 3, 1929, pp. 225–49. Europaeus was the pseudonym of Dr Ziemke, a senior official of the Foreign Ministry during the 'twenties.

32. Reports of the German Consul General in Jerusalem No. 974/661/38 and No. 884/48 of July 16 and 29, 1938, and the minutes of the Woodhead Committee of July 4, 1938, concerning requests of the Templar representatives, Pol. VII, 974, Politisches Archiv, A.A. Bonn.

33. The first appeal that the German Consul General in Jerusalem reports is dated March 31, 1933, i.e. two months after the rise of Hitler to power. The Mufti then suggested organizing an anti-Jewish boycott in the Moslem World.

34. Pol. VII, doc. No. 1541/375429–32/, Politisches Archiv., A.A. Bonn.

35. Files of the Unterstaatssekretar 1941/42, Politsches Archiv., A.A. Bonn.

36. Ibid., Politisches Archiv, A.A. Bonn.

# The 'Stern Gang' 1940-48 *

## Y. S. Brenner

The 'Fighters for the Freedom of Israel', commonly known as the 'Stern Gang,' was one of three Jewish paramilitary organisations operating in Palestine during the years between World War II and the establishment of the State of Israel in 1948.

The common origin of all three organisations; 'Haganah', 'Irgun', and the 'Stern Gang,' was the Jewish Defense Organization (Haganah) which was created during the Arab disturbances in 1929. When another Arab uprising against the British Mandatory Government in Palestine began in 1936, the right wing of the Jewish Defence Organisation disagreed with the general policy of mere defence laid down by the Jewish Agency.[1] In April 1937 it demanded retaliation against the Arab community whenever Jewish settlements were attacked by Arab marauders. As the Arab uprising, which had initially been an anti-British movement, became increasingly anti-Jewish, the right wing of the Jewish Defence Organisation started to carry out such retaliation. This wing, under its separate command, then became known by the name 'The National Military Organisation in the Land of Israel' (Irgum Zvei Leumi be Erez Israel, or simply the 'Irgun').

While the Haganah remained the military force at the disposal of the Jewish Agency, the Irgun kept a close liaison with the right wing — the Revisionist Party, led from Europe by V. Jabotinsky — of the world Zionist Organisation. Direct command over the Irgun was divided between the military head, David Raziel, and the political head, Abraham Stern. Even before the beginning of World War II, differences of opinion had already arisen between

*See revisions on p.277

Jabotinsky and Stern about the Irgun's attitude towards the British. Stern maintained that British interests in the Middle East were by their very nature diametrically opposed to the future development of the Jewish community in Palestine and he therefore wished to use the Irgun as a nucleus of a Jewish anti-British rebellion. Jabotinsky believed that Britain could be made to realise that her interests would best be served by a powerful pro-British Jewish stronghold in the area. He wanted to use the Irgun to demonstrate the strength of the Jews in Palestine and the military possibilities of a friendly Jewish force safeguarding British interests in the Arab world. Stern was prepared to accept help from all quarters, including Fascist Italy, while Jabotinsky was ready to accept the support of countries like Poland and Rumania, who would have been glad to see their Jewish population migrate to Palestine, but not of outspokenly anti-British countries like Italy and the Soviet Union.

On the outbreak of war in 1939 and the publication of the British White Paper restricting Jewish immigration, land purchase and settlement in Palestine, which tolled the death-knell of Jewish hopes for further expansion, the rift between Stern and Jabotinsky widened. The position of the Jewish community in general at the time was summarised by the Chairman of the Zionist Executive Ben Gurion, in the words: 'We shall fight the White Paper as if there were no war with Germany and we shall fight the Germans as if there were no White Paper.' In effect, the Jewish Agency confined itself to protests against the Mandatory policy of preventing immigration and advocated the recruitment of Palestinian Jews into the British Armed Forces. Jabotinsky supported a similar policy and ordered the Irgun to suspend all anti-British activities in Palestine for the duration of the war. Consequently, Raziel, the Irgun's military chief, collaborated with the British forces in commando-type raids in Iraq, in one of which he was subsequently killed. Stern, however, maintained that anti-British activities should be intensified: as the British were engaged in a struggle against Germany, they would more easily yield to Jewish demands. It must however be said that Stern had no doubts about the ultimate British victory over the Germans. In contrast to the general belief in Palestine that the Jewish participation in the anti-German war was not only morally obligatory but would also be duly rewarded by the British once the war was won, Stern was of the opinion that the Jews should join the British army only after a political settlement had been reached. This clash of policies brought about a split within the Irgun in January-August-1940, which left Stern with a small minority of supporters. Stern's group dropped the word 'Erez' from the name of the organisation and called themselves 'Irgun Zvai Leumi be-Israel' — an insignificant change which was designed to retain as nearly as possible the original name. In their own words, their difference from the majority organisation lay in the definition of the enemy. The majority of the Irgun considered the Arabs to be their ultimate adversary, Stern's splinter group looked upon the Arabs as mere rivals and on the British as the real enemy.

## (1)

In the atmosphere which prevailed in Palestine at the time Stern's policy was suicidal, as subsequent events in 1941 and 1942 were to show very clearly. In fact, though strongly opposed to the British policy on immigration to Palestine, the Jewish community was neither anti-British nor ready to shun its moral obligation to fight the Germans. Even the Irgun, which now partially collaborated with the British, did all in its power to prevent its former associates from carrying out acts of sabotage. The Irgun had at that time a special branch to combat Communism (formed after the Ribbentrop-Molotov pact of August 1939), which had established some connection with the British C.I.D. This branch was now also activated against Stern's splinter group, although, of course, they were right-wing and not left-wing extremists.

Even within the Stern group itself differences of opinion continued. Two of the leading personalities, Sterlitz and Zeroni, demanded a suspension of anti-British activities and favoured a policy of mere non-cooperation with the Mandatory Government while Stern wanted a limited period of peace to reorganise his group. The rank and file, however, demanded action. Sterlitz and Zeroni were expelled and when soon afterwards their pictures were circulated in the press by the police they simply gave themselves up. Stern understood that unless some activity began, the group would disintegrate and its members would join the British army to fight against Germany. The commencement of the anti-British fight, however, raised the immediate problem of funds.

The Haganah was allotted money from the defence funds of the Jewish Agency. The Irgun was financed partly by its political supporters (mainly right-wing industrialists) and partly by contributions from Jews living in the United States. Stern's group had no sources of income and, apart from the meagre salaries of some of the members in their civilian occupations, had to rely on robberies. The first small robberies were not attributed to the group. Then came the hold-up of the Anglo-Palestine Bank in Tel-Aviv, for which one of the known members was arrested and sentenced to fifteen years imprisonment.[2] A large-scale attempt in 1941 to rob the Ottoman Bank in Jaffa failed, and a third attempt, to rob the cashier of a Trade Union Cooperative in 1942, proved disastrous for the group. This was not only because the perpetrators were caught, but also because two Jewish bystanders were accidentally shot in the chase. This episode, together with the incident of No. 8 Yael Street, Tel-Aviv, during the same year, finally made the Stern group appear to the general public as nothing better than a band of senseless assassins. At No. 8 Yael Street an electrically detonated bomb, which was planted to assassinate two British Intelligence officers, accidentally killed instead two well-liked Jewish police inspectors. Only a few days after this event, on February 12, 1942, Stern himself was discovered and shot dead by a British police officer.[3] Shortly before Stern's death, four members of the group were discovered in a room in the north of Tel-Aviv and were shot by British policemen. Two of the four survived and claimed that they had all been unarmed at the time the police entered and that the only revolver which was later produced at their trial was planted there by the police.[4]

These two events — the massacre of 27th January in the north of Tel-Aviv and the death of Stern on 12th February in the south of the town — had a far reaching effect on the future of the organisation which was now led by Stern's deputy Zelnik. First, the organisation became obsessed with feelings of revenge and gave priority over all other activities to the assassination of the Police Sgts. who were implicated in the two events. Secondly, and probably most significantly in view of subsequent developments, the members of the group became convinced that they would be killed if captured by the police, and therefore decided to be armed at all times and to 'take one with them' if stopped by the security forces.

Meanwhile the other organisations, Irgun and Haganah, continued in their struggle against the White Paper on Jewish immigration by bringing illegally shiploads of Jewish refugees to the shores of Palestine. One of these ships, the *Struma*, sailing from Constanza in Rumania, reached Istanbul and was there detained by the Turkish authorities. An attempt to get permission from the Palestine Government to bring the passengers to Palestine failed and the vessel was sent back into the Black Sea. A few hours later it sank.[5] The news of the death of the 675 passengers in February 1942, shocked the Jewish community in Palestine and made the climate of opinion a little less unfavourable for the Stern Group than it had been two weeks earlier when Stern was killed. The group attributed the direct responsibility for the *Struma* tragedy and the decision to send the Jews back to Europe to Sir Harold MacMichael, the High Commissioner for Palestine, and to Lord Moyne, the British Minister-Resident in Cairo. The assassination of these two now had top priority in the Organization's plans. Meanwhile, attempts to kill police Sgt. M. near Tel-Aviv, and to wipe out the whole command of the Palestine police force at a funeral in Jerusalem, failed. Soon afterwards seven members of the group were arrested in Haifa, two others were arrested in Jerusalem and Friedman-Yellin, who was later to become the leader of the organisation, was arrested in Syria. Faced with all these disasters Zelnik surrendered to the police. In effect the organisation ceased to exist.

(2)

Of all the original members who had seceded from the Irgun in Palestine only two active men remained. The rest were either imprisoned, dead, or had left the organisation altogether. There was, however, a reserve of so far inactive members. These were either very young people or new immigrants from Poland, who had deserted from General Anders' army while it was stationed in Palestine, and were not yet familiar with the country. In addition there was a group of six women. The Polish group consisted of about fifteen members. The rest, i.e. the younger members, were scattered: four in Ramat-Gan, one in Jerusalem, and seven in Haifa. Some time later they were joined by two more Polish deserters, one of whom was an expert in constructing booby-traps and similar devices. Another source of man-power was a small group of ex-Irgun members, led by a man called Tuvia, who held similar ideas to those of Stern but had not joined Stern's group because he thought that the time for anti-British action had not yet come. When he finally changed his mind he still hesitated to join Stern's men. The many arrests and failures led him to believe that too many provocateurs had infiltrated into Stern's group to make it a safe vehicle for his purpose. Only later were the groups united.

The two active members of the original group who had survived took upon themselves to rebuild the organisation. They established contact with the so far inactive reserve and recruited new members. They also decided to stop all robberies until they were again ready to strike out at the British. They devoted most of their energy to freeing their leaders from prison. By this time Russia had entered the war and some of the Stern Group leaders, including Friedman-Yellin, had become increasingly favourably disposed towards socialism. The hard core of the organisation still consisted of right wing extremists but some of the leaders and certainly some of the newcomers were leftists. At no time was any plan discussed for the regime to be established after the departure of the British, and so there was nothing necessarily unstable about this strange political combination. The aims were negative — the elimination of British rule in Palestine — and in this all wings could stand united. In time the group also dropped the military formalities and changed its name from 'The National Military Organisation in Israel' to 'The Fighters for the Freedom of Israel' (F.F.I.). New members were no longer recruited exclusively from the 'Beitar' (the Revisionists youth organisation) as formerly, but also from other youth movements including those of the extreme left.

While Friedman-Yellin, though still in prison, established his leadership over the organisation, two other leaders managed to escape and put themselves at the head of the members outside. One of these two was Ysernitsky and the other Giladi. According to F.F.I. sources Giladi was a man of great physical courage but without moral scruples and with autocratic manners. Under his leadership new robberies were planned and a programme to assassinate the heads of the Jewish community was worked out in some detail. In addition, he was about to carry out some internal 'purges' in the F.F.I., when a secret meeting of some ten members decided to kill him before it was too late. He was eliminated even before Friedman-Yellin's permission was obtained. This episode convinced the organisation that one-man rule was too risky to be continued and a centre, a collective leadership, was set up. This centre consisted of Friedman-Yellin, who drew up policy, Dr. Scheib, a nationalist, who was in charge of propaganda, Ysernitsky, who was the general administrator, and Posner, who was in charge of finance.

While Giladi had been contemplating his purges, Ysernitsky had re-organised the group. Branches were set up throughout the country; rules of secrecy were laid down; a unit of full-time functionaries was enlisted to be a permanent striking force. An illegal printing press produced pamphlets which were stuck with glue on walls in all towns by groups of schoolboys specially organised for this purpose. It was also during this period that the events of 1942, when unarmed members of the group were shot by the police, were recalled with a double purpose: first, to make sure that no members of the group fall into the hands of the police alive, in Friedman-Yellin's words, 'to put an end to the prisons,' and secondly, to put before every policeman the alternative of either running the risk of being killed or ignoring suspects if he happened to come across them. A by-product of this policy of 'no surrender' was that it stirred the immagination of many young people in the country. The sheer physical courage displayed by the members of the F.F.I. in their encounters with the police soon became one of the group's most powerful propaganda weapons.

(3)

On the first day of November 1943, twenty members of the organisation escaped from a detention camp in Latrun. One of them was Friedman-Yellin. They had dug a 233 feet-long tunnel and walked out unnoticed. No one was caught though one of them was killed in an encounter with the police two days later. On rejoining the organisation outside Friedman-Yellin found himself at the head of a well organised force, which, thanks to the efforts of Ysernitsky bore little resemblance to the old 'Stern Group'. Again, however, the first actions failed, — an attempt to kill Sir Harold MacMichael, the High Commissioner for Palestine, and to wipe out the command of the Haifa police.

Soon afterwards, in January 1944, a major event took place. The Irgun, under the command of M. Begin, formally declared war on the British administration in Palestine and resumed attacks on British installations. The F.F.I. was no longer isolated in the Jewish community; it now had a powerful ally. The immediate cause for the Irgun's declaration of war was, in Begin's own words, 'The two fundamental facts — the campaign of extermination of the Jews of Europe and the barred gates (of Palestine) in the very days of that Campaign.[6] There was, however, no question of reunification. The two groups differed not only in their internal political sympathies but also in their aims and methods. The Irgun was by this time fighting only the 'British policy of suppression in Palestine'. In fact its leaders would have been content with a change in British immigration laws. They had no wish to 'burn all bridges' with Great Britain. In keeping with this point of view, the Irgun demolished the government immigration offices in Haifa, Tel-Aviv and Jerusalem but went out of its way to make sure that no British lives were lost in these operations. The F.F.I. (Stern Group) did not believe that British policy could be changed. In its view nothing short of total British withdrawal from Palestine could solve the problem. Consequently the F.F.I. saw no political reason to spare the lives of Englishmen as long as they remained in Palestine.

Meanwhile the policy of active resistance to arrest claimed its first casualties. A police inspector and a police Sergeant were shot dead while inspecting the identity cards of two F.F.I. men in Tel-Aviv. Two British police officers were wounded and a Jewish police sergeant was killed when they went to search a room in which a wounded F.F.I., man was hidden in Haifa. A battle took place between two F.F.I. men and an army unit which surrounded their hiding place in Javniel. When the two wounded men ran out of ammunition they shot themselves with their two last bullets. Finally on 19th March 1944 a member of the F.F.I., who would have aroused no suspicion had he not observed the organisation's instruction to carry arms at all times, was stopped by policemen in an armoured car and subsequently killed. This incident cast some doubt upon the advisability of being armed and resisting arrest in all cases.

During the same month the news of the elimination of the European Jews reached Palestine. There were only a few Jews left in German-occupied Europe and they were prevented from escaping to safety by the British immigration laws. The public became less inclined to cooperate with the British police and the climate of opinion began to move in favour of the Irgun and the F.F.I. While the Irgun simultaneously attacked the C.I.D. headquarters in Tel-Aviv, Haifa and Jerusalem, and the Jewish Agency proclaimed a day of protest and fasting, the F.F.I. initiated its first major campaign. The more favourable climate of public opinion towards the terrorists in the Jewish community and the wish to avenge Elisha (the F.F.I. man shot in Tel-Aviv on 19th March) by the members of his group, provided the necessary conditions for putting the plan into practice. A campaign was initiated to 'drive the British out of the Jewish towns'. The method employed was very simple. Small groups of F.F.I. men, armed with concealed sub-machine-guns and pistols patrolled the streets and opened fire whenever they met armed British police or army personnel. The Irgun dissociated itself from this campaign and the Haganah even went as far as taking an active part in trying to prevent it.

The British authorities retaliated by mass arrests, declarations of curfews in Jewish towns, and the imposition of the death penalty for carrying fire-arms. These counter-measures, which were aimed at intimidating the terrorists and turning the molested Jewish population against them, proved a complete failure. The population which was indeed harassed by the Government's anti-terrorist policy of the 'strong hand' began to move along the path which led eventually to the complete disruption of British-Jewish relations in Palestine. In fact the British anti-terrorist campaign back-fired; the Jewish towns were declared out of bounds for British army personnel off duty and the F.F.I. had won its first victory.

In the following months the Organization also scored a victory on its propaganda front. On 29 May 1944 at the trial of an F.F.I. man, found in possession of a revolver, the accused suddenly admitted to having carried a revolver but claimed that he had permission to do so from the only legal authority in the country, namely; the command of the 'Fighters for the Freedom of Israel'. He was sentenced to seven years imprisonment. At other trials which followed[7] all the accused took the same line of defence. They challenged the legality of the court ('Englishmen have the right to pass judgement in England but not here'), and made long political statements. Naturally the trials were reported in the press. Through the press reports the Organization's point of view and propaganda reached everybody in the country and the Jews in the U.S.A. On 20 June 1944 the death sentence was passed for the first time on a member of the F.F.I. The Organisation threatened to make a blood bath if the sentence was carried out but the military commander in Palestine commuted the death penalty to life imprisonment in this case.

## (4)

During the trials a blue print of the F.F.I.'s plans and political philosophy developed and reached the general public. They may be summarised in the following manner: In order to achieve the ultimate aim of an independent Jewish State in Palestine the British had to be made to withdraw from the country. The interests which made them reluctant to go were, according to the Stern Group's analysis, (1) their military base in the Middle East, (2) the oil refinery installations at the terminus of the Iraq Petroleum Company's pipe-line in Haifa, and (3) economic interests — for example the I.C.I., Shell, and financial establishments in Palestine. From this analysis of British motives for hanging on to the country followed the F.F.I.'s own plan of action: (1) Palestine was to be rendered useless as a military base by constant threat of attack on army installations and camps; by continuous harassing of road and rail transport by mines; and by restricting the soldiers to their camps for fear of being murdered; (2) the oil interests were to be eliminated by the destruction of the oil refinery installations and the demolition of the pipe-line; (3) the economic interests were to be undermined by frequent acts of sabotage and robberies against British or British-insured firms.

Meanwhile, another attempt on the life of the High Commissioner, Sir Harold MacMichael, was made on August 8, 1944. His convoy of three cars — his own car, a truck with soldiers, and an armoured police car, was forced to go slow by a group of Public Works Department workers on a mountain road some five miles outside Jerusalem. As soon as the convoy slowed down it was attacked by the P.W.D. workers who were of course F.F.I. men disguised for the purpose. In the exchange of fire Sir Harold MacMichael was wounded but escaped with his life. Less fortunate were two Jewish detectives and the much hated British Sgt. W. who were all shot by the F.F.I. during the same month. On October 18th 1944, two hundred and fifty-one Irgun and F.F.I. men were gathered from various prisons and camps and sent to a detention camp in Eritrea. Both organisations looked upon this as a deliberate act to challenge the Jews' rights to Palestine. Shortly after this, on November 6th, Lord Moyne, the British Minister-Resident for the Middle East, was shot dead by two members of the F.F.I. in Cairo.

The two assassins, Beit-Zuri, a student of the Hebrew University, and Hakim, a 'deserter' from the British Army, were caught by the Egyptian police and sent for trial in Cairo. The trial started on January 10th 1945. As in the F.F.I. trials in Palestine, the accused preferred to make a political statement instead of conducting a judicial defence. During the hearings Beit-Zuri, speaking in English, made one statement which was to influence developments in the F.F.I. He said: 'It is wrong to assume that we [the two accused] represent Zionism. In fact we represent, and we are, the real owners of Palestine and as such we are engaged in a struggle to free our country from the alien rulers who have taken possession of it.[8] Whether this dissociation from Zionism was merely designed to reassure the Egyptian public, or whether it was meant to be a true statement of policy, it was henceforth taken up as a political lead by a great body of opinion within the F.F.I. It appears that the trial had also some influence on the Egyptian national movement. Between November 6th 1944, the date of the assassination of Lord Moyne, and January 18th 1945, when judgement was given in the assassins' case, several events took place in Egypt. The Prime Minister Ahmed Mahir who succeeded Nahhas Pasha when the Wafd fell from power was murdered because of his pro-British attitude, and soon afterwards the first draft of the Egyptian Government's written demand for the withdrawal of all British troops from Egypt and the recognition of the 'unity of the Nile Valley' was drawn-up, though it was only published several months later. On the 18th of January the two F.F.I. men were condemned to death. Between the proclamation of the sentence and the execution the Egyptian press seemed to indicate that the two assassins might be granted a pardon, but Churchill's speech in Parliament on 27th February 1945, put an end to these hopes. In his speech Churchill demanded the tightening of security in Egypt and the hastening of the execution of people convicted of political murder. The two men were executed on March 22, 1945.

The attitude of the Egyptian nationalists during and after the Cairo trial gave rise to the idea of a 'Semitic Bloc'. At the time, some members of the F.F.I. believed in a union of all the semitic peoples of the Middle East — Jews and Arabs — in an armed struggle for the areas' independence. These ideas were again taken by one part of the Organization as mere tactics, while another part liked to see in them a first move towards genuine Jewish-Arab cooperation. In any case these ideas paved the way for the introduction of the first Palestinian Arabs to membership in the F.F.I.

## (5)

The news of Lord Moyne's assassination shocked Jews all over the world. In London Professor Weizmann, the President of the World Zionist Movement, said that he was more shaken by this assassination than by the death of his own son who was killed in action while serving with the R.A.F. He later assured Churchill that Palestine Jewry 'will go to the utmost limit of its power to cut out this evil (terrorism) from its midst.'[9] The reaction in Palestine was similar; 'Davar', the most influential paper in the country, wrote that the terrorists had destroyed the hopes of the Jewish people and the Jewish people must therefore forsake them. All other papers agreed with 'Davar' and even the right-wing newspaper 'Hamashkif', which was connected with the Irgun, wrote that the crime in Cairo was a disservice to the Jewish cause.[10] Most important of all was the Jewish Agency's official statement which proclaimed that 'together with all the civilized world, the Jewish community was shocked to hear of this most obnoxious crime...' and continued that 'the wave of terror may kill the prospects of our whole political struggle and destroy our internal peace...'. The proclamation ended with an appeal to the community 'to cast out all the members of this underground gang and deny them shelter and assistance; not to submit to their threats; to give full assistance to the authorities in the prevention of acts of terror and the elimination of its perpetrators...'

The leadership of the Jewish community made full use of the forebodings occasioned by the death of Lord Moyne to launch a large-scale attack, (which was given the code name 'open season') on the Irgun. Thousands of Haganah members were mobilised and concentrated in the big towns to carry out an anti-terrorist campaign of kidnappings and denunciations to the British police of members of the Irgun. Ben-Gurion, who had drafted a four point plan for this purpose, which included instructions that 'anybody connected with these gangs... must be driven out of his job... (or) expelled from school...' justified his collaboration with the British in this matter in the words: '...It would be stupid and suicidal if, because of our just grievances in other spheres against the country's existing regime, we should refrain from accepting its help and from helping it in fields where we have, to the extent that we have, a common interest. ...Without helping the authorities and without being helped by them we shall not succeed in destroying this plague...'.[11]

Yet, while the Irgun, who had not even been informed in advance of the F.F.I.'s plan to assassinate Lord Moyne, and had indeed dissociated itself from it, came under the heavy attack of the Haganah, members of the F.F.I. were walking the streets of Tel-Aviv and other towns undisturbed. The Irgun leaders told the leader of the Haganah, when the anti-terrorist campaign started, that they would neither accept Ben-Gurion's *diktat* nor retaliate against the Haganah and thus plunge the country into civil war. In Begin's own words:[12] 'We said there would be no civil war but, in fact, throughout the whole country, a one-sided civil war raged.' The leaders of the F.F.I., however, thought otherwise. At a meeting between Eliyahu Golomb, commander of the Haganah and Friedman-Yellin, in November 1944, Yellin agreed that he would suspend anti-British operations until sentence was passed on Lord Moyne's assassins so as not to prejudice their chance of a pardon. He also allayed Golomb's fears that the F.F.I. might assassinate Churchill and warned the Haganah that if attacked, the F.F.I. would retaliate by shooting Haganah leaders and informers.[13]

This dreadful situation continued for several months but in time uncommitted public opinion in Palestine became less and less enthusiastic in supporting the anti-terrorist campaign. Finally, certain political events in the U.K. brought about a complete change in the situation. By the summer of 1945, Jewish-British collaboration in Palestine neared its end.

(6)

The final breach was closely related to the General elections in England. Before the elections the Labour Party fostered the illusion that, once in power, it would support the creation of a Jewish national home in Palestine. Even Attlee himself had written that 'The Labour Party recalls with pride that in the days of the Great War they associated themselves with the ideal of a National Home in Palestine for the Jewish people and that ever since... have repeatedly affirmed their enthusiastic support for the effort towards its realisation. They... will never falter in their active co-operation with the work now going forward in Palestine.'[14] It was only natural that the Hebrew press should entertain high hopes from a Labour victory at the general elections. Golomb, the leader of the Haganah had no doubts whatsoever that once Labour came into power in Britain, part of the Jewish demands were sure to be satisfied. His confidence sprang from the traditional friendship for Zionism shown by the British Labour movement. He had implicit trust in the decision of the Blackpool Conference of the Labour Party which demanded the establishment of a Jewish State in Palestine. Friedman-Yellin's view remained that British governments may change, but 'British interests remain forever' — but he was ready to restrain the F.F.I. until after the election.

When the news of the Labour victory reached Tel-Aviv, the population was overjoyed to an extent which was to be equalled only at the time of the U.N.O. decision to establish a Jewish State in Palestine. But a few weeks after the election Ernest Bevin shattered all the illusions fostered for many years. Bevin made it clear that there was to be no friendship towards the Zionist movement and that he did not consider himself bound by the Blackpool resolution. With the disillusionment the 'open season' operation and the collaboration between the Haganah and the British authorities against the terrorists came to an end. Soon a meeting between the leaders of the three organisations, Haganah, Irgun, and F.F.I., was held to study the possibilities of cooperation. The Haganah was represented by M. Sneh[15] and I. Galili;[16] the Irgun by M. Begin;[17] and the F.F.I. by Friedman-Yellin. According to Begin,[18] Sneh and Galili proposed a complete merger of all organisations at this first meeting. The F.F.I. was apparently ready to agree to this but the 'Irgun' hesitated; no conclusion was reached. On November 1st 1945, a second meeting was held and it was then agreed that the three organisations should continue their independent existence but should agree to forego, for the sake of unity in the armed struggle, all independent operations except those for the confiscation of arms and money. The two meetings found an echo in the special White Paper on 'Violence in Palestine' in which the secret telegrams from the leader of the Haganah to his colleagues abroad which were intercepted by British Intelligence, were published. One of these telegrams, dated 23 September 1945 read:

'It has also been suggested that we cause one serious incident. We would then issue a declaration to the effect that this is only a warning and an indication of much more serious incidents that would threaten the safety of all British interests in the country... The Stern Group have expressed their willingness to join us completely on the basis of our programme of activities. If there is such a union, we may assume that we can prevent independent action even by the I.Z.L. [Irgun]'.

A second telegram, dated 1st November 1945, read:

'We have come to a working agreement with the dissident organisations, [the Irgun and F.F.I.] according to which we shall assign certain tasks to them under our command. They will act only according to our plan.'

Even before this agreement was ratified three British boats engaged in the detection of illegal immigrants were sunk by the Haganah and railway lines were cut at 186 points by some 500 explosions which suspended all rail traffic, in the country.' No one was wounded or arrested during the night these operations were carried out. During the same night the Irgun also attacked Lydda railway station, causing damage and a number of British casualties, and the F.F.I. attacked the oil refineries in Haifa. Although the Haganah had no objection to the Irgun's attack in Lydda, it opposed the F.F.I.'s attack on the refineries but was unable to prevent it because the agreement had not come into force. After this, however, and until July 1946, when the Haganah stopped fighting, all military operations of the Irgun and F.F.I. were carried out only according to plans approved by the Haganah. The plans were submitted to Y. Sadeh, commander of the Haganah's elite force (Palmach), who did not concern himself with the details of the operations. For a time the F.F.I. became part of the Jewish general effort and quite respectable.

For eight months all three organisations concentrated on attacking major British installations. This required from the F.F.I. a greater concentration of arms and men and a change in the methods of operation. This can be illustrated by the F.F.I.'s first large-scale attack, in which as many as 30 members took part. The attack, which was carried out simultaneously at three R.A.F. bases by the F.F.I. and the 'Irgun,' caused the destruction of thirty British military aircraft.

Some thirty members of the F.F.I., mostly known to each other only by their code names, assembled after dark at a meeting point half way between Tel-Aviv and the air base. The meeting point was an orchard. The men were divided into three groups of about ten each. One group wore British uniforms and drove in a stolen army truck into the air base, taking up positions close to the arsenal and billets of the three hundred personnel stationed there. A second group took up positions at a point outside the airfield, close to the runways. The ten remaining men, carrying rucksacks with explosives, crawled under cover of darkness to the airplanes on the runway, hiding from the armoured car patrols and from the searchlights on the guard posts. Each of the men picked a Spitfire and tied his explosives to it. When the commander of this unit had checked that all was ready he gave the order to light the fuses and retreat. As nine of the planes blew up, the unit which had been posted next to the army billets opened fire to cover the retreat of the saboteurs. The moment they had reached safety, the second cover-unit outside the fence opened fire to cover the retreat of the first cover-unit near the billets. When the two units rejoined each other, the general retreat through the orchards to a pre-arranged checking point continued. There was little risk of the assailants meeting any civilians on their way who might identify them, as the country had been under dusk-to-dusk curfew for some days. At this point the arms were collected for storage and the unarmed men, dispersed, and when morning came, separately joined the general rush of people going to work.

By January 1946 the number and dimensions of these attacks had grown to such proportions that they began to interest even the Russian newspapers *Isvestia* and *Pravda*. This fact prompted the F.F.I. to make its first official statement of foreign policy. A document called 'Outline for a Hebrew Foreign Policy' was published, which took notice of the rivalry between Britain and the United States of America in the Middle East and of the clash of interests between Britain and the Soviet Union in the same area. It was favourably disposed towards the Soviet Union and hoped for its support in the struggle for independence. This attitude was acceptable both to the right and to the left elements in the F.F.I. As on previous similar occasions the right saw in it a mere tactical measure. In the left it raised hopes of advance towards extreme socialism, though it should be borne in mind that the break between Stalin and Tito had not yet come about and people like Gomulka and Dimitrov were still in grace.

Meanwhile, several things occurred which, though not directly connected with the F.F.I., were to be of tremendous importance for the organisation's future freedom of action. On November 13, 1945, Ernest Bevin, the Labour Government's Foreign Secretary, spoke in Parliament. He officially repudiated the promises of the Labour Party and offered the Jews, instead of the abrogation of the White Paper, and relief for the Jews in the detention camps of Europe, a new commission of inquiry. To add insult to injury, at the press conference which followed his declaration in Parliament he also said: 'If the Jews, with all their sufferings, want to get too much at the head of the queue, you have the danger of another anti-Semitic reaction through it all'.[19] The memory of the extermination of six million Jews in Europe was too fresh to let such a remark go unheeded. Practically the whole population of Palestine came out into the streets of the big cities to protest. Some hotheads, who did not belong to any of the three organisations, set fire to government buildings and caused some damage. Units of the 6th Airborne Division were called into Tel-Aviv to put an end to the demonstrations. They opened fire on an unarmed crowd, killed seven people and wounded many more. Incidentally, not one terrorist was among the casualties. A few days later a number of kibbuzim were surrounded by British forces which intended to carry out large scale searches for illegal arms. The settlers offered passive resistance. They were joined in this by thousands of people who swarmed to the besieged kibbuzim on horseback, on foot and by truck, from all over the country, to prevent any discoveries. Unarmed men and women threw themselves in front of tanks and armoured vehicles. Again, nine people were killed by the military, scores were wounded and hundreds arrested. The worst two incidents, however, occurred in late June and July 1946. On Saturday 29 June, the government launched a carefully prepared all-out attack to break the back of the united resistance movement. Tens of thousands of British soldiers fanned out over the whole country, imposed a curfew and led thousands of Jews to detention camps.[20] Some of the leaders of the Jewish Agency and the 'Haganah' were arrested, in accordance with well prepared lists. Among the arrested was M. Shertok. The blow to the Haganah's elite force, the Palmach, was considerable, as about half its manpower was detained for several months. A month later, following the Irgun's attack on the British G.H.Q., at the King David hotel in Jerusalem on July 22, Tel-Aviv was occupied by nearly two divisions of infantry and armoured units, which were accompanied by police and C.I.D. men. A day and night curfew was imposed and anybody leaving his house ran the risk of being shot without warning. Only after several days were people permitted to leave their homes for one or two hours daily to enable them to buy food. Almost every house in the city was searched and almost every individual interrogated. The F.F.I. and Irgun were hardly affected at all. They had been underground for some time and the police had no good lists or pictures of their members. As the country had been divided by army cordons into almost impregnable sectors, the F.F.I. simply issued instructions that local members in the various sectors should carry out operations at their own discretion.

Although, following the 'Black Saturday' (29 June 1946), the Haganah suspended operations of a military nature against the British forces in Palestine until their final departure, the period of united struggle in the resistance movement greatly benefited the F.F.I. This was so for three main reasons; First, the F.F.I. had become more acceptable in the public eye, because the Haganah, the recognised Jewish armed force, had engaged in the same kind of warfare as they did. Secondly, as the British forces had indiscriminately killed unarmed people in Tel-Aviv and elsewhere, and had sometimes behaved in a most unpopular manner, even those who were strongly opposed to violence did no longer regard it as their duty to assist the police in the prevention of acts of terrorism and the apprehension of the perpetrators. Finally, the political situation in general had deteriorated rather than improved. The survivors of the European holocaust were not permitted to land in Palestine, and their many relatives and acquaintances there felt personally, as well as politically, outraged by the British policy of 'closed gates'. These feelings were later brought to a pitch by a wanton piece of tactlessness, when 4,000 illegal would-be immigrants from the 'Exodus' were sent back to Hamburg in Germany, and not to Cyprus as had been the practice until then.

During the 'honeymoon' of the united resistance, the F.F.I. learned some lessons which were to influence its methods of operation in the years to come. An attempt by the Haganah in February 1946 to take over for a few hours the whole town of Tel-Aviv and to prevent British forces from entering it, with the aim of facilitating the landing of illegal immigrants, failed. The ship *Wingate* was unable to dock and the Haganah's cordon around the town was broken. Similarly, a large scale attack by the F.F.I. in May 1946 on the railway workshops and installations near Haifa, which had been successful as far as the operation itself was concerned, led to the death of eleven and the capture of eighteen assailants. Among the captured were four women. This disaster severely crippled the organisation's operational force, which at this time had a strength of less than two-hundred experienced fighters. These and several other similar incidents confirmed the opinion within the F.F.I. that large scale encounters with the 6th Airborne Division, though not with other British units, were too costly to be repeated at this stage.

The Irgun, which at all times was more interested in spectacular military exploits and was still very careful to spare British lives as far as possible, continued with large scale attacks while the F.F.I. reverted once more to tactics of disguise and inventiveness in its operations. Indeed, the F.F.I. had no reason to risk men in open battle with the better trained British forces. Its plan to bring about the British withdrawal from Palestine, based on the destruction of economic and oil interests and the undermining of the safety of British military bases in the Middle East, did not necessarily require the employment of standard military tactics. Road and rail transport could be interrupted and the flow of oil stopped by groups of not more than two or three men armed with sub-machine guns and dynamite; camps and army installations could be made unsafe by a single man with forged documents, wearing British uniform, in a stolen army truck loaded with T.N.T.

The differences in method which distinguished the F.F.I. from the Irgun in this period were well illustrated by the example of the well-known Acre prison break. The F.F.I. favoured a 'quiet' escape through a tunnel which was to

link the prison cells with the mediaeval labyrinth of underground passages which were still, unknown to the police,
in good repair underneath the castle upon which the prison
was built.[21] The Irgun preferred a commando raid on the
fortress, a major military operation which was to win the
greatest possible publicity and demonstrate their military
capabilities. The Irgun's plan was adopted and successfully
carried out at the price of a number of casualties.

Between September 1946 and May 1948, when the State of
Israel finally came into existence, well over a hundred acts of
sabotage were carried out by the F.F.I. Most of these were
directed against military transport and army personnel.
They were greatly facilitated by the British anti-terrorist
measures and by the introduction of martial law in March
1947. This paradox can be illustrated by the law which
forbade the use of inter-urban roads during night time by
civilian motor transport. Until this law came into force the
F.F.I. man out to attack British road transport had to stay
with his mine near the highway and detonate it electrically
to make sure that he did not harm civilians. Once all non-
military vehicles had been banned from the roads, the F.F.I.
man could plant a great number of mines and leave the
danger zone even before the first exploded. The introduction of martial law affected the F.F.I. indirectly by
forcing the Irgun, which had so far done its best to avoid
loss of British lives, to revert to some of the methods hitherto
adopted by the Stern Group alone.

Here are a few outstanding examples of the kind of attacks
the F.F.I. carried out between the proclamation of martial
law in Palestine and the day of the final withdrawal of the
British forces in May 1948. On March 13, 1947, the F.F.I.
destroyed two oil transport trains, one near the Arab town
of Qalqilia and another in Jerusalem. On March 24, it
robbed the Tel-Aviv Branch of the Discount Bank of £27,000.
On March 30, it set fire to 30,000 tons of fuel oil at the
Consolidated Refinery's oil storage plant near Haifa. On
April 22, a train carrying army personnel was attacked near
Rehovoth. On April 24, the Headquarters of the British
Mobile Force in Sarona Security Zone near Tel-Aviv was
destroyed. On August 8, trains were attacked near Haifa
and Hederah. On September 26, the Tel-Aviv Branch of
Barclays Bank was robbed of £45,000. On November 13,

British army personnel off duty were attacked in Jerusalem and suffered twenty-eight casualties, in retaliation for the shooting by British forces of three school girls and one school-boy training with the F.F.I. near Ra'anana. On February 22, 1948 an all-out F.F.I. attack on British forces was carried out in Jerusalem. On February 29, 1948 twenty-five soldiers were killed and thirty-five wounded in an F.F.I. attack on a troop transport near Rehovoth. On April 28, the F.F.I. robbed the Tel-Aviv Branch of Barclay's Bank of £ 200,000.

During this period of all-out lawlessness two major political events took place. First, on 13 November 1945 Bevin announced that the U.S. and The British Governments had decided to appoint a joint Committee to examine both the position and desires of the Jews of Europe and the situation of the Jews and Arabs in Palestine. Some six months later, on May 1st. 1946 the Anglo-American Commission made its report. The general conclusion was that the only practicable policy was to continue the British Mandate over Palestine pending the drafting of a new mandate by the United Nations. As to the Jewish problem in liberated Europe the commission supported the immediate admission of 100,000 Jewish refugees to Palestine. Naturally both Arabs and Jews picked out the recommendations they liked and rejected the rest. The Jews concentrated on the proposal to admit the 100,000 immigrants immediately and the F.F.I. agreed to suspend operations in order not to prejudice the implementation of this proposal. But Bevin decided that the Commission's report should be implemented as a whole and not divided into separate recommendations. Attlee, speaking in the House of Commons, emphasized that 'It is clear from the facts presented in the Report regarding the illegal armies maintained in Palestine... that it would not be possible... to admit so large a body of immigrants unless and until these formations have been disbanded and their arms surrendered'. Since disarmament was out of the question this was tantamount to a rejection of the Anglo-American Committee's proposal. After some hesitation, while the position of the British government was being clarified, the rule of violence returned to the country.

The second major political event was the setting up of the United Nations Special Committee on Palestine,

(UNSCOP). 'At British request the U.N. Assembly in
April 1947, set up this commitee and on November 29
adopted its recommendations for partition of the Holy Land
into separate Jewish and Arab States. Such a 'solution'
was wholly unacceptable to both sides. Arabs opened
hostilities against the Jewish settlements. In March, 1948,
the U.S.A. abandoned the partition plan it had sponsored...
and proposed another special Assembly session to consider
a U.N. trusteeship. The Assembly met on April 16. It
could agree on nothing... On May 14, 1948, the day before
the day when Britain had announced it would abandon the
Mandate, the Zionists declared the independence of Israel.
The Arab States promptly declared war, invaded Palestine,
and were promptly defeated...'[22]

The United Nations decision, the British withdrawal
from Palestine and the Arab hostilities caught the F.F.I.
completely by surprise. Until the last moment in May 1948
the organisation did not believe that the British would really
give up. The Arab hostilities caused even greater confusion
than the British withdrawal. For years the F.F.I. had
refused to look upon the Arabs as enemies. On the contrary,
at least the left wing members had always hoped to have
them as partners. Suddenly, together with the rest of the
whole Jewish population, the F.F.I. was faced with this
new danger. For the first few days following the 29th of
November the confusion was so great that members did not
know whether to cooperate with the Haganah in repulsing
Arab attacks or not. Finally efforts were divided between
attacks on British arms stores and Arab military concentrations.

As the 15th of May drew closer the F.F.I. was still vacillat-
ing. There appeared to be three alternative courses open
once the Jewish State in part of Palestine was to come into
existence: one, to disband the organisation as its leadership
had always promised to do during the years of resistance,
and then to join the Israeli forces en bloc; two, to instruct
the members to join the Israeli army separately as individuals but retain some secret connections; three, to keep
an independent force in Jerusalem which, under the United
Nations decision, was not to become an integral part of the
State of Israel, to disband the rest of the organisation in the
areas governed by Israel and to instruct the members there

to join the Israeli army as a unit. The third of these alternatives was finally adopted, largely due to pressure from the rank and file, who were decidedly for joining the army and fighting amongst their comrades from the earlier years. On May 28, 1948, many seeing each other for the first time, some 850 F.F.I. men marched together to an army recruiting camp near Tel-Aviv and joined the regular Israeli force. With the exception of a small contingent of some 150 men in Jerusalem, the F.F.I. or Stern Group, ceased to exist.

(8)

Before concluding this discussion of the Stern Group it seems appropriate to mention four much publicised acts of violence in Palestine which have been too often attributed to the 'Stern Gang' but which in fact were not carried out by it. These were the assassination of Count Folke Bernadotte, the whipping of a British Major and three N.C.O.s, the hanging of two British sergeants, and the destruction, with heavy loss of life, of the British H.Q. at the King David Hotel in Jerusalem.

Count Bernadotte was shot dead in Jerusalem by a group of extreme right wing fanatics, who called themselves the 'Homeland Front'. The three assassins were in all likelihood ex-members of the F.F.I., but certainly did not act under instructions from Friedman-Yellin and Ysernitzky. As subsequent events showed, neither of these two leaders of the F.F.I. could have known of or condoned the assassination beforehand.

The whipping of the Major and three N.C.O.s was carried out by the Irgun, who publicly took full responsibility for the act. The affair began with the imposition of a sentence of 15 years in prison and, eighteen lashes on two seventeen-year-old members of the Irgun. The two were sentenced by a British military tribunal under emergency regulations for carrying arms. The Irgun viewed the last part of the sentence as a deliberate humiliation. As the whip seemed in all colonial countries the symbol of British rule the Irgun decided that the only suitable way to retaliate in this case was to pay in the same coin. Duly, a warning in English was published and posted on the walls in order to deter the British from using the whip.[23] On a Friday evening, in

K

December 1946, one of the two boys was whipped. Following this, on December 29th, the Irgun caught four Englishmen and lashed them in retribution. The second boy, who had been sentenced to the same treatment, was not whipped, and indeed never again was the whip used in Palestine after this incident. The public, not only in Palestine, and the Irgun considered this affair a service to human dignity and self-respect.

In January 1947 a military tribunal sentenced to death by hanging a member of the Irgun named Dov Gruner. This man, who had an exemplary war record in the British army, was found wounded after an Irgun attack on a police fortification in Ramat-Gan. When on January 25th 1947 the sentence was confirmed, the Irgun, maintaining that Gruner was a prisoner of war in the hands of the British, captured two hostages, Major Collins and Justice Windham. Following this the execution of Gruner was postponed by the C.-in-C. Palestine and the two hostages were freed.[24] During March four other members of the Irgun were sentenced to death by hanging. The Irgun, still maintaining that the captives were prisoners of war, issued a warning that 'the British would have to bear the consequences of their crime if the men were executed'. In the meantime the Government promised not to execute anybody until a Privy Council decision was reached about the Gruner case. Yet on April 16th, while the postponement was still in force, Gruner and three others were suddenly hanged in Acre prison. Two others, one F.F.I. man who was found guilty of carrying a hand-grenade and one Irgun man, committed suicide by exploding a bomb in their prison cell several minutes before they were to be taken for execution. Then, a further, three members of the Irgun were sentenced to death. The Irgun was by this time convinced that the only way to save their lives was to take hostages. The first attempt to take hostages was foiled by the interference of the Haganah. This forced the Irgun, for lack of time before the execution, to content themselves with the capture of two sergeants instead of officers as hostages for their men under sentence of death. On July 23, the three Irgun members were hanged and a day later the Irgun hanged the two sergeants. This was the last hanging of anybody in Palestine.

The southern wing of the King David Hotel in Jerusalem had served since the war as military G.H.Q., and Secretariat of the Civil Government. An attack on this objective had already been discussed by the united resistance leadership in the spring of 1946 and it was then agreed that thirty minutes should be allowed between the introduction of explosives and their detonation to permit the evacuation of the building. The operation was to be carried out by the Irgun, which had submitted the plan, and was to cause as little loss of life as possible. It was further decided that this attack should be timed to coincide with another operation about half a mile south of the King David Hotel which was to be carried out by the F.F.I. After many delays both attacks were confirmed by the united resistance command on July 1st 1946, two days after the British 'monster' operation of the 'Black Saturday'. Following confirmation the attacks had twice to be cancelled for technical reasons and, on the actual day of the execution on July 22nd, had to be delayed for one hour, from 11 a.m. to 12 noon. This postponment was the result of the F.F.I.'s failure to arrive in time for their attack on 'David Bros. Building.[25] At 12 a.m. the Irgun could risk delaying the final assault no longer and as soon as the explosives were set it issued a warning to evacuate the building. The warning was given by means of three telephone calls; one, to the management of the King David Hotel, a second to the editor of the 'Palestine Post' newspaper, and a third to the French Consulate, which promptly opened all windows to prevent them from being shattered by the blast.[26] For reasons which are still a mystery the building was not evacuated and more than two hundred people were killed or injured in the explosion. Fifteen of the victims were Jews and several more alien civilians. Bound by its previous agreement with the united resistance command no prompt communique was issued by the Irgun admitting responsibility for the attack, and as the Irgun's disinclination to cause loss of life was well known, the King David Hotel operation was sometimes attributed to the F.F.I.

(9)

In conclusion it must be said that any assessment of the contribution of the 'Stern Group', or indeed that of any of the secret armies in bringing about the withdrawal of the British forces from Palestine can be only conjecture until the relevant documents have been published by the British Government. Yet several things can be learned from a study of the Stern Group: Firstly *terrorism as a means of political pressure can thrive only if public opinion is favourably disposed towards the terrorists' aims, and neutral towards their methods.* This point is illustrated by the Stern Group's fortunes in the period from 1940 to 1943. During these years public opinion did not identify itself either with the group's aims or with its methods, and consequently the Organization had virtually ceased to exist by the end of 1942. Secondly, once the authorities are distrusted because of some real or immaginary grievances, public opinion becomes a little less unfavourably inclined towards the terrorists' aims, though not towards their methods. At this point the terrorists are well on their way to success. Any measures taken by the authorities to fight terrorism are bound to cause some degree of hardship to the public; if there were no political grievances the public may suffer it as the lesser of two evils but if political differences exist a self-sustaining vicious circle develops. The terrorists force the government to act, the government causes hardship to the community, the community becomes increasingly annoyed with the authorities and finally neutral in their struggle with the terrorists. In the end public opinion becomes reconciled even to the terrorists' methods once the government gives its oponents an opportunity to accuse its forces, rightly or wrongly, of using similar methods. At this stage only two alternative courses are open to the authorities, short of the physical annihilation of the com- munity it governs, either to satisfy some or all of the public's demands, which need not be the same as the terrorists', and thus restore the trust and cooperation between the public and the government, or, alternatively, to identify the whole community with the terrorists and fight terrorism by collective punishment and intimidation. The first course may or may not be practicable, the second plays straight into the hands of the terrorists. The latter who are but a small minority, have then succeeded in imposing their policy on the whole community by forcing the authority's hand. When such a situation has developed the terrorist has no longer to fear detection and is free to strike at the authorities at his own convenience. In fact only a major political change can at this point save the situation and any indecision or delay on the part of the government in implementing it can result only in futile loss of life. Thirdly, the 'terrorist' as distinct from the 'partisan' is often a city man. Usually he is sophisticated with an academic or at least good education,[27] but above all he is an individualist in his way of both thinking and acting. His individualism is the strength as well as the weakness of the group to which he belongs; the strength because neither the arrest nor the extermination of the organisation's leadership can put an end to its existence; the weakness because the leadership can never have absolute control over the organisation. In effect the leadership more frequently reflects the ideas and feelings of the rank and file, rather than directs them.

Finally, terrorism in Palestine was a reflection of the international 'terrorism', lawlessness and disrespect for human life which characterised the 1940s. The Jewish terrorists were trained by, or were taught the methods of, the British commandos, the Russian 'descent forces', the Polish and Jugoslav partisans and the French Resistance fighters. The general public's sensitivity to the loss of life had been blunted by years of war during which all countries acted on the principle that all means were justified by the ends. The Germans massacred Jews, Poles and Russians. The Allies dropped their atom bombs on Hiroshima and Nagasaki, destroyed towns from the air all over Europe and encouraged underground fighters everywhere to cause destruction and loss of life to the best of their ability. If ends justified the means everywhere else why not in Palestine ? What better aim could there be for Jews, six million of whom had been murdered while the world stood by doing almost nothing to save them, than the creation of a Jewish State to care for the survivors ?

---

[1] The legally recognised elected representative body of the Jewish community.

The sources upon which this article is based are the news-sheets of the Stern Groupe *Ha-Hazit* and later *Ha-Ma'as* and a number of special brochures like *Qawwei yisod le-mediniuth hutz 'ivrith* (which is an outline of the Group's foreign policy), and *Milhama o ma'avaq*, and some of my own recollections from these years. There are, in addition, the contemporary newspapers, and Y. Bana'i's voluminous work, *Hayyalim almonim* (Tel-Aviv 1958) which is the best summary of the Group's activities. Other books which shed some light on aspects of the Organization are M. Samuelewisz, *Be-Yamim adumim* (Tel-Aviv, 1950); Dr. I. Sheib ('Eldad') *Ma'aser richon* (Tel-Aviv, 1950); Avner, *Memoirs of an Assassin* (London 1959); Geula Cohen, *Sippara*

*Shel lohemeth* (Tel-Aviv 1961); ·and Gerolt Frank, *The Deed* (London 1963). For the general background see Yehuda Bauer, *Diplomacy and Underground in Zionism 1939-45* (in Hebrew, Merchavia 1963). Most of the original material relating to the Organisation is now deposited with the 'Ya'ir' Lehi Institute and Lehi Archive, Tel-Aviv.

[2] He has since claimed that, although he took part in the hold-up he was convicted on false evidence.

[3] The papers reported that Stern was shot while trying to escape. The Stern Group maintained that he was shot in cold blood by the police.

[4] Stern Group publications accuse the police of shooting the men and planting the revolver afterwards.

[5] Albert M. Hyamson in his book *Palestine under the Mandate* (London 1950) writes about the *Struma* p. 154 '...the vessel (was sent) back into the Black Sea, where she was, a few hours later, sunk by a mine or torpedo, or fell to pieces.'

[6] M. Begin, *The Revolt*, (London, 1951), p. 38.

[7] The trials: M. Tabory, 29 May 1944 (7 years prison); D. Hameiri, 19 June 1944 (12 years prison); Miss Ch. Shapiro, 19 June 1944 (4 years prison); A. Spilmann, 20 June 1944 (10 years prison); M. Samuelewisz, 26 June 1944 (death penalty later commuted to life imprisonment).
During the same period Dr. Scheib, the member of the centre, was also arrested but not tried and sent to a detention camp. This left Friedman-Yellin and Ysernitsky alone in charge of the Organization's centre.

[8] See also speech of Tawfiq Dos Pasha, counsel for the accused.

[9] Quoted by Col. R. Meinertzhagen, *Middle East Diary*, (London 1959), p. 194.

[10] Because it would undermine the fact that a Jewish state in Palestine would be useful to British interests. (Hamashkif).

[11] See Bauer, *op. cit.*, p. 211. Mr. Ben-Gurions' words are quoted from Begin, *op. cit.*

[12] M. Begin, *op. cit.*, p. 152.

[13] Y. Banayi, *Hayyalim almonim*, (Israel 1958), p. 315.

[14] Quoted by Colonel R. Meinertzhagen, *op. cit.*, p. 198.

[15] At the time spokesman for the moderate right - now Communist M.P.

[16] At the time spokesman for the 'activist' left - now left-Socialist M.P.

[17] At the time leader of the Irgun - now M.P. for the right wing Heruth party.

[18] M. Begin, *op. cit.*, p. 185.

[19] Quoted from Ch. Weizmann, *Trial and Error*, London 1950, p. 541.

[20] The total Jewish population in Palestine in 1947 was roughly 600,000; British army personnel at the same time numbered some 85.000 men.

[21] These underground passages were later shown to the press and to archaeologists by members of the F.F.I.

[22] F. L. Schuman, *International Politics*, New-York, Toronto, London, 1953, p. 218.

[23] M. Begin, *op. cit.*, page 233: 'Incidentally, on one of the posters containing our warning a British soldier scrawled in big letters: Please don't forget my Sergeant Major'. Unlike the soldier of the Airborne Division who had scrawled his threat to 'kill 60 million Jews', this particular Tommy thoughtfully added his full name, unit and regimental number'.

[24] Justice Windham's behaviour must have profoundly impressed his captors because even Begin speaks of him in his book as an outstanding gentleman.

[25] This delay was caused by a breakdown near the Arab village of Abu-Gosh of the truck which brought the F.F.I. men and equipment to Jerusalem.

[26] The French consulate was the building closest to the King David Hotel.

[27] This observation may not be universally correct because, as it was pointed out to me, the 'terrorists' in Morocco 1955-56 were drawn from an urban proletariat and not from the intelligentsia.

# Arab Immigration into Pre-State Israel: 1922-1931

*Fred M. Gottheil**

As an historical event of major consequence, it is not surprising that there are at least two conflicting accounts concerning immigration into Palestine prior to the formation of the State of Israel. One account, for example, depicts Jewish immigration into Palestine primarily in terms of filling up vast empty spaces of sparsely populated land.[1] Much of this description centers upon the drainage of the northern marshes and the reclamation of the desert. Essentially, it is an account of man versus nature. Only parenthetically does it consider Arab immigration or the impact of Jewish immigration on the resident Arab population.

By contrast, a second version shifts the focus of discussion to population displacement. It describes the sàme Jewish immigration as creating in Palestine a demographic overcapacity situation with the indigenous Arab population being forced off the settled land.[2] In this case, it is an account of man versus man for control and ownership of extremely limited natural resources.[3] Both descriptions survive today as historical summaries of pre-Israel Palestine.

Although there is substantial disagreement in the two accounts concerning the *impact* of immigration, there is no disagreement as to its *source*. Both emphasize its Jewish origins. Almost completely lost in these accounts is an analysis of concurrent Arab immigration. References to such immigration are made only in passing and the conclusion reached is that for purposes of permanent settlement, Arab immigration was insignificant.[4]

This conclusion, however, has not gone completely unchallenged. The Royal Institute for International Affairs, for example, commenting on the growth of the Palestinian population prior to World War II, states: 'The number of Arabs who entered Palestine illegally from Syria and Transjordan is unknown. But probably considerable.'[5] Professor Harold Laski makes a similar observation: 'There has been large-scale and both assisted and unassisted Jewish emigration to Palestine; but it is important also to note that there has been large-scale Arab emigration from the surrounding countries.'[6] Underscoring the point, C. S. Jarvis, Governor of the Sinai from 1923-1936, noted: 'This illegal immigration was not only going on from the Sinai, but also from Trans-Jordan and Syria and it is very difficult to make a case out for the misery of the Arabs if at the same time their compatriots from adjoining States could not be kept from going in to share that misery.'[7] Even the Simpson Report acknowledged Arab immigration in this form:

> Another serious feature of immigration is the number of persons who
> evade the frontier control and enter Palestine without formality of any

*The author acknowledges the helpful comments of Professors Haim Barkai and Nahum Gross of the Hebrew University on an earlier draft of this paper.

kind. It is exceedingly difficult to maintain any effective control of the various frontiers of Palestine. At the present time such controls as exists is carried out at police posts on the roads. The immigrant who wishes to evade the control naturally leaves the road before reaching the frontier and takes to the footpaths over the Hills . . . The Chief Immigration Officer has brought to notice that illicit immigration through Syria and across the northern frontier of Palestine is material. [8]

Other writers make this same point. [9] Although Arab immigration has been described as 'considerable,' 'large-scale,' and 'material,' such descriptions are nonetheless lacking in precision. [10]

This paper presents some statistical evidence concerning Arab immigration into Palestine. The following issues will be considered: What, in 1922, was the Arab population what in was to become Israel and how rapidly did this population grow? What per cent of this growth can be attributed to natural increase and what per cent to immigration? How do the demographic patterns in pre-State Israel compare with those in non-Israel Palestine during the 1922-1931 period, and what explanations can be offered to explain divergent patterns? Although data will be presented for all of Palestine, a distinction will be drawn between Arab immigration into the part of Palestine that later becomes Israel and the non-Israel sector of Palestine. The analysis will emphasize the former.

THE APPLICATION OF PALESTINE CENSUS DATA TO PRE-STATE ISRAEL: 1922-1931

Census data for Palestine are available only for the year 1922 and 1931. Prior to 1922, there existed, at best, educated guesses. [11] Since 1931, population estimates were derived by applying natural rates of growth and *registered* immigration to the 1931 numbers. [12] Because these population estimates make no attempt to measure unrecorded immigration, the reliability of these numbers is considerably less than those of the census years. [13] For this reason, the analysis here is restricted to the census period 1922-1931.

The transfer of these census data to pre-State Israel is complicated by the character of the Israel borders which were not entirely aligned with the administrative subdistricts of Palestine upon which the statistical

TABLE 1
PALESTINE AND ISRAEL
(by subdistrict)

| Subdistricts entirely within Israel | Subdistricts partially within Israel | Subdistricts entirely outside Israel |
| --- | --- | --- |
| Safad | Jenin | Nablus |
| Acre | Tulkarm | Ramallah |
| Nazareth | Jerusalem | Jericho |
| Haifa | Hebron | |
| Beisan | Gaza | |
| Jaffa | Bethlehem | |
| Ramle | | |
| Beersheba | | |
| Tiberias | | |

Source: *Survey of Palestine*, Vol. I, 1946, p. 145.

reporting of population was made. In 1922, population data for Palestine was arranged by the British Mandatory Government in eighteen sub-districts according to urban or rural location and according to religion. The relationship between these subdistricts and the State of Israel is illustrated in Table 1.

The problem of identifying the 1922 Arab population as pre-State Israel or non-Israel Palestine is thus reduced to an intra-subdistrict analysis of population allocation in the six subdistricts that are only partially included in the State of Israel. A disaggregation of the census data from the subdistrict level to the village level for those subdistricts whose domain includes the Israel border permits a reclassification of the Palestine census data into Israeli Arab and non-Israeli Arab population. The results are seen in Table 2.[14]

TABLE 2

ARAB SETTLED POPULATION 1922 AND 1931 IN
PRE-STATE ISRAEL AND NON-ISRAEL PALESTINE
(by subdistricts)

| Subdistrict | Pre-State Israel | | Non-Israel Palestine | |
|---|---|---|---|---|
| | 1922 | 1931 | 1922 | 1931 |
| Safad | 18,720 | 35,751 | | |
| Acre | 34,276 | 43,465 | | |
| Nazareth | 20,713 | 24,090 | | |
| Haifa | 45,712 | 69,136 | | |
| Beisan | 9,925 | 13,087 | | |
| Jaffa | 39,866 | 73,927 | | |
| Ramle | 44,465 | 61,329 | | |
| Beersheba | 2,258 | 2,948 | | |
| Tiberias | 14,245 | 18,877 | | |
| Jenin | 5,430 | 7,014 | 27,978 | 34,239 |
| Tulkarm | 13,424 | 17,016 | 21,477 | 28,581 |
| Jerusalem | 18,799 | 29,201 | 35,272 | 45,266 |
| Hebron | 11,246 | 14,359 | 41,881 | 53,114 |
| Gaza | 42,563 | 52,763 | 29,055 | 52,288 |
| Bethlehem | 224 | 325 | 22,554 | 21,444 |
| Nablus | | | 56,482 | 68,477 |
| Ramallah | | | 28,948 | 37,771 |
| Jericho | | | 1,888 | 3,192 |
| Totals | 321,866 | 463,283 | 265,535 | 334,372 |

Source: Barron, J. B., *Report and General Abstracts of the Census of 1922*, Jerusalem, Government Printer, m.d. Mills, E., *Census of Palestine 1931, Population of Villages, Towns, and Administrative Areas*, Jerusalem, 1932.

ARAB POPULATION IN PRE-STATE ISRAEL: 1922-1931

Total Arab settled population in the pre-State Israel sector of Palestine increased during the 1922-1931 period from 321,866 to 463,288, or by 141,422. This population increase reflects both natural increase and increase through immigration. Since natural rates of growth for the Arab population of Palestine are available for the 1922-1931 period (Table 3), the relative contributions of natural increase and immigration can be measured.

TABLE 3
ANNUAL RATES OF NATURAL INCREASE OF MOSLEM, CHRISTIAN,
AND OTHER NON-JEWISH SETTLED POPULATION
(1922–1931)

|      | Moslem | Christian | Others |      | Moslem | Christian | Others |
|------|--------|-----------|--------|------|--------|-----------|--------|
| 1922 | 2·49   | 1·91      | 2·48   | 1927 | 2·10   | 1·84      | 2·20   |
| 1923 | 2·15   | 1·98      | 2·15   | 1928 | 2·34   | 2·10      | 2·38   |
| 1924 | 2·47   | 2·34      | 2·03   | 1929 | 2·34   | 1·96      | 1·63   |
| 1925 | 2·18   | 1·81      | 2·63   | 1930 | 2·81   | 2·21      | 2·47   |
| 1926 | 2·90   | 2·16      | 1·84   | 1931 | 2·74   | 2·28      | 3·35   |

Source: Survey of Palestine, Government of Palestine, Government Printer, Palestine, 1946, Vol. III, p. 1176. These rates, averaged, for 1922–1925 and 1926–1930, appear in Palestine Blue Book, 1938, Government Printer, Jerusalem, p. 144 and Palestine, Office of Statistics, General Monthly Bulletin of Current Statistics of Palestine, Jerusalem, January, 1937, p. 4.

Applying these rates to the 1922 population, we derive for 1931 a population size of 398,498[15] This size would obtain if natural increase were the only source of population growth. The actual 1931 population, derived from the 1931 census data, however, is 463,288 or 64,790 more than can be explained by the natural increase. Since 10,000 represents simply a transfer of territory from Syria to the subdistrict of Safad, the 54,790 residual is imputed to the Arab immigration from the non-Israel sector of Palestine and from the surrounding Arab countries.[16]

Arab immigration thus appears to be substantial, as Laski, Jarvis, Simpson and others suggested. The 1922-1931 Arab immigration alone represents 11·8 per cent of the total Arab settled population of 1931 and as much as 38·7 per cent of the total 1922-1931 Arab population growth. This immigration size is no less impressive when compared to the 94,162 Jewish immigration during the same period.[17] The Arab immigration accounts for 36·8 per cent of total immigration into pre-State Israel.

PRE-STATE ISRAEL AND NON-ISRAEL PALESTINE IMMIGRATION: A COMPARISON

The demographic character of the pre-State Israel 1922-1931 period contrasts sharply with that of non-Israel Palestine. This is shown in Table 4.

TABLE 4
ARAB SETTLED POPULATION IN PRE-STATE ISRAEL AND
NON-ISRAEL PALESTINE (1922–1931)

|      | Population Measure | Pre-State Israel | Non-Israel Palestine |
|------|--------------------|------------------|----------------------|
| 1922 | actual             | 321,866          | 265,535              |
| 1931 | actual             | 463,288          | 334,372              |
| 1931 | natural            | 397,728          | 329,695              |
| 1931 | immigration 1922–1931 | 54,790        | 4,677                |

The population increase for non-Israel Palestine was 4,677 greater than what would have been obtained through natural increase alone. This number compares with the 54,790 immigration for pre-State Israel. The 1922-1931 immigration to non-Israel Palestine constitutes only 1·4 per cent of its 1931 population size and 6·8 per cent of the total increase for the period. The conclusion derived from the comparative analysis is that while immigration was an important contributor to population growth in pre-State Israel, it was of minor consequence in the non-Israel sector of Palestine.

Although the contrast between the two sectors of Palestine is clear, still, both sectors record for the period a net inflow of population. This outcome contrasts with the experience of the surrounding Arab countries, where, for the 1922-1931 period, emigration in some cases of substantial numbers, are reported.[18]

## IMMIGRATION AND ECONOMIC DEVELOPMENT

The explanation for these diverging patterns of population growth and immigration can be found in the growing disparities of economic performance in pre-State Israel, non-Israel Palestine, and the Arab States.

That migration is highly synchronized with international investment and with disparities in the rates of economic growth in different regions has been well established.[19] Although the statistical record of economic activity in the Middle East is severely limited for the period 1922-1931, a consensus of economic reporting does appear to suggest that an Arab migration of 54,790 to pre-State Israel and 4,677 to non-Israel Palestine should be considered as something less than a total surprise.[20]

In contrast to the 'economic paralysis' that seems to have characterized the Arab economies,[21] Palestine had been undergoing substantial economic growth. Capital stock, largely imported, increased by 327 per cent while net domestic product rose, at constant prices, by 410 per cent.[22] The importance of Jewish-owned enterprises, located primarily in pre-State Israel, can hardly be overstated. Their number increased during 1922-1937 from 1,850 to 6,007.[23] Moreover, 75 per cent of the entire industrial work-force in 1927 was employed by such firms and 60 per cent of the force was Arab.[24]

The rapid economic development in Palestine was not the exclusive property of the Jewish sector. The extent of Arab participation in the industrialization process is reflected in the growth, from 1918-1928, of 1,373 new Arab-owned enterprises.[25] Although clearly of a smaller scale than the Jewish enterprise, these nonetheless represented over 60 per cent of the total enterprises established during the 1918-1928 period.[26]

Economic conditions in Syria, Iraq, Lebanon, and Trans-Jordan appear to have been substantially different. In Syria, for example, the growth of new industry and the conversion of handicraft production to mechanization had been insufficient to absorb the surplus labour generated by the decline in overall industrial and handicraft production.[27] In the agricultural sector, progress appeared to have been equally unattractive. The persistence of agricultural backwardness is attributed to the continuation of primitive technology, excessive peasant indebtedness, climatic conditions, and the skewed distribution of land holdings.[28]

Similar descriptions are offered for Iraq[29] and Transjordan: the latter described as 'a parasite existing on the permanent subsidy of Britain and the civil administration of Palestine' with no attempts being made toward industrialization of the modernization of agriculture.[30] Industrial activity in Egypt appeared to have been hardly more successful. Capital in corporate enterprise increased by two per cent annually between 1920-1930

TABLE 5

PER CAPITA INCOME, RELATIVE WAGES, CONSUMPTION OF FOODSTUFFS, NET PRODUCTIVITY PER MALE EARNER IN AGRICULTURE, AND THE VALUE OF AGRICULTURAL AND INDUSTRIAL MACHINERY IMPORTS IN SELECTED MIDDLE-EAST ECONOMIES (1932–1936)

| | Per capita[a] income (L) 1936 | Industrial[b] daily wages 1933–1935 (mils) | Per capita[a] Consumption of foodstuff (I.U.) 1934–1936 | Net productivity[a] per male earner in agriculture (I.U.) 1934–1936 | Machinery imports[c] (Palestine = 100) 1932–1934 | |
| --- | --- | --- | --- | --- | --- | --- |
| | | | | | agricultural | industrial |
| Egypt | 12 | na | 16·0 | 90·1 | 10 | 16 |
| Syria | 13 | 50–310 | 19·0 | 97·6 | 23 | 17 |
| Iraq | 10 | 40–60 | 13·8 | 93·2 | 10 | 16 |
| TransJordan | na | na | na | 90·1 | na | na |
| Palestine | 19 | | | | 100 | 100 |
| Arabs | | 70–500 | 22·9 | 186·3 | | |

*Source:* (a) Alfred Bonne, *Economic Development of the Middle East*, Kegan Paul, Trench, Truber & Co., London, 1943, pp. 21, 47, 62. The International Unit (I.U.) is defined as the amount of goods and services that could be purchased for one dollar in the USA over the average of the decade 1925–1934. (b) David Horowitz and Rita Hinden, *Economic Survey of Palestine*, Hapoel-Hazair Co-operative Press, Tel-Aviv, 1938, p. 207. 1933 for Syria and Iraq; 1934 for Palestine and 1935 for Lebanon. (c) David Horowitz, 'Palestine and the Middle East: An Essay in Regional Economy,' *Palestine and the Middle East Magazine*, Tel-Aviv October/November, 1943, p. 8. 1935–1938 for Iraq.

and although investment in agriculture did increase, per capita agricultural output actually declined.[31]

Although comparative statistics for the Middle East for 1922-1931 are virtually impossible to construct because of limited comparable data, some regional estimates for 1932-1936 can serve at least as an indicator of comparative economic performance for the few preceding years. Such a comparison is offered in Tables 5 and 6.

TABLE 6
AVERAGE PER CAPITA GOVERNMENT EXPENDITURE
1929 (in Palestine Mils)

| Item | Palestine | Iraq | Syria | TransJordan |
|------|-----------|------|-------|-------------|
| General Adm. | 608 | 377 | 537 | 400 |
| Army and Police | 610 | 525 | 460 | 410 |
| Total Unproductive | 1290 | 902 | 997 | 810 |
| Education | 150 | 80 | 80 | 70 |
| Health | 110 | 70 | 40 | 40 |
| Economy | 80 | 115 | 30 | 57 |
| Survey | 80 | 14 | 63 | 30 |
| Public Works | 330 | 142 | 283 | 110 |
| Total Productive | 750 | 421 | 496 | 307 |

Source: Grunwald, K., The Government Finances of the Mandated Territories in the Near East, Palestine Economic Society, May 1932, p. 100.

The economic portrait shown in Tables 5 and 6 seem clear enough. Consumption of foodstuffs in Palestine among Arabs was 143 per cent of the Egyptian, 121 per cent of the Syrian, and 166 per cent of the Iraqi consumption. Net agricultural productivity was 207 per cent of both the Egyptian and Transjordanian, 191 per cent of the Syrian and 200 per cent of the Iraqi. Since a capital goods industry was virtually non-existent in the Middle East, the value of machine imports indicates, to some degree, the rate of increase in industrialization and mechanization of agriculture. Syrian, Egyptian and Iraqi agricultural machinery imports were 23, 10 and 10 per cent of the Palestine imports; industrial machinery imports were 17, 16 and 16 per cent.

Disparities between Palestine and the Arab States appear also in the investment outlays in the public sector.

On almost every budget item, and particularly on items of industrial and social overhead capital, per capita expenditures in Palestine were higher than in any of the Arab States. Productive expenditures were, in 1929, for Palestine, 151 per cent of the Syrian, 178 per cent of the Iraqi and 244 per cent of the TransJordanian expenditures. In terms of government revenues, Palestine's per capita tax was 156 per cent of Syria's, 167 per cent of Iraq's and 295 per cent of TransJordan's.[32]

While the comparative evidence offered above is admittedly incomplete, the simple observation that significant disparities in economic activity between Palestine and the Arab States is clearly not without substance.

CONCLUSIONS

Arab immigration into Palestine, and specifically into pre-State Israel during the census period 1922-1931 reflects, to some degree, the different levels of economic activity within Palestine and between it and the contiguous Arab States. Arab immigration accounted for 38·7 per cent of the total increase in Arab settled population in pre-State Israel, and constituted 11·8 per cent of its 1931 population. Although numerically less than the Jewish immigration during the period, the significance of Arab immigration is nonetheless emphasized by its comparison with the Jewish population inflow. Arab immigration composed 36·8 per cent of the total immigration into pre-State Israel. The situation in non-Israel Palestine was somewhat different. There, Arab migration was positive, but inconsequential.

NOTES

1. 'Regions that but a few years ago were barren sand dunes, bare hills or pestilential swamps, have been converted into fertile agricultural land dotted with pleasing villages and where people can live in the faith of their fathers and the children grow up happily. The labour was arduous, but it was cheerfully, even joyfully undertaken and it was lightened by the generous help given by Jews all over the world.' Sir John Russell in forward to Lowdermilk, W. C., *Palestine: Land of Promise*, London, Gollancz, 1945.

2. 'The increase in Jewish immigration was accompanied by large-scale acquisition of land and large-scale dispossession of Arabs. Thousands of Arab farm families, driven from the land which they and their ancestors had lived, were forced to go to the towns. The Jews aimed at controlling the economic life of the country. A landless and distorted class was created.' Rousan, Mahmoud, *Palestine and the Internationalization of Jerusalem*, The Ministry of Culture and Guidance, Government of Iraq, Bagdad, 1965, p. 31.

3. It is this second version that is reflected in the Shaw (*Palestine Commission on the Disturbances of August, 1929*, Cmd. 3530, London, 1930) and Simpson (*Palestine Report on Immigration, Land Settlement, and Development*, Cmd. 3686, London, 1930). Commission Reports which subsequently formed the basis of British policy restricting Jewish immigration into Palestine during the 1930s and 1940s.

4. It is noteworthy that this conclusion is represented in Arab, Jewish, and British writing alike. See, for example, Hopkins, L., 'Population,' *Economic Organization of Palestine*, edited by Himadeh, Sa'id, American Press, Beirut, 1938, p. 19; Ruppin, A., 'Population of Palestine,' *Palestine and Near East Economic Magazine*, Nos. 5 and 6, 1927, p. 130; and *Survey of Palestine*, Vol. I, Government of Palestine, Government Printer, 1946, p. 212.

5. *Great Britain and Palestine*, 1915–1945, Royal Institute for International Affairs, Information Papers no. 20, London, p. 64.

6. 'Palestine: The Economic Aspect,' *Palestine's Economic Future*, Ed. J. B. Brown, P. L. Humphries and Company Limited, London, 1946, p. 34.

7. *United Empire*, Vol. 28, p. 633.

8. *Palestine Report on Immigration, Land Settlement, and Development*, London, 1930, pp. 126 and 138.

9. See Horowitz, D., 'Arab Economy in Palestine,' *Palestine's Economic Future*, P. L. Humphries Co., London, 1946, p. 65; Gervasi, F., *To Whom Palestine?*, D. Appleton-Century, New York 1946, p. 79; Nemirovsky, M., 'Jewish Immigration and Arab Population', *Jews and Arabs in Palestine*, Ed. Sereni, E., and Ashery, R., Hehalutz Press, New York, 1936, p. 81; Jewish Agency for Palestine, *Memorandum submitted to the Palestine Royal Commission*, London, 1936, p. 109.

10. The few estimates offered simply mention numbers. No documentation is presented. Nonetheless, the numbers are of interest: Gervasi mentions 60,000–80,000 for 1926–1946, *op. cit.*, p. 79, 20,000–30,000 is recorded for 1922–1927 by the *Jewish Plan for Palestine: Memoranda and Statements presented by The Jewish Agency for Palestine to the United Nations Special Committee on Palestine*, Jerusalem, 1947, p. 115. 40,000 for 1919–1944 is mentioned in Nathan, R., Gass, O., and Creamer, D., *Palestine: Problems and Promise*, Public Affairs Press, Washington, 1946, p. 136. David Horowitz and Rita Hinden write: 'The official net immigration figures are obviously an underestimate, as they include neither illegal Jewish immigrants nor the steady influx of Arabs from the surrounding countries. The official net immigration for 1922–1936 is

about 250,000, whereas the figure we arrive at . . . was 322,000 – a difference of nearly 30 per cent.' *Economic Survey of Palestine*, Hapoel-Hazair Co-operative Press. Tel-Aviv, 1938, p. 28.

11. A. M. Carr-Saunders, for example, estimates Arab population in Palestine in 1919 at 642,000. *World Population*, Clarendon Press, 1936, p. 307.

12. See *Survey of Palestine*, Government of Palestine, Government Printer, Palestine, 1946, Vol. I, p. 140; Hovne, A., *Labor Force in Israel*, The Maurice Falk Institute for Economic Research in Israel, Jerusalem, 1961, p. 29.

13. 'There has been unrecorded illegal immigration both of Jews and of Arabs in the period since the census of 1931, but no estimate of its volume will be possible until the next census is taken.' *Report by His Majesty's Government on Palestine and Transjordan*, London, 1937, p. 221. No census was taken.

14. The transformation of population data in the form of Moslems, Christians and other non-Jews to Arab population was made according to the equation: Arab Population $= 0.82$ Christian $+ 1.00$ Moslem $+ 0.90$ other non-Jews. *Palestine Blue Book 1938*, Government Printer, Jerusalem, n.d., p. 328. The distinction between settled and total population is made by excluding the nomadic tribes of the Beersheba subdistrict. Mills, E., op. cit., Preface to the Census of Palestine 1931.

15. Other estimates of rates of natural increase for the Moslem population have been made. The 1931 Arab population that would obtain using the substantially higher estimates of the *Reports* modifies only slightly our results. The $11.8$ per cent of Arab immigration to 1931 actual Arab population is reduced to $9.2$ per cent; the $38.7$ per cent of total population growth 1922–1931 that is immigration is reduced to $30.2$ per cent; and the $36.8$ per cent of total immigration for 1922–1931 that is Arab is reduced to $31.1$ per cent. This compares with Horowitz and Hinden's estimate of 23 per cent for 1922–1936 non-Jewish immigration as a per cent of total non-Jewish population growth 1922–1936. *Economic Survey of Palestine*, Hapoel Hazair Co-operative Press, Tel-Aviv, 1938, p. 22.

| | Palestine and Trans-Jordan Reports | Survey of Palestine 'true-rate' | | Palestine and Trans-Jordan Reports | Survey of Palestine 'true-rate' |
|---|---|---|---|---|---|
| 1922 | | na | 1927 | 2·85 | 1·44 |
| 1923 | 2·18 | na | 1928 | 2·50 | 1·32 |
| 1924 | 3·37 | na | 1929 | | 1·77 |
| 1925 | 2·97 | na | 1930 | 2·90 | 2·12 |
| 1926 | 3·48 | 1·67 | 1931 | | 2·02 |

*Source: Report: Palestine and Trans-Jordan*, His Majesty's Stationery Office, London: *Reports* 1922 through 1931. *Survey of Palestine*, Vol. III, Government of Palestine, Government Printer, Palestine, 1946, p. 1177.

16. Although no analysis was made of such a residual, it was nonetheless recognized in the Royal Commission Report of 1937. The Report states: 'A discrepancy arose at the census of 1931 between the expected and enumerated population due to incomplete recording of births and deaths and of migration, and possibly to faulty enumeration of suspicious and primitive people.' *Memoranda prepared by the Government of Palestine for the use of the Palestine Royal Commission*, His Majesty's Stationery Office, London, 1937, Colonial no. 133, p. 2.

17. Ibid., p. 8.

18.

ESTIMATES OF SYRIAN AND LEBANESE
EMIGRATION (1921–1939)

| | Origin | Gross emigration |
|---|---|---|
| 1921–28a | Syria | 89,407 |
| 1922–27b | Syria | 46,500 |
| 1925–38c | Syria | 38,302 |
| 1925–38c | Lebanon | 49,586 |
| 1920–39d | Syria | 54,000 |
| 1923–31e | Syria and Lebanon | 97,892 |

*Source:* (a) Hurwitz, D., 'The Agrarian Problem of the Fellahin,' *Jews and Arabs in Palestine*, Ed., Sereni and Ashery, Hechalutz Press, New York, 1936, p. 54; (b) *The*

*Jewish Plan for Palestine: Memoranda and Statements Presented to the United Nations Special Committee on Palestine*, Jerusalem, 1947, p. 115; (c) Granott, A., *The Land System in Palestine*, Eyre and Spottiswoode, London, 1952, p. 47; (d) Helbaoui, Y., *L'Economie Syrienne et les problemes de son developpement*, Bosc Frères, Lyon, 1955. (e) Widmer, R., 'Population,' *Economic Organization of Syria*, Ed., Himadeh, S., American Press, Beirut, 1936, p. 16.

19. See, for example, Thomas, B. 'Migration and International Investment,' *Economics of International Migration*, Ed., Thomas, B., McMillan, London, 1958; and Kuznets, S., and Dorothy S. Thomas, 'Internal Migration and Economic Growth,' *Selected Studies of Migration Since World War II*, Milbank Memorial Fund, New York, 1958, p. 199.

20. There is no way of separating out the migration from non-Israel Palestine to pre-State Israel although it is clear that such migration did take place. The *Survey of Palestine*, for example, comments: 'Internal migrations have probably operated in the same way, the coastal plain and other regions *of more rapid economic development* attracting immigration from the hill regions,' Vol. III., op. cit., p. 1150. My italics.

21. The term 'economic paralysis' belongs to Z. Y. Herschlag, *Introduction to the Modern Economic History of the Middle East*, E. J. Brill, Leiden, 1964, p. 231. Herschlag's is perhaps the best analysis of Middle East economic development for the pre-World War II period, but here too, the scarcity of statistical evidence is apparent. See his section 'The Economy of the Mandated Territories – Syria, Lebanon, Iraq and TransJordan – Between the Two World Wars,' pp. 225–275.

22. Szereszewski, Robert, *Essays on the Structure of the Jewish Economy in Palestine and Israel*, The Maurice Falk Institute for Economic Research in Israel, Jerusalem, 1968, pp. 82.

23. Gervasi, F., op. cit., p. 104.

24. Grunwald, K., 'The Industrialization of the Near East,' *Bulletin of the Palestine Economic Society*, February, 1934, Volume 6, Number 3, pp. 78–79.

25. Horowitz, D., and Hinden, R., *op. cit.*, p. 208.

26. Himadeh, S., 'Industry,' *Economic Organization of Palestine*, Ed., Himadeh, S., American Press, Beirut, 1938, p. 230.

27. Himadeh, S., op. cit., p. 172.

28. Ibid., p. 115.

29. *Progress of Iraq 1920–1931: Special Report*, Colonial no. 58, His Majesty's Stationery Office, London, 1931, pp. 205–217, 235–240. See also, Young, E. H., *Reports on Economic Conditions and Policy and Loan Policy*, Government Press, June 1930, Baghdad, p. 4. Young, lamenting the lack of statistical data, 'surmises' a process of slow accumulation of wealth.

30. Herschlag, Z. Y., op. cit., p. 237.

31. O'Brien, P., *The Revolution in Egypt's Economic System*, Oxford University Press, 1966, p. 210.

32. Grunwald, K., *The Government Finances of the Mandated Territories in the Near East*, Palestine Economic Society, May 1932, Volume 6, Number 1, p. 97.

# Crop-Sharing Economics in Mandatory Palestine - Part I[1]

*Ya'akov Firestone*

INTRODUCTION

Agricultural production in large areas of the Middle East is conducted to this day on the basis of crop-sharing arrangements.[2] Until very recently, those arrangements reflected relations of dependence and mutual obligations that were social and political as well as economic in nature.[3] The purpose of this article is to shed some light on those obligations by analyzing the forms of tenure that existed under the British Mandate on the lands of the 'Abdul Hâdî family at the villages of 'Arrâbeh in the northwest foothills of Samaria and Zar'een in the Jezreel Valley. The study tends to show that economics does not adequately explain the relations of the 'Abdul Hâdî landowners with their crop-sharing farmers and peasants between the two world wars.[4] Our evidence derives from contemporary account books supplemented by the comments of surviving contemporaries. The main source are the accounts of Nazmî Hâjj Tawfeeq 'Abdul Hâdî, the biggest landowner at 'Arrâbeh and one of the biggest at Zar'een in those days.[5]

In the early nineteenth century 'Arrâbeh was a fortified place whose fighters and raiders often descended on the surrounding countryside in pocket wars and on looting expeditions.[6] Its sheikhly family, the 'Abdul Hâdîs, rose to regional primacy by allying themselves with the Egyptian occupants of Palestine in the 1830s and managed to retain their power and influence upon the return of the Ottomans, producing a number of leading personalities in the country's subsequent history. Progressively they acquired extensive lands in several districts of Northern Samaria. 'Arrâbeh remained the centre of gravity of their holdings and their influence, but as they rose to national prominence they moved their residence one by one to Jenin, Nablus and Jerusalem.

Under the British Mandate 'Arrâbeh no longer constituted a power centre but it was still the most important village in Northern Samaria, and by far the most outward-oriented. The peasants among its residents were largely husbandmen, smallholders and crop-sharing agriculturists devoting themselves primarily to the cultivation of wheat, barley, olives, Indian millet (*durra*) and sesame, as well as fruit and vegetables for home consumption. In addition to their hillside lands they held three or four thousand acres in the fertile Plain of 'Arrâbeh below, where most of the land belonged to the 'Abdul Hâdîs but after the First World War the secular trend was in the direction of disintegration by inheritance and selling out to the villagers. It was at that time that Nazmî Hâjj Tawfeeq 'Abdul Hâdî reconstituted a large part of the family's estates by buying up some of the disintegrating 'Abdul Hâdî property.

While 'Arrâbeh was a hill village with a long tradition of smallholder independence and warlike exploits, Zar'een, 13 miles to the north-east on the site of ancient Jezreel, was a lowland settlement of the *mushâ'* or jointly-owned type: each owner had a certain number of shares in the settlement's 5,300 acres of cultivable land, and this arable was periodically reassigned among them. The stress was on field crops, with some irrigable land. By the end of the Ottoman period the 'Abdul Hâdîs had taken over ownership of the bulk of the lands, and title to these was vested in various members of the wide-branching family residing at Jenin, Nablus and 'Arrâbeh. The villagers were largely migrants from the hill country and perhaps seden-tarizing semi-nomads. Almost all of them cultivated land on crop-sharing arrangements with the 'Abdul Hâdîs and moved accordingly with their landlords whenever the arable was reassigned among the latter.[7] Their social condition was low; nor were there among them, as at 'Arrâbeh, relatives or retainers of the 'Abdul Hâdîs. One might have expected different agrarian relations than at 'Arrâbeh. Yet in principle the forms and conditions of tenure on absentee landlord property were very nearly the same in those two so very different villages which had little in common except 'Abdul Hâdî landlordship.

CROP-SHARING AND CO-CULTIVATION

Realizing that production consisted in combining resources, the countryside in the Levant traditionally conceived of agriculture as a compact between factors of production.[8] In 'Arrâbeh and in Zar'een under the British Mandate those were generally held to be land, labour, seed and ploughing stock. For irrigated crops, water was a fifth factor. The owners of those factors shared in the product in proportion to the number of factors each had contributed. If one of them, for instance, had supplied the land, the ploughing stock and the seed and the other the labour, in principle they divided the crop between them in a ratio of three to one. Obligations to third parties incurred in the course of production were shared by the owners of the collaborating factors in the same proportion as was the product.[9]

The recognized list of factors was not always and everywhere the same. Relative scarcities had something to do with this. Scarce factors could be broken up into components and earn a higher share. Ploughing stock, which held one share out of four in our list and accordingly received in principle one-fourth of the produce at 'Arrâbeh and Zar'een under the Mandate, could in other circumstances be replaced by two separate factors: ploughing animals and equipment. This raised the list of factors to five and could give the ploughing stock two-fifths of the product while lowering the shares of land, labour and seed from one-fourth to one-fifth each. Nor was it an ironclad rule that all factors must in practice be remunerated equally—after all, on the market their respective values were quite disparate and fluctuated from place to place—but it constituted the basic starting principle of crop division.[10]

In 'Arrâbeh and Zar'een between the two World Wars, land, labour, seed and ploughing stock were in fact each held to be entitled to one-fourth of the crop. But it must be borne in mind that, in almost all cases that have come to my attention dating back all the way to the late nineteenth century, provision of the ploughing stock seems to have implied provision of the seed by the same party.[11] The Arabic word *shadd*, which means *inter alia* the harnessing of animals and was used in the villages for taking on the task of cultivation on a given plot, or on the lands of a given landowner or village, seems to have included, in an agrarian context, the connotation of contributing the seed as well.[12] In keeping with this, the party supplying the ploughing stock in any crop-sharing relationship, the *shaddâd*, was awarded the share of the product due the seed as well as the share due the ploughing stock.

In other words, the crop-sharing factors at 'Arrâbeh and at Zar'een boiled down to the three that are acknowledged in classical Western economics: land and labour, each in principle entitled to one-fourth of the product, and capital, which got the rest as behooved an under-capitalized economy. But notwithstanding this apparent simplicity, the crop-sharing compact between the three factors was in no way symmetrical, for within it, Muslim law as well as village custom allotted a special place to the relation of land to the other factors.

Muslim law considered that in all crop-sharing relationships the parties supplying the land and the labour respectively had formed an association called co-cultivation (*muzâra'a*).[13] Co-cultivation was one of a large class of institutions characteristic of Middle Eastern agriculture, commerce and industry that all consisted in associations between an employer and a worker, or a landlord and a tenant, in which the former farmed out capital or land to the latter and assigned him a share in the income. This was neither share-cropping nor share-tenancy: Muslim jurisprudence outlawed share-rents and share-wages because they were indeterminate and also because they meant paying a man in the fruits of his labour.[14] According to the jurists, the allocation of income in shares was really quite valid only in a partnership (*sharika*).[15] The farming-out associations were difficult to admit to the rank of full partnerships because they lacked the prerequisite of contractual equality between partners: the respective contributions of the owner of the resources and the man who farmed them were not comparable, nor did the latter share in the ownership of the capital.[16] But they very nearly qualified as partnerships (and elsewhere we have, accordingly, called them 'quasi-*sharika* contracts') because the relationship between the parties was fiduciary. At any rate, the jurists of Islam often discussed them in the same context as partnerships, and popular usage equated them with the latter.[17] Co-cultivation was a typical quasi-partnership by all these criteria: the association between landlord and cultivator implied solidarity and mutual responsibility, and the landlord spoke of his farmer as 'partner' (*shareek*).[18] The jurists devoted detailed treatment to the *muzâra'a*, which may well have been the most important of all quasi-partnership institutions in the Middle Eastern economy, due to the preponderance of grain farming.[19]

But of the several parties to the crop-sharing compact that we discussed earlier, who was to be thus singled out as the landlord's 'quasi-partner' in co-cultivation? If occupancy was by a farmer supplying his own seed, work animals and labourers and therefore getting three-fourths or four-fifths of the crop, who provided the labour as far as the landlord was concerned—the lowly labourer on quarter-share or fifth-share, or the *shaddâd*? We shall see later that the question was not at all academic. There was an evident dualism between the bilateral association of the *muzâra'a* and the multiplicity of parties in the crop-sharing compact.

This dualism is readily illustrated by an example from the classic 'Five-Village Survey' conducted in 1944 by the Palestine Office of Statistics. Several villagers co-owning a parcel of land, each in different proportions due to the Muslim system of inheritance, cultivated it jointly, each contributing seed and labour. Upon bringing in the crop they first set aside the rent-shares to which each was entitled, then divided the rest of the produce among each other.[20] There were, in other words, two consecutive divisions of the crop, corresponding to two superimposed contracts. One was between the basically passive function of land ownership, entitled to its rent-share (*qism al-ard*), and the active function of cultivation, the dynamic aspect of which is epitomized, incidentally—in Northern Samaria, at least—by the choice of the word *shadd*, which denotes bearing down on something forcefully. Here, then, was the concrete counterpart to the juridical relationship of 'co-cultivation'. But then came another division: the joint cultivators apportioned the remainder of the crop among themselves in proportion to the active factors of production they had invested, in tangible application of the crop-sharing compact.

The common denominator between the two divisions—and the two contracts—was the *shaddâd*, the entrepreneur. In the west the crop 'follows the ground': it belongs to the landowner or to his lessee, even if they have not sown it. In Muslim law the crop 'follows the seed': in principle it belongs to the owner of the seed.[21] In concrete terms, it was not the landlord but the *shaddâd* who had possession of the crop on the threshing-floor and allocated the payments due to outside claimants as well as to the holders of the land and labour shares. And conceptually, it is in terms of what was happening to the capital share, not to the land share, that we must visualize agrarian institutions and transactions in Northern Samaria.

It now becomes a simple task to classify the forms of tenure on absentee land at 'Arrâbeh and Zar'een. If the landlord retained the capital share— if he was his own *shaddâd*—the only other crop-sharer was a mere worker with nothing but his hands. This was cropping, which required the landlord's frequent presence on his farm—a marginal version, indeed, of co-cultivation, hardly to be conceived as resembling a partnership.

The landlord who wished to absent himself but still to retain a measure of involvement and control could choose, instead, to farm out the operation and part of the capital. This he did by delegating the operation to a man on the spot and co-opting him to responsibility for the stock by making over to him a share in it with the value of which he was debited. This was referred to as 'partnership in the *shadd*': we shall call it joint-farming rather than joint cultivation, to differentiate it from the case of peasants actually cultivating together a joint holding or a piece of common property.

The landlord could also decide to retain none of the capital and to limit himself to providing the land, in which case as far as he was concerned the farmer supplied animals, equipment, seed and labour. This was share-rent farming. His share-rent farmer in turn could, if he wished, cultivate the farm with his family's help, take on croppers, be an absentee and operate the farm through a joint-farming arrangement, or yet sub-rent the land or part of it on shares to smaller operators.

The landlord least committed to his land could drop the crop-sharing arrangement and collect his rent in cash. This was a lease, and the resulting form of tenure was tenancy as we know it. Finally, the landlord could sell out altogether.

It will be readily apparent that the above represents a functional order of decreasing responsibility for production in which a landlord progressively divested himself of his role in farming—and of his function in village life. We will take up the forms of tenure in that order because it also applies chronologically to the history of the 'Abdul Hâdîs with respect to 'Arrâbeh (and partly with respect to Zar'een where they never resided) in the century that followed their rise to power under Egyptian rule. As they moved out of the village one by one and city-born sons and grandsons succeeded their 'Arrâbeh-bred fathers, more and more members of the family opted for such agrarian arrangements in the ancestral village as would require less involvement on their part with the peasant community and a way of life from which they had become estranged. In the process, all the branches of the family went through most of the forms of tenure we noted above, though they did so at different speeds and in different periods, some of them leaving the village in the mid-nineteenth century while others tarried through the period of the Mandate.

## THE CROPPER

The only form of tenure that presupposed no co-cultivation compact in the agriculture of Northern Samaria was the family farm. In principle, this did not have to be a very small holding. What mattered was that the owners of the land—they were, more often than not, brothers who held their property in common—had enough manpower in the family to do their own ploughing and at the same time did not recoil from it in view of the stigma that attached to it. What we call the family farm could employ daily labour for weeding and harvesting, or even odd-job help paid in grain or oil; so long as this was a wage and not a share in the crop, there was no association underlying production at the farm, just a contract of hire.

Yet family farms appear to have been confined to such small holdings as afforded a bare subsistence. Above that limit, even where there was enough manpower in the family to do the ploughing, fathers tended to direct their sons into business or other off-farm occupations and only one or two remained, to attend to management and overseeing. Much the same seems to have applied on rented holdings, i.e. among share-rent farmers. To be considered a 'landowner' (*mallâk*) or a 'farmer' (*muzâri'*) one had to divest oneself of the labour function and to take on croppers.

In every agrarian economy there is a class of workers who stand a notch above the daily labourers because they have been promised a season's tenure. A further notch up the agrarian ladder is attained if this tenure is guaranteed by means of a share in the crop. In the South of the U.S. such workers are called croppers—defined as crop-share tenants whose landlord furnishes all their work animals or tractor power and who usually work under close supervision, the land assigned to them usually being part of a larger enterprise.[22]

The Middle East has a similar institution. It has been studied most closely in North Africa where it is known as *khammâsa* from the Arabic word for 'five', as the cropper traditionally got one-fifth of the crop. In the Levant the name one seems to come across most often is *murâba‘a* or *murabba‘a*, from the word for 'four', because the cropper received one-fourth.[23] This did not always apply, by any means. In the Aleppo district in 1858, for instance, the most usual arrangement was that peasants whose landlords supplied them with seed, oxen and money for the purchase and repair of equipment received half the crop.[24] In Northern Samaria under the Mandate, however, the cropper's share was again nominally one-fourth, which accorded with the number of recognized factors of production in the crop-sharing compact that we described earlier, but was subject, as we shall see, to significant variations.

Cropping is the most controversial of all the 'quasi-partnerships' for the Muslim jurists. On the one hand, the association between landlord and cropper is undeniably a compact for joint cultivation and for dividing the product in shares. On the other hand, in view of the low value attaching to his labour, the cropper cannot really exercise any control in the association. Accordingly, some jurists hold cropping to be a share-wage contract and hence basically illicit, although others argue for recognizing it as a valid co-cultivation compact.[25]

A look into the cropper's condition in Northern Samaria under the British Mandate fully vindicates this legal dualism. Socially and occupationally, there was little difference between him and any other regular farm worker paid in kind. His special place in the agrarian scheme of things and his marginal position in the complex association between landlord, farmer and worker emerge only after close study of the crop division accounts which will have to be postponed until we consider the joint-farm.

Some indication of the cropper's marginal status as an associate is afforded by the fact that at 'Arrâbeh and Zar‘een he was never referred to as *shareek* or partner. The term used was *harrâth* or cultivator, literally 'ploughman'—and indeed ploughing was his first responsibility.

In principle every farm had one cropper per *feddân*. A *feddân* was a team of plough animals and hence the amount of land that one team could plough the required number of times in the course of the ploughing season: once for the plots to be put under winter crops and two or preferably three times for those ear-marked for summer or rotation crops. In smallholding areas such as the hillside lands of 'Arrâbeh, the area that one team could handle varied from year to year and from place to place depending on the strength of the animals, the terrain, the season's tilth and the dispersion of the cultivated parcels. There was therefore little point in using the term *feddân* to denote any fixed unit of area, and the word meant little more than a unit of ploughing power input. Areas and farm sizes were expressed in terms of the number of measures (*kayl*) of seed (*bzâr*) that it took to put them under wheat, and the agrarian term for such land was accordingly '*bzâr-kayl* land'. Jointly-owned settlements, on the other hand, were '*feddân* land' par excellence: here ownership was in undivided shares and at each reassignment or reapportionment the community strove to allot identical shares of each type of land, to every *feddân* of locally standardized area. Historically the *feddân* of most such communities could be expected to increase or to decrease somewhat depending on the total area the settlement currently had under cultivation; but at any one time the *feddâns* were all equal in size and value. Here then the *feddân* meant at one and the same time a holding; the right of the farmer to own and work his plough and team and to take part in the periodic reapportionments of currently cultivable land; and a physical area of currently and locally standardized size. In principle this area was as much as a team could handle; but here too neither the power of the individual team nor the year's weather were constant, and in practice one team was not always equal to the task. Where much of a jointly-owned settlement had been taken over by absentee landowners, as at Zar'een, the area that each of them owned was expressed in terms of local *feddâns;* on each of these the landlord or his farmer had one cropper; if need be, one or more additional ploughboys (*atbâ'*) usually of inferior tenure status, supplied the rest of the input required on the farm. In the Plain of 'Arrâbeh too, as well as in the Plain of Esdraelon, on larger property where the use of ploughmen could be planned with some efficiency, the area owned by each landowner was referred to in terms of *feddâns* and this corresponded normally to the number of croppers he employed.[26]

The cropper also sowed, planted and carried out a range of other duties only partly set by custom. Many a cropper quit—some were said to have done so in the middle of the season, even though they thereby forfeited their entire share of the crop—in disagreement over work demanded of him, such as taking the plough animals out to pasture at night. A particular bone of contention was the work required of the cropper's wife or sister.[27] In many parts of Samaria a cropper was expected to supply a woman (*qâ'ima*) along with himself for the crop-share that he received, and unmarried croppers were not taken on unless they brought along a female relative or undertook to pay a year's wages for a woman who would feed and water the livestock, plant and thin summer crops, help the hired women with the weeding, prepare food for the harvest hands, sift grain at the threshing floor, etc. The woman's duties varied even more than the cropper's, for as one advances along the Beduin-villager-townsman continuum the *purdah* gets tighter: the women are more cloistered but they also perform much less farm work. For instance, in Zar'een it was the croppers' women who carried sacks of split straw from the threshing floor to winter storage places; in 'Arrâbeh this was done by beasts of burden.[28]

The croppers on each farm received their fourth of the crop (which they divided equally unless some of them had not worked full-time or for the whole season) only after deduction of their share of the crop taxes and of other fees and charges incurred in producing the crop.[29] They also reimbursed the landlord or the farmer for one-fourth of all wages paid out in the course of the season to non-cropper labour such as weeders and harvestmen.[30]

In return for all this, it was understood that the farm was responsible for

the cropper's livelihood. When wheat failed on account of poorly distributed rains, and it would have been better conservation practice to fallow
the land, it was the practice among the small peasants at 'Arrâbeh to sow
millet in the spring, a soil-depleting practice that imposed itself on them
because they would suffer hunger the following winter unless they laid in
some grain: croppers could and did insist that the farmer employing them
sow millet too for their sake.[31]

The cropper was entitled to get his necessities from his employer during
the season on account of his share of the coming crop.[32] He paid no
interest on this. He also got regular advances (not gifts) at holiday time
('*eediyya*). If his debt got out of hand owing to a succession of bad years
and, come harvest, he did not have enough grain to spare from his share
in order to pay off the debt, he could carry the unpaid portion over to the
following harvest, and beyond.[33] It is not clear to what extent interest was
charged on such debts.[34] All employers gave interest-free credit, within
limits, to their croppers.[35] Much of it took the form of charge accounts at
local stores; I was told this cost the landlord nothing because his credit
there was interest-free.[36] The explanation seems to be that the landlord's
sales of the grain on his estates to the district's merchants generated credit
for him at village stores through the instrumentality of the transfer of debt
or cession of credit (*hawâla*) which was highly developed in Islam and
apparently widely used in the Levant as an instrument of payment.[37] The
*hawâla* appears very frequently in Nazmî's notebooks.

None of this, however, was a prerogative of croppers as against other
workers, for they were all in a sense members of a traditional agrarian
household. A regular worker of some standing was provided with his
necessities regardless of the kind of contract he had, and in the traditional
districts of the Levant under the Mandates one often came across employment relationships that were close and personal, the master maintaining
his worker to the extent of caring for him when he was sick.[38] What is
more, evidence from North Africa suggests that the cash, the food and the
clothing received by croppers in the course of the season were considered
not advances, but wages paid in instalments.[39] This disposes of any
imputation of special privilege for the croppers, and also casts into
further relief the practical similarity between cropping and employment.
In Nazmî's accounts, it is true, the advances to croppers were entered as
loans (*qirda*) and duly paid back (*sidâd*) at the division of the crop between
the parties; but the same procedure was followed in Northern Samaria
with other workers paid in kind, for their wages too were not due before
the end of the season. There was, of course, the difference that the cropper
got a share of the crop while the other workers got an agreed quantity of
grain, oil or cash; but this was largely academic except perhaps in years of
plenty, for the cropper's actual take was geared to his subsistence and a
fluctuating debt accommodated the difference between that and his
contractual share year after year.

In North Africa the cropper was invested with gifts, and the employer's
responsibility for his welfare included even loans so that he could take a
wife.[40] But this too can probably be attributed to the relation of patronage
and dependence between a traditional master and members of his house-

hold rather than considered something specific to crop-sharing. In any case, the records at 'Arrâbeh show no positive evidence of such practices. Perhaps they were traditions that had died out by the time of the Mandate.

All in all, it seems that in the traditional agrarian society of the Middle East there was little to differentiate the socio-economic condition of the cropper from that of any other regular worker living as a dependant of the master and accorded his protection and a measure of his patronage, except perhaps that the cropper may have enjoyed a greater measure of trust, responsibility, and possibly security of tenure, and that his wage, of course, was in principle a share of the crop. To put it functionally, the more important and responsible tasks on the farm, such as ploughing, were entrusted to a worker whose pay was linked to the output of the enterprise as an expression of this responsibility and who enjoyed somewhat higher status. If we wish to inquire into the special features of cropping as an institution it is to the agrarian contract, as reflected in accounts showing the division of the crop between the parties, that we will have to look.

### THE JOINT-FARM PARTNERSHIP

Owner operation with the aid of croppers became difficult once the owner had moved to town under the pressure of business, or politics, or simply for social promotion. The cropper could hardly be left to be his own boss: Nazmî's books record just one case of a cropper who managed his *feddân* and those of his sons, at Zar'een in 1932.[41] There were salaried agents, probably rare at 'Arrâbeh, but they could not be asked to take on entrepreneurial functions.[42] Someone was needed to plan and direct farm operations, particularly at harvest-time.

The absentee 'Abdul Hâdîs attempted various solutions. Some went to the village each year for much of the spring and summer, when it was the landowner's ironclad right to spend the night, like Boaz, on the threshing-floor. Since most properties were co-owned by several brothers, only one of them needed take the task on himself; but the estates of some 'Abdul Hâdî branches were scattered over several parts of Northern Samaria and the adjacent valleys so that more than one brother was required to cover the territory. Various land exchanges that took place on a regional scale between the various branches of the family and consolidated the properties of each in a smaller number of villages probably stemmed largely from the need to cut down on such management and overseeing commitments. But ultimately, inevitably, the properties were farmed out to local peasants: on joint-farm contracts if the landowner retained a more active interest in his property, and, where this was not the case, on the share-rent contract we shall examine later.[43]

We noted earlier that the association between landlord and crop-sharing worker or peasant that the Muslims termed co-cultivation (*muzâra'a*) was what we call a quasi-partnership, an association for farming out resources for a share of the income.[44] Such quasi-partnerships flourished in many branches of the rural economy of the Levant, beginning with raising silkworms and tending groves and ending with the operation of strings of camels. In the period of transition beginning in the mid-nineteenth century, when the traditional economy of rural Samaria was aroused to greater activity under the impact of the market, many of these associations took on a new form: they no longer merely resembled partnerships but set out to meet the requirement of Muslim jurisprudence that in a partnership each partner really owns a share of the stock. This was achieved by granting the worker or entrepreneur a share in the capital and debiting him its value which he paid up in the course of the association or upon its dissolution.[45] This accession to the ownership of capital by plain workers and peasants facilitated the expansion of the economy in the period of transition.[46]

The joint-farm represented the application of this form of association to agriculture, or more precisely to the capital factor in the crop-sharing compact. Hence the name 'partnership in the *shadd*' (*sharika bil-shadd*). One partner, the capital owner, contributed or financed the bulk of the ploughing stock and seed; the other, whom we shall call the joint-farmer, operated the farm and was granted and debited an agreed share in the capital, toward which he often contributed some stock of his own such as oxen and seed. The partners paid off the contributors of land and labour in the crop-sharing compact, then shared in the expenses of the capital share and in the income in proportion to their respective agreed shares in the capital. The better the joint-farmer's economic standing, the bigger the share of capital that he took on. The capital owner could be the land-lord or a rent-share farmer; the joint-farmer could himself be the cropper, or perform the work through his family, or have it done by croppers.

The joint-farm was a widespread institution at 'Arrâbeh about 1930, it seems—not only on absentee-owned land but on the properties of local peasant land-owners as well. As the years went by, it became increasingly difficult to get workers who were satisfied with a cropper's share; they insisted on a joint-farmer's contract. We were shown with the aid of cost calculations based on contemporary prices how the acqustion of part of the capital share greatly increased the worker's income yet required almost no investment on his part, since it was the capital owner—in this case, the peasant landowner—who put up most of the outlay until threshing time.[47] These calculations, derived from the personal experience of one peasant landowner, were borne out by the implications of the figures for Nazmî's farms which we shall analyze closely later.

The circumstances in which a joint-farm was set up, and the mechanics of its establishment, are illustrated by a case from the village of Soulam, across the Plain of Esdraelon from Zar'een. Most of the land at Soulam was owned by the Sursoq family of Beirut who had acquired the bulk of the Plain from 1872 onward.[48] The Sursoqs awarded their land in the Plain to local dwellers and to migrants from the hills of Samaria on rent-shares of only one-fifth of the crop—actually one-tenth, for this included the government tithe—yet although they were prepared to advance seed and plough animals to their farmers and even gave them free housing at such places as Jaloud, the peasants' meagre resources were seldom adequate to the risks of farming in an area of marginal settlement and Beduin raids: in prey to usurers, repeatedly they abandoned the land.[49] About the turn of the century the Sursoqs' local agent awarded several hundred acres at Soulam to a tough family from 'Arrâbeh, the sons of Najeeb Yahyâ 'Atârî, each of whom farmed a few *feddâns* with croppers. As was customary, one of the 'Atârî brothers, Husayn, resided in 'Arrâbeh to take care of the family land and business there; but he also farmed a holding in Soulam.[50] In 1922 he either secured no croppers for that holding or had no one in the family to oversee the croppers, for he took on a joint-farmer, Ibrâhîm Khateeb.

As capital owner, Husayn contributed the lion's share of the stock: a work-horse worth £E25, four oxen worth £E78, £E7 to purchase an ox in Nazareth, and also £E11 for barley feed and seed, £E1.800 for vetch grown for grain (*kersenneh* or *Vicia ervilia*) £E0.500 for millet feed, £E0.500 for chickpea seed £E1.500 for choice sesame seed (*zaree'a*). Ibrâhîm, on the other hand, had an ox worth £E10, a cow worth £E9 which was sold off soon after, and a donkey worth £E4. The total assets were £E148.300 of which Ibrâhîm had contributed £E23; he was assigned a one-third share in the capital and debited £E26.440 as the difference between it and the actual value of his contribution.[51]

The joint-farm accounts we have for 'Arrâbeh and Zar'een are more complex for the 'Abdul Hâdîs were themselves landlords, so that if they operated joint-farms on their own land they collected the rent-share as well as whatever proportion of the revenue corresponded to the share of the capital they retained in their joint-farm contract. The mechanics of the relationship emerge from the accounts recorded in Nazmî Hâjj Tawfeeq 'Abdul Hâdî's notebook for 88 joint-farms operations conducted on an annual basis in the two villages between 1919 and 1941.

## THE DIVISION OF THE CROP

We noted earlier that the capital owner on a joint-farm could be either the landlord himself or a share-rent farmer. Nazmî operated in both capacities: most of the land he farmed was his, but there was also some in which he owned only an undivided fraction—many 'Abdul Hâdî properties were still co-owned at the time by brothers or cousins—and some that he share-rented from close relatives, to accommodate them and to achieve economies of scale for himself since individual holdings were fragmented and scattered. Finally, several of Nazmî's joint-farmers had some land of their own, and their joint-farms with him also took in their property: this too involved a share-rent compact (the joint-farmer here playing the role of landowner) underlying the joint-farm compact.

The division of the crop recorded in Nazmî's accounts brings out clearly this share-rent relationship to his landholding relatives and partners. In all accounts allocating the crop on their land, the first disbursement after settlement of debts to camel-drivers, watchmen, etc., was the landlord's rent-share—in Nazmî's day this was uniformly one-fourth of the crop—set apart at the threshing-floor. In a second stage of division, the cropper's share of one-fourth was paid out, and the rest was divided between Nazmî and his joint-farmer in proportion to their shares in the capital.

But the cropper's fourth was not one-fourth of the whole crop; it was levied only on what remained after the rent-share had been assigned to the landlord.[51] In other words, the croppers got only three-sixteenth of the crop—from which Nazmî deducted one-fourth of the crop taxes, of all external fees and obligations, and of the casual wage-labour bill. This formula was followed in all of Nazmî's accounts with 'Abdul Hâdî land-owners until the record ends in 1941.

At first sight this appears quite consistent with our conception of the association for co-cultivation and the crop-sharing compact as two separate, superimposed contracts connected only through the person of the *shaddâd*—in this case, of Nazmî and his joint-farmer as partners in the *shadd*. But a difficulty arises. The separateness of the two contracts would have been sufficiently established if the partners in the *shadd* had confined themselves to representing *either* the croppers in the compact with the landlord *or* the landlord in the compact with the croppers. The fact that they seemed to do both, collecting a share in the croppers' name in the division of the crop with the landlord, and a rent-share in the landlord's name in the division with the croppers, is difficult to explain away as mere exploitation of the croppers by the partners in the *shadd*.

Two facts may point to a possible explanation. One is that, as we have already noted, in the late nineteenth and early twentieth centuries the Sursoqs' rent-share in the Plain of Esdraelon had been one-fifth; the other is that according to one legal authority the share that landlords collected from their tenants in Mandatory Palestine, while varying in value, was known as the *khums* or fifth.[53] If this indicates that at 'Arrâbeh too the rent-share had at one time been one-fifth, our difficulty is resolved. We could then postulate that before Nazmî's time the crop-sharing compact at 'Arrâbeh had been held to consist of five factors, or at any rate that the product had been divided into five shares, as was the tradition in North Africa; that landlord and croppers had each received one-fifth of the crop; and that in keeping with the practice of two consecutive divisions this meant reserving one-fifth for the landlord and remitting one-fourth of the rest, i.e. one-fifth of the original crop, to the croppers. When, in the period of the Nazmî accounts, the rent-share increased to one-fourth, the practice of remitting a quarter of the rest to the croppers could have continued either by inertia or through the farmer's desire to recoup part of the rent increase from the croppers. We do, in fact, have testimony that before the First World War the cropper's customary share had been one-fifth, although the evidence is not from 'Arrâbeh or Zar'een.[54]

So much for the accounts of Nazmî and his joint-farmers with his land-lord relatives. On land farmed by the two partners but belonging to Nazmî's joint-farmers the procedure was exactly the same—until 1936, as we shall see. First the landowner, i.e. the joint-farmer, took his rent of one-fourth of the total crop; then the croppers got one-fourth of what remained; finally the partners in the *shadd* divided the rest.[55] In other words, on the oint-farmer's property both Nazmî and his joint-farmer paid rent—the latter, of course, to himself—and it was only on the remainder of the product that they granted one-fourth to the croppers.

On the land that belonged to Nazmî, however, the division was quite different. After payment of external obligations it proceeded as follows: (1) allocation of the crop between Nazmî and his joint-farmer in pro-portion to their shares in the capital; (2) payment by the joint-farmer of one-fourth of his share to Nazmî as the latter's rent-share—but Nazmî (unlike the joint-farmer where the latter was landowner) paid no rent to himself; (3) payment by each of the partners in the *shadd* of their obligations to the croppers.[56] Here it will be noted that while the joint-farmer deducted the rent-share he paid to Nazmî before allotting the croppers one-fourth of the remainder, Nazmî, who paid no rent, turned over regularly to the croppers a full fourth of his portion (though not of the rent that he got from his joint-farmer).[57]

On the face of it, the situation would seem to have called for the same division of the crop—with a simple reversal of roles between Nazmi and his joint-farmer—whether the land belonged to the one or the other.[58] The difference in the division formula teaches us that their agrarian roles were not the same—because within the joint-farm partnership the power relationship was understandably unequal, and it was Nazmî, not his peasant joint-farmer, who played the part of initiator and responsible moving spirit.

We noted earlier that the crop 'followed the seed', that it was the *shaddâd* who played an active role in co-cultivation, and that it is in terms of what was happening to the capital share, not to the land share, that one must visualize agrarian institutions and transactions in Mandatory Northern Samaria. In the West, a landlord contemplating the equivalent of joint-farming would have rented his land to some consortium of his joint-farmer and himself. That was exactly what the peasant joint-farmer had done on his own property, where he remained in the passive role of land-owner instead of setting up a joint-farming relationship on the lines of the position on Nazmî's property. Nazmî, for his part, had set up no consor-tium on his land, and had farmed out to his joint-farmer not his land but part of his capital. That part of the capital carried wih it an obligation to pay a pro-rated portion of the payments due to the holders of the land and labour shares on the farm. The other part of the capital remained with Nazmî, quite outside the purview of the joint-farming relationship which was concerned only with the part of the capital that had been farmed out to the joint-farmer. The part remaining with Nazmî was, in effect, a land-owner-operated farm (except that, being a unit of capital rather than of land, it could have no territorial extent) on which of course Nazmî had no contractual obligation to pay rent to himself.[59] Only the obligation to the croppers remained; and with respect to them, on this part of the capital Nazmî was an owner-operator and could hardly claim from them a portion of a rent he had not paid.

Notwithstanding its formal character as a partnership, then, the joint-farm contract was asymmetrical: while Nazmî was concerned with the capital share that he had farmed out to his joint-farmer, the latter was not concerned with the share that had remained with Nazmî. Hence the uni-lateral character of the farm's financing, which will be discussed in the next section; hence also some rather unexpected implications about the croppers' share.

We just noted that while on the land belonging to the joint-farmer the croppers received a gross three-sixteenths of the crop, on Nazmî's property they got a gross three-sixteenths of the joint-farmer's portion of the capital share but a gross one-fourth, i.e. 33 per cent more, of Nazmî's portion. The higher the capital share acquired by the joint-farmer from Nazmî, then, the lower was the croppers' aggregate take from the whole of Nazmî's land; and the higher the proportion of the joint-farm's land that was owned by the joint-farmer (or yet by Nazmî's relatives) as against by Nazmî, the lower the croppers' aggregate take from the whole joint-farm. In fact, from 1927 through 1932 we have accounts for two adjacent farms in 'Arrâbeh in one of which Nazmî held half the capital and about two-thirds of the land, and in the other two-thirds of the capital and about three-quarters of the land, creating a difference of about 5 per cent in the croppers' effective aggregate share between the two farms that persisted year by year.

Accustomed as we are to economic determinism, we may find it surprising that the croppers' share should have been a function of something so extraneous to the labour supply and the croppers' bargaining power as the distribution of land and capital among the farm's owners and managers. Yet so it was. More surprising yet, it seems that, in the short run at least, the croppers' share varied with this distribution only and not with economic factors. For, subject only to the differences between categories of ownership that we have sketched out at the beginning of this section, the formula for allocating the crop was identical on all of Nazmî's farms, at 'Arrâbeh and at Zar'een, irrespective of the significant differences in social and economic conditions between the two villages, or of the disparities in the croppers' work load on different farms. We assume the work load did vary to a certain extent with social and economic conditions, providing some outlet for supply and demand pressures on the labour market; but that, of course, cannot be traced in our accounts; and, in view of the rule of one cropper per *feddân* and the *feddân*'s fixed area at Zar'een, such an outlet could only have operated with considerable rigidity. Over longer terms, of course, changes must have taken place in the cropper's share in response to economic conditions; but one would tend to speculate that in the traditional period such responses had been delayed, diffuse, and therefore limited to stimuli of substantial magnitude and duration.

Be that as it may, the superimposition of the share-rent on the institution of the joint-farm resulted, given the asymmetry of the partnership in the latter, in a difference of one-third between the rate paid the croppers by Nazmî and by his joint-farmers. Yet for a long while no one seemed to react to the apparent irrationality of this mechanism. It does not seem farfetched to suggest that perhaps an association had formed in the popular mind between this difference and the 'Abdul Hâdî landlords' *noblesse oblige* as sheikhs or as 'efendis', the social class to which they were assigned.

The first inkling of a change came in 1933, perhaps in the wake of a tremor in the labour market as employment expanded in the implanted sector and in the more developed districts of Palestine. That year, and in 1934 as well, on one of Nazmî's three or four joint-farms at Zar'een the croppers—a man and his sons—got a gross full fourth of the crop. One of the accounts bears the explanatory remark 'because they are so good'.[60] Closer examination reveals that this was the same man who had managed his *feddân* and those of his sons the previous year, at which time he had naturally received a full fourth of the crop since there was no joint-farmer in the picture; and now that he was subject to one a cut in his income seemed hardly in place.[61] It was therefore a special situation, but it may well have come to the knowledge of the croppers on other farms.

In 1934 Nazmî established at Zar'een a joint-farm in which the joint-farmer held one-half of the capital. On the other farms the joint-farmer held only one-third or one-fourth of the capital, giving the croppers higher effective shares. In the past such differentials appear to have been accepted, as we have seen, as a matter of course; but in 1935 a bonus was given to the croppers on the new farm to bring their share up exactly to the effective rate of 11/48 that the croppers got where the joint-farmer held one-third of the capital. The bonus was paid out of the joint-farmer's share: after all, Nazmî was already paying a full fourth of his.[62] On the farm where the joint-farmer held one-fourth of the capital, the croppers retained their higher effective rate.[63]

We have no accounts for 1936. The harvest of 1937 was bountiful, and the croppers were evidently so delighted with it that they pressed no claims for adjustments; but in 1938 and 1939 the bonus reappears, showing that by then the croppers were both conscious of the differential mechanism that we have sketched here and able to do something about it.[64] In Zar'een, then, a 'floor' of 11/48 of the crop—very close to the one-fourth that the croppers had in the past received from Nazmî alone—was put under their effective rate of income beginning in 1935.

'Arrâbeh was more outward-oriented than Zar'een; its villagers had more skills and personal connections, enabling an unusually large number to become absorbed in the economy of Haifa and in other urban employment. Small wonder, then, that at 'Arrâbeh the 'cropper revolution' was more thorough than at Zar'een; what is enlightening is that the croppers' demands were met at Nazmî's expense rather than at the joint-farmers.'

As of 1936, at all of Nazmî's joint-farms at 'Arrâbeh the croppers were assigned a full fourth of the grass crop—subject to payment of external obligations, of one-fourth of the wage bill, etc. Then the landowner—i.e., Nazmî or his joint-farmer, as the case might be—got one-fourth of the remainder.[65] In other words, whereas formerly Nazmî and his joint-farmer had passed on to the croppers part of the burden of the rent paid to whichever of the two was landowner, now they passed on to the landowner part of the burden of the share they allotted to the croppers. (In their joint-farming capacity, as partners in the *shadd*, their share of the crop remained the same).

Since Nazmî's joint-farmers, particularly from 1936 onward, were peasants with little land of their own, the parties actually affected by this change were the croppers and Nazmî. He had deferred to their demand that their share of the entire crop be raised to the level of the share they had received in the past from him alone; but this reform was implemented by cutting his own income rather than by making any demand of the joint-farmer (except where the latter was landowner). One might argue that Nazmî needed his joint-farmer even more than his croppers in view of the limited availability of good farmers. But the real question is why Nazmî kept up his joint-farms at all in the 1930s, and, *a fortiori*, how he could guarantee to both joint-farmers and croppers a stated minimum share of the income, at a time when, as we shall see in Part II of this article, he bore the brunt of the financing burden, quite out of proportion to his nominal share in the capital, and in addition farming was proving a losing proposition year after year.

NOTES

1.  This article is based on field work conducted from 1968 to 1971 on the social and economic history of the rural district of 'Arrâbeh. The research was funded by National Defense Foreign Language Fellowships and by a grant from the Center for Middle Eastern Studies at Harvard University. I owe more than words can express to Hajj Qâsem Hâjj Muhammad Qäsem 'Abdul Hâdî, Mr Bâsem Nazmî 'Abdul Hâdî, Professor Gabriel Baer, Mr Albert Hourani and Mr Edward Wheeler: this article would not have been written without the help of each and everyone of them. The interest of Professor David S. Landes in this research is gratefully acknowledged. Above all, my thanks go to the kind and generous people of 'Arrâbeh who steered me so graciously into the beginnings of an understanding of their institutions.

2.  Cf. Ann K. S. Lambton, *Landlord and Peasant in Persia*, London, 1953, pp. 295-336.

3.  Jacques Berque, *Les Nawâzil el-Muzâra'a du Mi'yâr al-Wazzânî*, Rabat, 1940, pp. 73-76; Henri Schirmer, *Le Sahara*, Paris, 1893, pp. 297-299; Augustin Bernard and N. Lacroix, *L'evolution du nomadisme en Algerie*, Alger, 1906, pp. 178-179; Louis Milliot, *L'association agricole chez les Musulmans du Maghreb*, Paris, 1911, pp. 201-202; Pierre Bourdieu, *The Algerians*, Boston, 1962, pp. 78-80; Jacques Weulersse, *Paysans de Syrie et du Proche-Orient*, Paris, 1946, pp. 60-64, 115-117; Doreen Warriner, *Land Reform and Development in the Middle East*, London, 1957, pp. 135-138; cf. Marc Bloch, *Les caractères originaux de l'histoire rurale française*, Vol. I, Paris, 1964, pp. 152-153.

4.  Needless to say, it would be inadvisable to generalize too freely from these forms of tenure and the socio-economic relations they reflect. Different agrarian patterns are established where, as in our case, a deeply-rooted sheikhly family moves out of the village, selling out its land progressively to the peasants, than where the village land is passing under the control of money-lending city merchants, a process that was actually taking place in another part of Samaria during the period with which we are dealing. (For differences in landowner attitudes to their tenants see Jean Duvignaud, *Change at Shebika*, New York, 1970, p. 90). Nor are the landlord-tenant relationships of the period of the British Mandate necessarily representative of more traditional times, for the economy was undergoing transition to the age of the market (for the related effects of the establishment of security on the alienation of rural land to creditors, see Milliot, *op. cit.*, pp. 216-7.) At present we are not in a position to avail ourselves of data pertaining to earlier periods, but documents relating to the first two decades of the twentieth century have been collected and await collation and interpretation.

5.  The accounts were kindly lent to me by Nazmî's son, Mr Bâsem Nazmî 'Abdul Hâdî of Nablus, to whom I owe a debt of gratitude for the many evenings he sat up with me, at a time of greatly unsettled conditions, interpreting the entries until I began to find my feet in the agrarian and commercial concepts that underlay them and among the personalities and events to which they referred.

6.  Mary Eliza Rogers, *Domestic Life in Palestine*, Cincinnati, 1865, p. 236; James Finn, *Stirring Times*, Vol. II, London, 1878, p. 168; W. M. Thomson, *The Land and the Book*, London, 1905 ed., p. 465.

7.  From Mr 'Awnî Ra'ouf 'Abdul Hâdî of Nablus, June 3, 1969. We may envisage two types of relationship between a *mushâ'* settlement and absentee landlords. Under the first, the landlord collected his rent-share from all the cultivators. The village lands being undivided, he could do so even if he owned only a fraction of the land. For instance, if his fraction was one-half and the accepted rent-share was one-fifth of the crop, the landlord would collect one-tenth of the crops on each threshing floor. Should such a landlord transfer his title to others through sale or succession, it stands to reason that his successors would continue to collect the one-tenth from each threshing-floor, then divide the combined proceeds among themselves in the proportion in which each

landlord held title to the land. Under such circumstances the landlords would not be concerned with the periodic reassignment of locations among the cultivators.

But in a case such as Zar'een, where the *mushâ'* land jointly owned by the cultivators was bought out or taken over progressively from the individual owners, as each non-resident owner acquired a share in the lands of the village he was concurrently under-stood to have taken over the right to the periodic reassignment of locations that went with that share: any such reapportionment was henceforth among the new owners (and those cultivators who had not lost their land) and there could be no reassignment among cultivators independent of it. In fact, one of the big landowners at Zar'een, Mr Khaleel Hilmî 'Abdul Hâdî of Nablus (August 20, 1970) recalled only one or two reapportion-ments in the course of decades, a contributory factor being the owners' expectation of imminent surveyed settlement of title to the lands.

8. It is instructive in this connection that in Moroccan customary law land had no rent value whatever in cash (Berque, *op. cit.*, pp. 72-3). In other words, land had value only in the context of collaboration among the factors of production that could fructify it. In customary African tenure there is no market for land (Montague Yudelman, *Africans on the Land*, Cambridge, Mass., 1964, p. 14); it is considered 'virtually a free good' (Kenneth R. Parsons, 'Customary Land Tenure and the Development of African Agriculture', *FAO Report RP 14*, Rome, 1971, reproduced as *LTC No. 77* by the Land Tenure Center, Madison, Wis. 1971, p. 36).

9. Typical obligations to third parties in Northern Samaria were crop taxes, camel drivers' fees for bringing in the crop (at 'Arrâbeh, not at Zar'een, where this was done by the farm's own donkeys), fees to watchmen in the fields and at the threshing-floor, etc. Such obligations varied substantially from place to place; for an example from 'Arrâbeh in 1928 cf. another leaf from the notebooks of Nazmî Hâjj Tawfeeq 'Abdul Hâdî (hereafter referred to as *Notebooks*): Volume AIV, p. 484. The payments were usually disbursed in kind from the crop before it was divided among the parties con-tributing the factors of production; failing that, they were pro-rated among them. Thus the crop tax (tithe, or *'ushr*) was generally taken from the threshing-floor under the Ottomans, but when cash payments, based on estimations at the threshing-floor and an official redemption rate, were substituted in the first years of the Mandate (A. Granovsky, *Land Taxation in Palestine*, Jerusalem, 1927, p. 26), at 'Arrâbeh and Zar'een the tithe was paid by the landlord or farmer and pro-rated among the factors of pro-duction. In Nazmî's accounts the debit on this score was usually set off against each party's share of the receipts from sesame, the local cash crop (see Notebooks, AIV, pp. 470, 461) if any had been grown. The consolidated Rural Property Tax that replaced as of 1935 the dual structure of tithe on crops and property taxes on land in Mandatory Palestine was legally payable by the landowner (A. Granovsky, *The Fiscal System of Palestine*, Jerusalem, 1935, p. 178) but on Nazmî's farms it too was pro-rated among the factors of production and if possible set off against the receipts from sesame (*Notebooks*, AIV, p. 110). See Part II of this article, n. 20.

10. Cf. Milliot, *op. cit.*, p. 22; Lambton, *op. cit.*, p. 306; Berque, *op. cit.*, p. 71. Paul Ward English, *City and Village in Iran: Settlement and Economy in the Kirman Basin*, Madison, Wis., 1966, pp. 88-9. For the crop divisions actually obtaining in various districts of the Levant just after the Second World War see 'Isâm 'Ashour, 'Nizâm al-Murâba'a fî Sûrya waLubnân waFalasteen', *al-Abhath*, Vol. I, no. 3 (1948), pp. 37-41.

11. See also Rev. George E. Post, 'Essays on the Sects and Nationalities of Syria and Palestine', Palestine Exploration Fund, *Quarterly Statement*, 1891, p. 109. This need not imply that such was the practice in other parts of the Levant, or even of Palestine; cf. Louise E. Sweet, *Tell Toqaan, A Syrian Village*, Ann Arbor, 1960, p. 65.

12. Hâjj Qâsem Hâjj Muhammad Qâsem 'Abdul Hâdî of Nablus, August 19, 1969; Mr Muhammad Hasan 'Alî of 'Arrâbeh, May 27, 1969; Samuel Bergheim, 'Land Tenure in Palestine', Palestine Exploration Fund, *Quarterly Statement*, 1894, pp. 192-3.

13. Ottoman Civil Code (*Mejelle*) Art. 1431. For discussion of the *muzâra'a* as a contract see David Santillana, *Istituzioni di diritto musulmano malichita, con riguardo anche al sistema sciafiita*, Vol. II, Rome, 1938, pp. 303-9; Charles Hamilton's trans-lation of al-Marghînânî's *Hedaya*, 2d ed. by Standish Grove Grady, London, 1870, pp. 579-85; O. Pesle, *La société et le partage dans le rite malékite*, Casablanca 1948, pp. 45-9; Berque, *op. cit.*, pp. 85-135.

14. Félix Arin, *Recherches historiques sur les operations usuraires et aléatoires en droit musulman*, Paris, 1909, pp. 39-42; Milliot, *op. cit.*, pp. 11-12; Santillana, *op. cit.*, II, pp. 56, 259-60, 303-4; *Hedaya, op. cit.*, pp. 499, 501, 579.

15. *Hedaya*, pp. 226, 580; Louis Milliot, *Introduction à l'étude du droit musulman*, Paris, 1953, p. 662.

16. Octave Pesle, *Les contrats de louage chez les malékites de l'Afrique du Nord*, Rabat, 1938, p. 108; Pesle, *op. cit.*, 1948, p. 46; Milliot, *op. cit.*, 1953, p. 662; Santillana, *op. cit.*, II, p. 308.

17. See the present writer's forthcoming article on 'Production and Trade in an Islamic Context; Sharika Contracts in the Transitional Economy of Northern Samaria' in the *International Journal of Middle East Studies*, Vol. VI., No. 2.

18. See, among others, Dominique Chevallier, 'Aspects sociaux de la Question d'Orient: aux origines des troubles agraires libanais en 1858', *Annales* 14 (1959) pp. 35-64; Duvignaud, *op. cit.*, pp. 12, 26; Sweet, *op. cit.*, p. 65.

19. Santillana, *op. cit.*, II, pp. 303-9; *Hedaya*, pp. 579-84; Milliot, *op. cit.*, 1911, pp. 17-33.

20. Palestine, Office of Statistics, *General Monthly Bulletin of Current Statistics of Palestine*, Dec. 1945, p. 764.

21. *Hedaya*, p. 581. The sower's right to his crop is unaffected by whether or not he had any rights in the ground in which he sowed, although if he did not, he must of course pay a fair rent or compensation (but see Pesle, *op. cit.*, 1938, pp. 120-1). Under the traditional tenure system in Nigeria anyone who plants a crop may harvest the product (Parsons, *op. cit.*, p. 52). All this may help explain the attitude of the semi-nomadic and semi-settled sower to the niceties of property boundaries.

22. *United States Census of Agriculture*, 1950, Vol. I, any Part, pp. xviii-xix.

23. A. Latron, *La vie rurale en Syrie et au Liban*, Beirut, 1936, p. 85; Sweet, *op. cit.*, p. 65. But in this article on crop-sharing in the Levant (*al-Abhâth*, I:3 (1948), pp. 32-48; 4, pp. 47-69; II:1 (1949), pp. 61-72) 'Ashour employs the word *murâba'a* to designate all crop-sharing, more specifically the form we call share-rent farming. *Murâba'a* is also the term employed for crop-sharing in general by Abdulla M. Lutfiyya in *Baytîn, A Jordanian Village*, Paris, 1956, pp. 106-7.

24. Great Britain, *Parliamentary Papers*, 1859, 2d Session, Vol. XXX, p. 431.

25. Santillana, *op. cit.*, II, pp. 307-9. A particularly copious juristic literature has accumulated on the subject in North Africa. For a partial listing of the sources for just one Moroccan school see Berque, *op. cit.*, pp. 60-1. For the various points of view see Pesle, *op. cit.*, 1938, pp. 180-5; Milliot, *op. cit.*, 1911(, pp. 20-4; Berque, *op. cit.*, 111-8. For the *khammâsa* contract in North Africa in practice see Milliot, *op. cit.*, 1911, pp. 81-95.

26. Latron, *op. cit.*, p. 16; Mr 'Awnî Ra'ouf 'Abdul Hâdî, June 3, 1969; Mr Bâsem Nazmî 'Abdul Hâdî, Sept. 8, 1969; Elihu Grant, *The People of Palestine*, Philadelphia 1921 ed., p. 132; Mr Muhammad Hasan 'Alî, June 24, 1970; Hâjj 'Aqqâb As'ad of 'Arrâbeh, May 19, 1969. The Ottoman authorities recognized three separate land area values for the Syrian *feddan* (Roumî, khattät and statistical) which they standardized at 200, 130 and 165 dunams respectively (Vital Cuinet, *Syrie, Liban et Palistine, Georgraphie administrative, statistique, descriptive et raisonnee*, Paris, 1896, p. 373.Cf. the values of the Chiflik—'about 70 to 80 dunams of superior, 100 dunams of middling, and 130 dunams of inferior land'—in Art. 131 of the *Ottoman Land Code*, trans. F. Ongley, London, 1892, p. 68.) The dunam was the equivalent of 0.09193 hectares, or just under one-fourth of an acre; under the Mandate it was gradually superseded by the 'metric dunam' of 0.1 hectares. For values of the *feddân* in Palestine see Claude R. Conder, *Tent Work in Palestine*, Vol. II, London, 1879, pp. 252-256, and Government of Palestine, *Report of a Committee on the Economic Condition of Agriculturists in Palestine*, Jerusalem, 1930, p. 21. The latter recorded a range from 24 metric dunams to the *feddân* in a village of the Acre Sub-District to 300 metric dunams to the *feddân roumî* in a village near Nablus; and indeed at Zar'een in the 1930s each of the 85 *roumî feddâns* of cultivable land worked out to 254 metric danams (Central Zionist Archives, Jerusalem, KKL 5, Box 1001, file on land purchases at Yizra'el-Zar'een 1935-1937, correspondence of June 21 and 24, 1936, between the Head Office of the Jewish National Fund and Yehoshua Hankin of the Palestine Land Development Company.)

The *kayl* was the basic unit in the duodecimal system of dry measure in use in the

Levant (cf. Latron, Appendix I.) In Samaria the system was 1 *kayl* = 2 *'ilbeh* = 6 *mudd* = 12 *ṣâ'* = 24 *rub'iyya* = 48 *thumniyya* (cf. Cuinet, p. 372.) One *kayl* averaged 170 lbs. for wheat, 152 for Indian millet, 127 for barley and sesame, according to local informants, but variations were considerable: we found differences of up to 8 per cent between shipments of sesame coming in by the *kayl* to Nazmî's store at Nablus in 1941 and then weighed in (*Notebooks*, AIV, p. 73) but in 'Arrâbeh we were assured by Mr Muhammad Hasan 'Alî and Hâjj Dheeb As'ad Hasan that the range could have been 20-25 per cent—for one thing, buyers were entitled to top their measures as high as they could, a skill that was greatly appreciated and cultivated (for excellent descriptions of grain measuring see Palestine Exploration Fund, *Quarterly Statement*, 1881, pp. 325-6 (Rev. Jas. Neal) and Rev. T. C. Wilson, *Peasant Life in the Holy Land*, London, 1906, p. 212); for another, in a good year grain kernels were.

We found that the *kayl* as a measure of area—the *bzâr-kayl*, or the acreage usually sown with a *kayl* of wheat—works out to the same area as the English acre of today (more or less, for shallower soils required denser seeding). Since the acre, in turn, is defined as the amount of land that a team of oxen could plough in one day, one is set to wondering which came first: the measure of area or the dry measure of the same name.

27.  From Mr Mahmoud 'Abdul Fattâh 'Abdul Ghanî of 'Arrâbeh, July 7, 1970.

28.  From Hâjj Qâsem Hâjj Muhammad Qâsem 'Abdul Hâdî, August 19, 1969; Mr Khaleel Hilmî 'Abdul Hâdî, June 3, 1971; Mr Mahmoud Muhammad 'Abed Ibraheem of 'Arrâbeh, December 14, 1970.

29.  See above, p. 4 and n. 9.

30.  *Notebooks*, AIV, p. 386 (Zar'een, 1931), p. 135 ('Arrâbeh, 1938). Cf. Latron, *op. cit.*, p. 85. In 'Arrâbeh and Zar'een this wage bill was called 'joint expenditure' (*maṣrouf mushtarak*) to show that farmer and cropper were jointly responsible for it. In Algeria, where the cropper got a fifth of the crop, he paid one-fifth of the farm's cash expenditure (Berque, *op. cit.*, p. 76).

31.  From Mr Muhammad Hasan 'Alî, May 31, 1970.

32.  This was repaid at the accounting that followed the threshing as the end of the year's operations. Cf. Rev. F. A. Klein, 'Life, Habits, and Customs of the Fellahin of Palestine', Palestine Exploration Fund, *Quarterly Statement*, 1883, p. 45; Sweet, *op. cit.*, p. 65.

33.  *Notebooks*, AIV, p. 285 (grain vetch at 'Arrâbeh, 1933) and p. 253 (barley at 'Arrâbeh, 1934).

34.  Nazmî kept special accounts (*Notebooks*, Volumes AI, AII) for debts owed to him, where annual entries often showed interest charges. In all his accounts with croppers we saw such a charge only once—for two 'Arrâbeh croppers about 1933 on what appeared to be an old debt. The interest rate was 30 per cent (*Notebooks*, AII, p. 266).

35.  From Mr Khaleel Hilmî 'Abdul Hâdî of Nablus, June 3, 1971. Cf. Milliot, *op. cit.*, 1911; p. 84.

36.  From Hâjj Dheeb As'ad Hasan of 'Arrâbeh. For the interest rates of the time see Part II of this article, n. 9.

37.  Santillana, *op. cit.*, II, pp. 200-7; *Hedaya*, pp. 332-4; *Mejelle*, Art. 673-700.

38.  Latron, *op. cit.*, p. 85.

39.  Milliot, *op. cit.*, 1911, p. 84.

40.  Berque, *op. cit.*, p. 77; Milliot, *op. cit.*, 1953, pp. 660-1; *op. cit.*, p. 84.

41.  *Notebooks*, AIV, pp. 358-9, 340, 315-6. Mr Huhammad Hasan 'Alî, who served as Nazmî's agent and recalled the man, stated (October 14, 1969) that he had received no remuneration for this beyond his one-fourth of the crop. A full fourth, of course, was more than other croppers got on joint-farms at the time (see below, pp. 13-16).

42.  Salaried agents were more like custodians, and took little initiative. Commission agents specialized in commercial operations. Pesle's perspicacious point that in Islamic lands partners seldom delegated management to third parties (*op. cit.*, 1948, pp. 57-8) is another way of saying that, where it could not be carried on by the owner of the resources, entrepreneurship tended to take the form of farming out. See the article referred to in n. 16 above.

43.  See Part II of the present article.

44.  See above, p. 5.

45.  Muslim jurisprudence considered the resulting form of association a partnership

in property in which only one partner worked. Cf. *Mejelle*, Art. 1370-1371.

46. See my forthcoming article referred to in n. 17 above.

47. From Mr Mahmoud 'Abdul Fattâh 'Abdul Ghanî, December 21, 1969 and March 10, 1970.

48. Laurence Oliphant, *The Land of Gilead with Excursions in the Lebanon*, Edinburgh, 1880, p. 330; *Haifa or Life in Modern Palestine*, Edinburgh, 1887, p. 42; A. Granott, *The Land System in Palestine*, London, 1952, pp. 80-1.

49. Oliphant, *op. cit.*, 1880, pp. 330-2; Great Britain, *Report of the Commission on the Palestine Disturbances of August, 1929, Minutes of Evidence*, Vol. I, pp. 452 (11,488), 466 (11,749-11,750); Mr Kâmil Hasan Zu'bî of Soulam, April 28, 1971; Hâjj Dheeb As'ad Hasan of 'Arrâbeh. Oliphant (p. 330) mentions a payment of 10 mejidies per *feddân* to the Sursoqs in addition to the rent-share but does not specify whether it was annual or a one-time â sum. At the turn of the century the best grades of whate sold at Ramallah for three piastres per *ruttl*, i.e. per six and one-quarter pounds (Grant, *op. cit.*, p. 79): assuming a gross return of two piastres per *ruttl* to the farmer, at 19 piastres to the mejidie this would make the 10 mejidies equivalent to 95 *ruttls* of wheat, or $3\frac{1}{2}$ *kayls* (see n. 26 above). As we have seen ,one *kayl* seeded an acre. Since a yield of $3\frac{1}{2}$:1 could be achieved except in a very poor year (see Part II of this article) and there were 50 to 75 acres to the *feddân Roumî* that seems to have been the usual *feddân* in the Plain of Esdraelon, it appears that an imposition of 10 mejidies would not have raised the rent-share of a *feddân* substantially even if it were annual.

50. From Mr Fâris Muhammad Najeeb 'Atârî of 'Arrâbeh, July 1, 1971.

51. From the accounts of Husayn Najeeb 'Atârî, kindly lent to us by his son Saleem of 'Arrâbeh, entries of 1922.

52. For one of many examples see *Notebooks*, AIV, p. 469 ('Arrâbeh, 1927).

53. Moses J. Doukhan, 'Land Tenure' in Sa'id B. Himadeh, ed., *Economic Organization of Palestine*, Beirut, 1938, p. 94. According to T. Canaan ('The Saqr Bedouin of Bisan', *Journal of the Palestine Oriental Society*, XVI, 1936, p. 25) on Sultan Abdul Hamid's lands in the Beisan valley, the 20 per cent paid by the farmers consisted of a land tax of 10 per cent and a rent to the Sultan of 10 per cent of the income.

55. For one of many examples see Notebooks, AIV, p. 479 ('Arrâbeh, 1927).

56. The page that is photographed here from the notebooks of Nazmî 'Abdul Hâdî (AIV, p. 393) is an unusually informative one in several respects in addition to the list of external obligations that we noted in n. 9 above. It shows how the shares were arrived at for all the crop-sharing parties. It proves that the three croppers got their shares from the landlord and his joint-farmer and not from the crop as a whole, indicating graphically that labour was employed by capital and not associated with the other factors of production on an equal footing as predicated by the traditional concept of a crop-sharing compact (p. 4 above) or on a basis of partnership with land as envisaged by the Shar'i institution of co-cultivation (p. 5 above.) The photograph also shows that the croppers divided their share among themselves in equal parts; that the grain they had borrowed from their employers was deducted directly from that share, and that two of the croppers were probably members of the joint-farmer's family since he collected their takings. It also gives marketing dates for the wheat—immediately after the harvest, implying a scarzcity, otherwise Nazmî would probably have held on to the grain to await the seasonal rise in prices.

For other examples of the division on Nazmî's land see *Notebooks*, AIV, pp. 468 ('Arrâbeh, 1928) and 426 (Zar'een, 1929).

57. This follows clearly from all crop division accounts on Nazmî's land before 1936, but at Zar'een the difference is occasionally actually spelled out (*Notebooks*, pp. 102, 393) because on his farms there Nazmî often kept his joint-farmers' and croppers' accounts as well as his own (see Part II of the present article).

58. This did happen once, on one 'Arrâbeh farm, but only for one season, in 1934 (*Notebooks*, p. 245).

59. Since so much land in Palestine was co-owned in undivided shares, the statement in parentheses should not be taken to mean that if the unit were of land rather than of capital it would necessarily have territorial extent either.

60. *'Liannahum mumtâzeen.'*

61. See above, p. 11 and n. 41.

62.  *Notebooks*, AIV, pp. 190-1. The bonus entry reads 'share differential' (*farq qism*).

63.  *Notebooks*, AIV, p. 189.

64.  *Notebooks*, AIV, pp. 102, 116. In 1940 the joint-farmer's half-shares in the farm's capital was cut to one-third for reasons we do not know, so there was no further occasion to 'level up' the croppers' share on his farm.

65.  For a page showing crop division on this post-1936 model both on Nazmî's land and on the property of one of his joint-farmers, see *Notebooks*, AIV, p. 93 ('Arrâbeh 1939).

# Crop-Sharing Economics in Mandatory Palestine— Part II

### Ya'akov Firestone

The first part of this article showed that crop division in Mandatory Palestine incorporated two superimposed principles of tenure. The first of these was the crop-sharing compact between the traditionally acknowledged factors of production that shared in the produce: land, seed, ploughing stock and labour. In Northern Samaria both capital factors— seed and ploughing stock—were contributed by one party, who was said to have been awarded the *shadd* or cultivation. In other words, he was the farmer.

The second principle of tenure was the *muzāra'a* or co-cultivation compact between landowner and cultivator. In this compact the cultivator (the farmer) represented the other factors of production as far as the landowner was concerned, and assigned him his rent-share of the crop. Only as a second step was the rest of the crop divided among the other factors of production: and here the farmer represented the landlord. All in all, the farmer constituted the link between the two compacts and the linchpin of the landholding system. Accordingly, it is in terms of where the capital came from under each form of tenure, that we have found it most productive to visualize agrarian institutions and to follow the evolution of the land system in this article.

We then classified the forms of tenure in Northern Samaria under the Mandate in descending order of involvement in farming on the part of the landowner:

(a) cropping: the landowner retained the capital (the stock) the labour being performed by croppers;

(b) joint-farming (partnership in the *shadd*): the landowner, who owned the stock, appointed a villager to operate the farm, made over a share in the stock to him, debited him its value, and split with him the crop share due to the seed and to the ploughing stock under the crop-sharing compact. The operator, whom we shall call joint-farmer, could either perform the labour himself or take on croppers;

(c) share-rent farming: the landowner provided only the land, the farmer supplying the whole capital. The farmer in turn could, if he wished, take on joint-farmers or croppers or sub-farm out the land;

(d) tenancy, in which cash replaced the share-rent.

We were able to analyse crop division procedures on the basis of the accounts of Nāẓmi Hājj Tawfeeq 'Abdul Hādi who owned extensive lands both in the hill village of 'Arrābeh in Northern Samaria and in the lowland settlement of Zar'een in the Plain of Esdraelon. We learned from them that Naẓmi awarded the croppers (crop-sharing labourers) a much larger part of his share of the crop than did Naẓmi's joint-farmers. This differential persisted until the mid-1930's when the croppers apparently secured its elimination—again, at the expense of Naẓmi, not of his joint-farmers. We also saw that while in principle the joint-farming form of association

175

was a full partnership in the farm's capital, in fact the agrarian roles of the capital owner or investor (in the case Naẓmi, the landowner) and his joint-farmer were not the same. It was Naẓmi, not his peasant joint-farmer, who played the part of initiator and responsible moving spirit in the relationship—which fitted in with the difference between their respective roles as far as the cropper were concerned. We now go on to some of the other implications of this asymmetry in the joint-farming partnership.

FINANCING THE JOINT-FARM

In principle, capital owner and joint-farmer apportioned among themselves all of the joint-farm's capital expenditure, such as equipment repairs, and all investment, such as providing seed, in proportion to their agreed shares in the capital.[1] In practice, however, when circumstances were unfavourable it seems that it was the capital owner who shouldered the bulk of the outlay. Similarly, while ideally the function of management should presumably have been mainly the preserve of the joint-farmer, since he was the operator, in practice, if we are to judge by Naẓmi, the capital owner took an active part in it. At Zar'een in particular it was often Naẓmi who sold the produce, assigning the joint-farmers and croppers their shares, and he who bought supplies and debited his partners.

A revealing example of the extent to which Naẓmi took the financing upon himself is afforded by one of the six joint-farms he operated at 'Arrābeh in 1933/34—with Shlāsh Hājj Rajā Abou Ṣalāḥ.[2] When it was set up, presumably in the fall of 1933, Naẓmi assigned to it six oxen assessed at an aggregate £P22.250 (two of them had apparently been bought for the purpose at the livestock markets of Jenin and Tulkarm) and a work horse and mare worth £P16.800; all Shlāsh had were an ox, a cow, a horse and a donkey valued together at £P14.950. The partnership was on a 1:1 basis (Shlāsh was to own half the capital) and each partner's share was accordingly entered at £P27.160.[3] Naẓmi shouldered the difference of £P12.210.[4] By April 8, 1934, Shlāsh had borrowed seed, split straw and cash to the tune of an additional £P25.030[5]. In return, he had delivered to Naẓmi £P11.810 in early grain and split straw, presumably from his share of the harvest then taking place. He had also laid out £P4.320 in capital expenses of which Naẓmi consequently owed him half. Accordingly, his debt had gone up to £P23.245.[6] This was the season for barley and wheat to come in but Shlāsh apparently intended to lay in the whole crop for his own use—it was poor, as we will see, and it came on top of three bad years—instead of paying off any more of his debt with it.[7] At all events, a promissory note was drawn up to Naẓmi for the whole £P23.245.[8] Thereupon Naẓmi began to charge him interest: in his accounts receivable of 1934, Shlāsh's debt is upped from £P23.240 to £P25.330. This was 9% p.a., the legal interest rate; the same was charged to another 'Arrābeh joint-farmer of Naẓmi's that year; in 1932 a joint-farmer had been debited 17½%, but an ordinance empowering the courts to reopen money-lending transactions involving interest higher than the legal rate had since been gazetted.[9]

Shlāsh borrowed another £P7 (possibly £P9) in instalments of £P1 to £P3 in the rest of April and in May, also pocketing £P2.250 as his share on an exchange of livestock and taking £P0.150 for harness collars and £P0.770 for a threshing drag from Naẓmi.[10] That season the farm also incurred £1P5.060 in mower fees and in wages to day-labour. After deduction of the croppers' quarter of the debt, Shlāsh owed half of the rest, or £P5.647½.[11] This presumably raised his debt to Naẓmi by £P13.567½ (or £P15.567½.)

This pattern was typical of Naẓmi's joint-farming in Zar'een and often in 'Arrābeh. To judge by Naẓmi's systematic debiting in all his accounts, a joint-farmer—perhaps in his capacity as the farm's actual operator—was supposed to disburse all of the farm's running expenses out of his pocket until the final accounting between the partners at the crop division upon conclusion of the threshing.[12] In practice, however, the capital owner apparently provided most of the stock, covered running expenses and kept his farmer in food through the season to boot. Once the crop was in, perhaps the joint-farmer was in a position to pay back those advances, cover a share of the season's expenses that was proportional to his holding of the capital, and perhaps even reduce the original debt; but during the season his outlay on the farm was far lower than the capital owner's, so that his return was proportionally far higher. To what extent was this true on the Shlāsh farm in 1933/34?

It seems well-nigh impossible to calculate Shlāsh's outlay directly, for Naẓmi's accounts were not kept with that object in mind. However, we do have for that season one account in which Naẓmi itemized £P110.640 he had laid out for Shlāsh's farm—work animals, seed, advances to his joint-farmer—until about the time Shlāsh's promissory note was drawn up.[13] Adding the later figures we have just reviewed, we find that Naẓmi invested at least £P129.855 on his behalf and Shlāsh's during the season, of which £P93.042½ was on his account alone.[14] Since they were 1:1 partners, and on the assumption Shlāsh invested nothing on Naẓmi's account beyond the figures included by Naẓmi, then Shlāsh must have laid out £P56.230 that season. This was only 42% as much as Naẓmi, and only 30% of the partners' joint investment instead of 50%.

What did those investments yield? The grain obtained by Naẓmi and Shlāsh that season is shown in the threshing-floor accounts between the parties.[15] To convert those earnings in kind into money we may refer to sales prices entered by Naẓmi in connection with that year's harvest on his various farms.[16] We may then calculate each party's return under the heads of rent, capital and labour.[17] The result is that Naẓmi received £P55.689 on his capital and Shlāsh £P55.539 on his.[18] Naẓmi got £P31.894 in rent-shares on his land, and Shlāsh £P12.880 on his. The croppers received £P41.579 in produce for their labour. The livestock of each partner in the *shadd* was worth £P24.910 at purchase prices, each having pocketed £P2.250 on an exchange of animals.

This still does not enable us to calculate rates of return accurately. We do not know in what months the seed, feed and cash put in by each of the partners were mobilized.[19] We cannot be sure that Naẓmi had not laid out other sums not included here, such as personal loans to croppers. We have no record of the tithes and property taxes on the farm that year, though we do know they were at least partly remitted.[20] We cannot tell the value of such unaccounted produce as milk, split straw, or vegetables grown for home consumption. The grain prices on which we have based our calculations are subject to some margin of error.[21]

Notwithstanding these qualifications, it cannot be disputed that the season had entailed far graver losses for Naẓmi than for his joint-farmer. He had mobilized at least £P133.620, or £P40 more than his nominal investment.[22] He had obtained (like Shlāsh) £P56 in crops (net of rent, which we did not include in the outlay since it was paid out of the crop receipts) and retained £P25 worth of livestock. Another £P38 remained uncollected as a loan to Shlāsh, would be unavailable to Naẓmi for at least another year, and was probably costing him twice as much in interest as the 9% he was charging Shlāsh for it.[23]

For Shlāsh it was the reverse situation. Even the £P56.230 at which we arrived indirectly as his outlay was in fact exaggerated. For one thing, it included £P11.810 in grain and split straw delivered in April, out of the new crop—a repayment, if anything, rather than an investment. Other such elements may have entered our sum. The only cash outlay we do know Shlāsh incurred was £P4.320; he had also, of course, contributed his livestock and an undetermined amount of seed. For the rest, even when he needed £P0.100 to shoe a horse he came to Naẓmi or to his agent; so did most of the other joint-farmers.[24]

There is indeed something arbitrary—yet essential, if we are to understand the import of the joint-farm for its capital owner 'investor'—about attempting to force these agrarian facts of life into the accounting patterns of capitalistic agriculture. What counted for Shlāsh was the plain fact that he had been in a weak economic position at the outset of the season—a few scraggy animals, some seed and perhaps not enough grain to last his family through the winter, was all he had—and that the joint-farm with Naẓmi had improved that position immeasurably. He had been tided over with easy credit. He had achieved a crop income of over £P55 on a very small actual outlay. The value of his capital holding had gone up from £P15 to £P25 in addition to £P2 pocketed in cash. His debt to Naẓmi stood at only £P40 including interest through the following summer, and even then there would be no urgency about repaying it. Finally, he had doubtless attained higher status by becoming the joint-farmer of the biggest landowner in the district.[25]

Needless to say, to Shlāsh his income of £P56 was not capital he would re-invest but grain needed to feed his family and sow his fields, so that the following season his indebtedness might rise higher. But this did not affect the striking contrast between what the joint-farm meant to the capital owner, for whom it represented a losing operation with the added disadvantage of tying up further capital in high-risk, low-return personal loans to peasants, and to the joint-farmer, to whom it had yielded capital gain on easy credit plus prestige and a degree of economic security. Given a modicum of farming prosperity, the joint-farmer was, in such circumstances, inevitably on his way to the ownership of more capital.[26]

Such financing of the joint-farmer by the capital owner was probably an integral feature of most joint-farms. The accounts of Husayn Najeeb

'Aṭāri with Ibrāhīm Khateeb at Soulam in 1922 to which we referred in Part I also show that within a few months of setting up the joint-farm Husayn had advanced to Ibrāhīm an additional £E20.810 in cash, sesame seed, wheat for his household and money to sharpen ploughshares and to purchase a new plough.[27]

Three of the six joint-farms that Naẓmī operated at 'Arrābeh in 1933/34 were founded that season, so that the accounts involving them list all stock acquisitions and other purchases along with the prices paid, making it possible to calculate the year's profits and losses with the same degree of accuracy as on the Shlāsh farm.[28] In both we find the same burden of financing by the capital owner and the same ultimate financial loss. To what extent were those two features typical of joint-farms at 'Arrābeh in the 1930's?[29]

As far as financing went, we have already mentioned that by 1934 three diastrous seasons had left the peasant with no resources to spare for any outlay, so that it was up to the capital owner to put up all the funds needed to make a go of the farm. This did not necessarily apply everywhere. At Zar'een, to be sure, all of Naẓmī's farms fitted this pattern. In 'Arrābeh, however, we have many cases of joint-farmers pulling their own weight. One of these was Ali Maḥmoud Abou Jalboush, whose accounts with Naẓmī for 1930 are typical. 'Ali seems to have covered expenses on the farm as they came along, and at the same time Naẓmī kept up a stream of £P2, £P3 and £P5 remittances to him so that the end of the season saw 'Ali owing Naẓmī exactly £P2.160.[30] A similar pattern characterized Naẓmī's joint-farms with Muḥammad Hasan Ali, his agent in 'Arrābeh and a merchant in his own right who had cash even in bad years. Clearly, the joint-farm did not always demand of the landlord heavy subsidies to the joint-farmer and the croppers. But it rarely seems to have involved profits—at least, not in the 1930's.

THE PROFITABILITY OF FARMING

From 1929 to 1936 Arab farming in Palestine, traditionally afflicted by poor yields and a high burden of indebtedness, went through a period of extreme hardship well calculated to discourage investors thoroughly owing to a combination of consecutive crop failures with the competition of agricultural imports seeking entry at depressed world prices.[31] At the same time, the national economy prospered, affording the rural population relief from the farm problem through expanding employment in the colonial sector and the urban economy. But this only served to underscore the apparent senselessness of investment in the hill country's agriculture at a time of remunerative alternative uses for capital. The position of 'Abdul Hādī landowners who had capital tied up in joint-farms in their ancestral village was no different.

We were able to draw up a time series of wheat yields for one of Naẓmī's joint farms in the village—probably the one that was closest to his heart—for the seasons 1933/34 through 1937/38 by juxtaposing the amounts set aside for seed each year with the following year's crop.[32] The results (to the nearest *kayl*) are as follows:

| Season | Kayls Set Aside For Seed | Kayls Harvested | Yield Ratio |
|---|---|---|---|
| 1933/34 | 26 | 83 | 3.2:1 |
| 1934/35 | 35 | 175 | 5.0:1 |
| 1935/36 | 32 | 145 | 4.5:1 |
| 1936/37 | 35 | 177 | 5.0:1 |
| 1937/38 | 29 | 54 | 1.9:1 |
| Five-Year Average | 31.4 | 126.8 | 4.0:1 |

No other farm produced such a complete series, but data for individual farms over spans of one or two years confirmed the above yields fully. So did the recollections of Naẓmī's agent in 'Arrābeh, and also the yield ratios Naẓmī himself compiled in his notebooks.[33] Further, we may assume that yields at any one of his farms, unless it was unusually badly managed, were representative of his lands as a whole. for it was his practice to apportion his 'Arrābeh lands among his various joint-farms in such a manner as to give each of them parcels in as many types of land as possible.[34]

In 1933/34, then—the year on which our analysis of the Shlāsh farm is based—yields were indeed below average. For Palestine as a whole it was not a bad farm year, but in certain districts, particularly in Samaria, hot and dry winds in the spring and attacks of *Scythris temperatella* did considerable damage.[35] 'Arrābeh must have been in one of those districts. But the figures in our table are eye-opening with respect to the whole time series.

Naẓmī's notebooks provide us with plentiful data on livestock and crop prices, on equipment and repair costs, on financing patterns and tenure arrangements from 1919 to 1920 and from 1927 to 1941. However, the three farms that were founded in 1933/34 are the only ones for which lists of purchase prices are provided. We cannot therefore compute returns directly for any other year.[36] But there is nothing to prevent us from projecting our findings for 1933/34 to the whole five-year time series for which we have consecutive wheat yields, for prices did not in fact vary greatly between 1933 and 1938. Assuming little departure from the standard stock required on a farm the type of Shlāsh's, we may construct the following schematic table if $C(1+r)^t = P$, where C is the original capital, r the rate of return and P the product, with t arbitrarily set at one:

| Season | Original Capital | Yield Ratio | Crop Value | Product | | Return |
|---|---|---|---|---|---|---|
| 1933/34 | £P93.5 | 3.2:1 | £P56 | £P25 + £P56 | = £P81 | —12.8% |
| 1934/35 | £P93.5 | 5.0:1 | £P83 | £P25 + £P83 | = £P108 | 15.5% |
| 1935/36 | £P93.5 | 4.5:1 | £P74.7 | £P25 + £P74.7 | = £P99.7 | 6.6% |
| 1936/37 | £P93.5 | 5.0:1 | £P83 | £P25 + £P83 | = £P108 | 15.5% |
| 1937/38 | £P93.5 | 1.9:1 | £P32 | £P25 + £P32 | = £P57 | —39.0% |
| Five-Yr. Ave. | £P93.5 | 4.0:1 | £P70 | £P25 + £P70 | = £P95 | 1.6% |

This demonstrates how pitifully low was the rate of return that an investor could expect on a joint-farm at 'Arrabeh in the 1930's—even where the joint-farmer took up his share of the burden of financing and no loans had to be provided to the peasants, which would have reduced the return even more. But the above table must not be taken as more than a schematic presentation. For one thing, it is based on the yield of wheat, which accounted for only about two-fifths of the product value at the Shlāsh farm in 1934. For another, in very good years the revenue rose far beyond what the improvement in wheat yields suggests, for then it became possible to produce sesame, the district's cash crop *par excellence*, on most of the fallow half of the farm's acreage. At the same time, such very good years were rare, at least in the 1930's, when Nazmi's income from sesame at 'Arrābeh averaged out over the decade to only about £P10 per farm p.a.

We have no doubt that low output was at the core of the joint-farm's economic difficulties. Back in the 1880's the Palestinian fellah's crop was said to average sixfold; twelvefold was considered very good.[37] In 1930 the Johnson-Crosbie Committee investigating the economic condition of agriculturists collected estimates for average wheat yields that ranged from 57 to 86 kg. per dunam (1000 sq. m.)[38] At standard sowing rates this meant a countrywide all-time average yield ranging between 3.5:1 and 5.5:1. On 'Arrābeh's fertile plain yields should have been higher: indeed, one veteran farmer insisted that in good years in the Mandatory period the crop had exceeded the equivalent of a ton per acre (a twelvefold yield, at traditional seeding rates) while another, with a reputation as an expert agriculturist, still put it at three-quarters of a ton.[39] Yet Nazmi's joint-farm yields, on his excellent land, had not exceeded fivefold even in the bountiful years of 1935 and 1937.[40]

The eye of the master feeds the flock. Ascribing this poor record to the carelessness and mismanagement that went with absentee landlordism, the expert agriculturist from 'Arrābeh quoted the fellah adage, 'He profits in farming whose plough-ox is the son of his own cow and whose ploughman is the son of his own wife'.[41] The landowner's profit per acre clearly dropped as he moved along the continuum that we have traced from family farm to joint-farm. A family farmer took the entire product for himself—if he had no debts—paying out only a few pennies for harvest hands and woman weeders. When he took on croppers he did not just give up one-fourth of the crop to them: he also faced a drop in income due to ignorance, indifference and pilfering on their part. The disadvantages grew more pronounced in the joint-farm stage, for the landowner forewent a further substantial share of the crop and, at the same time, by abandoning day-to-day control of the farm, courted further deterioration yet retained in practice the burden of financing the operation and, to top it all, supplied personal credit to croppers and joint-farmer alike. In 1934 Nazmi 'Abdul Hādi, owed £P1595.635 to all his creditors and was charged on it an average interest rate of 9%.[42] Of the £P785.345 that he held as against this in accounts receivable, £P360.300 was owed to him by joint-farmers and croppers. Of this, on £P303.360 he apparently received no interest that year.[43]

One evident reason for the popularity of the joint-farm in 'Arrābeh until the 1930's was that its partnership structure provided flexible financing for the under-equipped and poorly managed subsistence farm of Northern Samaria in its attempt to withstand the challenges of the age of the modern market. But even the joint-farm was not equipped for the crisis

in field-crop farming that hit the country in the 1930's, when the mobiliza-
tion of new resources became an annual necessity rather than an occasional
stopgap. And so, many of the 'Abdul Hādī family's absentee owners pulled
out of joint-farming one by one, and in the late 1930's Naẓmī was one of
but a few still joint-farming at 'Arrābeh. Clearly, it was not the prospect
of easy earnings that kept him at it until his death in 1942.[44] Yet every year
between 1932 and 1942 he operated seven to nine joint-farms there and at
Zar'een.[45]

While it is difficult to entertain an economic motivation for this, a social
and political explanation is not far to seek. 'Arrābeh was the cradle of the
'Abdul Hādīs, the anchor of their political support in the entire region,
the home base on which they fell back again and again in time of trouble.
When they lost the governorship of a town in the power play of mid-19th
century Ottoman administration, it is to 'Arrābeh that they temporarily
repaired. When, during the 'Revolt of the Bands' of 1938, they decided to
resist the pressure of the bands for contributions, it is 'Arrābeh which,
alone, stood up to the entire surrounding countryside and, equipped with
British arms, earned the label of traitor to the national cause to support
them. Within 'Arrābeh's complex social and political structure of clans
and social classes, there was constant jockeying for influence between the
major 'Abdul Hādī branches and personalities of each period, some based
in Jenin and others in Nablus, through most of the years between 1840 and
1948. At times, when there were two recognized 'Abdul Hādī camps
headed by competing personalities—at the turn of the century, for instance—the struggle within 'Arrābeh assumed critical proportions and
blood flowed among the peasantry, with resultant out-migrations that have
etched themselves on the village's social and demographic history. Small
wonder, then, if the joint-farm, perfect opportunity for a patron-client
relationship, assumed pivotal importance as a lever of influence in such
circumstances. Its establishment was, indeed, a crucial stage in the evolution of a local sheikly family into an absentee class exercising its economic
and political control of the home village in new ways.

SHARE-RENT FARMING
We noted in Part I of this article that the concept of a compact of co-
cultivation (muzāra'a) took in a whole range of forms of association, each
of which allotted the factors of production differently but always in such a
manner that one party contributed the land and another the labour. We
reviewed two such forms: cropping and joint-farming. We shall now deal
with the most common of these arrangements: the share-rent association,
in which one party supplied the land alone, for which he got a rent-share
of the crop, and the other party contributed his own or hired labour, as
well as seed, animals and tools.[46]

This was so much the best-known of the muzāra'a contracts in modern
Palestine that the share-rent farmer was commonly designated 'co-
cultivator' (muzāri'); he was also, along with the joint-farmer, referred to
as 'partner' (shareek).[47] As we saw in Part I, neither of those terms applied
to the cropper (harrāth) who owned nothing but his hands and whose
compact with his employer was farther removed from the notion of

partnership.

Writing in 1891, Post rendered the share-rent association as partnership in land'; the English translation of the Ottoman Civil Code renders the *muzāra's* as 'partnership in land and work.'[48] Both terms are closer to the reality of the share-rent relationship than are such words as sharecropper or share tenant which connote an inferiority of status that did not always apply. In 'Arrābeh for instance, during the exodus to town that began in the 1930's villagers of all classes rented out their land on shares, and among the takers were not only landless peasants but also prosperous farmers seeking to expand their operations who were often wealthier than their landlords.[49]

Statistically, the relationship in which it was the landlord who had the upper hand was by far the more significant. Palestine was not a land of great estates. As a rule, property consisted of scattered units of relatively modest size, and since yields were low, no great fortunes were built on rural domains; but a few families did control large aggregate areas as between their various branches—notably the 'Abdul Hādis with a total of about 15,000 acres.[50] The share-rent farm was understandably the leading form of tenure on such estates, the landowners often providing free housing and other facilities.[51] But among resident owners the share-rent farm was rare, in 'Arrābeh at least. If they did not cultivate their land themselves, they preferred operation by croppers of some form of joint farming.

In view of the disparity of power between large landlords and their tenants, one may well ask wherein lay the 'partnership' between them. The answer will become apparent if we contrast the share-rent farm with the cash-rent lease that has gradually been taking its place—in 'Arrābeh since about 1935.[52] The villagers discuss the share-rent (*qism*) in terms of the values of justice and trust. They point out that it is fairer than a cash rent (*damān*) since it reflects the considerable fluctuations that take place in crop yields. When they are asked whether it has survived anywhere, they give you a list of men who still farm 'Abdul Hādi land on shares 'because they are trustworthy.'[53] Cash rents, on the other hand, are discussed in terms of monetary advantage: one is told how landowners were able to demand their rent in cash during the Second World War because of soaring prices and higher farm profits, and especially after 1948 and the flow of refugees that it brought; how the peasants for their part tried harder under cash leases than under share-rent farming, knowing that the whole of the extra income they might make would be theirs; how the economy profited because peasants who paid cash rents took better care of the land.[54]

But the distinction between the money lease and share-rent farming went considerably beyond the values that they embodied and into very practical differences. While under a lease the tenant was authorized to sublet the land at a profit, a share-rent farmer who sub-farmed out to others some of his land remitted to the landowner the whole of the rent-share he had collected for it, making him the landowner's trustee rather than a middleman.[55] And while a lease was a contract between two persons, a rent-share could be collected at the threshing-floor by any member of the landowner's family: I was told of the guardian of the young heirs to a considerable estate who switched to cash rents only because one of his wards would make the rounds of the farmers, collect advances on the rent-share, and spend them on drink. All in all, there was a telling contrast between the fiduciary and organic character of the share-rent association, in keeping with its character as an integral part of the crop-sharing compact, and the purely contractual, market-oriented cash tenancy that succeeded it.

We noted in Part I that under the Mandate the acknowledged factors of production held to collaborate in turning out the crop were four in number in Northern Samaria, and that the rent-share was accordingly one-fourth of the crop.[56] But about the turn of the century, as we saw, it was likely to have been one-fifth.[57] These shares applied to the valley land, where most of the share-renting took place. Hill land, shallower and much harder to cultivate, rated less. Plots within the village's built-up area— *jadr al-balad*, denoted in the Ottoman land registers as *köy civarina*—rated more because they were watered by sewage, manured by farm animals and much easier of access. Toward the close of the Mandate period, hill soils had gone up to one-fourth of the crop, and the better land in the Plain of 'Arrabeh to one-third.[58] The reason lay in that the prosperity of the Second World War had conspired to raise land values with the advent of tractor ploughing. The latter greatly alleviated a number of problems such as weed control, difficult access to many cultivated lands and, specifically in 'Arrabeh, the challenge posed by the heaviness of what is otherwise the best soil in the district.[59]

Many of the 'Abdul Hādi landowners who had moved out of 'Arrabeh and retained their land there chose to farm it out by rent-share contract rather than by joint-farming. By the 20th century, at which time the involvement of many branches of the family with the home village of yore had greatly decreased, the share-rent farm seems to have been by far the more prevalent. Even those who did set up joint-farms rented out some of their land on shares.[60] Naẓmi did so with his poorer land and less accessible plots.[61]

The transition from own management to share-renting was in any case not of one piece. Some of the absentee 'Abdul Hādis retained more or less direct management of their properties right down to 1948. Others went through the joint-farm as a stage. Others yet at first let out their lands gradually, parcelling them out to various share-rent farmers, but later, as their connections with the old village grew tenuous, consolidated all their land in it in a contract with a single farmer.[62] The recipient often allocated sub-farms from it to smaller operators.[63]

It goes without saying that in the rent-share association the landlord's responsibilities to his farmer were a good deal more restricted than in the joint-farm, which was after all a full partnership. Yet the absentee landlord who opted for the share-rent relationship could and did exercise patronage as unmistakably as the one who practiced joint-farming.[64] The normal share-rent contract in the district ran for two years. This was so because the traditional rotation was the two-field system, and one of the two years, during which several ploughings and weeding were required for the summer or rotation crop and left the soil in good tilth, was considered an investment in the other. But the 'Abdul Hādis retained their share-rent farmers for years, sometimes for decades.[65] What was more, several of our informants maintained that the 'Abdul Hādis contented themselves with lower rent shares than did other owners of land of similar quality; one villager pointed out that this concession was an encouragement to the kind of trustworthy farmers that an absentee landlord required, and one big 'Abdul Hādi landowner explained that he had always taken a little less than the going share from his farmer 'to keep him happy.'[66]

In other words, the 'Abdul Hādis were bidding for loyalty. Their concessions were a recognition of mutual dependence between each of them and the particular village families that farmed his land and were accordingly allied with him. One may conclude that the 'Abdul Hādis patronized their share-rent farmers by granting them greater security of tenure, and perhaps lower rents, just as they patronized their joint-farmers by giving them financing, and their croppers by allowing them a bigger share of the crop than the joint-farmers allowed them.

The motives were apparent. To begin with, in a community that bubbled over continuously with feuds and intrigues, an absentee landowner required at least one devoted family on the spot to safeguard his interests. The importance of this was shown during one of the feuds that erupted in 'Arrābeh between the two World Wars, pitting the village's powerful local sheikh against a big absentee landowner. Both were of the 'Abdul Hādi family. A central episode was the sheikh's 'removing his neighbour's landmark,' i.e. moving boundary stones in order to reduce his rival's property.[67] The landowner did not dare retaliate because he did not reside in the village and hence was not equipped to meet any situation that might arise.[68] Had he had trusted men of violence on the spot he might have acted through them.

This need for local supporters was accentuated by the local, regional and national political ambitions of many of the 'Abdul Hādis. Their farmers, along with other peasants they patronized, served as their eyes, their ears, their mouthpieces and their hands in the vital arena of influence that 'Arrābeh was to them.[69] And underpinning the whole relationship was the organic personal bond which had grown out of the 'Abdul Hādis' history as the village's sheikly family and later as 'its' *efendis:* a combination of considerations of power, profit and prestige, ties of affection and devotion, *noblesse oblige* and, last but not least, common pride in 'Arrābeh and its tradition of fighting and looting prowess.

## CONCLUSION

In modern society economic institutions must be approached in economic terms because the actions men take to provide for their livelihood are largely motivated by self-interest and rationally oriented to it. In a traditional society, a description of economic patterns may be couched in economic terms, but any meaningful analysis of economic life must make far-reaching allowance for non-economic desires and values and non-rational behaviour patterns that may have primacy even in those activities by which the livelihood of men is insured.

N

Communities moving from the traditional to the modern model occupy a middle ground in this respect. Analysis predicated on self-interest and some measure of rational behaviour will give us important insights into them but must suffer from unpredictable limitations. Historical research on such a community finds itself shadow-boxing much of the time: where is it sound to adduce rational economic motivation? Where could it be dangerously misleading? Due to the fragmentary nature of our information about the past, historical judgments are often so nicely balanced that a misreading of the evidence could vitiate the entire would-be reconstruction of a society.

With regard to crop-sharing economics in Northern Samaria under the British Mandate the evidence is indeed Janus-faced. The observer's conclusions can easily be coloured by unwarranted assumptions about the society with which he is dealing, and he may become the victim of his own framework in classifying his data. Granott, for instance, in his comprehensive study of the land system of Palestine, intimates there were only two kinds of landowners: those, presumably mainly Westerners, who were interested in the proper agricultural condition of their property, and those who speculated on the price of land by acquiring their properties and meantime ground the faces of the peasantry.[70] Nowhere in his conceptual scheme does there appear to be room for traditional aspects of landlordship such as seem to have obtained at 'Arrābeh and Zar'een.[71]

Clearly, we need to put some order into our assumptions about economic behaviour in rural Arab society in Palestine in the period of transition to the age of the modern market. Specifically, on our reading of the workings of the crop-sharing system in Northern Samaria, there are three aspects of modern economic behaviour that did not wholly apply to that society. The first is motivation by self-interest; the second is rationality in the pursuit of economic goals; the third is a belief in the rationality of economic activity. We believe that those are three cardinal respects in which the traditional agrarian Arab society of some more distant past had differed from modern industrial society. But since the interpretation of much human behaviour lies entirely in the beholder's eye, we cannot tell from our evidence to what extent agrarian relations at 'Arrābeh and Zar'een had moved along the continuum from that traditional model to the modern one.[72]

The traditional crop-sharing system was by definition *Gemeinschaft*, not *Gesellschaft*, but the organic mutuality with which it invested the notion of dependence may slip between the historian's fingers. What a traditional age treated as evidence of solidarity will today more likely be interpreted as enlightened self-interest to consolidate one's economic or political position. The financing Naẓmi 'Abdul Hādī provided for his joint-farmers may be viewed as a conscious bid to enlist entrepreneurs, or yet as an obligation of the power-seeking patron toward his client, rather than as the fulfilment of traditional solidary human relationships. The concessions the 'Abdul Hādīs granted their share-rent farmers can be considered entirely in terms of self-interest: I have myself mustered evidence for this in the course of this study.

But that evidence, it will be noted, is entirely circumstantial. Drawing a verdict on its basis in full historical conscience is another matter. If a capital owner on a joint-farm took losses repeatedly to keep his peasant partners on the farm, can this be wholly explained in terms of power and prestige? If a landlord granted his farmers reductions over accepted share-rents, to what extent was he buying political support, and to what extent was he proudly following a tradition of collaboration between his father and the farmer's father? Reciprocally, was the peasant's loyalty to him so mercenary that his political allegiance required cementing by economic advantages? Those are all intangibles, into which each of us will read as much self-interest as he pleases.

The second area in respect to which there is a see-sawing quality about our judgments is the rationality of action. To be able to explain agrarian relations in terms presupposing that each party pursued its advantage, we must first assume that the parties perceived their advantages and were, further, psychologically prepared for rational action in pursuing them. But this corresponded neither to the normative values of Arab culture, which placed a high premium on spontaneous and even improvident magnanimity and denounced calculation, nor to the existential traits of a national character that could give away a tract of land in a surge of generosity, sell it in a fit of spite, or set fire to it in a flush of anger.

Finally, neither perception of a rational course of action nor the ability to follow it suffice without some belief in its effectiveness. Before penetration by the cash economy spearheaded new ways of thinking and new motivations in Northern Samaria, croppers on adjacent farms gave little thought to differences in work loads, and even less to effective rates of remuneration, for those were givens to which they felt their actions were irrelevant. They saw no correlation between their toil and their standard of living: they were 'working for' bread, as they would have said in Arabic, not 'earning their' bread, as we would say in English. In urban employment, on the other hand, and, beginning in the 1930's, in those areas where the rural economy was expanding to meet the build-up of demand generated in the cities and in the implanted sector, rewards did bear a relation to inputs: a reorientation of goals and behaviour patterns was inevitable, and it proceeded quickly as of the Second World War.

Asked why the 'Abdul Hādis had largely switched to cash rents in the 1930's, an 'Arrābeh villager explained: 'Because they realized that they were being robbed.' In other words, during the century when 'Abdul Hādi land had been farmed out on share-rent, either there had been no cheating or else it had been irrelevant to a network of relationships quite impervious to mechanistic accounting. But then the village had tasted of the Tree of Knowledge:

And the eyes of them both were opened, and they knew that they were naked; and they sewed fig-leaves together, and made themselves aprons.

The Arab villager of Palestine was ready to take his place in modern society.

NOTES

1. *Notebooks* of Naẓmī Ḥājj Tawfeeq 'Abdul Hādī, Vol. AIC, p. 134 ('Arrābeh, 1938.) Those capital expenses were termed 'private' (*maṣāreef khāṣṣa*) in order to distinguish them from the 'joint expenditure' on day-labour wages to which the croppers had to contribute (see Part I of this article).

2. Five of the six farms were Naẓmī's own (*Notebooks*, Vol. AIV, pp. 261, 257, 253, 245.) On the sixth (*Notebooks*, Vol. M, pp. 1-9) he was apparently agent for the capital owner who was his father-in-law. The fact that Shlāsh required consistent financing is instructive, for he was among 'Arrābeh's rather more prosperous peasants: he owned 7½ acres under olives, 2 acres of good and 11 acres of poor field crop land (Jenin Property Tax Office, 1935 Rural Property Tax Distribution Lists, Registers for 'Arrābeh, Vol. IV, Folio 71) as well as 6-7 acres of manured and watered plots within the village's built-up area, according to his son Qāsim of 'Arrābeh.

3. The discrepancy was apparently due to an arithmetic error of £P0.050 that was corrected by spring, as can be seen.

4. *Notebooks*, AIV, p. 296.

5. Of this, £P13.275 was accounted for by over a ton of wheat purchased from or through Naẓmī at £P0.900 per *kayl*, (see Part I of this article, n. 25) i.e. well above the average wholesale prices of £P10.500 and 9.600 officially recorded for 1933 and 1934 respectively (Palestine Office of Statistics, *Statistical Abstract of Palestine, 1936*, Jerusalem, 1937, p. 59) and 50% more than the prices paid on the farm at harvest time in 1934 (see below, n. 16). The wheat was probably for seed: on p. 287 Naẓmī lists an acquisition of seed for himself at the same price. It was probably purchased from his own stores (selected wheat, purchased outside, would probably have been entered as *zaree'a*) so that the profit he made on it as a trader must be borne in mind as a compensatory element for the depressive influence it exerted on his rate of return as a farmer; and he would have achieved this same profit had he sold the wheat to anyone else, since at the time the farm purchased it—presumably in the winter—it must have been the going price.

6. *Notebooks*, AIV, pp. 297, 296.

7. Palestine, *Annual Report of the Department of Agriculture and Forests for the Year Ending March, 1934*, Jerusalem 1934, p. 18.

8. *Notebooks*, AI, p. 297.

9. *Notebooks*, AII, p. 237; AIV, p. 411; Usurious Loans Ordinance No. 20 of 1934, Leon Rotenberg, ed., *Laws of Palestine, 1934-35*, Vol. I, Tel Aviv 1936, pp. 342-343. Interest is severely forbidden in Islam, and in Northern Samaria there are persons in all walks of life who will to this day have nothing to do with it in any form although many ways of evading the ban have been available through the centuries. It is likely that, in Islam as in Europe, it is this prohibition that was responsible for the popularity of the commenda and other such institutions. But under the French-patterned Ottoman Code of Commerce, promulgated in 1850 for the convenience of Western businessmen and of those who dealt with them, interest was perfectly legal (cf. George Young, *Corps de droit Ottoman*, Vol. VII, Oxford 1906, p. 70n.) and Ottoman laws continued in effect under the British Mandate unless specifically amended or repealed. The legal rate of 9% on ordinary and commercial debts dated back to 1887 (C. A. Hooper, *The Commercial Law of Iraq and Palestine*, Baghdad 1929, pp. 226-227); higher rates were illegal; but unofficially usually flourished (cf. Elihu Grant, *The People of Palestine*, Philadelphia 1921 ed., pp. 205-206). Under the Mandate 30% p.a. was very common and 50% for three months not unusual (Government of Palestine, *Report by Mr C. F. Strickland of the Indian Civil Service on the Possibility of Introducing a System of Agricultural Co-operation in Palestine*, 1930, n. p., p. 2; Government of Palestine, *Report of A Committee on the Economic Condition of Agriculturists in Palestine*, Jerusalem 1930, p. 42; cf. John Hope Simpson, *Palestine: Report on Immigration, Land Settlement and Development*, London 1930, Cmd. 3686 of 1930, p. 68). The rate of interest that members of the 'Abdul Hādī family seemed to charge each other most often, to judge by NaЕm.'s records, was 15-17½% in the 1930's (*Notebooks*, AII, pp. 263, 242, 209) but the women of the family, who acted as repositories of cash as well as of real property for their brothers and nephews in line with the patrilineality of the Arab family, often charged them from 15% down to 10% and 6% (*Notebooks*, AII, pp. 282-283, 279, 242). The interest that Naẓmī charged others seems to have varied greatly, depending not only on his relationship with

the borrower but also, it seems, on economic conditions affecting the latter's ability to pay: in the bad year of 1934 he appears to have remitted the interest charges due him on nearly all his accounts with peasants (see *Notebooks*, AII, pp. 237-238) except one case that seems to have involved a lawsuit (*Notebooks*, AII, p. 166).

10. *Notebooks*, AIV, p. 269.

11. *Ibid.*, p. 246.

12. See Part I of this article, n. 32.

13. *Notebooks*, AIV, p. 287.

14. Adding to the £P110.640 the £P7.920 representing the minimum advanced to Shlâsh after that and the £P15.060 in mower fees and daily wages, we get a total outlay of £P133.620 on Nazmi's part. Of this, we saw, Shlâsh owed an aggregate £P36.812* (or more) before interest, and the croppers £P3.675.

15. *Notebooks*, AIV, pp. 249-247. The crops entered were, in order of value, wheat, barley, Indian millet (*Sorghum cernuum*, in Arabic *durra baydã*, grown in 'Arrâbeh largely in years of poor or late rain, mainly as a substitute for wheat) vetch (*Vicia ervilia*, in Arabic *kersenneh*, grown for its grain and used for feed), lentils and chickpeas.

16. *Notebooks*, AIV, pp. 297, 249 and 248 for vetch, lentils and chickpeas respectively, on the farm with Shlâsh; p. 268 for barley and millet on the farm with Muhammad 'Ali 'Abdurraheem in 'Arrâbeh; pp. 267-266 for wheat received in share-rent at Sandala in the Plain of Esdraelon and sold probably in Jenin. For all the crops except wheat the prices obtained from the above accounts seem to be the prices at harvest-time, and if there were any minor differences in time or as between farms they probably did not exceed a few percent. For wheat, however (which at the price of £P0.600 per *kayl* used in our table accounts for about two-fifths of the farm's income) our margin of error may easily be 10% or more. £P0.600 appears to be the first price at which Nazmi sold the wheat from Sandala after the harvest; but at Sandala it ripens earlier than in the hills, and an entry lower down the same page of accounts shows a sale price of £P0.550 per *kayl* which may for all we know be closer to the price that ruled by the time wheat ripened at 'Arrâbeh. The average wholesale price in Palestine that year was £P9.600 per metric ton (see above, n. 5) i.e. ca. £P0.750 per *kayl*.

17. To arrive at these figures we followed the principles of crop division that emerge from Nazmi's accounts and that we summarized in Part I. There was, first, that part of the farm where the land belonged to Nazmi. Here the crop division figures on pp. 249-247 show that for each crop the heap of grain obtained on the threshing-floor was divided into two equal halves, one for Nazmi and one for Shlâsh and the croppers together. This was so because that is how the principles of crop division described earlier (Part I, pp. 14-15) work out where the rent-share is one-fourth and the capital holding ratio between capital owner and joint-farmer happens to be 1:1. There is no indication in the accounts of how the second heap was divided between Shlâsh and the croppers, which we need to know in order to find out his return on his outlay. But we know Shlâsh's rent payment to Nazmi was one-fourth of Shlâsh's portion and therefore worked out to 4/32 of the net crop (i.e. after payment of external obligations); that the croppers got one-fourth of what remained for Shlâsh's portion, giving them 3/32 of the net crop, plus a full one-fourth of Nazmi's portion for another 4/32, making their aggregate share of the crop 7/32; and that after the two deductions for rent and for the croppers Shlâsh was therefore left with 9/32 of the net crop, which checks with the threshing-floor assignment of a heap of half the net crop to him and the croppers together.

How, now, are we to establish Nazmi's return on his capital? We must divide his heap of half the net crop into three discrete components: what he got in rent on Shlâsh's half of the crop, which, as we have just seen, was 4/32; what Nazmi should have paid himself in rent on his own half of the crop; and the rest, which would be what his capital had earned. Since Nazmi paid no rent to himself in his accounts, it is up to us to select the principle on the basis of which we shall determine the rent. Should it be a full fourth of Nazmi's half of the net crop—even though he, unlike Shlâsh, already paid out a full fourth to the croppers? Or should it be a fourth of what remained after his payment of that full fourth—even though that would mean charging Nazmi a lower rent (3/32 of the net crop) than Shlâsh paid? We opted for the latter course because it seems more consistent with the basic principle of a partnership—equal returns on the capital owner's and the joint-farmer's equal capital holdings in the farm—as well as with the historical evolution that did in fact take place in 1936, when the labour share supplanted the rent-share in primacy and the latter was determined by the principle we have chosen here (see Part I, p. 17).

As for the part of the farm where the land belonged to Shlāsh, in keeping with the principles we discussed (in part I, pp. 13-15) one-fourth of the crop was allotted to Shlāsh, one-fourth of the remainder went to the croppers, and the rest was divided equally between Naẓmi and Shlāsh.

The results may be summarized as follows (on the land belonging to Shlāsh only wheat, barley and vetch were grown that season):

| | Wheat | Barley | Indian Millet | Vetch | Lentils | Chick-peas | Total |
|---|---|---|---|---|---|---|---|
| Price used as basis for calculations, £P per *kayl* (see n. 114) | .600 | .320 | .300 | .560 | .840 | .500 | |
| Income on Naẓmi's land, £P: | 52.425 | 26.213 | 31.675 | 15.178 | 11.615 | 9.145 | 145.801 |
| Croppers' share (7/32) | 11.468 | 5.734 | 6.992 | 3.321 | 2.442 | 2.000 | 31.894 |
| Shlāsh's capital share (9/32) | 14.744 | 7.372 | 8.909 | 4.268 | 3.140 | 2.573 | 41.006 |
| Naẓmi's est. rent share (7/32) | 11.468 | 5.734 | 6.929 | 3.321 | 2.442 | 2.000 | 31.894 |
| Naẓmi's est. cap. share (9/32) | 14.744 | 7.372 | 8.909 | 4.268 | 3.140 | 2.573 | 41.006 |
| Income on Shlāsh's land, £P: | 29.450 | 12.800 | | 9.520* | | | 51.770* |
| Shlāsh's rent share (1/4) | 7.300 | 3.200 | | 2.380 | | | 12.880 |
| Croppers' share (3/16) | 5.500 | 2.400 | | 1.785 | | | 9.685 |
| Shlāsh's capital share (9/32) | 8.250† | 3.600 | | 2.683 | | | 14.533 |
| Naẓmi's capital share (9/32) | 8.400† | 3.600 | | 2.683 | | | 14.683 |
| Total net income in £P, by crop | 81.875 | 39.013 | 31.675 | 24.698 | 11.165 | 9.145 | 197.571 |

*Our cash value equivalents for the shares do not work out to exact fractions of the whole because the crop was divided in kind to the nearest *thumniyya* (see Part I, n. 25).

†Some of the wheat came from a field where the sharers divided the crop before threshing. Upon threshing Naẓmi found he had 3/8 of the grain instead of 9/32 (*Notebooks*, AIV, p. 247). Our cash values have been adjusted accordingly.

18. The reason for the difference is the small wheat field that was divided before threshing (see end of previous footnote).

19. Even if we knew the time of the investments, at this stage it is not possible to tell in what direction pressure was exerted on the rate of return when an investor's capital was mobilized in the wintertime rather than held available since summer. It is true that both money and grain were of little use in farming before the approach of winter, when their prices rose; but this probably did not apply to livestock, the prices of which apparently fluctuated, with feeding costs a factor precisely in the fall. On the other hand, the interest-free credit that was built into the village economy at the private, retail and wholesale level, and the persistence of barter, may have greatly mitigated many of these factors. The village lived on an annual cycle and the economy was still geared to that.

20. See Part I, n. 9. Beginning in 1927 a 'commuted tithe' gradually replaced the tithe that had been assessed each year. Under the new system, each farmer's annual payment was to be the average of the tithes his farm had paid in the four years preceding the introduction of the commuted tithe into the district; but owing to the bad harvests and low farm prices of the 1930's, payment was repeatedly waived or partly remitted (A. Granovsky, *The Fiscal System of Palestine*, Jerusalem 1935, pp. 160-167). In 1933/34 the summer crop payment was wholly remitted and the remission on the winter crop payment was set at 25% and up depending on the village (Palestine, *Memoranda Prepared by the Government of Palestine for the use of the Palestine Royal Commission*, Vol. I, (Jerusalem 1936?) p. 51). If Naẓmi paid any winter tithe, it may have gone unrecorded here because no sesame was harvested. Naẓmi's property taxes that year are listed in his accounts but not broken down by farms, for in 'Arrābeh it was the landlord who paid them and we may neglect them here since we are dealing with Naẓmi's return on his capital, not on his land. In Zar'een not only the tithe but also the property tax was pro-rated among all the sharers in the crop (*Notebooks*, AIV, p. 276).

21. For the margin of error in our crop price estimates see n. 16 above. The reader will note we made no allowance for depreciation of the livestock: we assumed some animals grew stronger as others grew older, and the stock renewed itself.

22. See n. 14 above.

23. See n. 9 above and p. 181 below.

24. *Notebooks*, AIV, p. 297. Absentee landowners in the villages of Northern Samaria had recourse to cousins, friends and clients to disburse money to their farmers and generally represent their interests. See Part I, n. 42.

25. We do not include the rent that Shlāsh got for his land in this list of benefits: he would have found some alternative use for it if he had not set up the joint-farm with Naẓmi, for 'Arrābeh's good lands are said to have remained cultivated even in years of heavy out-migration.

26. See Part I, pp. 11-12.

27. Accounts of Ḥusayn Najeeb 'Aṭāri (courtesy of his son Saleem Ḥusayn) entries for 1922.

28. This was a period of tenant changeovers for Naẓmi at 'Arrābeh as well as Zar'een. Some of these must have been sudden—witness the farm he had operated at 'Arrābeh for years with the sons of Maḥmoud Abou Jalboush, to judge by the entries of 1932 in his books. There are accounts for the early crops—lentils and grain vetch—and even after the barley had been threshed it appears the parties had no intimation of impending dissolution, for they put away seed for the following year. Yet the horses had barely eaten a quarter of a ton of barley before the partnership was terminated (*Notebooks*, AIV, p. 324). There are no records of division of the wheat crop, leading one to suspect the initiative was the joint-farmers' and they thereby forfeited their share. The Abou Jalboush farm does not reappear in Naẓmi's notebooks.

29. For all we know, at Zar'een the economics of farming were different and operations more profitable. We have no lists of purchase values for stock and seed at any of the farms there.

30. *Notebooks*, AIV, pp. 415-413.

31. For documentation on the problems of Arab farming in Palestine in the 1930's see Government of Palestine, *Report of A Committee . . .*, pp. 2-27, 39-46; Hope Simpson, pp. 60-73; Palestine, *Memoranda Prepared . . .*, Vol. I, pp. 42-43; Vol. II, pp. 29-30; A. Granovsky, *The Fiscal . . .*, pp. 42-45, 165, 168-171; Montague Brown, 'Agriculture', in Sa'id B. Himadah, ed., *Economic Organization of Palestine*, Beirut 1938, pp. 129-130; (Government of Palestine), *A Survey of Palestine for the Information of the Anglo-American Committee of Inquiry*, Vol. I, Jerusalem 1946, pp. 272-289. Very pertinent, if in places somewhat influenced by the prosperity of the Second World War, are the following sections of the 'Survey of Social and Economic Conditions in Arab Villages, 1944' in Palestine, Office of Statistics, *General Monthly Bulletin of Current Statistics of Palestine;* July 1945, pp. 426-440; December, 1945, pp. 745-764; January-March, 1946, pp. 46-56; October, 1946, pp. 554-573; comments in *A Survey of Palestine . . .*, Vol. III, Jerusalem 1946, pp. 1197-1213.

32. *Notebooks*, pp. 282, 260, 202, 172, 160. This was the joint farm with Muḥammad Ḥasan 'Ali. It must be borne in mind that the amount set aside for seed was the planning for the following season, not necessarily the amount that turned out to be actually sown. On the face of it the planning would tend to be met, for it was always in terms of amounts of seed and not of physical area (see Part I, pp. 8-9) so that the cropper would be expected to sow until the seed ran out; but as he broadcast and the rate depended on his habit and judgment at times the amount allotted did not suffice for the land available, or vice-versa (Mr. Muḥammad Ḥasan 'Ali, January 4, 1970). In the former case the land left over was sometimes added to the part of the rotation reserved, depending mainly on the rainfall, for summer crops, legumes or fallow; but sometimes it was seeded with wheat acquired beyond the amount originally put side, in which case yields were even lower than our calculations show. Where there was seed left over, this might have been due to the cropper's low seeding rate, in which case our bias was downward; but it is more likely that part of the allotted seed went unused because drought or heavy rain made it impractical to prepare enough land or to sow what was originally envisaged; the margin of error would then on the face of it still be on the side of understating the actual yields; but this would be true only in the narrow sense of yields *per acre sown*, as the crop *per farm* dropped sharply, of course, in such disaster years.

For some implications of yield ratios see B. H. Slicher van Bath, *The Agrarian History of Western Europe, A.D. 500-1850*, Arnold 1963, pp. 18-23 and appendices.

33. The agent, Mr. Muḥammad Ḥasan 'Ali, discussed yields in general with me quite independently of the data concerning the joint farm with him in Naẓmi's notebooks, which he had not consulted. He put a good crop of wheat such as was attained once in two or three years in those days at the equivalent of 1000 lbs. per acre, and a poor crop at about half of that (October 8, 1969). This made the average yield in good year 6:1 and in poor ones 3:1, for as noted +in Part I, the *kayl* weighed about 175lbs. and one

*kayl* of wheat was seeded over an area of more or less one acre (according to Mr. Muḥammad Ṣâleḥ Muṣliḥ of 'Arrâbeh on December 16, 1969, seeding quantities under the Mandate had ranged from one *kayl* to three-quarters of an acre in shallow hill soil all the way down to one *kayl* to an acre and a quarter where the land was good and the farmer knew how to seed sparingly.) In Naẓmi's own table of yields for all his lands (*Notebooks*, AIV, pp. 6-7) the good land in the plain is designated as yielding sixfold, the very best land sevenfold, and hill land one-and-a-half or threefold. This was presumably based on an average year since the figures are so schematic. My special thanks go to Mr. Muḥammad Ṣâleḥ Muṣliḥ for figuring out, where all others had failed, that these unlabelled entries represented a table of yields.

34. In line with the principle of allotting to each cultivator indentical shares of each type of land that we noted in connection with the *mushâ'* (Part I of this article, p. 14) Naẓmi seems to have divided every plot he farmed (except for those that were smaller than roughly six acres, to judge by his seeding tables) into sections assigned to at least two different joint-farmers (see *Notebooks*, AIV, pp. 347 and 346 for such seeding tables for the 1932 and 1933 seasons in 'Arrâbeh.) The division was effected by mesauring off the parts with a rope, and the resultant parcels were rotated every other year. According to Mr. Muhammad Hasan 'Ali this was to promote competition between the croppers of 'rival' joint-farms to outdo each other in yields, for which the winners each received a tunic (*qumbaz*) of silk from Naẓmi (October 8, 1969).

35. Palestine, *Annual Report of the Department of Agriculture and Forests for the Year Ending March, 1935*, p. 18. *Scythris temperatella (al-doodeh)* is a wheat and barley worm that frequently infested the region.

36. Naẓmi's accounts for 1919 and 1920 also give full lists of investments with purchase values (*Notebooks*, AI, p. 25; AIV, pp. 10-15). The return on capital and, it appears, on the land as well, had also been low then, it seems; but those were years of rapidly shifting price levels from which one can hardly generalize.

37. Rev. F. A. Klein, 'Life, Habits, and Customs of the Fellahin of Palestine,' Palestine Exploration Fund, *Quarterly Statement*, 1883, p. 45; cf. Vital Cuinet, *Syrie Liban et Palestine—Géographie administrative, statistique, descriptive et raisonnée*, Paris 1896, pp. 345-346.

38. Government of Palestine, *Report of A Committee . . .*, p. 9. Official countrywide statistics (including Jewish agriculture) for crop areas and yields between 1935 and 1944 work out to much lower averages, due partly, presumably, to under-reporting and partly to the greater weight of the arid districts of Palestine in the countryside statistics than in the sample 104 villages where questionnaires were filled in for the 1930 Committee. The highest countrywide average in those ten years, in 1937, was 57 kg. per metric dunam; the lowest, in 1938, was 22 (Palestine Office of Statistics, *Statistical Abstract of Palestine*, 1939, Jerusalem 1940, p. 41).

39. Mr. Maḥmoud 'Abdul Fattâḥ 'Abdul Ghani, October 8, 1969; Mr. Muḥammad Ṣâliḥ Muṣliḥ, October 16, 1969. In the hill soils of the village threefold was considered a good average (Mr. Maḥmoud 'Abdul Fattâḥ, 'Abdul Ghani, July 7, 1970; cf. n. 33 above).

40. See above, pp. 11-12 and n. 33; Palestine, *Annual Report of the Department o Agriculture and Forests for the Year Ending March, 1936*, p. 21, and same for the year ending March, 1938, p. 5.

41. From Mr. Muḥammad Ṣâleḥ Muṣliḥ, May 31, 1970.

42. *Notebooks*, AII, p. 242.

43. *Ibid.*, pp. 237-238. See n. 9 and p. 178 above.

44. The Second World War, with its soaring demand for produce as well as for labour, changed all that, making farming more profitable and setting off a veritable revolution in all aspects of economic life. Landlords who had held on to their lands until then instead of succumbing to the temptation of selling them when they had brought in so little, proved far-sighted indeed.

45. It is apposite to ask whether two administrative reforms enacted in the 1930's might not have helped move landlords to continue joint-farming even when it had proved unremunerative. One of these was the unified Rural Property Tax enacted by ordinance in 1935 (for the clearest presentation see Palestine Office of Statistics, *General Monthly . . .* December 1945, pp. 747-748, 750; see also A. Granovsky, *The Fiscal . . .*, pp. 171-204); the other was the tightened-up *Cultivators (Protection) Ordinance* No. 37 of 1933 (text

in Moses Doukhan, ed., Laws of Palestine, 1933, Tel Aviv 1934, pp. 72-83). For the Rural Property Tax penalized non-cultivation by substituting a land tax for a system based mainly on crop taxation (n. 20 above) while tightened cultivator protection might have discouraged a landlord from renting out land—and therefore worked in favour of joint-farming it instead—for fear the rent-share farmer might become a 'statutory tenant' whom it would later prove impossible to remove (cf. Palestine, *Report of the Committee Appointed to Consider the Necessity of Amending the Cultivators (Protection) Ordinance*, Jerusalem 1943, pp. 3-6). However, landowners impelled by the Property Tax to keep their land under cultivation could do so equally well by taking share-rent farmers or lease tenants rather than joint-farmers. As for statutory cultivator protection, its main purpose was to protect tenants against eviction when ownership of the land was being transferred (Palestine, *Memoranda Prepared . . .*, Vol. I, p. 57—the secret memorandum on the 'Protection of Small Owners,' Vol. III, p. 13, makes this even clearer). In any case very little use was being made of the Ordinance in the hill country (*Ibid.*, Vol. I, p. 57).

46.   For a survey of the main features of this institution in the Levant see A. Latron, *La vie rurale en Syrie et au Liban*, Beirut 1936, pp. 48-58.

47.   Cf. Rev. George E. Post, 'Essays on the Sects and Nationalities of Syria and Palestine,' Palestine Exploration Fund, *Quarterly Statement*, 1891, pp. 105, 109.

48.   *Ibid.*, p. 109; C. A. Hooper, *The Civil Law of Palestine and Transjordan*, Vo. I, Jerusalem 1933, p. 369.

49.   From Mr. Muhammad Sâleh Muslih, May 31, 1970; cf. H. H. Mann, *The Social Framework of Agriculture*, Bombay 1967, pp. 92-93; J. H. Boeke, *Economics and Economic Policy of Dual Societies*, New York 1953, p. 58, quoting D. H. Burger.

50.   Ya'aqov Shim'onî, *'Arvei Eretz-Yisrael*, Tel Aviv 1946/47, p. 168n.

51.   Post, p. 109; Latron, p. 53; 'Isâm 'Âshour, 'Nizâm al-Murâba'a fee Soureeâ waLubnân waFalasteen', *al-Abhâth*, vol. ii, 1949, no. 1, pp. 61-62; Mr. Mahmoud 'Abdul Fattâh 'Abdul Ghanî, March 10, 1970; cf. Part I of the present article.

52.   Mr. Mahmoud 'Abdul Fattâh 'Abdul Ghanî, March 10, 1970.

53.   From Mr. Fâris Mousâ Ahmad Qâsem of 'Arrâbeh, June 8, 1971.

54.   From Mr. Jameel Raf'at Fayad 'Abdul Hâdî of Nablus, March 12, 1971; Mr. Muhammad 'Abdul 'Afoo 'Assâf of 'Arrâbeh, August 11, 1970.

55.   From Mr. Muhammad 'Abdul 'Afoo 'Assâf. This stemmed from the fact that for a given plot the rent-share, set by local convention, could not assume two values like a price that is raised by a middleman.

56.   See i. a. Notebooks, AIV, p. 146.

57.   Part I of the present article, p. 14.

58.   From Mr. Khaleel Hilnî 'Abdul Hâdî of Nablus, June 3, 1971. After 1948, with the influx of refugees from the area that became Israel, the rent-share on good land shot up to one-half; but Mr. Jameel Raf'at Fayâd 'Abdul Hâdî maintains that his branch of the family collected a full half at Kfeirat, adjoining 'Arrâbeh, under the Mandate as well. For Palestine as a whole, in 1930 the commonest rent-share was about 30% of the crop (Government of Palestine, *Report of A Committee . . .*, pp. 10-11); for 1944, the 'Five-Village Survey' conducted by the Palestine Office of Statistics uses two-fifths of the total produce as an example of the rate of rent prevailing in the Ramleh Sub-District (Palestine, Office of Statistics, *General Monthly . . .*, December 1945, p. 764).

The wide discrepancy between the landlord's share on fertile and less fertile lands is a widespread phenomenon. In early 18th-century France, good land rated a rent-share of at least one-sixth but poor land only one-15th or one-20th (Georges d'Avenel, *Découvertes d'histoire sociale, 1200-1900*, Paris 1910, p. 52).

59.   From Mr. Muhammad 'Abdurrahmân Shehâb of 'Arrâbeh, April 7, 1970. See n. 61 below.

60.   The Arabic word for 'share' is *qism*. Landowner and share-rent farmer referred to each other reciprocally as *qassâm*. Nazmi 'Abdul Hâdî designated the plots that he rented out on shares as *qusoumât* (*Notebooks*, AIC, p. 146).

61.   From Mr. Jameel Raf'at 'Abdul Hâdî, March 12, 1971; Mr. Muhammad Hasan 'Ali 'Arrâbeh's lands take up 10,000 acres, within which a large landowner's properties were scattered in a dozen or more locations (Rural Property Tax Taxpayers' Lists for 1935 for 'Arrâbeh at the Finance Office in Jenin). Moving with work animals, it took a

couple of hours to reach some of the cultivated lands from the village, and since the croppers also had to bring in the horses and oxen from pasture before they could start the ploughing day's work, it made little sense to assign to one farm properties that were too widely scattered (Mr. Mahmoud 'Abdul Fattâh 'Abdul Ghanî, September 25, 1970) particularly since those were themselves often fragmented, requiring an excessive proportion of the limited number of days in which the weather and the condition of the ground made ploughing possible to be spent moving from plot to plot. It was a measure of a joint-farmer's skill, according to Mr. Muhammad 'Abdul 'Afoo 'Assâf, to shunt off into share-rent arrangements with other farmers those of his landlord's lands that were too distant to farm profitably.

62.  From Messrs. Jameel Raf'at Fayâd and Khaleel Yusuf Hasan 'Abdul Hâdî of Nablus, March 12, 1971.

63.  From Hâjj Maḥmoud Hâjj Najee Hunayti of 'Arrâbeh, Dec. 12, 1969.

64.  For a shrewd insight into the relation between share tenancy and personal dependence in modern society see Marc Bloch, *Lès caractères originaux de l'histoire rurale française*, Vol. I, Paris 1964, pp. 152-153.

65.  From Messrs. Fâris Mousâ Aḥmâd Qâsim and Muhammad 'Abdurraḥmân Shehâb, April 13, 1970; Great Britain, *Report of the Commission on the Palestine Disturbances of August 1929. Minutes of Evidence*, Vol. I, p. 459 (11,589); Mr. Khaleel Hilmi 'Abdul Hâdî, August 20, 1970.

66.  From Mr. Fâris Mousâ Aḥmad Qâsim, June 8, 1971; Mr. Khaleel Hilmi 'Abdul Hâdî., June 3, 1971. 'Abdul Badi landowners were reported to have often taken one-fourth whereas local peasant landowners collected one-third; nor did the absentee landlords usually collect their share of the split straw—for which as town-dwellers they had little use but which was often a peasant's most important livestock feed (Mr. Dheeb As'ad Hasan).

67.  From Hâjj Dheeb As'ad Hasan.

68.  From Mr. Muhammad 'Abdul 'Afoo 'Assâf, August 11, 1970.

69.  In the period of independence after 1948 they also helped 'bring in the vote' when members of the 'Abdul Hâdî family ran for elective office (From Mr. Sâdiq Sâleḥ Nowfal of 'Arrâbeh, April 8, 1970).

70.  A. Granott, *The Land System in Palestine*, London 1952, pp. 54-83.

71.  Cf. Clifford Geertz, 'Social Change and Economic Modernization in Two Indonesian Towns' in Everett E. Hagen, *On the Theory of Social Change*, Homewood, Ill. 1962, pp. 399-400.

72.  The typology of polar models and continua between them along which one may place a given community was systematized by Robert Redfield, *The Little Community*, Uppsala 1955, pp. 139-143.

# Changes in the Settlement Pattern of Judea and Samaria during Jordanian Rule

*Elisha Efrat*

From the War of 1948 until the Six Day War in 1967, Judea and Samaria were cut off from Israel by the Israel-Jordanian armistice lines. The two regions forming an integral part of cis-Jordanian Palestine have thus been deprived of their contacts with the adjacent Coastal Plain and Gaza Strip as well of their outlet to the Mediterranean. Their sole remaining contacts were with the Kingdom of Jordan (Fig. 1). To adapt to these enforced and unnatural political conditions, both the rural and urban settlement structure had to undergo far-reaching changes, which it is intended in this article to describe and analyse against the physical, economic and social background of the area.

## PHYSICAL BACKGROUND

Judea and Samaria form part of Palestine's central massif, Judea comprising the Hebron and Jerusalem mountains and Samaria covering the area from Jerusalem to Jenin (Fig. 1). Both together cover an area of about 2,200 sq.miles (5,700 sq.km.).[1]

Mount Hebron forms a wide crest with two synclines on both sides, the lowland in the west and the desert in the east. Rising to a height of 3,000 ft. (1,000 m.) it runs in a north-east - south-west direction. Hebron is located on the flat crest which continues to the north, declining gradually to 2,100 ft. (700 m.) in the vicinity of Jerusalem. To the west a tectonic fold line provides a gradual 1,000-1,500 ft. (500-550 m.) high slope. In the east another fold forms the transition from the crest to the Judean desert.

The mountains of Samaria fall of gradually from south. They extend from the hills of Jerusalem up to the Jezreel Valley in the north, and border on the Jordan Valley in the east and the Coastal Plain in the west. In contrast to the compact Hebron mountain, the Samarian mountains, whose average height is 1,650 ft. (550 m.), are dissected by rifts and valleys underlining the topographical differences between one section and another.

## GEOGRAPHICAL LAYOUT OF VILLAGES

In Mount Hebron the layout of the rural settlements follows a linear, concentrated pattern, in line with the geographic structure. Owing to the strong effects of the desert, the rainfall in the eastern part is down to 4-12 inch (100-300 mm.), with sparse vegetation, little soil, and springs but few and far between. Human settlement accordingly does not extend

196

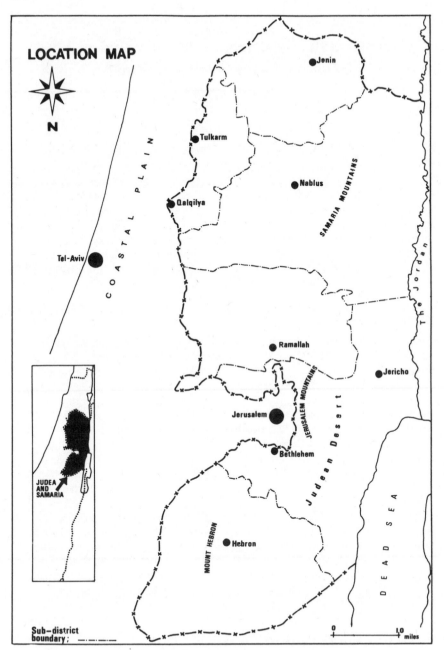

FIG. 1. Location map.

beyond a line running about 3 miles (5 km.) east of the watershed. In the south, too, the influence of the 'Negev' makes itself felt, and settlement tends to dwindle on the fringes of the desert penetrating into the Hebron mountains.[2] The villages on the mountain crest run parallel with the watershed, but are located at some distance from it, where soft stones are available for building, rather than in the fertile soil of the crest proper. To the west a further series of villages is located along the tectonic fold line running parallel with the mountain. This location, besides the topographical advantage, also offers them access to water sources.[3]

The largest villages with a population of 3,500-5,000 tend to be located in the south-east, while the villages in the central part of Mount Hebron usually have only 500-1,000 inhabitants each. The larger size of the outlying villages is probably due to the need of the farm population to ward off marauding desert nomads and the gradual settlement of bedouin in the more prosperous villages where they have since merged with the farmers.[4]

In Mount Hebron we thus find a compact settlement pattern, along well defined axes corresponding to the geographic layout and the agricultural potential of the region (Figs. 2 and 3).

No such compact layout is found in Samaria, where the settlements are dispersed practically over the entire region, in line with its dissected topographic structure. They are located on hilltops, domes and ridges dominating the surrounding countryside and offering a good strategic position. The valleys with their rich alluvial soil are generally uninhabited, being left free for intensive cultivation.[5] The numerous springs which are the outcome of the fault lines characteristic of the Samarian mountains facilitate the extensive dispersion of the population. Most of the villages are small, with 500-1,000 inhabitants, and only a small minority number 3,000-5,000 inhabitants (Figs. 2 and 3).

CHANGES IN NUMBER AND LOCATION OF VILLAGES

Table 1 shows the number of villages in Samaria and Judea at the end of the British Mandate (1947) and of Jordanian rule (1967).

The figures show a total increase of 132 villages or 50 per cent, which is, however, unequally divided between Judea and Samaria, the one showing an increase of 144 per cent as against only 25 per cent in the other. Although most of the increase in Judea is made up of small villages, their impact on the overall settlement structure is considerable.

From the sub-district distribution (Table 2) it appears that in Judea both the Hebron and Jerusalem sub-districts received a major increment, whereas in Samaria the increase was primarily concentrated in the northern Jenin sub-district.

On comparing the village dispersion at the beginning and at the end of this period it becomes evident that a maximum effort was made in the intervening twenty years to settle the Judean region, especially along the former southern and south-western border with Israel as well as on the fringes of the desert, in the eastern sections of Mount Hebron and the

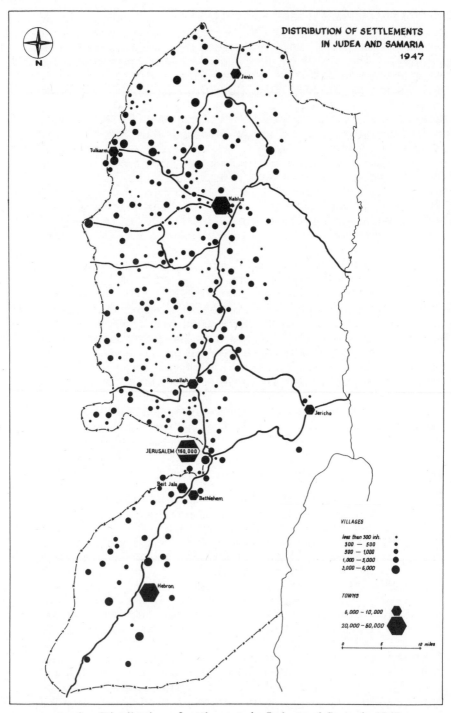

FIG. 2.   Distribution of settlements in Judea and Samaria 1947.

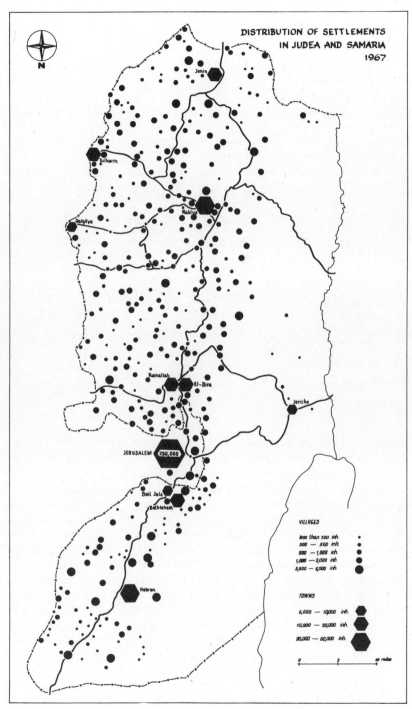

FIG. 3.  Distribution of settlements in Judea and Samaria 1967.

TABLE 1

VILLAGES IN JUDEA AND SAMARIA

|  | 1947* | 1967** | Increase | |
|---|---|---|---|---|
|  |  |  | Total | Per cent |
| Judea | 54 | 132 | 78 | 144 |
| Samaria | 210 | 264 | 54 | 25 |
|  | 264 | 396 | 132 | 50 |

* Based on mandatory Village Statistics, 1945.

** Based on Population Census of Judea and Samaria, 1967, conducted by the Israel Army Command.

TABLE 2

VILLAGE SETTLEMENTS IN JUDEA AND SAMARIA BY SUB-DISTRICT

| Sub-district | 1947 | 1967 | Increase | |
|---|---|---|---|---|
|  |  |  | Total | Per cent |
| Nablus | 91 | 97 | 6 | 6.5 |
| Jenin | 29 | 55 | 26 | 89 |
| Tulkarm | 34 | 42 | 8 | 23.5 |
| Ramallah | 56 | 70 | 14 | 25 |
| Jerusalem | 34 | 66 | 32 | 94 |
| Hebron | 20 | 66 | 46 | 230 |
| Total | 264 | 396 | 132 | 50 |

Jerusalem Hills. In Samaria the distribution was less lop-sided, though here, too, more new villages were founded near the armistice lines in the north and west than in the east. The older villages near the armistice line underwent considerable demographic and physical changes. Cut off from their lands in the Coastal Plain, they began to cultivate the less fertile foothills, and being unable to sell their produce either to Israel in the west or to potential markets in the east, in the absence of proper communication and transport facilities, their production and standard of living declined. Villages assumed an inner-directed, eastward orientation. In many of them the reasons of early location on hilltops disappeared. There is evidence which shows disintegration of the clustered village. Many villages even create new neighbourhood units and sprawl towards other sites even not always connected with water sources. Subsequently the emigration of young men to the oil principalities on the Persian Gulf led to a renewed influx of funds, stimulating construction and enlarging the built-up area of the initially improverished villages.[7] The building of new and expansion of existing roads along the border, primarily for defence purposes, also enhanced the status of the villages located there. However, despite deliberate settlement efforts, geographic factors continued to play a predominant role, and only few new settlements sprang up along the threshold of the desert and the shores of the Dead Sea, as well as in the Jordan Valley with its problematic soil conditions and paucity of water sources[8] (Figs. 2 and 3).

## CHANGES IN RURAL POPULATION

In Table 3 is a comparison of the rural population in 1947 and 1967.

TABLE 3

THE POPULATION OF JUDEA AND SAMARIA BY SUB-DISTRICT

| Sub-district | 1947* | 1967** | Percentage increase |
|---|---|---|---|
| Nablus | 62,500 | 152,400 | 144 |
| Jenin | 49,000 | 78,300 | 60 |
| Tulkarm | 35,000 | 72,300 | 106 |
| Ramallah | 50,700 | 88,800 | 75 |
| Jerusalem | 39,400 | 88,400 | 124 |
| Hebron | 47,000 | 118,300 | 151 |
| | 283,600 | 598,500 | 111 |
| Judea | 86,400 | 206,700 | 139 |
| Samaria | 197,200 | 391,800 | 99 |

\* Estimate based on mandatory Village Statistics, 1945, rounded off to nearest hundred.

\*\*Figures of Population Census, 1967, conducted by the Israel Army Command, rounded off to nearest hundred.

Thus the rural population went up from 283,600 in 1947 to 598,000 by 1967, an increase of 111 per cent in twenty years. The increase was more marked in Judea (139 per cent) than in Samaria (99 per cent), apparently as a result of the internal migration of refugees and sedentary tendencies among the nomadic population. Whereas in 1947 the population was more or less evenly spread over the different sub-districts, two of them, Nablus and Hebron, are found to predominate by the end of the period, with a respective increase of 144 and 151 per cent. The population has thus tended to concentrate in the two principal nodes in the north and the south as well as along the armistice lines.

It should further be noted that in mandatory times the villages showed a distribution such that the majority had 500-1,000 inhabitants and only a small minority either less than 500 or more than 3,000. Now, on the other hand, a disproportionately high share has only 100-300 inhabitants.

An analysis by population growth groups shows that most of the villages existing in mandatory times experienced a population increase (Fig. 4). The highest proportion went up by 100-200 inhabitants (22 per cent). Next come villages which increased by up to 100, 200-300 and 500-1,000 inhabitants (17 per cent). An extraordinary growth of

o

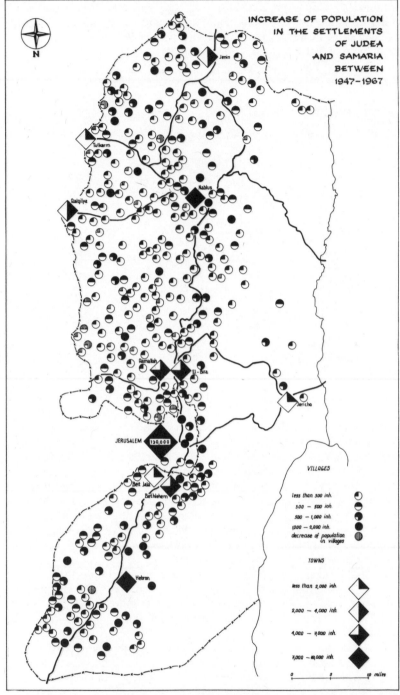

INCREASE OF POPULATION
IN THE SETTLEMENTS
OF JUDEA
AND SAMARIA
BETWEEN
1947–1967

N

Jenin

Tulkarm

Nablus

Qalqilye

Ramallah

El - Bira

Jericho

JERUSALEM  130,000

Beit Jala

Bethlehem

Hebron

VILLAGES

less than 300 inh.
300 — 500 inh.
500 — 1,000 inh.
1,000 — 2,000 inh.
decrease of population
in villages

TOWNS

less than 2,000 inh.

2,000 — 4,000 inh.

4,000 — 7,000 inh.

7,000 — 10,000 inh.

0          5          10 miles

FIG. 4.   Increase of population in the settlements of Judea and Samaria
between 1947–1967.

1,000-2,000 inhabitants occurred in sixteen, and of 2,000 and more in nine villages.

Geographically, most of the villages whose population grew by up to 100 inhabitants are located in Central Samaria. These are small villages whose growth is apparently due to natural increase. In Judea some of the new settlements along the armistice line belong to this group. In Samaria an increase by 100-200 inhabitants took place mainly in villages facing the Jezreel Valley and the Coastal Plain, along the armistice line and in Judea on the south-western slopes of Mount Hebron. Apart from the natural increase, the population of these villages was apparently boosted by the Jordanian government, for security reasons. The villages whose population grew by 500-1,000 inhabitants had also previously been of a substantial size, as were those growing by 1,000-2,000 or more which in addition are located on the fringes of the desert, in the midst of the fertile agricultural lands of Samaria or in the vicinity of a major city.

THE GEOGRAPHICAL LAYOUT OF THE TOWNS

On the whole the towns in Judea follow the watershed, from Hebron to Bethlehem and Beit Jala via Jerusalem to Ramallah and El-Bira. They are located on the mountain crest, each constituting a service, administrative, agricultural, marketing and commercial centre for the surrounding villages. While Jerusalem has the central function of being the capital city of both Judea and Samaria, Hebron is the main centre of the southern Judean mountains, while Bethlehem and Beit Jala, on the one side, and Ramallah and El-Bira, on the other, form secondary centres which are economically and otherwise dependent on Jerusalem. Thus Judea has a linear urban lay-out characterised by a functional division between the various towns.

In Samaria, on the other hand, the towns have developed primarily on the edge of the mountains facing the Coastal Plain and the Jezreel Valley or as intra- or inter-regional communications centres. The urban system is largely focused on Nablus, with Jenin as a subsidiary centre in the north, Tulkarm in the west, and Qalqilya in the south west.

None of the towns of Judea and Samaria is particularly big, and their share in the population is not very considerable. A comparison of their population figures in 1947 and 1967 is given below (Table 5), (Figs. 2 and 3).

From this breakdown it may be seen that:

(1) The urban population grew by a mere 42 per cent compared with a 111 per cent increase of the rural population (Table 3), so that the index of urbanisation, which has reached 87 per cent in Israel, is still very low with a marked predominance of the rural areas.

(2) As before, all the towns are very small, with the biggest of them - Hebron and Nablus - having a population of about 40,000.

(3) Although two villages, Qalqilya and El-Bira, were promoted to urban status, their population was less than 10,000.

(4) In Judea the towns grew less than in Samaria while the villages grew

204

## TABLE 4
### RURAL POPULATION GROWTH IN JUDEA AND SAMARIA, BY GROWTH GROUPS AND SUB-DISTRICTS

| Sub-district | Up to 100 | 100–200 | 200–300 | 300–400 | 400–500 | 500–1,000 | 1,000–2,000 | 2,000+ | Total villages | Percent |
|---|---|---|---|---|---|---|---|---|---|---|
| Nablus | 19 | 27 | 19 | 11 | 6 | 9 | 6 | 0 | 97 | 26.5 |
| Jenin | 6 | 5 | 10 | 6 | 5 | 10 | 2 | 1 | 45 | 12 |
| Tulkarm | 5 | 11 | 5 | 3 | 2 | 8 | 2 | 0 | 36 | 10 |
| Ramallah | 14 | 11 | 11 | 8 | 4 | 8 | 1 | 0 | 57 | 15.5 |
| Jerusalem | 9 | 12 | 11 | 7 | 6 | 16 | 1 | 4 | 66 | 18 |
| Hebron | 9 | 15 | 6 | 14 | 2 | 11 | 4 | 4 | 65 | 18 |
| Total | 62 | 81 | 62 | 49 | 25 | 62 | 16 | 9 | 366* | 100 |
| Percent | 17 | 22 | 17 | 13.5 | 7 | 17 | 4 | 2.5 | 100 | |

* Thirty villages which were abandoned or whose population decreased were not included.

TABLE 5

THE URBAN POPULATION OF JUDEA AND SAMARIA

|  | 1947* | 1967** | Percentage increase |
|---|---|---|---|
| Jenin | 4,000 | 8,346 | 109 |
| Nablus | 23,250 | 41,537 | 78 |
| Tulkarm | 8,000 | 10,157 | 27 |
| Qalqilya | (5,850)*** | 8,922 | 52 |
| Ramallah | 5,000 | 12,030 | 141 |
| El Bira | (2,920)*** | 9,568 | 228 |
| East Jerusalem | 65,000**** | 65,857 | — |
| Bethlehem | 9,000 | 14,439 | 60 |
| Beit Jala | 3,700 | 6,041 | 63 |
| Hebron | 24,600 | 38,091 | 55 |
| Jericho | 3,000 | 5,200 | 73 |
| Total | 154,320 | 220,188 | 42 |

* Estimate based on mandatory Village Statistics, 1945, rounded off to the nearest hundred.

** Population Census, 1967, conducted by the Israel Army Command.

*** Village in 1947.

**** Comprising those parts of Jerusalem annexed in 1967 to 'Greater Jerusalem'.

more, apparently because of their more tenuous economic and social relations with Trans-Jordan, compared with the far closer links maintained by the Samarian towns.

(5) The urban growth was due more to the migration of refugees or rural-urban migration than to the natural increase of the town population.[9]

(6) East Jerusalem remained static except for the urban spread to the surrounding villages and to Ramallah and El-Bira.

(7) Jericho experienced an extraordinary growth thanks to its location on the road between Trans-Jordan and Jerusalem and its winter resort function.

CHANGES IN THE INTERNAL STRUCTURE OF THE TOWNS

Most of the towns of Judea and Samaria experienced changes in the orientation of their urban sprawl and municipal boundaries as a result of the armistice lines sealing off Jordan from Israel. An analysis of the building trends revealed by some of them during the past twenty years may serve as an illustration of the general development (Fig. 5).

*East Jerusalem*

Under the British Mandate, East Jerusalem was a commercial and economic centre for the residents of Judea, Samaria and Trans-Jordan and provided an outlet to the Mediterranean via the roads leading through it to Jaffa and Haifa.[10] With the annexation of Judea and

206

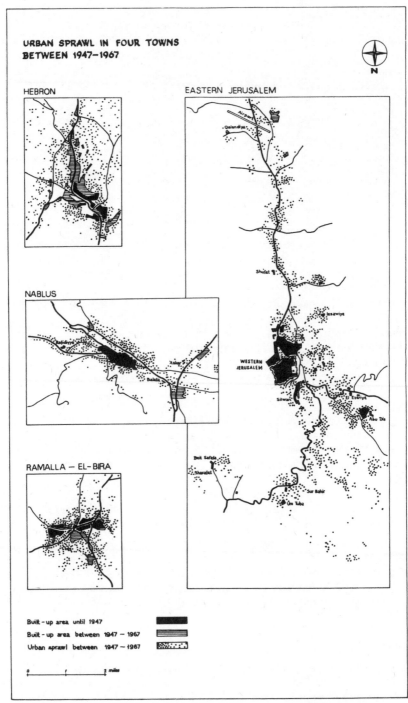

FIG. 5. Urban sprawl in four towns between 1947–1967.

Samaria by the Hashemite Kingdom, it became an economic backwater. All its supply lines were centred on 'Amman which drew its own goods from the ports of 'Aqaba and Beirut. The loss of the city's economic predominance also affected its orientation. Since to the east and south-east the topography was not amenable to urban development, most of the development took place in a northerly direction along the mountain crests and on both sides of the Jerusalem-Ramallah road. Since communications with Bethlehem were impaired there was little development towards the south of the city.

Considerable efforts were invested in improving housing conditions and the standard of services in the Old City which has always been the main residential quarter of Jerusalem's Arab population. The lack of adequate commercial and industrial facilities in the eastern section of Jerusalem led to the re-zoning of areas in the northern part of the city which had formerly been designated for residential purposes. In view of the altered conditions the government of Jordan set about replanning the Jerusalem region, fixing its boundaries along a circular line stretching from the Qalandiya Airfield in the north to the village of Sur Bahir in the south, so as to compromise an area of 32,500 areas.

East Jerusalem under Jordanian rule therefore had to adapt to the artificial boundaries hemming in its natural expansion. Turning its back upon its natural economic base in the west, it had to spread out towards north, south and east. The main planning concepts were dispersion along the mountain crest, the development of new settlement nodes on the flat outrunners of the central ridge and their connection by means of a main road along the north-south axis bypassing the Old City, and the development of an eastern traffic artery to Trans-Jordan (Fig. 5).[11]

## Hebron

At one time Hebron had consisted of the inner core of the Old City and some few buildings around it, all straddling the main highway. At the beginning of the century further developments were carried out to the north-west along the highway to Bethlehem and Jerusalem. The new, more spacious and taller buildings also enhanced the town's economic activities. The main expansion, however, took place during the nineteen years of Jordanian rule when the city received a population increment of about 13,500. Its standard of living rose, not least because of the influx of funds from emigrants returning from the oil principalities. About 1,800 new houses were built in this period, about 500 of them in the surrounding agricultural area.[12] Most of the development still was along the Jerusalem highway, over a stretch of three miles (about 5 km.) and at a depth of 600 ft. (about 200 m.) either way. To the south-east, however, the city expanded by only about one mile (1.6 km.), having been cut off from Beersheba, the marketing centre of the bedouins (Fig. 5).

*Nablus*

The original core of Nablus, the second largest city in Judea and Samaria after Jerusalem, is a compact, unplanned warren of buildings hemmed in between two mountains. The influx of refugees from the Coastal Plain provided a considerable impetus for expansion while at the same time the city lost its western zone of influence. It therefore had to develop an eastward orientation and strengthen its economic and social ties with 'Amman. The regional road leading to the east was expanded and the town began to spread out in a new direction previously barred by the presence of an ancient tel, a power station and a prison. During six years alone, from 1961 until 1967, over 1,000 houses were built,[13] many of them with money earned in Kuwait. The building boom also spread to the refugee camps and the suburbs on the Nablus-'Amman and Nablus-Jerusalem highways (Fig. 5).

*Ramallah*

Until 1947 Ramallah was densely built up, especially along the road to El-Bira and about half a mile (800 m.) to the north and to the south of it. Again, with the growing wealth of the population earned in foreign fields, new and better-spaced buildings went up and the satellite town of El-Bira began to be developed. As buildings sprawled over onto formerly agricultural areas these were retroactively annexed to form part of the municipal boundaries. Though the new developments are totally unplanned they show a certain orientation towards Jerusalem, especially its northern neighbourhoods, which have begun to merge with Ramallah into a continuous built-up strip along the mountain crest (Fig. 5).

These few examples are enough to indicate that the towns of Judea and Samaria responded in different ways to the region's severance from its natural outlets and surroundings, each according to its specific regional functions and geographic conditions. It may, moreover, be noted that they were all affected by the exogenous economic factor of emigration to the Arab oil principalities. Throughout urban growth was sporadic. No attempt was made to adopt a modern approach to land uses, zoning and the construction of modern, functional neighbourhoods. The towns developed without an appropriate industrial base or adequate public institutions. Many of the residents still have an agrarian background, being landlords and farmers. Physical expansion thus did not go hand in hand with the development of urban functions and occupations. Moreover, the city boundaries were mostly determined haphazardly through the incorporation of rural areas on which buildings happened to be put up, so that the towns tend to sprawl out at low density.

CONCLUSIONS

1. During the nineteen years of Jordanian rule in Judea and Samaria rural growth exceeded urban growth, as is evidenced by the number of

new villages and the rural population increase. In spite of some urban development reflected in the growth of the urban population and of the built-up areas, there is as yet no perceivable process of urbanisation.

2. The impassable armistice lines between Israel and Jordan resulted in changes in the rural and urban settlement structure of Judea and Samaria, necessitated by the new artificial conditions. A large number of new villages was founded along these lines, border settlements underwent a major expansion, as did villages located along new security roads, and hilly areas were cultivated instead of the fields in the Coastal Plain which were no longer accessible. In the towns the built-up areas were reoriented in line with the new foci of attraction while a building boom was set off by residents forced through lack of local employment to emigrate to the Arab oil principalities and investing their earnings in this way.

3. Since the Hashemite Kingdom of Jordan did almost nothing to stimulate the economy and develop local resources, looking upon Judea and Samaria merely as a strategic front or buffer zone, development was largely dictated by the dominant geographic characteristics of the area. In the absence of new water sources, mineral exploitation and industrial development, the region had to contend with desert conditions in the east, the artificial boundary in the west, north and south, and its own inhospitable topography. The resulting modified settlement pattern was thus unfavourably affected by the armistice lines on the one hand and the lack of economic progress on the other.

NOTES

1. For further details, see E. Orni and E. Efrat, *Geography of Israel* (Third Revised Edition, Israel University Press, Jerusalem, 1971), pp. 398–419.

2. Z. Meshel, 'The Southern Section of Mount Hebron', *Teva Va'Aretz* (Nature and Land) (in Hebrew), Vol. 11 (1969), pp. 118–124.

3. E. Efrat, 'Settlement Distribution in Judea and Samaria', *The New East*, (in Hebrew) Vol. 20, 3 (79) (1970), pp. 257–265.

4. A. Shmueli, 'The Settlement of the Bedouin of the Judean Desert' (in Hebrew) (Gomé Publ. House, Tel Aviv, 1970), pp. 140.

5. Y. Dan, 'The Soils of the Judean and Samarian Mountains', (The Vulcani Agricultural Research Institute, Rehovot, 1968), pp. 17; and 'Atlas of Israel', Geomorphology, Soil Map, II/3 (1970).

6. Based on 'List of Settlements in the West Bank' (The Israel Land Authority, August, 1967), also showing the land holdings of each village.

7. M. Brawer, 'Changes in Location and Pattern of Border Villages', *Proceedings of the Symposium in Rural Geography* (University of Baroda, 1968), pp. 16.

8. E. Efrat, 'Judea and Samaria, Guidelines for Regional and Physical Planning' (The Ministry of the Interior, Jerusalem, 1970), pp. 67–86.

9. E. Cohen, 'The Towns in the Administered Areas' (The Hebrew University, Department of Sociology, Jerusalem, 1968), pp. 41.

10. H. Kendall, 'Jerusalem, The City Plan, Preservation and Development during the British Mandate 1918-1948' (London 1948).

11. E. Efrat, 'Changes in the Town Planning Concepts of Jerusalem, 1919-1969', *Environmental Planning* (the Israeli Association for Environmental Planning Quarterly, July-Sept. 1971), pp. 53–65.

12. Y. Karmon and A. Shmueli, *Hebron - The Image of a Mountain Town* (in Hebrew) (Gomé Publ. House, Tel Aviv, 1970), pp. 146.

# Rāshid Husain: Portrait of an Angry Young Arab

## Emile Marmorstein

In 1955 an anthology of Arabic poetry (*alwan min-shi'r al-arabi-yati fi Isra'il*) which included poems by Jews, Christians and Muslims, was published in Nazareth. The editor, Michel Hadad, in his foreword divided his contributors into three groups. He ingeniously referred to those who had written poetry before and after their incorporation within the Zionist State, as *al-mukhadhramun*—a term originally applied to pagan poets who continued to write poetry after the triumph of Islam. In the second group he placed immigrant Jewish poets from Arab countries (*al-qadimun*), and in the third " those whose poetic gifts had developed during the years of this new era " (*al-nashi'un*). This third group consisted almost entirely of the sons of villagers with the ambition and the means to provide their sons with a secular education.

One of the young Muslim contributors was Rashid Husain Mahmud. According to the short biography under the photograph of a fresh and alert-looking face, " he was born in Masmas, one of the villages of the Northern Triangle, in 1936 and went to the elementary school in Um al-Fahum. He left for his own village on the foundation of the state and is now in his final year at the Nazareth school. He began composing poetry when he was sixteen. The Israel broadcasting station has broadcast and the local press has published a little of his production. He has been influenced by the poetry of Abu'l-'Ala and Abu Madi. His poetry is marked by sympathy with others and awareness of the difficulties of the people ". The choice of these two mentors is clearly relevant to the experience of those Palestinian Muslims who found themselves reduced from majority to minority status. For the scepticism and pessimism of Abu'l-'Ala

211

al-Ma'arri (973-1057) reflect an age of social decay and political anarchy in Islam while Iliya Abu Madi (1889-1957) who emigrated in 1911 to the U.S.A., represents the capacity of Arabic literature both to survive in and to be enriched by a non-Arab environment.

After a brief but stormy career as a teacher, he devoted himself to poetry and literature. Moreover, he began to mix politically as well as socially and culturally with Jews. Reviewing " *Sawarikh* " (Rockets), his second volume of poetry, Eliahu Khazum, an Iraqi Jewish critic, reported that " apart from being the most promising Arab poet in Israel, he seems the only one interested in the study of Hebrew, and recently during a Histadruth-sponsored meeting of Arab and Jewish writers, he pleasantly surprised the packed hall of the ' Milo ' writers' club in Tel Aviv by reciting the first poem he wrote in Hebrew" (*Jerusalem Post* 25.9.58). Since then he has translated plays and books from Arabic into Hebrew and vice versa and, through English and Hebrew, introduced Arab readers to the work of Brecht, the Turkish poet Nazim Hikmet, the Persian Ashub, Lumumba and other ' progressive ' writers. Moreover, his prolific contributions to the press gave rise to the complaint that " from being a poet with a bent for journalism, he has become a journalist with a bent for poetry "; but he himself has insisted that his flow of poetry shows no sign of drying up (*al-Yaum* 29 April, 1959).

Now the society of the Zionist state can almost be described as a federation of the factions among which the Jews of Eastern Europe had divided their political allegiance; and fame as well as many other more tangible advantages depends to a considerable extent on party patronage. Rashid Husain joined the United Workers' Party (Mapam), successor to the Marxist ' Young Watchman ' (*hash-shomer ha-sa'ir*) that had in mandatory times preferred a binational Jewish-Arab State to partition. In the fifties, Mapam which had admitted Arabs to full membership, established branches in Arab towns and villages, induced hundreds of young Arabs to attend agricultural-ideological courses in its collectives and initiated a number of cultural and economic projects of benefit to Arabs; and the results of the 1959 elections showed that Mapam doubled its percentage of the vote in predominantly Arab districts at the expense of its main rivals, the non-Marxist Labour Party (Mapai) and the communists. (The decline of the communist share of the Arab poll was commonly attributed to the deterioration of Jamal 'Abdu'n-Nasir's relationship with international communism). This is not surprising; leaving aside its connection with the Palestine problem,

Mapam's Titoism is fashionable among the politically conscious elements in the Arab World and, indeed, in the whole assembly of " developing countries ".

For Rashid Husain whose Islam is almost as secularised as Mapam's Judaism, his party membership involved a minimal sacrifice of his inherited religion. " I do not pray ", he admitted, " and I do not go to the mosque and I know that in this I am disobeying the will of God. I am a lax believer and thousands of people like me are lax in fulfilling the divine precepts. But these disobedient thousands did not keep silent about what our pious judges who pray and fast, have kept silent ". (al-Mirsad 1 May, 1961). Such is the tone familiarly employed by secularizers of all religious traditions when the dignitaries of their ancestral faiths reject the often costly luxury of dramatic gestures against the powerful in favour of the more discreet and often more effective path of private intervention, negotiation and prayer. That people who do not practise their religion are the ethical superiors of those who do, is a common secularist implication; and, in one of his poems in the above-mentioned anthology, Rashid Husain implies it when he denounces fasters for their hopes of Paradise and fears of Hell and advises them rather to care for orphans and refrain from lies. However, he appears readier than most Jewish Mapamniks to confess doubts of the outcome of secularization—though his doubts, not unlike their unspoken ones, stem not from a residue of faith but rather from nostalgic memories of the atmosphere of his youth when adults appeared to him to take their religion seriously and to be the better and happier for it. One of his allegories begins during the Ramadan of 1945 with a revolt led by Sha'ban, the eight month of the Islamic calendar, against Ramadan (the ninth month) which is envisaged as gorged with the food heaped up by the faithful while the other months remain famished and resentful of the allocation of all the food grown during them to the nights of the month when the fasters break their fast. Addressing the others, Sha'ban makes a demagogic speech on the subject. " You know, my brothers, that our mother, the year, bore us equal in rights and responsibilities; but vanity has blinded our brother Ramadan to this fact. He is, therefore, satisfied while we are hungry, he sleeps while we remain awake and he is idle while we but multiply effort through toil. We are deprived of most of our rights, nay of the fairest of those rights—bread (applause). You know, my brothers, that before Ramadan I spread my shadow over this earth. Imagine, gentlemen, that even during

the days of my power and authority I cannot find satisfaction in a
morsel. Whenever I enter a home, I hear its owner tell his sons:
' save the delicious food for Ramadan, save the meat for Ramadan, save and save everything good for Ramadan '. As for
wretched Sha'ban who has come upon them as a guest, nobody
pays any attention to him except a crowd of madmen and
lovers ". He then proposes an appeal to the Creator to put
Ramadan on the same level as themselves. " We must enter every
house and persuade its inhabitants that food is delicious and that
the Fast is merely an old custom. Winter and summer, spring and
autumn, we must try to discourage people from honouring Ramadan. This task, my brothers, must be completed within ten years.
We sow and we shall reap, we grind and we knead and we bake
throughout the days of the year and we have more right than
Ramadan to that for which we have toiled ". The scene changes to
Ramadan in the year 1956. Sha'ban is gorged with food and Ramadan, who is hungry, has a sorry tale to tell. The neglect of the
physical side of fasting has been accompanied by a disregard of its
moral aspects. " The days of thy brother Ramadan, O Sha'ban, are
not merely those on which people hunger in daytime in order to be
satisfied after nightfall. They are the days of the renewal of the
spiritual forces after matter has almost exhausted them. They are
days of struggle between faith and unbelief during which the spirit
is cleansed from its impurities of base matter in a stream of lasting
endurance and of the faith that is clothed in light. What grieves me,
Sha'ban, is that people no longer reflect on the meaning of fasting
but dismiss it as an ' old custom ' which the age has consumed. If
any of them fasts, he sleeps the length of his day or spends it in
playing cards and listening to songs—as if he regards fasting only
as a burden unjustly imposed upon him and the whole of his intention is to escape the punishment which he sees involved in failure to
fast. Such people, my brother, merely go hungry: they do not fast.
Ten years ago I found a welcome wherever I went and people
compelled me to taste their food. Today I have become burdensome
upon everybody. Yesterday I entered the house of one of the judges
while he was saying that he would have supper at five. I went out
with grief in my heart to the house of a rich merchant: he had gone
to the cinema before six. I entered many houses and all their inhabitants had forgotten that I was their guest: they had eaten their food
at four. I saw some small boys who were fasting the whole day and

I looked at them and smiled encouragingly; but it turned out that I had come to the poor quarter where they were fasting in their thousands without love in their fasting or awareness of its meaning but simply in order to economise on food. That is what I heard them say; so I drew back without tasting their food out of sympathy for them and compassion for their misery and wretchedness ". Sha'ban was moved by this recital. "Although he felt that his revolt had succeeded, he hoped from the depths of his heart that history would go back ten years in order to wipe out from its page that call to revolt. He felt his tears flow down his cheeks and there began to appear before his eyes a mass of poor people who used to be happy in the month of Ramadan ten years ago when the rich really fasted and did not merely go hungry as they do today if they fast " (al-Mujtama' May, 1956).

His attitude to the cognate problem of the position of women in society is less ambivalent. In a conversation with Yusuf Isma'il on the Tel Aviv beach, he professed admiration for Jewish women. " Here we have all the varieties of beauty that exist in the world. Oriental beauty, American, Polish and English together. The whole of the beautiful half of the world is to be found in the beauty show that is our country ". Asked whether in his opinion " our youth is doing its duty in the cause of female emancipation " he gave the following answer:

" No . . . women want freedom but they are afraid of what people say; and our youth are the kind of people who frighten women by telling tales about them. If a woman says ' Good-morning ' to one of them, he tells his friends that she is his sweetheart. If she stands by his side for a moment, he says that she wants him to kiss her. He really means that he wants it ".

Questioned further as to his personal handling of the problem, he laughingly replied that, as he was still a bachelor, he had not had the chance to practise what he preached; but he promised that, when the opportunity arose, he would grant his wife a reasonable measure of freedom. " I call for freedom to be given to educated women " (al-Yaum 29 April, 1960). Yet, refuting at roughly the same time what appeared to him to be aspersions on Arab morals in the film of Leon Uris' novel Exodus, he proclaimed with pride " that there is no dance-hall in Nazareth, that not one girl is employed in a Nazareth restaurant, that no girl is allowed to walk out in Nazareth in the company of a man other than her husband, her betrothed or

a near relation " (al-Mirsad 21 April, 1960). However, within traditional Islamic morality a zest for procreation is invariably em-
bedded; and, judging from a poem called 'The Horses' (al-Fajr
January-February, 1961), he is inclined to attribute the stagnation
and squalor of Arab village society mainly to the general admiration
for fecundity:

I

In other lands
    The child is born small
    So warmth and light do they heap upon his days
    Then of the tale of the sun do they tell him in lines
    So that the child that was small
    Becomes a man . . . a great man


.  .  .


In our villages the child is born a prince
    So night and vows upon his eyes they heap
    And on his tender skin they build castles
    So the child that was a prince
    Becomes a dwarf . . . a little man
    Who drinks mud and chews fruit peel


.  .  .


In other lands
    The child grows up and with him all the qualities unfold
    And stars and hopes unfold upon his brow
    In our villages . . . among the wreaths of smoke the child grows
    So that congratulations on the child may grow
    That they may say: " Fair women's dream has Heaven's ward
      become "
    Or "A bridegroom . . . the age of wedlock has the boy attained "


.  .  .


So there floods my country a generation of bridegrooms
    A generation of big children . . . like horses
    Their minds are filled with shapes of ashen thought
    So with Su'ad the hopes are ended
    With the feet of Su'ad
    With henna on the palm of Su'ad

Should my people beget the child as a child
   They would not cast mud in his eyes
   Perhaps on my country's soil there would shine
   A new generation of knights . . . in my country
   As small children would children be born
   Then men they would become and fill the night with fire
   Perhaps around me eagles I might glimpse
   Not birds that ape the eagles

         .   .   .

In other countries people worry about the end
   In our villages people worry about the beginning
   One is concerned that the wife should bear a male
   That they may say : " She comes of fine stock
   She has born a male child
   Whose face is the moon's face "
   That they may say: "A powerful stallion is her husband . . .
      a man "
   Or " an Arab steed . . . an unconquerable hero
   His firstborn is a male
   Whose face is like the moon's "
   After this though their son be a shepherd of flies
   Though he be a worm of the earth and all the dust that's in it
   Though he be mute . . . blind . . . though he be an owl in a ruin
   Though his father die and though his mother die
   And though she died from joy at his encounter
   Still he is born a male
   Whose face is the face of the moon
   His mother of noble breed . . . a mare that does not falter
   Her husband a thorough-bred stallion . . . a victorious hero

         .   .   .

My country . . . tell me when, O my country
   Will you smother us with light and not with slumber
   As you have smothered us in honey and in milk
   So may the slave-market be demolished
   And the black horses leap to the fire
   So when the flocks of birds encircle
   Lo and behold they are falcons and eagles

Membership of Mapam provided the young poet with a forum
in the shape of the Arabic newspapers, periodicals and a publishing
company founded and maintained by the party. An investigation of
his contribution in poetry and prose to the weekly *al-Mirsad*

(founded in 1951), the illustrated fortnightly *al-Musawwar* (founded in 1960) and the cultural monthly *al-Fajr* (founded in 1958) of which he has been literary editor, shows how extensively he has taken advantage of it. Moreover, English rendering of a few of his articles and poems in the Mapam-sponsored *New Outlook* have conveyed a pasteurized impression of him to a wider circle of readers at home and abroad. In brief, from being an impecunious young teacher, harassed by trying to teach poor village boys in decrepit schoolrooms without sufficient textbooks and conducting a running fight with the Zionist supervisors of Arab education and the Arab section of the Teachers' Union, he has been transformed into a celebrity; and his European tour in the winter of 1960/61 testified to Mapam's confidence in his loyalty and appreciation of his efforts. Yet Rashid Husain has resisted the temptation to rest on his laurels. His talent and imagination have developed. The austere style of his earlier poems has been varied by a greater freedom in his use of the traditional metres. Both in this respect as well as in his turn to satire, he has followed the mainly Lebanese fashion that originally derives from the poetry of the American Arabs—though not from Abu Madi himself. In his prose, he effectively combines the kindred traditions of gallows humour whereby both Syrian Arabs and Eastern European Jews helped themselves to endure trouble, prefacing most of his slashing denunciations in *al-Mirsad* by paragraphs containing old Ottoman or Judaeo-German jokes or a rhetorical summary of the Arab condition under Zionist rule e.g.

" When I think of the past years through which we have lived . . . And when I think of the chastisement we have eaten and drunk . . . and when I think of what has been lost or forbidden to us, then when I think of the way we faced all this—when I think of all this, I cannot help smiling. We are not the first people to be ill-treated . . . yet the ill-treatment to which we have been exposed over the length of the past years is of a strange kind. By means of the law our lands have been seized . . . and by means of the law military government has been imposed on us . . . and by means of the law the endowments (*awqaf*) of God continue to complain about their case to God . . . and, nevertheless, by means of the law we can speak . . . and protest . . . and by means of the law we can complain of the military governor . . . and by means of the law we can write . . . and cry out . . . and demonstrate against all this. It is a strange situation. Whenever I think about it, I keep on smiling " (*al-Mirsad* 14 April, 1960).

Rashid Husain has certainly taken advantage of a situation outside the experience of religious and linguistic minorities in independent Middle Eastern countries. Their disappointments may well have been greeted with explanations such as

" Because they are of the line of Ishmael and not of the line of Isaac, because they are of the new oppressed and not of the new arrivals, for all this and because of all this and as a result of all this they fail in the matriculation examinations " (*al-Mirsad* 8 December, 1960)

but they were not published in newspapers. But Rashid Husain does not confine himself to drawing attention to instances of discrimination, humiliation and arbitrary decision. Ranging downwards from Ben Gurion whom he accused of standing on his head politically as well as physically (*al-Mirsad* 24 November, 1960), whom he informed that all his friends were weary of him and asking why he did not go (*al-Mirsad* 19 January, 1961) and whom he likened to Tshombe (*al-Mirsad* 30 June, 1961), through the cabinet and the higher ranks of the bureaucracy to their Arab collaborators, he wields his scourge devastatingly and entertainingly. Not that he is incapable of generosity—even towards the Arab adherents of Mapai: he praised their courage in joining the campaign against a project for the amalgamation of scattered plots of agricultural land that was suspected of being directed exclusively against Arab farmers (*al-Mirsad* 19 January, 1961). Again, protesting against the dismissal of a Jewish official in charge of Arab trade union affairs, he alleged that the real reason was not the fall of Lavon, the dismissed official's patron in the Trade Union Federation (*Histadruth*), but the military government's resentment of a man who had turned against the view that the stick was the only language intelligible to Arabs (*al-Mirsad* 19 May, 1961); and his spirited demand for the resignation of an official in charge of Arab education was accompanied by the compliment that, although he was a good man and would undoubtedly be replaced by a worse, the forces hindering his efforts were too powerful for him to overcome (*al-Mirsad* 15 December, 1960).

Most—but not all—of his attacks on the government attitude to the Arabs of the State were published at times when Mapam remained outside the ruling coalition. He addresses himself to "Jewish compatriots " (*al-muwatinun al-yahud*) as a citizen of a democracy, a member of the working class movement and an opponent of " those who colonized both our peoples and humiliated them to-gether " (al-Mirsad 21 April, 1960), appealing especially to the workers' parties that profess to favour friendship and brotherhood between the two peoples, to be true to themselves. " The principles of these very parties are in danger; and if these parties are not stirred up because of us fellow-citizens, perhaps they will be stirred because of their principles " (al-Mirsad 28 April, 1960). As for the neighbouring countries, peace is being prevented by Ben Gurion's bellicose policy; but, should the Zionists agree to re-admit Arab refugees on a realistic basis and support Arab causes rather than the ' imperialists ' at the United Nations, a compromise might result.

His assessment of the morale of the Arabs of his own age-group in the Zionist state is scathing. It is a ' lost generation ' that aims only at being left in peace to earn a living (al-Musawwar 9 October, 1960). The ' crisis of the intellectuals ' is one of his favourite themes: they are pretentious and slothful. Every secondary school graduate claims to be an ' intellectual ' (muthaqqaf) and every occasional contributor to a newspaper or magazine an author (adib); and even the few capable of producing poetry or short stories rarely go be-yond conversation about their literary plans. Yet if they are slothful, submissive, aimless and apprehensive about their posts, the fault is not entirely theirs. They were children when the catastrophe over-took them; and they had been assured that the Jews would be thrown into the sea. The youth of every defeated country experiences despair in exactly the same way. The Arab countries reacted to the calamity by banishing ' the old leadership ' from the political scene and replacing it with ' a new leadership ' that offered youth an ' example ' and an opportunity for constructive effort. But in the Zionist state ' the old leadership ' was re-imposed on the Arabs by their conquerors; the men who had spent money entrusted to them for the purchase of arms on wine, women and song, i.e., those who had been responsible for the catastrophe, were given authority over the victims. In ' From a Deputy's daughter ' (Al-Fajr, February, 1962) perhaps the most venomous of his poems, he seeks to illus-trate this alleged relationship between collaborators with Mapai on the one hand and the ' youth ' and the ' people ' on the other:

Father . . . our garden is fruitful
Our pomegranates bloom . . . and the apples ripen
Even the box-thorn planted round the hedge . . . is in blossom
And wafts its perfume in the air in waves of ambergris
Why have you not borne fruit . . . like my garden that is fruitful
Why have you not grown?

. . .

Why are you apart from the people among Caesar's plantations
His steed you provide with its needs of fodder and sugar
And you squeeze the tears of the exiled to water his grey colt
The heart of the homeless you pierce . . . to feed his tawny cat
Why should his colt grow and why should his cat grow
And you remain as you are and not grow?

. . .

Father, I beg you, do not be angry . . . for the like of my sin is
    venial
For when I jot down my thoughts . . . I feel that I am growing
That I am more free
And I sense that I am like the people . . . not a statue of marble
Like them I am angry with Caesar your master

. . .

When I call my neighbours so that we may gossip
They say: in your house the flies spend their holidays . . . they
    are encamped
And I say: maybe but . . . it is the sweetness . . . the sugar
And they say: no . . . the blood of the simple keeps watch in
    your house

. . .

How much was your red gown, my girl-friends ask me
And I weep, father, I weep and call out: its colour's green
A peasant's daughter screams: we have lost field and threshing-
    floor
Another little girl calls out: your father evicted my elder
    brother
And I sense that my gown is coloured red by tears

I have become lonely, my father, I lie ever sleepless
I the most exiled . . . and you the least liberator
Above your dark brow I almost see the horses of the Turk
And in your eyes a Mameluke who leads you where he decides
To the level of the earth you descend . . . you are getting
    smaller, father, smaller
As if the bones of our dead that Caesar has confiscated
Force you to their graves that you agreed should be desecrated
Force you to see what replaces them . . . buried

      . . .

Father, forgive me . . . when will you grow
Betrayal of the simple, did you not know, will not be forgiven
True they are on the earth . . . as seed that is scattered
More abundant than their wealth is the wealth before you
True with the watchful cloud is our dwelling
That on earth are their houses . . . on its dust that is yellow
But you did not understand . . . therefore you did not grow
Were not the sea above the earth . . . that cloud would not give
    rain

      . . .

My father I beg you to grow
Our apples bloom . . . and the pomegranates ripen
Even the box-thorn of the garden wafts ambergris around us
And around me the poor grow . . . the blind and the sightless
And the public scribe grows . . . the beetroot-seller grows
And you when oh when will you grow?

      . . .

Almost all the content of Rashid Husain's writing is in complete
harmony with the views of his patron. The party openly demands
equal rights for Arabs, denounces the powers represented by the
'Turk' and the 'Mameluke', laments Lumumba and execrates
Tshombe, cheers for the Algerians and all 'National Liberation
Movements', attacks rival parties in the State and condemns the
servility of Arabs who adhere to them. But Rashid Husain makes
no attempt to conceal his identification of the 'example' that should
inspire Arab youth. When he charged, for instance, the Arabic Service of the 'Voice of Israel' with partiality in favour of Qasim,
Husain, Bourguiba, the Imam of the Yemen and Sa'ud and hostility
towards Jamal 'Abdu'n-Nasir exclusively, he explained this state of
affairs by means of an assertion that, while all of them were equally
opposed to Zionism, only the last-named had persistently developed

his country, fought against 'imperialism' and worked for Arab unity (*al-Mirsad* 2 February, 1961). Here, both he and Mapam are in a dilemma: prudence might have dictated silence about the 'example' and concentration on the 'menace'; for Mapam remains, notwithstanding its bi-national past, a Zionist party and its quarrel with Jamal 'Abdu'n-Nasir and, for that matter, the Ba'th and the late Abdu'l-Karim Qasim, with all of whom it is in general ideological agreement, concerns ownership of a disputed stretch of territory in the Holy Land. But Rashid Husain, a brave man and one clearly allergic to silence, has sensed an artistic challenge to present his own dilemma in a literary form. A clue is provided by his fondness for symbolism in the light of which he is inclined to interpret the writings of others. One might quote from his review of a novel entitled *Asmahan* by Ibrahim Musa Ibrahim which was published by the Mapam 'Arab Publishing Company' in 1962. The plot is a simple one. Amal, an unhappy girl living with her married sister Huda, dislikes Munir, her brother-in-law, and then falls in love with him. In order to separate her from Munir, she tells Huda that she and Munir have had a passionate love affair. Amal's confession that this story is completely untrue, comes too late. Huda dies in the belief that Munir has been unfaithful to her. The novel ends with an account of Amal's journey to Europe in Munir's company.

One might think that a plot of this kind could have been concocted by any Arabic writer anywhere in the Middle East; but the fact that the author is by origin an Iraqi Jew has enabled Rashid Husain to detect a layer of symbolism beneath the structure of this tragic romance.

"Huda's household might be a symbol for Israel. Huda as well as her children might be a symbol for Western Jews in Israel. Munir—Huda's husband—might be a symbol for the rulers of Israel. Amal—the heroine of the story—might be a symbol for the Eastern Jew who senses estrangement and discrimination. The mutual feeling between Huda and Amal might be a symbol of the mutual feeling between the ordinary Western Jew and the ordinary Eastern Jew—between two unconnected persons. The relationship between Munir on the one side and Huda, Amal and the children on the other might be a symbol of the relationship between ruler and ruled with Munir's rude behaviour symbolizing the rude and dictatorial behaviour occasionally displayed by the rulers of our country. Amal's desire to attract Munir might be a symbolical expression of the desire of members of the Eastern communities here also to secure higher government posts and to obtain proper and just consideration on the part of the rulers. Finally, Amal's destruction of her sister's life and happiness might be a symbolic warning that feelings of estrangement, deprivation and discrimination among members of the Eastern community will lead them in a negative direction ".

(al-Fajr May 1962)

The daring with which Rashid Husain claims to have unravelled the two " tragedies ", the author's and the unfortunate Huda's, prompts an attempt to apply similar treatment to one of his own efforts—with, it is hoped, more plausible results. More than two years before the review appeared, he himself wrote a fable entitled " From an Animal Psychologist's Files " (al-Fajr January 1960). It begins with a description of the grandfather's love of animals to which the psychologist's specialization in that branch could be traced. His grandfather had been so passionately fond of animals that he had been compelled to pay blood-money to the family of a ploughman whom he had struck down with his cudgel when he saw him ill-treating his ass-colt; but, he adds characteristically, the grandfather's affection had extended to the ploughman's wife as well. However, the grandson graduated with distinction and opened a clinic furnished in the latest fashion.

" The first case that I had to deal with, was a violent love affair between a young cat and a full-grown mouse. I arrived one morning at the clinic to find the two lovers seated on one of the benches and exchanging passionate kisses. I wondered how the visitors had got into the room seeing that the door and windows were all closed and I finally discovered that the mouse had taken the liberty of gnawing the wood of the door. His friend had then helped him to widen the hole. So they both entered and sat in silence. As a psychologist in a position to investigate irregular behaviour, I investigated the behaviour of the couple in the light of psychology and I refrained from remonstrating with them for breaking into the clinic. Sometimes the mouse spoke, at other times the cat. They both lived in one house, both ate the remnants of one table and both drank from one place. Their first encounter had been a violent one in which the cat used her teeth and claws and the mouse twisted and turned. As often happens among human beings, hostility turned into friendship and then into a violent love that swept them off their feet . . .

The first obstacle in the path of the lovers was the objection of the owner of the house to this love. He thought that the old mouse was threatening the security of the house and he also thought that it was the cat's duty to defend its security by keeping the mouse imprisoned in his hole. Should the mouse persist in causing trouble, the cat was in duty bound to exterminate him. The second obstacle was the joint opposition of the family of the cat and the family of the mouse to this love. Both parties threatened the lovers that they would avenge the family honour if they persisted in their error which conflicted with inherited animal traditions.

" Such was the case related to me by the two lovers. As a result, both the mouse and the cat were suffering from complexes. The mouse could not refrain from stealing cheese while the cat was torn between her duty to prevent the mouse from exercising his natural right and her love for him. The mouse was now under suspicion of conveying military secrets to his family which was hostile to the owner of the house. He was suspected of disclosing the secret of military stores of cheese, milk and bread, and he was sentenced to death *in absentia* on a charge of damaging security to the extent of high treason. The cat was entrusted with the task of implementing the sentence of execution on her precious lover . . . Those who do not know the real meaning of the word ' animalism ' will have a good laugh. In fact, ' animalism ' bears the same relation to animals as ' humanity ' to human beings. Almost in tears the mouse said to me :

' This is our story sir . . . a first-class animal tragedy . . . even human beings would be ashamed to do what my family and the family of my beloved are doing.'

I wanted to slap his face for his impudence . . . but I remembered the ploughman whom my grandfather had felled because of the donkey . . . and my grandfather seemed to be standing behind me and to be now about to fell a respectable doctor because of a mouse. I therefore controlled my temper and kept quiet. Moments of silence prevailed which were finally interrupted by the cat saying:

' Listen, sir. Why don't you ring up the owner of the house and ask him to forgive us? Here's the number.'

The idea appealed to me and I quickly dialled. Seconds later I heard a voice reply and when I asked the owner of the voice for the master of the house, I was told that he was speaking. With all the skill at my command, I explained to him the case of the mouse and the cat. I was astonished to hear him laugh and say:

'Listen, sir, the fact is that the mouse was one of our best agents and used to convey to the cat information about all the mice that infiltrated from their cells or were plotting against us to plunder the food supplies.'

Though I was feeling rather confused, I said:

'Absurd . . .'

'First listen to the rest of the story. In recognition of the mouse's service, the cat used to allow him to wander about the house as much as he wished and we were aware of this secret agreement. But later the mouse gave himself away. His mates had grown afraid of talking in front of him. In other words, he was no longer of any use to us. So an order was issued for his execution. What do you think about that? '

I screamed in reply:

'But this is barbarous and in my capacity as a physician I will inform the police.'

He replied scornfully:

'The police, sir, are now surrounding your house in order to arrest the criminals and I request you to allow them entry.'

I tried to say something else but he had cut me off. So I put down the receiver and went back to the fond sweethearts. What was I to tell them? They were looking at me sadly and I felt more inclined to oblige them than their master. Should I conceal them? Would I not then be charged with damaging security? The pair noticed my distress and confusion and the mouse trembling with fear asked me what he had said. I had no alternative but to tell them the truth. When I had finished, silence descended on the room. The mouse looked this way and that as if in search of a way of escape. The cat's eyes glistened and her fur stood on end like spikes. Then she turned to her precious lover:

'What is it? Do you want to escape?'

The wretched mouse looked at her in panic and froze in his place. He tried to speak but could not and had to be content with shaking his head in denial. Then we heard footsteps approach the room. It must be the police coming to arrest the fugitives. I felt my heart throb powerfully in fear. Suddenly the mouse leapt from his place . . . and the cat followed him with a horrifying leap with her claws sunk in his back. I paid no attention to the knocks on the door. I was frozen in my place intent on watching the outcome of the tragedy between the lovers. The cat said:

' So that's how it is. In the moment of trouble you want to escape, you scoundrel!'

The mouse trembling with anxiety replied:

' By the life of my grandfather's head I did not want to escape. I wanted to attack the policemen in order to protect you.'

The cat said savagely:

' The policemen are coming from the door and you jumped towards the window. Even on the point of death you keep on lying.'

When he did not answer, she buffeted his head with her paw and put a question to him:

'Answer . . . do you still love me?'

As though he expected deliverance through his speech, the mouse said:

' Yes . . . by the life of my grandfather's head I love you.'

Her eyes flashed and she said:

'As long as you love me, I have more right to your flesh than any other cat . . . I could not get you alive . . . then dead shall you be mine.'

When the policeman entered, the mouse was firmly lodged in the stomach of his beloved. The officer angrily asked:

' Where is the other criminal?'

The cat said with a smile:

' I have carried out the sentence of execution on the traitor. Since dawn I have been following him from one lane to another. At last I feared that he might escape. So I called him and pretended that I was in love with him. Then we came here and I asked the doctor to contact the owner in order to let him know where we were and he sent you to us.'

I felt my head spin. Even animals have spies and traitors and detectives among them . . . even the animals for whom my grandfather had killed a man. I slumped in the chair in a faint."

The characters in this fable can easily be identified. If the owner of the house is Mapai with the military administration at its command, the cat is Mapam which was then in the ruling coalition, and Arab Mapamniks must be the mouse. Mapam's campaign for the brotherhood of the two peoples, which is obviously represented by the fervour of the love affair, faces hostility from the cat's relatives, i.e., other Zionists by whom Mapam is accused of encouraging Arabs to denounce the State and its government, and from the relatives of the mouse, i.e., communists and others who have charged their political rivals with collaboration with a Zionist party. The disclosure by the owner of the house that the mouse is now distrusted by other mice may indicate the fear that, should Arab Mapamniks fail to promote the party's success among Arab voters, they too or perhaps only their cultural apparatus will be considered expendable. When the cat engulfs the mouse after insisting on a declaration of love, one cannot help thinking of the allocation of considerable areas of confiscated Arab land to Mapam collectives; and her boasts of her treachery hints at the suspicion that Mapam may be secretly justifying the licence given to its Arabs as a combination of a safety-valve and a security operation, and at resentment of the party's failure to withdraw its representatives from the coalition in the face of Mapai's determination to maintain military government in the Arab areas. Finally, the psychologist collapses because the author himself is seized with doubt as to whether he has not involuntarily participated in the betrayal.

. . .

His forebodings have been justified. *Al-Mirsad* which had become a daily in the spring of 1961, reverted to its weekly role soon after the August elections: both *al-Fajr* and *al-Musawwar* ceased to appear, for lack of financial support, in 1962;[2] and a little over two years after the publication of his fable Rashid Husain was expelled from the party. It is reported that his application to return to teaching was rejected and that he is now working on an Arabic translation, subsidized by the *Histadruth*, of the collected works of the most eminent of Zionist poets, Bialik.

[1] Rashid Husain was kind enough to allow me to translate passages from his poetry and prose.
[2] Al-Musawwar was revived in 1964.

# Intellectuals in Israeli Druze Society[1]

## Gabriel Ben-Dor

The direct involvement of intellectuals in the politics of the developing countries is an intuitively obvious phenomenon, well brought out in the writings of theorists concerned with political development in the 1960's.[2] More recently, it is increasingly conspicuous that on the one hand the intellectuals seem to lose power to the military, and on the other the earlier hopes in regard to their modernizing activities have not materialized. The ruling élites of most Middle Eastern, African and Asian countries tend to be alliances of officers and bureaucrats, and the prevalence of the intellectuals at the highest echelons of governmental power in the stages preceding and succeeding independence[3] has drastically decreased. Apparently, the political capacity of the intellectuals has declined (at least vis-à-vis that of competing élites), or else it was seriously overestimated.

Similarly, those intellectuals who were or are able to hold power for fairly lengthy periods of time seem to disappoint those who put their faith in their conscientiousness, ideological orientation, leadership and political skills as effective instruments of modernization and purposeful social change. Although we have a good number of studies concentrating on the ideologies of such intellectual élites,[4] for a variety of reasons (probably heavily influenced by conditions and difficulties of research) we seem to know much less about what the intellectuals do when they are in power, when they attempt to attain power, or when they act in terms of putting ideological tenets into practice. Even less do we know about the dialectical relationship between ideology and practice,[5] i.e. about the mutual impact of notions about the ends and means of politics, and political activity on all levels.[6] One would like to know more about the way ideas and practices are shaped, not only in terms of philosophical traditions, foreign influences of socialization or social background, but also in terms of political realities.[7] In this paper, the analysis will proceed with this purpose in mind.

Intellectuals are defined in this paper as those who have acquired a formal education, and see it (at least partially) as a basis (whether in terms of skills, background, prestige or pure formal requirements) for a living or a profession.[8] No analytical distinction is made between 'old' and 'new', or 'sacral' and 'secular'[9] intellectuals, as it seems advisable to leave the differentiation and interrelationship between the various strata of the intellectual élite to empirical investigation. The military and bureaucrats as such will not be referred to as intellectuals, unless they satisfy the requirements of the definition as individuals or groups within their profession; on the other hand, students are included in this category, since they have already acquired some formal education, and they consider their studies a basis for advancement and livelihood.[10]

The case study presented and analyzed in this paper deals with intellectuals who are not only active in politics, but regard themselves – and are so regarded by others – as a vanguard destined to fulfil a crucial role in two key aspects of political development: innovation and integration. Their activity, therefore, can be evaluated (both in terms of ideology and of grass-root practice, at both the centre and the periphery) according to criteria of purposeful political and social change. Despite the differences between this case and a number of other instances of intellectuals in the politics of developing countries, a considerable degree of comparability (and thus potential theoretical significance) exists, and it enables the analyst to derive generalizations [10a] that seem relevant to a fair number of similar cases. Such generalizations, their limitations and their applicability will be dealt with in the concluding part of this paper.

TRADITIONAL DRUZE SOCIETY: THE LACK OF INTELLECTUALS

The Druze are a small minority concentrated on six mountain ranges in three Middle-Eastern countries:[11] in Syria, where 170,000 of them constitute 3 per cent of the population, in Lebanon, where there are 130,000 Druze (6·3 per cent of the population), and in Israel where 34,000 Druze make up 1·2 per cent of the population, and less than 10 per cent of the minorities. This paper will concentrate on the latter community.[12]

By all accounts, the Druze in Syria and Lebanon have played an influential, active role in coalition politics, in the military and various movements, out of all proportion to their small numerical strength.[13] They have always been known as a tightly-knit community, enjoying high degrees of solidarity, cohesion and the face-to-face loyalties of small groups. Geopolitically, they were characterized by semi-independence in mountain villages, which are characteristic places of dwelling for them even today. There was no urban stratum in traditional Druze society, and merchants, manufacturers and indeed professionals of any kind were virtually unknown.

The origins of the Druze religion[14] go back to eleventh-century Egypt, but new converts came exclusively from Syria and Lebanon. The Druze religion is an extremely complex and sophisticated doctrine, combining neo-Platonic philosophy, allegorical interpretations of reality, Persian influences and the traditions of Shi'ite sects of Islam, particularly the Isma'iliya. Moreover, many of the tenets of Druze religion are unknown even to the believers, as one of its major principles is secrecy, enshrouding truth and reality in deep layers of mystery. The principle of secrecy was coupled with the prohibition of conversion, after the first generation of the converts were subject to hostility and persecution. This further contributed to the solidarity and cohesiveness of the community.

Traditional Druze society was characterized by high levels of conflict, elaborate mechanisms of arbitration, low levels of differentiation, great effectiveness of military power, a relatively high degree of equality (both in terms of economic goods and political resources), and the predominance of the family[15] (which is extended, patriarchal, patrilineal and patrilocal)[16] as a primary unit of competition, loyalty, organization and identification, outside of which one's way to advancement is blocked. This was accompanied by a lack of 'free-floating' persons[17] and resources, and low levels of institutionalization.[18] Therefore, it is not surprising to conclude that intellectuals as individuals or as a group could not function; indeed, according to all accounts, no professional intellectuals ever existed among the Druzes.

To be sure, the community is divided into the initiated ('uqqal) and the uninitiated (juhhal = 'the ignorant ones'). Yet this differentiation is based not so much on knowledge, as on the access to knowledge on the basis of devotion, piety and demeanour. The juhhal are not expected to adhere to any but the simplest commandments, while the 'uqqal (who are distinguished by their white headgear) are expected to follow commandments, refrain from drinking, smoking and swearing, and carry themselves with dignity. Yet everyone (including women, who are shielded in the kinship group, due to the great sensitivity to honour and shame, but are in general respected much more than in the neighbouring communities)[19] can become an 'aqil (singular of 'uqqal) if he undertakes to undergo the stages of initiation, which make him eligible for participation in reading and discussing the secret writings of the sect. Although there is a more pious and respected group among the 'uqqal, called ajawid, these, too, are distinguished by conforming to certain norms of behaviour more than by possessing knowledge. Similarly, while there is normally a spiritual (ruhani) headman along with a secular (jismani)[20] one, the distinction is not sharp, and the two are likely to come from the same family. None of the religious leaders or sages expects to make a living out of his knowledge – indeed this is prohibited by religious commandments.[21] In summary, while there are degrees of differentiation along lines of religious status, they are not sharp, they do not correspond to socio-economic cleavages, and above all, they are based on piety and righteousness rather than on creating and transmitting knowledge for a living. Had an 'intellectual' attempted to act as such, he would have had no institutional bases of support inside the community, while the fierce particularism[22] and the peculiar state of semi-independence and semi-integration of the Druze vis-à-vis broader political frameworks would have taken away the ability to act as a Druze intellec·tual outside the community.[23]

THE EMERGENCE OF THE INTELLECTUALS AND THEIR IDEOLOGY IN THE DRUZE COMMUNITY IN ISRAEL[24]

The Druze in Israel today are a minority within a minority. They have made a more or less conscious decision to seek solutions to their problems (economic, political, demographic) within the framework of an Israeli state: the earlier fierce particularism is now mitigated by an ever-increasing reliance on the central government, and the realization that this trend is highly likely to grow in the future. The Druze, some of whom supported the Jewish forces long before the establishment of the state,[25] and who have been subject to compulsory conscription for two decades (at their own request), consider themselves to be undergoing a period of transition and change, which can be summarized as a process of integration (into Israeli society and polity) and innovation (technological progress, structural transformation of the economy, diversification of the socio-political framework toward democracy, equality and 'modernity'). In this complicated process of change, the major roles are allocated to the government, the military and education[26] (as well as its 'products', the intellectuals).[27]

More than 20,000 of the 34,000 Druze now living in Israel were born after the establishment of the state in 1948. At the end of 1968, the following distributions prevailed:

TABLE 1

THE DRUZE IN ISRAEL ACCORDING TO AGE

| Age | Percentage |
| --- | --- |
| 0–14 | 48·9 |
| 15–29 | 23·8 |
| 30–44 | 13·6 |
| 45–64 | 9·3 |
| 65 and over | 4·4 |

Adapted from *Statistical Abstract* 1969, No. 20, pp. 38–39, as quoted in Harari, *The Arabs in Israel: Statistics and Facts*, p. 15.

The extremely high percentage of young members in the community is a phenomenon underlined by the obvious intergenerational differences. According to the results of the 1961 census,[28] the rate of literacy among the Druze was 50 per cent (among Christians 76 per cent, and among Muslims 38 per cent). The difference between the generations in this respect is striking: while the rate of literacy among Druze 65 and over is only 31 per cent (among Christians 57 per cent, and among Muslims 22 per cent), in the relevant age group of 19 and under, 92 per cent of the Druze are literate (as are 96 per cent of the Christians, and 79 per cent of the Muslims).[29] The introduction of an elaborate educational network became necessary, and an entirely new cult of education as the key to the future has come into being. This has been accompanied by the appearance of a series of new political slogans, and indeed words such as 'progress', 'equality', and 'modernity' are ubiquitous in the rhetoric of Druze public figures. While education is not the only factor accounting for this phenomenon, it has certainly played a key role in its appearance.

The growth of the educational network, although often criticized as too slow, has been impressive. Since 1948, the number of Druze pupils has grown by 730 per cent (while in the same period the community has grown by 130 per cent). The percentage of girls among pupils has gone up from 10·2 to 40·6. The number of Druze teachers has increased from eight to 180, the number of female teachers from nought to twenty-three, the number of principals from two to thirteen. From one single university graduate, the student population grew to fifty in 1968–69, and it is sharply on the increase.[30] A few Druze have advanced to high ranks in the ministry of education, including Salman Fallah, the Druze scholar who is supervisor of secondary education in Arab schools. There are now Druze physicians, lawyers and one engineer. [31] The controversy over such issues as the establishment of secondary schools in the two areas of relatively heavy Druze population (the Carmel and Western Galilee) has reached universal proportions, to the extent that an American Jewish philanthropist donated a sum of $250,000 to help establish a secondary school in Yirka for the Druze population of the area. [32]

The expectations from education are high, to the extent that they seem to have become a matter of faith. Activity to improve the lot of Druze in higher education is fervent: there exists a vigorous and publicly well-known Council for the Advancement of Education in the Druze Community, that includes Druze and Jewish members, some of whom are quite prominent and influential. [33] Increasing the number of Druze students is considered a supreme goal, and vigorous efforts are exerted to make this possible. [34] Among Druze students, the belief in the efficacy of education is overwhelming: according to my survey, 54 per cent consider the improvements of education the most important challenge facing the community and they see the lack of adequate educational facilities as one of the two most important obstacles to progress and modernity, 54 per cent suggest education as the way to advance the Druze woman, and 36 per cent and 12 per cent respectively regard a university and a book as the most important symbols of modernity and progress.

Yet the rapid growth of education has introduced some highly visible imbalances. Even among the very same students experiencing their belief in education as the key to the future, twice as many (36 per cent) think that their chances of finding a 'suitable' job commensurate with their education are minimal, as those who think that their chances are good (18 per cent). [36] Although compared to other 'developing' countries [37] this percentage may not be too high, it signals the initial stages of an imbalance certain to grow as the number of students increases: the overwhelming majority of the Druze students major in the humanities and social sciences, and their community does not now possess an adequate infrastructure to absorb a considerable number of such graduates. Only a limited number of journalists and lawyers are needed, and the teaching profession does not appeal to most students, who consider it below their ability and training. [38] There is, therefore, a tendency to aim for a position in the civil service, or public institutions, positions normally requiring political background and connections. This presents a political problem: for the first time in Druze history in Israel, there exists an urban intelligentsia with a high degree of political consciousness, and with ambitions and expectations that probably cannot be satisfied within the existing political framework of the community. Eighty per cent of the students think there are serious disagreements (almost a third of them call this a 'deep gap') between them and the older generation, and almost 50 per cent of all students think it certain or probable that considering their educational background they will engage in political activity in the community. On numerous occasions, I have heard

R

students complain bitterly about their dependence on '*shaikhs*' and judges incomparably inferior to them in education and knowledge of the modern world. Although education gives them prestige, they would like to use it as a political resource to gain influence inside the community. The traditional Druze network of power relationships, however, has no place for the professional, free-floating intellectual at all, let alone in a position of influence. This contradiction between the seemingly harmless nature of education as an avenue of advancement for the young, and its increasingly painful political consequences, constitutes an important strain in Druze political life.

Education also emphasizes and sharpens another set of imbalances and strains, those relating to identity, citizenship, religion and language. Druze children go to Israeli schools, but many of them are in classes containing a sizeable proportion of Arab children; since they are Arabic-speaking, they are subject to the same curriculum as Arab children, a curriculum that gives rise to numerous complaints about the lack of a Druze content in terms of history and literature, not to mention the generally lower standards of the Arab schools as compared to their Jewish counterparts. In many of the Druze villages, there arose a movement to replace Arab teachers with Druze ones, and in 1968–69 the Ministry of Education organized a course to train Druze veterans for teaching, in order to satisfy the demand for Druze teachers. [39] Several Druze intellectuals have initiated the writing of a textbook of Druze history. [40] The Ministry of Education, encouraged by some Druze leaders, offered to begin the teaching of the Druze religion in schools, either in the school building or in the *khilwas*, [41] and under the direction of Druze religious leaders; but the latter declined, citing secrecy as the obstacle. [42] Thus far, then, the Druze school children have lacked an adequate curriculum orienting them to their community. A Druze teacher of literature bitterly complained that he had to teach Druze children only Arab poetry, but not Druze poems or songs. [43] The problem is particularly acute in mixed schools, where Druze children often encounter an attitude to their identity and duties blatantly contradictory to their upbringing at home: I was told by a Druze father that on one occasion his son had come home crying, badly upset and confused, as his teacher, an Arab nationalist, had almost labelled his father – an officer in the Israeli Army – a traitor to the nation to which the son was supposed to belong. The schools, therefore, bring into clear focus the imbalance between the status of the Druze as a minority on the one hand, and their status as a minority within a minority on the other, as their language is identical to that of the larger minority, but they are interested in asserting their separateness and in getting along with the majority.

It is not easy to find one's place as a Druze intellectual in Israel. One is a Druze, an Israeli, and an Arabic-speaking person at one and the same time. One has to come to terms with one's fellow Israelis, with the Druze across the border, and with the surrounding Arab world speaking one's own mother tongue. For an intellectual, and particularly the creative artist who heavily depends on words, the attraction of a potential audience of

100 million Arabs in the immediate vicinity, with whom one shares a common language, is powerful, although difficult (but apparently not impossible) to reconcile with one's status as a citizen of Israel. Thus, Arab nationalism as an ideology and its institutional manifestation in Israel, the New Communist List (*RAQAH*), are readily available as avenues of protests for the disenchanted. At least one major Druze intellectual, the poet Samih al-Qasem of Rameh, has chosen this avenue, and he now holds the post of literary editor of the Arabic weekly of RAQAH, *Al-Ittihad*. He is known as an Arab nationalist of extreme convictions, he is well-known and appreciated in the Arab world, and frequently participates in political activities in Israel. [44] While he is one of the very few who have chosen this way, the difficulty of coming to terms with one's identity, aggravated by the problems of the newly-emerging educated stratum, clearly puts a strain on the political position of the community, and gives added incentive to the attempts to find a satisfactory degree of integration accommodating the community.

The bewildering array of problems arising out of the rapid changes of recent years had led to recurring attempts to define the status of the Druze community in Israel, to delineate its future plans and options, and to justify systematically some courses of action as preferable to others. For the first time, there exists a professional stratum of men of letters who occupy themselves with such problems, and for the first time there has come into being a series of principles and guidelines apart from the tenets of religion, in the sense both that the origins of the new ideas are not necessarily to be found in religion, and in the sense that some of the ideas now put forth may, and do, challenge the authority and correctness of religious dogmas, as well as of religious leaders. Seen in this perspective, the emergence of a distinct political ideology not only reflects and demonstrates the strains and imbalances of Druze politics, but also adds further considerable strain of its own.

Optimally, those who regard ideology as a desirable and necessary instrument of modernization, progress or transformaton would like to see in it 'an explicit statement of political ends and means, capable of inspiring and guiding action: a general theory applicable to the problem of the day'. [45] Others contemptuously define ideologies as 'more or less conscious disguises of the real nature of the situation'. [46] Still others define ideology as 'a pattern of ideas which simultaneously provides for its adherents: (1) a self-definition, (2) a description of the current situation, its background and what is likely to follow, and (3) various imperatives which are deduced from the foregoing.' In this view, 'In ideology there is a strong tendency to merge fact and value', to superimpose upon 'things as they are the things that are desired'. [47] In a most influential essay, Clifford Geertz puts forth a theory of ideology as a cognitive map of the universe, arguing that

> ... ideology is a response to strain ... It is a loss of orientation that most directly gives rise to ideological activity, an inability, for lack of

usable models, to comprehend the universe of civic rights and responsibilities in which one finds oneself located . . .

It is . . . the attempt of ideologies to render otherwise incomprehensible social situations meaningful . . . Ideology . . . provides novel symbolic frames against which to match the myriad 'unfamiliar somethings', that, like a journey to a strange country, are produced by a transformation in political life. Whatever else ideologies may be . . . they are, most distinctively, maps of problematic social reality and matrices for the creation of collective conscience.[48]

The Druze intellectuals rarely give expression to an awareness of the requirements or purposes of a systematic ideology. As a rule, they do not attempt to build or utilize sophisticated theories.[49] The do, however, attempt occasionally to define ends and means; they do try to put forth a self-definition congruent with changing reality; and they are busy with drawing maps that could make confusing reality comprehensible and meaningful. Since the strains and imbalances are felt not only by the intellectuals, but also by the simplest inhabitants of the villages, receptivity to explanations and slogans definitely exists. The new vocabulary of progress and citizenship filters down to each village and can be heard in everyday conversation. Ideology may be primarily the preoccupation of the small, partly urban intelligentsia, but it is not monopolized or preempted by it. In fact, even the casual observer is struck by the linguistically sophisticated quasi-ideological formulations of the simplest Druze peasants when interviewed about political issues.[50]

A new vocabulary is very much in evidence. Words such as 'modernization', 'progress', 'equality', 'citizenship', 'democracy', and 'integration' are widely used and quoted. At times a heated debate is conducted on the relationship between these concepts and the teachings of Druze religion. Particular events or phenomena that arouse dissatisfaction are attacked and condemned on the grounds that they contradict the aforementioned concepts or ideals. Whatever the eventual outcome of the semantic change may be, it has already given a definite framework to the ongoing political arguments, and a somewhat formal structure – that is within the bounds of accepted ideals and, thus, criteria – to the process of longer-range planning and strategy.

Perhaps the most fundamental problem to be mentioned here is that of identity, orientation and self-definition. The difficult and confusing situation of multiple attachments, and the obvious hardship in reconciling religious and political loyalties of citizenship, have led to some very serious soul-searching. Briefly, this means that the question 'Who are the Druze?' and 'What does it mean to be a Druze?' must be answered. The answer, in turn, must take into consideration the religious status involved, and the relationships with the Druze in the neighbouring countries, as well as with the Arabs and the Israelis. Inasmuch as, according to my sample of students, the two most important characteristics of the Druze are loyalty (29 per cent) and religiousness (19 per cent), this is a difficult task indeed.

In discussing the subject with Druze, the 'Druze question' is often likened to the 'Jewish question' in terms of self-definition, political identity and relation between religion and nationalty.[51] Thus, the Druze religion is seen as the heart of Druze self-identity, as the one thing above all that holds the Druze community together. This is true with scholars and laymen, leaders and followers, intellectuals and peasants, *'uqqal* and *juhhal:* the word *din* (religion) is indeed on everyone's lips, and as pointed out above, religiousness is considered to be the most typical characteristic of a Druze. This reply was often given not only by Druzes who are not religious, but even by some who define themselves as 'anti-religious'.

Yet religious identity and political status are at times difficult to reconcile. Despite the very strong sense of identity, only 3 per cent of the respondents to the survey thought the ties with the Druze in Syria and Lebanon strong and permanent. Seventy-six per cent defined the ties as purely spiritual, 7 per cent thought the ties to be weak, and 13 per cent thought that there are almost no ties. Only 14 per cent responded favourably to the idea of a possible Druze state, while 54 per cent said they wouldn't be in favour of such a project, and 20 per cent said they didn't know what to think of it. While one or two of my informants went as far as saying that the idea of a Druze state was forbidden by the principles of Druze religion,[52] perhaps the best-known representative of the young generation thinks a Druze state would be the optimal solution to the Druze problem; but since that solution seems to him utopian, even he thinks that the task of the leadership is to concentrate on integrating the Druze community into Israeli society.[53]

The Druze in Lebanon and Syria remain, however, strongly influential reference groups to Israeli Druze. Some complaints are heard that Druze officers can advance in the Syrian Army more than in Israel, and the higher level of education among the Druze in Syria was manifest at the first meeting of Israeli Druze with the 7,000 Druze in five villages of the Golan Heights occupied in June 1967.[54] Much more important, Israeli Druze see among their co-religionists in Lebanon a higher level of sophistication, a satisfactory standing in the state, and a reasonable compromise between tradition and modernity. Mr Ramal quotes with pride and approval the enlightened and well-educated leadership in Lebanon, and the fact that it is honoured and respected by the heads of the state. Another well-known Druze leader, who was a candidate for the *Knesset* in the Labour Party list in the last elections, and now functions as the President's Adviser for Arab Affairs, looks upon the enlightened, but religious, reformism of the Druze leadership in Lebanon as the example to follow.[55] Druze judges in Israel rely heavily on the laws and verdicts regarding Druze personal status in Lebanon.

Since religion is defined as the heart of Druze identity, it fulfils a central role in what the Druze consider their ideology of modernization. The process of coming to terms with rapid, often unintended changes is extremely painful, and it is considered to be dangerous. Some fear that process will completely destroy Druze identity and will push Druze youths to a course of hiding or abandoning their attachment to the community. [56] Others fear that the separateness of the community – a fundamental feature of its existence – will be given up. Most Druze also have the uneasy feeling that some justification must be found for the particular changes now taking place, at the same time that reassurances must be given that, despite the changes, the essential core of Druze identity will remain the same. As a result, a frantic examination of religious principles goes on in order to prove that this or that feature of 'progress' not only does not contradict religion, but in fact is almost commanded by it.[57] This is not a movement for the reinterpretation of religious principles, but rather a tendency to cling to religious teachings as the justification of changes, and a re-assurance that *plus ça change, plus c'est la même chose*. The questions: 'If everything changes, are we still the same? If change is so constant, what is it that changes?' are answered by religion. What changes is a community held together by a common religion; it remains the same as long as religion does not change; other changes are possible if they can be recon-ciled with the teachings of religion. Since, however, many Druze are deter-mined to have both religion and change, there is strong pressure on religious leaders to find justification for the changes. Their reaction is mixed: some would like to go along with a long series of reforms, but others – according to the reformists – fear the challenge to their authority and thus object to reform on (false) religious grounds.[58] The vast majority of the community cannot participate in the debate, as the secrecy of their own religion and their lack of knowledge of it prevent them from judging the positions of those who do participate.[59] Even so, some educated Druze who are well-versed in the ways of the city, return to their villages and enter the stages of religious initiation, apparently motivated by the belief that only in religion can they find the solution to the twin problems of continuity and change. Still others now openly challenge religion and religious leaders as anti-progressive. The confusion over this issue is demonstrated by the responses to the question: 'What in your view is the relationship between the Druze religion and progress?' in the survey. Seventeen per cent thought religion contributes much to progress, 24 per cent thought it contributes something to progress, 20 per cent thought there is no connection between the two, 24 per cent thought religion hinders progress a little, and 14 per cent thought religion hinders progress very much.

The disagreement brought out by the results of the survey can be accounted for partially by the disagreements in the religious leadership, and by the various degrees of knowledge about religion. It is noteworthy that only 3 per cent consider religion to be the most important agent of modernization in the community, and only 4 per cent think the key to progress is to be found in the hands of the religious leadership. These figures indicate that the students do not necessarily agree with the attempts of the leadership to anchor changes in religious tradition. Many of the leaders may still be tied to the overwhelming source of mysterious power to be found in religion, that alone can distinguish between desirable and undesirable (indeed, permissible and non-permissible) change, and that alone can ensure that the community will not fall apart amidst change. The students agree only very partially. Some Druze leaders suggest that if they (students and youths) knew more about religion, even in relatively simple terms of commentary rather than the philosophical background, communication might be easier.[60] In any case, the tendency to look for justification of each change in particular relgious teachings,[61] leads to a situation in which every innovation, invention and change is expected to become the final state of affairs, based on religious dogmas. Particular changes are accepted and then are more or less reconciled to tradition; what this procedure does is to neglect the problem of change as such. Innovations are accepted as long as they are not considered 'real' innovations,[62] but the attitude toward innovation has not changed. Since the frozen dogmas are shielded from the believers, not much hope for a critical re-examination of them remains, unless religion becomes better known to the Druze,[63] so that instead of being the ultimate, unexamined and uncriticized arbiter of truth and error it can become itself the target of examination, analysis and criticism. 'When we remain conscious of the origins of concepts in beliefs about current utility, values or interests, or in statements of probability within competing or evolving paradigms, we keep alive the constant need for experimentation and re-examination and hence the potentials for transformation.'[64]

Most young Druze see the ongoing process of change as related to a general movement toward progress and modernity; that is, the perceive that the changes already visible, and those required to redress the equally visible imbalances in the community, will lead to a generally improved state of affairs that they label 'modernity' or 'progress'. The use of these words, as mentioned before, is quasi-universal. When asked whether they were satisfied with the rate of social and economic progress, none of the respondents to the survey answered 'very satisfied', while 37 per cent were satisfied, 56 per cent were dissatisfied, and 6 per cent were very disappointed. Similarly, none of the respondents was very satisfied with the present leadership of the community, while 17 per cent were satisfied, 63 per cent dissatisfied and 20 per cent were very disappointed.[65] The figures indicate that whatever rate of progress the Druze students see as satisfactorily achieved, they do not attribute it to the leadership. Neither do they expect much from traditional institutions in the future: only 3 per cent consider religion to be the most effective and important agent of modernization and progress, and only 10 per cent think that the key to progress and modernity is to be found in the hands of the present political or religious leadership.

Education, as mentioned before, is seen as both an end and a means. Both in the survey and in interviews with people it was striking to find to what extent the Druze – and not only the students among them – consider education both the essence of modernity and the way to achieve it.[66] Fifty-four per cent of the respondents to the survey consider the improvement of education the most important challenge facing the Druze community in Israel in the near future,[67] as compared to 20 per cent who emphasize the advancement of women, 14 per cent who pointed to integration into Israeli society,[68] and only 8 per cent who stressed economic development. As pointed out before, one of two most important obstacles to modernity is believed to be the lack of educational facilities and teachers, and almost half of the respondents consider a university and a book the most important symbols of progress and modernity.

What are progress and modernity? In addition to the 48 per cent who named a university or a book, 37 per cent identified equality as their most important symbol, and 9 per cent pointed to a parliament. Only 3 per cent thought political modernization is the most important challenge facing the community. When asked to identify the two most important signs of modern politics, the following replies were received:

TABLE 2

THE TWO MOST IMPORTANT SIGNS OF MODERN POLITICS AS IDENTIFIED BY DRUZE STUDENTS IN ISRAEL

| | |
|---|---|
| Democratically elected institutions | 25% |
| An educated and active public opinion | 15% |
| Educated and responsible leadership | 27% |
| Activity based on a man's worth and not his family or communal belonging | 19% |
| Equality between men and women | 4% |
| Social and economic equality | 8% |
| Lawful and organized administration | 4% |

Who is to carry out the activities necessary to achieve the goals of modernity and progress? Among the responding students, 17 per cent said they would definitely take part in political activities, 31 per cent said they would probably do so, while 48 per cent said they did not think so, and 3 per cent said they would definitely not engage in politics. When asked to identify the best and most important agent of modernization and progress, 26 per cent pointed to 'other' (mostly educational and some internal Druze) factors, 20 per cent pointed to the military, 13 per cent to the political parties, 3 per cent each to religion and the *Histadrut*,[69] but the largest number (35 per cent), stressed the role of the government. The tendency to attribute overwhelming importance to government is conspicuously demonstrated also in the following two tables summarizing the results of the survey:

TABLE 3

THE MOST SEVERE OBSTACLE HINDERING PROGRESS AND MODERNIZATION IN THE COMMUNITY, ACCORDING TO DRUZE STUDENTS

| | |
|---|---|
| Lack of educational facilities and teachers | 26% |
| Tradition and religion | 3% |
| The patriarchal and feudal structure | 10% |
| Economic backwardness and lack of industry | 14% |
| Lack of care by the Israeli authorities | 27% |
| Internal strife in the community | 7% |
| Lack of suitable leadership | 10% |
| The situation of women | 3% |

## TABLE 4
THE INSTITUTIONS AND FACTORS HOLDING THE KEY TO MODERNITY AND PROGRESS IN
THE DRUZE COMMUNITY IN ISRAEL, ACCORDING TO DRUZE STUDENTS

| | |
|---|---|
| Israeli institutions (government, *Histadrut*, parties, &c.) | 35% |
| The spiritual leadership of the community | 4% |
| The political leadership of the community | 6% |
| The young generation that served in the Army and acquired an education | 23% |
| The generation that is still in elementary and secondary school | 11% |
| The Druze woman | 11% |
| Others (independence of the community, the attitude of the Jewish people) | 8% |

Fundamentally, all want progress and modernity, the fundamental feature of which is education. Not much attention is paid to the political aspects of modernization,[70] which is seen as hindered by educational deficiencies and lack of adequate attention by the government. Since education is the key, a fair proportion of the educated generation wishes to participate in politics, yet the activity of the government is seen as even more important and potentially beneficial. This drastic *volte-face* in the attitude to government presents an astonishing contrast with traditional Druze society; however, its immediate impact may well be a feeling of inefficacy and thus lack of self-confidence. However important education may be, any time the government and education are considered together, the former is believed to be even more powerful. Since the government is all-powerful and holds the key to future progress, and since the present, uneducated leadership is seen as unsatisfactory, the logical solution is considered to be the support of the government for the educated young generation as against the traditional leadership. Yet the respondents of the survey[71] seem to believe that the opposite case is true: when asked to express their opinion on the often-heard charge that the state (through governmental and public institutions) cooperates (for reasons of political convenience) with the patriarchal-'feudal' forces of the community, and neglects the forces of progress and modernization, not a single respondent disagreed with the charge; 51 per cent thought the charge was definitely true, 41 per cent thought that it was at least partially true, and 7 per cent thought it to be true, although politically there was no other alternative.[72] The serious dissonance between the two key factors, the 'educated' and the government, imposes a serious strain on Druze political relationships, in that there is much frustration and bitterness at what is generally believed to be support by the government of the leadership, which is considered unsatisfactory.[73] The strain is conspicuous, and it derives from the penetration of the government as a new, overwhelming power: in traditional Druze society not only was such intergenerational hostility unimaginable, but no governmental or other non-Druze institutions would have been considered competent to 'make or break' an entire stratum of leaders not only in the centre but also at the periphery.

The neglect to search for ways of organizing and utilizing institutionalized power, either inside the community or along with Jewish elements, an option now clearly open, is remarkable. A certain mechanistic and deterministic view prevails as to progress and modernity being ushered in by education. This view is held by the older traditional leaders[70] as well as by the young political-science graduates of the universities, who for the most part see no relevant connection between their studies and the political problems of their community. No theories have emerged in a manner linking past and present, centre and periphery, problems and solutions, resources and activities. Educated Druze speak of creating a stratum of intellectuals who have honest principles and a sophisticated outlook,[75] but little or no attention is paid to the possibility of translating intellectual skills into components of purposeful political action. Young would-be reformers believe that education and government will put in motion a process that will almost automatically bring about the hoped-for results, a process that is likened to introducing new instruments of technology. A Druze student told a newspaperman: 'Just as the telephone and electricity have entered the village, so we will make political progress also enter the heads of the inhabitants'.[76]

The preoccupation with progress and modernity has also brought about a discernible change in the attitude toward one of the most conspicuous features of traditional Druze politics: conflict through factionalism. Earlier it was emphasized that the available tools of mediation and negotiation were considered sufficient to protect the community from the potentially damaging impact of large-scale conflict. Now, the mechanistic view of modernity is giving rise to slogans of unity. Some Druze believe factionalism allows too much manipulation by the authorities.[77] Others believe that factionalism has become suicidal, and that there is a danger of outright collapse in the villages still torn by inter-clan feuds.[78] Following the outbreak of violence in the wake of a blood-feud in the village of Abu Snan, one of the best-known young leaders challenged the religious leadership to put an end to internal feuds, and to regard this as a major task in the immediate future.[79] The speeches of the religious leaders indeed contain numerous exhortations to unity.[80] In analyzing the first issue of the journal published by the Labour Committee of the two Carmel villages, the reader is struck by the conspicuously frequent use of the words 'unity', 'unifying', and 'unification'.[81]

There is considerable disagreement on the meaning of 'unity'. Some Druze mean by this simply a reduction in inter-clan tensions. Others would like to see a gradual decline in the power of the units which underline factionalism, the kinship groups. The latter task appears to the observer to be truly revolutionary, while the informants are often reluctant to mention it on their own. Once the subject is raised, however, they all agree on its exceptional importance; yet practically none of them has clear and specific ideas as to the ways and means of carrying out such a revolution. Musbah Halaby,[82] in his own view one of the few exceptional persons who have been able to break away from the political hold of the family,[83] points out three tasks on the way to help 'anti-family modernization': the love of one's fellow men, emphasizing the public good rather than individual benefits, and 'liberalization of thinking'.[84] Shaikh Labib Abu Rukun says that while he cannot prophesy, he thinks that time will erode the base of the *hamulas*.[85] Indeed, the same cheerfully deterministic belief in the efficacy of time ushering in modernity prevails as to the eventual decline of the present devotion to kinship groups. Very little thought is given to the philosophical, psychological or political reasons accounting for the strength and endurance of the kinship system; consequently, even the few young Druze who emphasize building 'modern' political institutions,[86] have difficulty in pointing out how they plan to avoid the capture and subversion of such institutions by the traditional kinship units. Still, the verbal attack on the sanctity, usefulness and, eventually, the very survival of the *hamula* as the fundamental unit of political loyalty and competition, along with the professed change in the attitude toward conflict, impose a serious strain on the existing pattern of politics.

The picture depicted above represents faithfully the ideological position of the vast majority of those Druze in Israel who articulate and express such a position. There are, needless to say, patterns of dissent. We have already mentioned the availability of Arab nationalism and its institutional outlet, the Communist *RAQAH* party, as alternatives to the mainstream of Druze thinking. As pointed out before, this alternative has been taken advantage of only by a small handful of intellectuals, while the vast majority of those who occasionally vote for Communist candidates do so as a means of protest and bargaining, well within the framework of Israeli politics, rather than out of ideological convictions. Still, there are a few Israeli Druze who feel a closer identification with the Arabs. More often than not, these are the losers and the disappointed who no longer wish to participate in the mainstream of Druze politics. The conspicuous example of this is Shaikh Abdallah Khayr,[87] probably the wealthiest Druze in Israel, member of one of three most distinguished families in Galilee, and the first Palestinian Druze to achieve a university degree. Shaikh Abdallah, who was the first to organize a Druze institution in Palestine, was a District Officer during the British mandate, functioned as the chairman of the Tobacco Board in Israel, and was appointed the first chairman of the local council of Abu Snan, where his family is wealthy (and has a large proportion of well-educated members), but not very large. He lost the first election in his village,[88] and he is on bad terms with the authorities, who pick far less educated and experienced Druze than himself for important posts. Now Shaikh Abdallah, the man who founded the first Druze political organization in Palestine, claims that he identifies with educated, 'reasonable' men everywhere[89] and believes in the power of science and reason, and their eventual triumph. In terms of identity, however, he firmly believes that the Druze are Arabs, and he claims that Druze identity is a crude political fabrication for temporary advantage and convenience. He also believes that an eventual settlement between Israel and the Arabs will solve the Druze problem by enabling the Druze to return to their natural identity as Arabs.[90] He has generally nothing but contempt for the leaders of the community, both old and young, who seem to him ignorant (including the better-educated young politicians) and opportunistic. Shaikh

Abdallah totally denies 'Druzeness', so to speak, and dissents from the mainstream of Druze thinking altogether.

Perhaps the other side of the coin is best represented by two brothers living in a village in the Lower Galilee.[91] Their father, a liberally-minded Druze who cooperated with the *Haganah*, the major Jewish underground defence organization long before the establishment of the state, encouraged them to study. Indeed, both brothers attended a well-known Jewish high school in Haifa. The older brother is a university graduate and now teaches. Among his posts is a part-time one in a Jewish school. The younger brother studied at the University of Haifa while serving in the Army, and he plans to continue his studies, perhaps even for a higher (master's) degree. The two brothers are rather unhappy with much of what the mainstream of the Druze 'ideologues' has to say,[92] although the younger brother is active in the Druze organization.

The major point in the dissent of the brothers has to do with the identity of the Druze as individuals and as a group. They feel themselves to be above all citizens of the state, and would like to participate in public life on this basis. They accuse many of the young leaders of opportunism and careerism, and of using the name of the Druze community only for their personal advancement.[93] To this they strongly object: they advise the Druze to think and behave on a universalistic basis, as men and citizens, just like everyone else in the country. They express sorrow at the frequent use of such words as 'community' and 'minority', on account of their divisive and parochial political implications. They feel their 'Druzeness' is a matter of religion: in all other respects they are much like their fellow Israelis. They think this point should be explained to Druze youths rather early, so that minorities[94] can be slowly dissolved as outmoded, parochial groups. They do not advocate revolutionary steps, and would not like to see Druze girls leave the village for work or study.[95] They do, however, object, very strongly, to one prevailing feature central to Druze life and thinking, a feature they share with other Middle Easterners: emotionalism. The brothers consider the Druze to be excessively emotional, a short-coming that seriously undermines the rational, universalistic trend of thinking they would like to see emerge, both as a desirable development in its own right and as a step toward integrating the Druze fully into Israeli life. They calmly but firmly insist: 'Emotion ought to be burned'. While the mainstream of Druze ideology emphasizes integration *of* the community, and innovation *within* the community, the dissenting brothers advocate innovation in the sense of doing away with identification as a community, and behaving as member of a minority, and integration in the sense of full, unconditional citizenship,[96] again by liberating the Druze from their community and minority 'complex'. They have not given much thought to the particular strategies and conditions of purposeful political action in the direction to which they point, but they feel that the particularistic and parochial ways of the present leadership – again, both young and old – are not only incongruent with the ideals of universal, rational and civic-minded citizenship, but that they lead to outright opportunism and careerism.

THE POLITICS OF THE EDUCATED: THE REALITIES OF POWER

Having pointed out the overwhelming belief in the efficacy of education among the Druze. it is somewhat surprising to find that the educate élite has had a relatively slight impact on the politics of the community. To be sure, the presence of the intellectuals creates strains, changes the vocabulary and may lead to some inter-clan differentiaton, but on the whole, the impact of the intellectuals has been slight on the aspects of politics and society most important to them: the centres of power, the structure of political competition, and the traditional character of prevailing relationships. How can we account for the difficulties of Druze intellectuals in politics?

First of all, one must bear in mind that the degree of politicization among Druze intellectuals (as indeed among Druze throughout the centuries) is high.[97] The tendency, now observable, to devote oneself purely to an artistic or administrative career at the expense of public activity, is a recent phenomenon,[98] and it is very frequently a way of fulfilment for those whose hopes in terms of sociopolitical activities have not materialized. On the whole, the intellectuals do attempt to get involved in politics in a variety of ways: by organizing in the cities and, to a lesser extent, in the villages,[99] by allying themselves with powerful elements such as political parties or the *Histadrut*, and by attempting to build on the prestige and skills associated with their background.

Ever since the 1930's, when the first Druze intellectual in Palestine appeared,[100] there have been attempts to organize institutions that overtly or covertly (by their very existence as alternative, non-kinship based centres of power) challenge the traditional leadership.[101] Since the 1930's, the observer is struck by the weakness of these structures (to the point of quick disintegration) in a hostile environment. The traditional leadership has adroitly employed four strageties *vis-à-vis* the institutional threat: (a) *destroying* the institution by exerting pressures, invoking sanctions and mobilizing external (governmental and across-the-border Druze) support;[102] (b) *assimilating, subverting and penetrating* institutions and resources[103] (political parties, trade union branches and even industrial companies are captured and held in captivity by kinship groups, and ancient factionalism continues in a modern disguise); (c) *diverting* and *draining* the energies of potential or actual challenges to relatively harmless activities in the arts, business, studies and even the military; and (d) *co-optation*[104] by dispersing favours through the control of resources which government and public agencies have placed in the hands of the traditional leadership.

The ability of the traditional leadership to use these strategies skilfully and selectively demonstrates the dialectical character of the penetration of external factors: a non-authoritarian, manifold process which liberates energies and makes resources available in different, often contradictory directions. While, however, the traditional leaders have been able to utilize this situation to their advantage, the intellectuals have failed to realize and utilize their advantages. Having been unable or unwilling to fashion connections with sympathetic elements in the Jewish sector,[105] and having experienced many initial failures, they now find themselves in a situation where they fear that the process of change, which (on account of its dialectical character) seems to strengthen everyone, but also to make everyone feel somewhat threatened, may freeze at any moment to their disadvantage, to the point where they will be altogether eliminated from the centres of power. In order to prevent this, they feel that they must participate in the politics of leadership, even at the price of allying themselves with the traditional leaders through occasional patron-client relationships, or else through re-insertion in the traditional kinship groups or factions.

Hence, the astonishingly different standards at the centre and the periphery. Young leaders who appear to the Jewish public[106] as radical, extremist and even revolutionary are not only tolerated but at times even encouraged by the traditional leadership, as long as their attacks are directed at abstract notions of 'feudalism', 'patriarchalism', 'backwardness', and the vague 'shaikhs', or simply the 'elders', and not directly against actual personalities or concrete practices. As far as the older leadership is concerned, the activity of the young 'radicals' is useful, since (a) it constitutes a verbal safety-valve for discontent; (b) it presents an outward appearance of progressive and democratic political conflict, and (c) the criticism of the existing state of the community is seen as a powerful vehicle of pressure for extracting more benefits and resources from the government.

From the point of view of the young 'radicals', the tacit alliance with the elders is equally useful, since it makes their criticism 'respectable' and safe, in that they can voice their slogans without sanctions being invoked and without loss of resources. It is also useful because of the aforementioned feeling of the necessity to find allies in the leadership, on account of the inability or unwillingness to do so outside. The young intellectuals also feel above all that they are Druze, and are gratified to feel that their criticism is not considered destructive to their community. This alliance (which is often difficult to detect at first or second sight) frequently astonishes the observer, who encounters the young intellectuals in the city, where they bitterly criticise, indeed condemn, phenomena such as backwardness, ignorance, illiteracy, opportunism and the patriarchal structure of politics, yet when visiting the villages he notices the same critics 'eating out of the hands' of the very same patriarchal, 'backward', often illiterate or semiliterate old leaders. This alliance is known to the Druze, and to the careful analysts of Druze affairs. One of its consequences is cynicism on the part of Jewish officials when confronted with the arguments of the young 'radicals'.[107] A much more serious consequence is the astonishing degree of mistrust among the young activists, who freely condemn each other and trade charges of being one of the old leaders' tools,[108] thus undermining the capacity to cooperate for common goals in a stable framework. Even those Druze who sympathise with reforming ideals are sceptical about the young would-be reformers, as the inconsistent duality of vocal criticism in front of the Jewish public, on the one hand, and the quiet conformism in the villages, on the other, undermine both the credibility and the 'image' of the intellectual would-be leaders.[109] The different standards at the centre and periphery[110] certainly undermine the self-confidence of the young political activists, by casting doubts about the worth of their activities and the faith both in their eventual outcome and moral implications.

Mistrust, of course, feeds on itself.[111] The weakness of their institutionalized power deprives the intellectuals of the possibility of enjoying the achievements of their reform-oriented political activities in the foreseeable future. Mutual suspiciousness, well-congruent with the Druze tradition of searching for ever deeper layers of reality,[112] creates a feeling that one's fellow 'free-floating' reformer may well be neither free-floating nor a committed reformer. The sad realities ensuing cause a situation in which the perceived constant need to compromise and to change behaviour in order to conform to prevailing norms creates a feeling that the distinction between strategy and tactics, long-range goals and temporary compromise, persistence in reform (or 'revolution') and opportunism, becomes very murky indeed. The rhythm of political development (perceived in terms of integration and innovation) is uneven when the strength of the process at certain stages of the life-cycle (military service, studies at the university) is followed by its drastic weakening at other, often consecutive stages (return to the village, political activity in the villages). The taste of honey is often followed by the bitterness of frustration, and a good deal of cynicism and alienation (from previously held reformist goals) ensue.

The intellectuals seem to be caught in a vicious cycle. As long as the strength of traditional leaders and patterns continues, they can successfully resist and subvert penetrating institutions; on the other hand, they cannot be broken without building alternative (institutional) centres of power for the reformers. Yet the latter have been unable to do so without allying themselves with, and thus strengthening, the traditional leaders, groups and practices, as well as, in so doing, weakening themselves as a group capable of cooperation and effective political action. The breaking of this vicious cycle appears to be the primary task of the political innovator; yet the ideology, background and skills of the intellectuals have not thus far been made particularly relevant to this task.[113] While the intellectuals have not been completely eliminated from politics, what has happened is that some of them have been able to negotiate a good bargain for themselves through utilizing their standing, skills or prestige.[114] On the other hand, the results of their activities as groups oriented toward reform and change have been meagre and unimpressive. Their relative failure signifies the inability to utilize ideology as an effective guide to political realities; to the extent that this has been accompanied by mistrust, cynicism and alienation we may reply to Lord Acton that if power corrupts, weakness resulting from the lack of power may also corrupt.

NOTES

1. The empirical data in this paper are based on the results of field research lasting a year (1970–1971) for a doctoral dissertation at Princeton University. I am grateful to Professor Henry Bienen of Princeton University for helpful criticism of a draft of this paper.

2. Edward Shils, 'The Intellectuals in the Political Development of the New States', *World Politics*, XII (April, 1960); Harry J. Benda, 'Non-Western Intelligentsia as Political Elites', in John H. Kautsky (ed.), *Political Change in Underdeveloped Countries* (New York, 1962); Fred W. Riggs, *Administration in Developing Countries* (Boston, 1964) and James S. Coleman (ed.), *Education and Political Development* (Princeton, 1965). The latter work lists a large number of further studies in its annotated bibliography and references.

3. Shils, *op. cit.*; Benda, *op. cit.* Although the intellectuals participated in politics in many ways, the most conspicuous among them were the leaders of nationalist parties, many of which have been overthrown, barred or taken over by military regimes, as was the case in Ghana, Uganda or Syria.

4. See Paul E. Sigmund (ed.), *The Ideologies of the Developing Nations* (rev. ed. New York, 1967) and further works there listed. David E. Apter (ed.), *Ideology and Discontent* (New York, 1964) and Chaim I. Waxman (ed.), *The End of Ideology Debate* (New York, 1968).

5. Leonard Binder, *The Ideological Revolution in the Middle East* (New York, 1964); Alexander Gerschenkron, *Economic Backwardness in Historical Perspective* (Cambridge, 1962); Mary Matossian, 'Ideologies of Delayed Industrialization', *Economic Development and Cultural Change*, VI (April, 1958).

6. Therefore, the analysis of ideology detached from practice may not only divert attention from political realities, but it also may mislead or baffle the observer, as in cases where downright contradictory ideological principles seem to be held. Such cases can be explained only through relating ideology to the political process on several levels. See, for instance, William B. Quandt, *Revolution and Political Leadership: Algeria 1954–1968* (Cambridge, 1969).

7. Aristide R. Zolberg, *Creating Political Order* (Chicago, 1966); Henry Bienen 'What Does Political Development Mean in Africa?', *World Politics* (October, 1967).

8. This definition follows more or less the elastic and loose concept of 'intellectuals' as put forth in Shils, *op. cit.*

9. As in Edward Shils, 'The Intellectuals and the Powers: Some Perspectives for Comparative Analysis', *Comparative Studies in Society and History* I (1958–1959), or in a different way in Riggs, *op. cit.*

10. Cf. Douglas E. Ashford, *Second and Third Generation Elites in the Maghreb* (Washington, 1964); Coleman, *passim*; Shils, 'The Intellectuals in the Political Development of the New States'.

10a. A case study of course can neither establish nor decisively refute comprehensive theories (see Bernard E. Brown, 'The Case Method in Comparative Politics' in James B. Christoph and *idem* (ed.)), *Cases in Comparative Politics* (Boston, 1965), but it can and should generate generalizations that can be treated as theoretically-oriented hypotheses in need of refinement and testing.

11. These statistics are as of 1969. Source: *Hitpathut Hahinuh Baeda Hadruzit Beyisrael* (The Development of Education in the Druze Community in Israel, Ministry of Education, Jerusalem, 1969), pp. 7–8. See also *U.S. Army Handbook for Syria* (Washington, 1964), p. 11 and Gabriel Baer, *Population and Society in the Arab East* (London, 1964), pp. 109, 114.

12. The best sources for this are: Chaim Blanc, *Hadruzim* (The Druze, 2nd ed. Jerusalem, 1971); Salman H. Fallah, *Hadruzim Beeretz Yisrael* (The Druze in Palestine, Unpublished M.A. thesis, Hebrew University of Jerusalem, 1962); *idem*, 'The Druze Community in Israel', *New Outlook* V (June, 1962); *idem*, 'Druze Communal Organization in Israel', *New Outlook* X (March-April, 1967); Yitzhak Ben-Zvi, *Eretz-Yisrael Veyishuva Tahat Hashilton Haottomani* (Palestine and its Population Under Ottoman Rule, Jerusalem, 1966–1967); *idem*, 'Hevel Hadruzim Beyisrael', 'The Druze Region in

Israel', *Eretz Yisrael* II (1952–1953); Eliahu Epstein, 'Hadruzim Beeretz Yisrael (The Druze in Palestine)', *Yalkut Hamizrah Hatikhon*, 32–33 (1939); Zeev Wilnay, *Hamiutim Beyisrael* (The Minorities in Israel, Jerusalem, 1959). Yechiel Harari (ed.), *The Arabs in Israel: Statistics and Facts* (Givat Haviva, 1970); M. Harel, 'The History of Druze Settlements in Israel', *Bulletin of Druze Affairs* II (April 1959, in Arabic translation); Ori Sthendel, *Yisrael: Miutim* (Israel Minorities, Jerusalem, 1970); R. Baki, 'The Demography of the Muslim, Christian and Druze Population', *Hebrew Encyclopaedia* VI (1956–57), pp. 701–707; Benjamin Shidlowsky (ed.), *Hayishuvim Haarviim Wehadruziim Beyisrael* (The Arab and Druze Settlements in Israel, Jerusalem, 1969); Menashe Harel, *Yanuh, Kfar Druzi Bagalil* (Yanuh: A Druze Village in Galilee, Jerusalem, 1959); the annual Statistical Abstract and Statistical Yearbook of the Israeli Government and the annual *Majallat al-Akhbar al-Durziya* (Bulletin of Druze Affairs).

13. Philip K. Hitti, *The Origins of the Druze People and Religion* (New York, 1928); Capitaine N. Bouron, *Les Druzes: Histoire du Liban et de la Montagne Hauranaise* (Paris, 1930); C. F. Volney, *Travels through Syria and Egpyt* (2 vols. London, 1805); John Lewis Burckhardt, *Travels in Syria and the Holy Land* (London, 1822); Colonel Churchill, *Mount Lebanon: A Ten Years' Residence from 1842 to 1852* (2 vols. London, 1853); Richard F. Burton and Charles F. Drake, *Unexplored Syria* (London, 1872); Lawrence Oliphant, *The Land of Gilead* (Edinburgh, 1880); idem, *Haifa, or Life in Modern Palestine* (New York, 1887); Joseph T. Parfit, *Among the Druzes of Lebanon and Bashan* (London, 1917); William R. Polk, *The Opening of South Lebanon* (Cambridge, 1965); Albert Hourani, *Minorities in the Arab World* (London, 1947); Hanna Abu Rashid, *Jabal al-Duruz* (The Druze Mountain, 2 vols. 2nd ed., Beirut, 1961).

14. See the monumental 2-volume study by Sylvestre de Sacy, *Exposé de la Religion des Druzes Tiré des Livres Religieux de Cette Secte* (Paris, 1838).

15. Victor Ayoub, *Political Structure of a Middle East Community: A Druze Village in Mount Lebanon* (Unpublished Ph.D. dissertation, Harvard University, 1955); idem, 'Resolution of Conflict in a Lebanese Village', in Leonard Binder (ed.) *Politics in Lebanon* (New York, 1966).

16. Blanc, p. 138.

17. S. N. Eisenstadt, *The Political Systems of Empires* (New York, 1963).

18. According to various criteria, such as those in Samuel P. Huntington, 'Political Development and Political Decay', *World Politics* XVII (April ,1965).

19. Burton and Drake, *passim*; Oliphant, *Haifa, passim*; Churchill, *passim*; Volney, *passim;* Fallah, *Hadruzim*, Ch. 9.

20. Oliphant, *Haifa*, p. 143.

21. De Sacy, II, p. 665; Churchill, II, p. 229.

22. Chaim Blanc, 'Druze Particularism: Modern Aspects of an Old Problem', *Middle Eastern Affairs*, III (November, 1952); idem, 'Hadruzim: Bedaya Umtziut' (The Druzes: Fallacy and Reality) *Molad*, April, 1954.

23. This was true even relatively recently. See E. Lévi Provençal, *L'Emir Chekib Arslan* (Paris, 1948).

24. The sections on the contemporary period are based on data that include (in addition to the cited written sources) a large number of extensive, open-ended interviews with persons on various levels of political leadership and activity, participant-observation in universities, military bases, villages, political meetings and other occasions in places of gathering, analysis of correspondence and documents of Druze personalities and organizations, and the analysis of the results of a written questionnaire (containing 25 questions) distributed among the central sector of the Druze intelligentsia (Druze students at the University of Haifa), to which the response was 50 per cent. I am grateful to Mr. Salah Kheir, Secretary of the Druze Organization in Israel, and his associates for their help in distributing the questionnaire.

25. Blanc, *Hadruzim*, pp. 148–150; Fallah, *Hadruzim*, pp. 79–84; Musbah Halaby, *Brith Hadamin* (Alliance of Blood, Tel-Aviv, 1970) and interviews.

26. For statistical data on education, see in addition to the sources already quoted Uri Tahon, 'Hahinuh Baeda Hadruzit' (Education in the Druze Community), *Haaretz*, August 14, 1970.

S

27. The latter term has come to occupy an important place in the vocabulary of contemporary Druze politics – in itself a notable innovation.

28. As quoted in Shtendel, p. 13.

29. *Ibid.*, p. 14.

30. These details are based on *Hitpathut Hahinuh*, pp. 12, 19, 24 and Tahon's article in *Haaretz*, August 14, 1970. I have not been able to obtain official figures for the past two years, but according to a number of sources the number of students may well have almost doubled.

31. Several of these professionals I have been able to interview The press also emphasized occasions such as the graduation of the first Druze physician, Dr. Hamed Saab (e.g. in the *Bulletin of Druze Affairs*, II (April, 1969), and engineer, Salah Ramal (e.g. *Maariv*, September 28, 1970).

32. Jerusalem Post, February 3, 1971.

33. I was able to interview (several times) at length the Secretary of the Council, Muhammad Ramal, and have in my possession several documents regarding its activities.

34. I had the occasion to attend a dinner party in honour of the Dean of Tel-Aviv University in the home of the Druze Member of the *Knesset* where efforts were made to enable more Druze students to attend that university. (The *Knesset* [the Israeli Parliament, made up of 120 members] has always had at least one Druze member, who is extremely influential as a central figure in the community.)

36. 47 per cent think there are 'some chances'.

37. Cf. James S. Coleman (ed.), *Education and Political Development*.

38. Although there are among them some dedicated teachers, and recently a few have reached the rank of assistants and preceptors in the universities.

39. *Hitpathut Hahinuh*, p. 19, Interview with the Director of the Course, Deputy Principal of the Arab Teachers' College in Haifa, Mr. Najib Nabuani, March 11, 1971.

40. Personal information. Recently it has been announced that a Druze monthly is about to be published. This monthly is described as independent of any political ties, run by a group of young Druze (its editor is a lawyer, Mr. Kamal Kassem of Rameh) and intended to be a forum for the free exchange of ideas and information relevant to the community. The publication is to be named *al-Duruz* (The Druze). *Maariv*, October, 15, 1971.

41. These are the Druze houses of prayer.

42. *Hitpathut Hahinuh*, p. 24. Some Druze claim that the Ministry backed down because of the pressure of the spiritual leadership, after everything had been prepared to make the plan practicable. On account of similar pressures, a plan to establish an institute for training religious functionnaires was also rejected. Interview with Shaikh Labib Abu-Rukun, religious leader and judge, and former Member of the Knesset, Isfiya, February 24, 1971.

43. Documentary program on the village of Isfiya, Israel Television, January 11, 1971.

44. See, for instance, *Maariv*, October 25, 1970.

45. In the words of Manfred Halpern. Note also the following definition of ideology: '. . . it involves a philosophy of history, a view of man's present place in it, some estimate of probable lines of future development, and a set of prescriptions regarding how to hasten, retard and/or modify that developmental direction . . . it tends to specify a set of values that are more or less coherent and . . . it seeks to link given patterns of action to the achievement or maintenance of a future, or existing, state of affairs.' Joseph La Palombara, 'Decline of Ideology: A dissent and an Interpretation' in Chaim I. Waxman (ed.), *The End of Ideology Debate*, p. 320.

46. Karl Mannheim, *Ideology and Utopia* (New York, 1954), p. 49.

47. Mary Matossian, 'Ideologies of Delayed Industrialization', in John H. Kautsky (ed.), *Political Change in Underdeveloped Countries* (New York, 1962), p. 253.

48. Clifford Geertz, 'Ideology as a Cultural System', in David E. Apter (ed.), *Ideology and Discontent*, (New York, 1965) p. 64.

49. This is true despite the relatively high percentage of university graduates in the social sciences among them.

50. Personal observation. See also, *inter alia*, Doron Rosembloom, 'Avir Dalil Beharey Hadruzim' (Thin Air in the Druze Mountains), *Dvar Hashavua*, February 5, 1971.)

51. Interview with Druze workers in Kfar Sava, December 23, 1970. Of course, the parallel with the 'Muslim-Arab question' is almost as striking.

52. Interview with Mr. Nagib Nabuani, March 11, 1971.

53. Interview with Mr. Muhammad Ramal, March 11, 1971.

54. 'Hadruzim: Miut Leumi o Dati' (The Druze: a national or religious minority). Radio Israel, July 18, 1970 (Panel discussion).

55. Interview with Mr. Kamal Mansur, November 4, 1970. See also the Lebanese Druze periodical *al-Duha*.

56. There have been several cases of young Druze pretending to be Jews of oriental origins in order to secure social benefits, mostly during their military service, but thus far the cases of Druze actually leaving their community have been very few.

57. Interview with Mr. Fadel Mansur, Deputy Chairman of the Druze Organization, September 16, 1970.

58. Interview with Shaikh Labib Abu Rukun, February 24, 1971.

59. Information based on interviews with students, soldiers and workers.

60. Interviews with Shaikh Labib Abu Rukun and Mr. Zaki Kamal, Director of the Druze Religious Courts, December 25, 1970. See also the interview with Mr. Kamal in *Laiskah*, February 22, 1970.

61. For excellent examples, see the various articles in the annual *Majallat al-Akhbar al-Durziya* (Bulletin of Druze Affairs).

62. In the sense that they can be reconciled with existing dogmas.

63. As is suggested by a number of Druze leaders, including religious authorities such as Shaikh Labib Abu Rukun.

64. Manfred Halpern, 'Conflict, Violence and the Dialectics of Modernisation', (a paper delivered to the Panel on Violence of the American Political Science Association annual convention, Washington, 1968), p. 6.

65. It is noteworthy that despite these figures of the survey, practically all the outstanding leaders of the young generation, such as M. Ramal, K. Mansur and Z. Kamal take pains to emphasize that they are not against the present leadership, and they do not want to dislodge it from its position. Some speak vaguely of 'the old', or the '*shaikhs*' as the element retarding progress, but they rarely come out openly against the leadership.

66. One example to this overwhelming faith in the efficacy of education was given in discussing the question of women, the solution of which seems to most Druze purely a matter of education.

67. Among those who did not serve in the military, 79 per cent thought so. Apparently that section of the respondents was oriented more toward an academic or quasi-intellectual career.

68. The relatively low percentage of the respondents who pointed to this, as compared with the tremendous pre-occupation with the question by the leaders as well as practically all the informants interviewed can be explained probably by the interpretation of the question: some respondents may have thought that this has already been more or less achieved and thus does not constitute a major challenge any longer, and some may have wanted to emphasize specific goals rather than a general process.

69. The huge and powerful Federation of Trade Unions, which has recently increased its activities in the Druze sector.

70. This is true of the vast majority of my informants. Very few among them recognize, as does Muhammad Ramal, the importance of institutionalized power as one of the components of the capacity to innovate.

71. As well as the vast majority of the informants in interviews, including those who are considered to be part of the 'establishment' and the traditional power-structure.

72. Interviewing officials in governmental and public institutions, I found that many do not deny the charge at all, but claim that political realities deriving from the interests of the state necessitates this approach. Some officials, however, accuse the young Druze of looking for excuses for their lack of vigorous activity, courage and consistency. One such official claimed that he and his colleagues 'cannot carry out the revolution for them', and if he tried to do so, they would resist his efforts (along with the old, traditional leaders), on the grounds of defending the autonomy of the community. The fact that the young leaders enter into frequent alliances with the traditional leaders is seen by these officials as indications of an inconsistent and irresponsibly vocal attitude.

73. See the article by the spiritual leader of the community, Shaikh Amin Tarif, 'The Druze Community', *New Outlook*, V (April, 1962), in which he claims that 'the political and economic situation of our Community leave nothing to be desired'. (p. 85).

74. See the plans for the future by the Druze Member of the *Knesset* Jaber Maudi in *al-Anba* (the Arabic-language daily in Israel), December 11, 1970.

75. Interview with Mr. Zaki Kamal (a lawyer and the Director of the Druze Religious Courts in Israel), December 25, 1970.

76. *Maariv*, December 15, 1970.

77. Interview with Mr. Fadel Mansur, September 16, 1970.

78. Interview with Mr. Kamal Mansur, November 4, 1970.

79. M. Ramal, 'Nikmat Hadam Beabu Snan', (The Blood Feud in Abu Snan). *Haaretz*, August 1, 1970.

80. See the variety of speeches contained in the annual *Majallat al-Akhbar al-Durziya*.

81. *Carmel*, I (1971), *passim*. A second series of words also very frequently used in that issue have to do with 'initiative', and 'enterprise'.

82. A Druze journalist and author of a book commemorating the fallen Druze soldiers (*Brith Hadamim, op. cit.*) he is a member of the largest family in his village which controls the local council, yet he is active (despite pressures by his kin) in the local branch of the *Histadrut*, which is led by a member of the rival family. Interview, February 15, 1971.

83. In the list of candidates to the 1969 elections in his village, Daliat al-Carmel, there appears the name of another member of his family in the slate led by the head of the rival clan. *Habhirot Larashuyot Hamkomiot Basector Haarvi, 1969* (The Elections to the Local Authorities in the Arab Sector, 1969; Jerusalem: Section of Local Government, Department of the Minorities, Ministry of the Interior, 1969), p. 10.

84. Interview with Mr. Halaby.

85. Interview with Shaikh Labib Abu Rukun. *Hamula* is the Arabic term for clan, or extended family.

86. Ramal, *op. cit.*; Interview with Mr. Ramal.

87. Series of four interviews with Shaikh Abdallah Khayr.

88. He claims that the elections were corrupt and that votes were bought 'in the open market'.

89. Nevertheless, some educated men in his village told me that he had tried to prevent them from acquiring an education. A group of young Druze claimed contemptuously that since he is a millionaire, he identifies only with millionaires everywhere . . .

90. His son, curiously, works for the Ministry of Defence, despite the fathers' present reluctance to get involved in Israeli politics and public life.

91. Interview, December 26, 1970.

92. The older brother expressed his views partially in a letter to *Yediot Aharonot*, November 1, 1970.

93. *Ibid.*

94. Which is the framework within which the vast majority of Druze soldiers in the Israeli Army complete their service.

95. They said: 'We are in favour of granting Druze girls freedom – but not absolute freedom.' They did not see a contradiction between this view and the wish to see all Druze behave as Israelis.

96. They definitely disapprove, for instance, of the popular practice of citing military service as a basis on which benefits and rights are then requested. They see military

service as the obligation of all citizens, that entitles no-one to special benefits. Similarly, the rights of citizenship are due to every citizen, and thus no special merits or particularistic claims are necessarily desirable in order to secure them.

97. See, for instance, Oliphant, *The Land of Gilead*, p. 348.

98. It is particularly prevalent among Druzes who reside in Jerusalem or Tel-Aviv and are thus physically far removed from Druze politics in the North.

99. Personal information based on interviews and documents; see also, for instance, *Yediot Aharonot*, January 3, 1971.

100. Series of four interviews with Shaikh Abdallah Khair of Abu Snan, who kindly supplied me with copies of pertinent documents. See also Epstein, p. 39 and Fallah, *Hadruzim*, pp. 171–176.

101. For a few examples, see Fallah, *op. cit.*, Ch. 9. I relied also on personal information and documents.

102. For an example, see *Ibid.*, pp. 171–176.

103. Similarly to the process described in C. S. Whitaker, Jr. 'A Dysrhythmic Process of Political Change', *World Politics* XIX (October, 1967), and *idem, The Politics of Tradition: Continuity and Change in Northern Nigeria, 1946–1966* (Princeton, 1970).

104. Other than the fact that Druze alternative leaders are mostly co-opted into an informal network of alliances rather than an institutional machinery. This is not unlike the classic phenomenon of co-optation well-known to students of politics throughout the ages and brilliantly analyzed in Robert Michels, *Political Parties: A Sociological Study of the Oligarchical Tendencies of Modern Democracies* (New York, 1966).

105. Other than for attempts to find scolarships for Druze students or occasionally to redress particular grievances.

106. The exposure and sympathy of the Jewish public to the difficulties of the Druze community are remarkable: the Druze intellectuals have ample opportunities to communicate their views in the press, radio and television.

107. One of them told me that in his view (based on 'solid facts') one of the leading Druze critics of the 'establishment' would 'sell out' (i.e. abandon opposition to present policies and criticism of the status quo) for a license to engage in a much-coveted and profitable business.

108. This is a conspicuous feature of the numerous interviews I conducted with young activists and intellectuals. Without any hint on the interviewer's part the informants would say: 'You must have heard a lot of rumours about me from this or that young Druze leader, but you should not believe what he says, since he is a fake, he is nothing, he is but a tool of this or that *shaikh* or *hamula*.'

109. A thoughtful teacher in a small village told me that in his opinion none of the active spokesmen of the young generation will be a 'real' leader, as they simply do not conform to the Druze image of what a leader ought to be in terms of personality, stature, dignity and demeanour. The Arabic word for leader (*za'im*) is a combination of 'chief', 'boss', 'patron' and among the Druze a 'public figure with dignity'. See also Arnold Hottinger, '*Zuama* in Historical Perspective' in Binder (ed.) *Politics in Lebanon*.

110. Such inconsistency is manifest in numerous examples, particularly in regard to sensitive issues, where the farther removed the intellectual is from having to act, the more vocal is his criticism. For instance, one of the best-known young 'radicals' advocated, on a nationally-televised panel discussion, the use of police force if necessary to get all Druze girls to school (Israel Television, August 30, 1971), but the press reported that the very same 'revolutionary' begged, entreated and demanded that the scene in which his aunt had been photographed (for the same television programme) from a distance of 220 yards not be shown, as according to Druze tradition a woman is not allowed to have her picture taken! (*Maariv*, January 22, 1971).

111. For similar cases of mistrust among the members of the would-be 'modernizing' élite, see Lucian W. Pye, *Politics, Personality and Nation-Building: Burma's Search for Identity* (New Haven, 1968) and William B. Quandt, *Revolution and Political Leadership: Algeria 1954–1968*.

112. De Sacy, *passim*; Churchill, II, *passim*; Bouron, Part III.

113. The observer cannot help being struck by the extremely low degree of relevance university graduates (most of whom seem to major in Political Science or Middle Eastern Studies) see in their studies in regard to political problems they encounter.

114. This   is activity totally congruent with the traditional patterns of politics. In making statements of such nature, I am influenced by the ideas of Manfred Halpern, particularly in his 'Dialectics of Continuity, Change, Collaboration, Conflict and Justice in Traditional Muslim Societies'. (A paper presented to the Plenary Session of the Second Annual Meeting of the Middle East Studies Association, Austin, Texas, November 1968).

# The Political Status of Jerusalem in the Hashemite Kingdom of Jordan, 1948-1967

## Naim Sofer

THE RESIDUE OF THE PAST

The religious significance of Jerusalem, in the consciousness of Moslems in general and of the Palestinians in particular, had a great deal of bearing on the status of the city within the Kingdom of Jordan.

This importance of Jerusalem, as the first *Qibla* and third in rank according to the holiness of its mosques (after Mecca and Medina) has had its ups and downs ever since the days of Mohammed. In the days of the Crusaders a new dimension of importance was added to the city and a pan-Moslem effort was made, which eventually brought about the liberation of Jerusalem from the hands of the crusaders.

Whereas in the past the importance of Jerusalem was mainly religious, in modern times the city has taken on a nationalistic significance, brought about by the strife between the Arab and the Jewish communities during the days of the Mandate. Since the leadership of both sides was concentrated in Jerusalem, the focus of the struggle lay in the capital, and it centred mainly on the possession of the city and its holy places. Accordingly, many of the clashes flared up in Jerusalem and from there spread throughout the whole country as, for example, the Wailing Wall incident of 1929.

This religious and national importance of the city is a part of the Palestinian consciousness, which is renewed – every year afresh – by festivals such as Leilat el Asra' wa'l-Mi'raj which commemorates the night of the journey of Mohammed from Mecca to Jerusalem and his ascension to heaven. The Arab leaders fanned this religious and national consciousness during the days of the Mandate and stirred up the fury of the masses by accusing the Jews of plans to capture the Dome of the Rock. This incitement received added strength when the religious and political leadership passed into the hands of the Mufti of Jerusalem, Haj Amin al Husayni. The agitation bore fruit in the form of attacks, leading to bloodshed, on the Jewish population.

In the days of the Mandate Jerusalem was of importance in many spheres. It was the headquarters of the Mandatory government. It also served as the political headquarters of the Arabs through the Higher Arab Committee. Jerusalem was also their religious· headquarters; it was the seat of the Mufti of Jerusalem, as well as that of the Supreme Moslem Religious Council. It served, as well, as the social centre of Arab Palestine – for in this city the most honoured and important families were concentrated. And, finally, Jerusalem was the cultural centre of the whole country; it contained the best teachers' academies as well as law schools and high

255

schools. It was also the home of the radio broadcasting services with its attendant talent.

Jerusalem was the centre for foreign activities, and the Arab and other Moslem countries emphasized the importance of the city. During the Mandate, Jerusalem was host to pan-Moslem conferences, and the Arab countries appointed consulates there.[1] Important personages were buried in the Dome of the Rock: the King of Hijaz Husayn ibn Ali, founder of the Hashemite dynasty; Muhammad Ali, an Indian Moslem leader; Mussa Kazem al Husayni and his son Abd al-Qadir.

To the Transjordanians as well, Jerusalem served, during the days of the Mandate, as the centre of government. It was the residence of the British High Commissioner – who was responsible for Transjordan as well as Palestine – and, as a result, widespread administrative links between Transjordan and Jerusalem developed.

Along with the official bonds with the government of the Mandate, there developed relations with the Arab population. Jerusalem became one of the cultural centres for Transjordan. It served as a source of teachers, clerks and spiritual leaders, and students were sent to Jerusalem from Transjordan.

Jerusalem was not, in fact, the chief Arab centre. In this respect the cities of Damascus, Beirut and Cairo served more important functions; however it had a geographical advantage over the other cities, being closer to the centre of Transjordan and to its capital. In addition, crossing the border was scarcely a problem.

It should be emphasized that the links between the Transjordanians and Jerusalem in the days of the Mandate were almost one-sided. The Transjordanians needed the city and its services, while the Jerusalemites had practically no need of Transjordan, except as a source of income for a few people. Therefore the relations were limited to a small crust of the upper civil-service personnel and the higher reaches of the bourgeoisie.

King Abdullah had special bonds with Jerusalem, in addition to his official connections with the British government. First of all there was an emotional factor involved; his father, Husayn was buried there, and Abdullah would make pilgrimages to the grave. Perhaps even more important was the political factor, namely his ambition towards the end of his life to include Jerusalem in his realm. This late ambition grew and strengthened after his dreams of bringing one of the historic capitals – Mecca, Baghdad or Damascus – under his rule were shattered.[2] This ambition reached its height on the eve of the war of 1948. Even after he had taken Jerusalem, he did not relinquish his aim of including Damascus in his domain.

Abdullah had connections with Arab leaders in Jerusalem. These connections were mainly with the leaders of the opposition factions,[3] since the main recognized leadership was strongly opposed to his ambitions in Palestine.

As a result of the network of the relations between Transjordan and Jerusalem, the Transjordanians, too, became accustomed to viewing

Jerusalem as the centre of government. Especially since Amman in 1948 was a village of 45,000 inhabitants[4] while at the same time Jerusalem was a city of 160,000 inhabitants.[5]

## THE WAR OF 1948

The central question with regard to Jordan and the 1948 war is – what were King Abdullah's plans towards the end of the British Mandate? Did, Abdullah plan to accept the partition plan, reaching an agreement with the Jews? Or did he have separate plans for Jerusalem? Did he have any concrete plans?

A close examination of his actions before and on the eve of the 1948 war, as well as during the war, shows that Abdullah's attitude was pragmatic, and that he wanted to retain the power of manoeuvre; the vagueness of his declarations was, therefore, deliberate.[6]

Generally, Abdullah wanted to act on the basis of the partition plan, to enter into those territories allotted to the Arabs, and he informed the Jewish leadership accordingly, through various channels. The testimony of Haza' al-Majali, in this respect, bears a special weight.[7] Whereas most Arab sources condemn Abdullah for his acceptance of the partition plan, and one cannot know whether these accusations are well-founded, for they are prejudiced against him, Majali defends him, and tries to refute their accusations. Majali justifies Abdullah's support of the plan and presents it as a tactical step.

Glubb relates[8] the discussion between the British Secretary of State for Foreign Affairs, Bevin, and the Jordanian Prime Minister, Tawfiq Abu'l Huda, that took place in London in February 1948, and in the course of which the Jordanian Prime Minister confirmed that Jordan did not plan to enter territories other than those allotted to the Arabs by the partition plan. However, according to Majali, this commitment was undertaken without Abdullah's knowledge or consent; the latter found out about it only later, on May 16, 1948. It is possible that Tawfiq answered questions, under some pressure, and on the spur of the moment, and that the issue had not been previously decided upon by the King.

Majali relates that[9] Jordan suggested that only its army should enter Palestine, because Jordan was not a member of the UN and was not, therefore, bound by any UN decision, or by the partition plan. In other words, Abdullah foresaw a possibility of acting against the partition plan, depending on the outcome of the situation and circumstances. The Jordanians, however, were ready to carry out the resolution on the internationalization of Jerusalem, provided that the other side carried it out in full as well (the Jewish position was similar).

Jordan's readiness to carry out the UN resolution on the internationalization of Jerusalem, was based on military considerations. Glubb[10] gives a full account of those considerations about Jerusalem, and his main point is that a war in Jerusalem would bring about a full concentration of the military efforts on one front, and thus the Jordanian army would not be able to fight on other fronts. One should add, of course, political considerations as well, relating mainly to the British position which further supported the internationalization of Jerusalem.

The Jordanian hopes for the actual realization of the UN resolution brought about a deferment. The entrance of the Jordanian army into Jerusalem was delayed for four days, until the night of May 18. It actually started its operations only on the following morning.

The first two days of deferment occurred with Abdullah's knowledge and consent, but it was Glubb who decided on the last two days. In fact Glubb admits to having deferred the entrance of the army into Jerusalem, notwithstanding Abdullah's orders. [11] He writes that he took the responsibility of a deferment, hoping to reach a cease-fire in the meantime. During all this time, the Arabs of Jerusalem addressed desperate calls to Abdullah, asking him to save them. [12]

Arif el-Arif[13] relates that the Arabs of Jerusalem called these fateful days 'al-Ayam al-Hamra' (literally 'the red days', meaning the bloody days). One can still feel the emotion in these words.

Arif adds that the Jerusalemites had exhausted their ammunition, and didn't think of acquiring any, having relied upon the Jordanian army's entrance in Jerusalem on May 15.

Abdulllah al-Tall,[14] who was the commander of the Jerusalem contingent at that time, says that on May 17 at noon he received orders by phone, from King Abdullah to send a company to Jerusalem. After explanations, Abdullah agreed to dispatch the batallion stationed near Jericho to Jerusalem. Tall concluded from this direct order, received from the King, without a similar order from Glubb, that the King acted against Glubb's opinion. This conclusion is confirmed by Glubb himself, but contrary to Tall's assumption, Glubb had known about the King's orders. Tall relates that he had asked Glubb for permission to move his division stationed at Damya, but Glubb refused, saying that this matter did not concern him. [15] Tall concludes that there were conflicting views and grave disagreements between the King and Glubb.

As a result of the 1948 war, some important Arab quarters in Jerusalem remained in Jewish hands.

It is very important to understand the Palestinian attitude to the 1948 war, and the assessment of Abdullah's share in it. The accepted view is that Abdullah was a traitor to the Palestinian cause, because of his readiness to accept the partition plan, the internationalization of Jerusalem, and because of his direct contacts with the Jews. They regard the deferment of the entrance of the Jordanian army into Jerusalem as the direct cause for the loss of a great part of the city. They connect the defeat with the fact that the Jordanian army was led by a British officer – Glubb.

It is possible that, in the eyes of the Palestinians, only the 1967 war could compensate for the 1948 war. For, in contrast to the period of waiting in 1948, the Jordanian army hurried to start fighting a war with Israel in 1967, even though it could have been avoided. There are Palestinians, however, who view the Jordanian army's role in the 1967 war unfavourably, and believe that it did not act competently and effectively, because of King Husayn's policy. [16]

JERUSALEM AS THE CENTRE OF FOREIGN ACTIVITIES

After the annexation of Jerusalem to Jordan, the city continued to serve as a focal point for foreign activities, as it had during the days of the Mandate. The eyes of the Arab world were turned towards it during the war; it became the central theme in Israel-Jordan relations; it became a bone of contention on the international stage, and the fate of the city brought forth differences between Jordan and the rest of the Arab world.

In the relations of Jordan with Israel, Jerusalem occupied a central position. There were many instances of armed clashes, both because of the border that cut through the city and because of the Mount Scopus enclave. [17] The clashes stirred fears in the local population, as well as the Arab countries, for the future of the city. [18] The differences between the speed of development of the Israeli town (with 160,000 inhabitants) as compared with the slow pace of Arab Jerusalem (with 60,000) was striking, and embittered the citizens. The transfer of the foreign ministry of Israel, as well as the proclamation of Jerusalem as the capital of Israel, caused unrest and brought pressure on the Jordan government to take a similar step.

The Arab nations considered themselves, to a certain extent, as guardians of Jerusalem, because of its sanctity. They, therefore, took part in protests against Israel on the occasion of border clashes, and when Israel transferred its foreign ministry. [19] Certain of these states went so far as to spread accusations to the effect that the rulers of Jordan were ready to hand over the city to Israel. These accusations deepened the mistrust of the population toward the government.

The Arab states started up activities in Jerusalem. Inter-Arab meetings were held in connection with the problems of Palestine; committees of the Arab boycott; [20] a conference of the Arab Armistice Committees; [21] a meeting of those governments that were hosts to refugees. [22] In addition there were conferences, such as those of the Arab Women of Jerusalem, [23] and of the Moslem Brotherhood, [24] etc. Important Arab figures, who visited Jordan, made a point of visiting Jerusalem as well, thereby emphasizing its importance. Arab states established consulates in Jerusalem. [25] Some of the consulates served, at times, as centres of anti-government agitation, especially during the years 1955–1957, and the government of Jordan was forced to expel an Egyptian consul. [26]

Side by side with diplomatic activities, the Arab states acted in the fields of charity and of public works. The overhaul of the Aqsa mosque became an all-Moslem activity. [27] Sa'udi Arabia set up several charitable institutions in Jerusalem and, during the period when the relations between the two governments became strained, Sa'udi Arabia was forbidden to set up new charitable organizations. [28] Tourism to Jerusalem was also developed.

Besides the Moslem personages, who were buried in the *Haram* during the Mandate, there was buried there, in 1963, at his own request, Ahmad Hilmi, the head of the 'Government of All Palestine', who spent his last days in Lebanon.[29]

A bone of contention between the Arab states and Jordan was the problem of internationalization of Jerusalem. Jordan remained isolated in her opposition to internationalization. The other Arab states supported the scheme for a variety of reasons, in addition to the desire to harm Israel. Egypt and Syria wanted to harm Abdullah and his position in the annexed areas; Lebanon acted, mainly from Christian motives, while Iraq took the stand after some misgivings, that there should be unity among the Arab states in the United Nations.[30]

The scheme for internationalization placed Jerusalem at the centre of widespread international activity and added to the internal difficulties, for the very continuation of Jordan's government was thereby put into jeopardy.[31] A part of the city's population hoped for internationalization: there were those who owned property in the Iraeli part and who hoped to get back this property;[32] there were Christians who wanted to live under a non-Moslem rule, and who wished to increase their influence under such an international government. Concerning the ferment among the Christians there exist several specific testimonials.[33] Abdullah al-Tall, who was governor of Jerusalem in 1948–1949, informs us that a committee for the Arab Women of Jerusalem, which he formed in 1949, was headed by a Christian, Kamil Sham'un, 'to counteract the attempts of the Jews to sow discord between the Moslems and the Christians, especially in Jerusalem'.[34] This subject came up again at the time of the Pope's visit to Jerusalem in January 1964,[35] and one can surmise that this visit brought about some tension between the Moslems and the Christians in the town.

Jerusalem's unique position in the Arab and Moslem world interfered, therefore, with the quiet integration of the city within the State of Jordan.

JERUSALEM AS THE CENTRE OF INTERNAL AFFAIRS

Even under Jordanian rule Jerusalem retained its leadership of the Western bank of the Jordan and, to a certain extent, of the whole country. It remained the political, religious and cultural centre.

In the political field, Jerusalem remained the centre of the groups opposing the government. At first there were the members of the established opposition – the followers of the Mufti. Later the city served as the breeding ground of the Socialist Arab Renaissance Party (al-Ba'th), as well as the stronghold of the Communist Party.

In addition several religious parties had centres there: the Muslim Brotherhood, who held their annual conferences in Jerusalem, set up a permanent office as well as a commercial company for the development of the city. Jerusalem also housed the extremist Islamic Liberation Party (al-Tahrir).

Jerusalem also continued to be the religious centre. The 'Council of Religious Leaders' (al-Hay'a al-'ilmiya), which was set up afresh after the annexation, had its regular sessions there, in the building formerly belonging to the former Supreme Moslem Council. [36]

A kind of pilgrimage to the Aqsa mosque took place on the Fridays of Ramadan, and the number of worshippers reached 150,000, according to newspaper estimates. [37]

The Muslim Brotherhood, since 1953, instituted an all-Muslim Congress to commemorate the night of the ascension of Mohammad to the heavens, with the participation of representatives of many Moslem countries. [38]

Jerusalem also served as the national religious centre for the various Christian communities and housed the heads of the Christian churches.

In the cultural sphere Jerusalem stood out as an important national centre, surpassing Amman in certain respects. The chief daily newspapers, *Falastin* and *al Difa'* (which were already established in Jerusalem in the days of the Mandate), *al-Jihad* (founded in 1954) and *al-Manar* (founded in 1959) were published there. Whereas in Amman only one daily paper, of meagre contents, was published: *al Urdun* (founded in 1909). [39]

Thus Jerusalem influenced Jordanian public opinion to a major degree, and there was a natural tendency to stress the problems and demands of the city in a frequently disproportionate fashion.

The city had a large concentration of secondary schools, cultural and public institutions, and foreign-financed Christian schools.

The importance of Jerusalem in the political, religious and cultural spheres underlined the competition between the city and the capital, Amman.

### CLAIMS OF DISCRIMINATION

Jordanian rule over Jerusalem and over the whole of the Western bank, started off with mistrust and heavy suspicions on the part of the Palestinians, who were convinced that Abdullah was ready to betray them and that he had not used his full military capacity in the defence of the Arab parts of Palestine.

Ever since then, all of the authorities' steps were watched with suspicion and criticism, and everything was looked upon as intentional and deliberate discrimination, whether or not there was ground for these accusations.

The Jerusalemites' claims concentrated on the economic situation. Jerusalem's economic situation was precarious, owing to the war of 1948. In the days of the Mandate, the economic basis of the city was founded both on the presence of the staff of the central government, and on the economic 'hinterland' of the neighbouring villages, from which she was now cut off. In addition, some 40,000 inhabitants, who had in the past lived in the Israeli part of the city, were now refugees who increased the economic plight of Jerusalem. [40]

Since Amman was the capital, there was no way of preventing the transfer of the central government offices there and so Jerusalem was emptied of the chief offices that had been located there. The Jerusalemites could not accept this and the transfer of the government offices became one of the painful issues between them and the government. [41]

Another factor that played a decisive role in sharpening the feeling of bitterness and of being slighted, in the heart of the Jerusalemites, was the person of Abdullah al-Tall, who after serving as commander of a regiment on the Jerusalem front during the war, served as governor of Jerusalem in the period between August 29, 1948 and June 7, 1949.[42] Tall, according to his memoirs, spread the view that the authorities were allowing Jerusalem to be deprived of its advantages on purpose, because they considered the city to be foreign and internationalized. Therefore, supplies were delayed, a city council was not set up, and the government opposed transfer of offices to the city.[43]

These opinions were taken seriously by the citizens, both because of Tall's high position and his accurate knowledge of the mysteries of Jordanian policies, and because these rumours served to strengthen their complaints concerning the attitude of the authorities.

Tall himself quarrelled with his superiors, both in the army and in civilian government. In fact he was one of the main causes for the suspicious attitude of the authorities towards Jerusalem, as he admits in his memoirs.[44]

Since Tall was active during a decisive period, when the attitude of the Jordan government towards Jerusalem was being decided and formed, his activities had a long-range negative effect.

From the beginning of Jordanian rule, the Jerusalemites, as well as other Palestinians, complained of discrimination against the city. These complaints were continuously being voiced. The claims that were made included several points: the status of Jerusalem, discrimination in employment, and the economic situation. The inhabitants were especially sensitive concerning the status of the city, since they had formed hopes that Jerusalem would become the capital or, at least, a second capital. Administrative discrimination and the economic situation touched the private citizen, causing much bitter comment.

The main groups that took up the cause of Jerusalem were:

(a) *The press:* The newspapers took the lead in the campaign in the form of editorials. They made a point of publishing daily reports dealing with the economic situation; with the transferring of offices from the city; with the lowering of its status, emphasizing the broken promises.[45]

(b) *The parliament:* The representatives, especially those from Jerusalem, continuously raised the problems of the city and complained of its neglect and abandonment. Other representatives as well, especially Palestinians, echoed these complaints. The most noteworthy step was the memorandum of the fifteen Palestinian representatives who insisted on – among other things – the retention of Jerusalem's moral and material status.[46]

(c) *The municipality of Jerusalem:* The mayors of Jerusalem were among the main fighters for the improvement of the city's status.[47]

(d) *The Jerusalem Chamber of Commerce:* This body voiced considerable criticism concerning the economic problems of the city, and especially of the transfer of various offices.[48]

Owing to the deep feeling of neglect, little notice was taken of the considerable developments that took place in the city. Among these were: the doubling of the population; the development of a widespread tourist trade and the building of accommodation for visitors.[49]

### JERUSALEM AS A CENTRE OF THE OPPOSITION

Various factors contributed to turn Jerusalem into a centre of opposition to the government:

a. During the Mandate Jerusalem was the centre of Palestinian leadership. This leadership was inimical to Abdullah and his ambitions. The main leaders left and only second- and third-rate people were left, whose enmity towards Abdullah and the Jordanian government was strengthened by the war of 1948.

b. The cream of the Palestinian intelligentsia was concentrated in Jerusalem. It was among them that antagonism arose towards the undemocratic ways of the government, towards the limitations on the freedom of expression and of organization, and towards the concentration of government in the hands of the Transjordanians, whom they considered to be their inferiors.

c. The deterioration of the status of Jerusalem, and of its economic situation, created feelings of bitterness among the population.

d. The suppression of the opposition and the violent clashes which broke out in Jerusalem, further strained the relations with the government.

All these helped create a fertile breeding ground for an active opposition to government. Added to this came the detrimental effect of Abdullah al-Tall's activity at the beginning of Jordanian rule. Al-Tall organized and spurred the opposition forces in Jerusalem and its environs. He gave them the direction and the backing they had been sorely lacking, thereby replacing the leaders who had fled. It is doubtful whether the opposition would have succeeded in becoming organized without him, for the government suppressed them energetically, and quarrels about the leadership were always breaking out.

Tall acted with long-range considerations in mind. He endeavoured to undermine the Jordanian rulers, in whom he saw traitors to the nation, and he considered the Palestinians a vital element in his scheme to change the régime.

Tall based his activities on the 'Young men, who, in the past opposed imperlialism'. He worked systematically to get them into leading administrative posts. Among his ventures were the appointment of a municipal council in Jerusalem on his own initiative and the infiltration of his 'Young Liberals' into the council, the organization of the opposition delegation to the Jericho conference in December 1948. He also saw to it that the secret talks with Israel became known and made plans to sabotage them. And in general he sowed distrust in the government.

The personages whom Tall cultivated later became the mainstays of the Palestinian opposition. Among them were Abdullah al-Rimawi; Abdullah Nawas, Kamal Nasir (these three later became Ba'th leaders); Anwar al-Khatib; Yahya Hammuda; Dr Musa el-Husayni (who was later hanged because of his participation in the murder of Abdullah). The first evidence concerning his opposition activity is from November 1948, but it is reasonable to assume that it started earlier.[50]

Tall's doings finally brought about the climax in the rift between the Palestinians and the Transjordanians, namely, Abdullah's assassination. He was killed by a Jerusalemite, a member of the former Mufti's organization 'Al-Jihad al-Mukkadas'. The planning was done in Jerusalem by Dr Musa al-Husayni, a relative of the Mufti, whom Tall had cultivated while he was still in Jerusalem. The plot was developed by Tall from Cairo (where he had taken refuge) and there were clear indications during the trial that the Mufti himself had been behind Tall. Other members of Husayni's family were charged at the same trial, but were freed.[51]

The Municipality of Jerusalem remained a centre for the opposition. When the Mayor, Anwar el-Khatib, who had been nominated by Tall, was removed from office on July 22, 1950 most of the members of the council resigned.[52] When another mayor, 'Arif al-'Arif, joined the government of Majali, who wanted Jordan to join the Baghdad Pact, the members of the council decided that this was reason for him to resign.[53]

After the riots of December 1955, the city government decided to call a street after the name of a girl student who was killed by army bullets during the demonstrations.[54] And in 1961 the entire city council resigned as a result of differences of opinion concerning who would be in charge of the municipal water reservoirs.[55]

In the Parliament most of the representatives from Jerusalem took a strong stand with the opposition and were numbered among its leaders. Many of these persons were arrested at one time or another. Among the Jerusalem representatives were members of the Ba'th; members of the Mufti's party; National-Socialists; Communists and members of the Moslem Brotherhood.

The opposition was active and took a sharp stand against the authorities, especially in times when heavy-handed governments were in power, who suppressed and persecuted the opposition. This was the case in the days after Abdullah's assassination; after the decline of Mulqui's liberal government (May 19, 1953–May 19, 1954) and during the rise of Abu al-Huda's government. Also following the dismisssal of Nabulsi in April 1957 and after the murder of the Prime Minister, Majali, in August 1960.

On the other hand, the opposition cooperated with the government in the days of Mulqui and during Nabulsi's nationalist government.

The relations between Jerusalem and the authorities became a vicious circle. The stronger the opposition became in Jerusalem – the heavier became the yoke of the government; the greater the pressure of the authorities – the more the opposition gained in strength. The inevitable outcome was bloodshed.

CLASHES IN JERUSALEM

Jerusalem was one of the main centres of armed clashes with the authorities. (The other sore spot was Amman, which contained a large concentration of Palestinians.)

The opposition groups wanted Jerusalem to be the theatre of clashes with the government for a variety of reasons:

(a) Clashes in Jerusalem served to accent the differences between the population of the East and West banks of the Jordan.

(b) Riots in Jerusalem obtained a wide news coverage owing to world-wide interest and to the presence of many foreign reporters in the city.

(c) In Jerusalem it was easier to cause trouble than in Amman with its large concentrations of troops, both in the city and in the surrounding camps. In Jerusalem, on the other hand, the armed forces were limited for a variety of reasons, among which was the armistice agreement with Israel.

(d) Owing to world-wide interest in Jerusalem, the authorities were reluctant to exert all of their power to suppress riots in the city.

Therefore there were riots in Jerusalem during every period of strain in Jordan. The important riots are as follows:

(a) After the assassination of King Abdullah on July 20, 1951, in the Aqsa mosque in Jerusalem. In the wake of the murder, the soldiers of the Jordan army, most of them Beduins (and loyal to the King), ran riot. Many persons were killed and wounded.[56] A measure of the number of victims may be had from the denial of the representatives of the various communities of Jerusalem which appeared in the paper Al-Ahram, concerning the rumour of hundreds killed and thousands wounded, following the murder of Abdullah. The article claimed that no one was killed.[57] One of the accused at the murder trial said, in his evidence, that another accused was afraid to turn himself in 'because he was afraid of being beaten as they were beating the passers-by in the streets'. He referred to the soldiers of the Legion.[58]

(b) Following the attempt to bring Jordan into the Baghdad Pact in December 1955. These riots were the most serious of all. The Consulates of western powers were attacked and burned, and many people were killed and wounded.[59] As a result of these riots, the Majali government fell, and the attempts to join the Baghdad Pact failed. This was the first successful attempt of the opposition to achieve its goal through the use of force.

(c) After the dismissal of the Nabulsi government in April 1957. As a result of these demonstrations and riots that were concentrated in Jerusalem and in Amman, the Khalidi government fell within nine days. Martial Law was declared and military courts were set up in Amman and Jerusalem.[60]

(d) After the dismissal of the Governor of Jerusalem, Anwar Nuseiba,

T

in January 1963. Owing to the strikes and demonstrations the situation attained such serious dimensions, that King Husayn personally came to Jerusalem to intervene. The problem became one concerning the rift between Cis- and Trans-Jordan. The King convened Parliament and reprimanded the members for once again starting to talk about 'the two banks of the Jordan'. Finally the government (which meanwhile had changed) was forced to remove the new governor – a Transjordanian – and substitute in his stead one of the previous governors, the Palestinian, Daoud abu Ghazala. [61]

(e) Following the announcement of the triple alliance of Egypt-Syria-Iraq in April 1963. In the wake of the unrest and demonstrations, the authorities arrested three Jerusalem Representatives. [62] The ferment subsided after the cancelling of the programme because of the split between Egypt and Syria-Iraq. Otherwise we may be quite sure that the unrest would have increased.

These clashes aggravated the break between the inhabitants and the government, all the more so owing to the harsh measures taken after each flare-up. Foreign powers, especially Egypt, strove to exaggerate the incidents and to make it appear that Beduin soldiers were engaged in quelling the people of Cis-Jordan. The many victims that fell from the actions of the military, caused a blood-feud with the government, which prevented all attempts at reconciliation and liberalization. The Jordan government took on the aspects of a foreign, oppressive rule. Again, the emergence of the Palestine Entity idea sharpened the rift between the Palestinian and the Jordanian governments.

THE DEMAND TO MAKE JERUSALEM THE CAPITAL

Jerusalem was the capital of Palestine during the days of the Mandate. She had more inhabitants than Amman, and was of more importance politically, economically and culturally than the latter. In view of this, and in view of the weight of the past – also taking into account the emotional and national importance of Jerusalem in the eyes of the Arab world at the time of the 1948 war – it was but natural that the Palestinians should hope that after the official annexation of Cis-Jordan, Jerusalem would become the capital of the whole State of Jordan. In any event they thought that it should at least be declared as a recognized second national centre – a second capital of Jordan. [63] Especially since the number of Palestinians in the Kingdom was double that of the Transjordanians.

Jordanian laws provided a justification for this desire. There existed a law which stated that it would be possible to transfer the capital from Amman by means of a special statute. This clause, which appears in the present code of Jordan (in force since 1952), appeared as well in the previous code from 1946. It would appear, however, that many Palestinians, upon reading the new code, thought that this clause was a new addition, a result of the annexation.

In the days of King Abdullah, the Palestinians did not make an issue of transferring the capital to Jerusalem. In the first period, between May 1948 and April 1950, there was no call for such a demand, because Cis-Jordan was not yet officially annexed to Trans-Jordan. After this period, it may be assumed that the Palestinians thought it wise not to bring up the demand seriously because of two reasons: first, there was the question of the internationalization of Jerusalem; second, because of the great honour and respect that Abdullah paid the city – in fact, he treated Jerusalem as though it were a second capital.

After his murder, the demand for turning Jerusalem into the capital became stronger. This may be attributed to a deterioration in the relations between the government and the Palestinians in general, and the government and the Jerusalemites, in particular; and to a sharp decline in the status of the city. The demand came partly as a reaction to the bad relations between the authorities and the Cis-Jordanians.

An opportunity did not present itself immediately for making a demand to transfer the capital to Jerusalem, and the Palestinians had to wait for an appropriate moment. This moment was reached in 1953 when Israel transferred her foreign ministry to that city. Then the demand was made to take a similar step, in order to safeguard the status of Arab Jerusalem.[64] In this way, the demand was camouflaged as an anti-Israel step and not as a Palestinian demand, directed against the Jordanian rulers.

The demands concerning the status of Jerusalem became increasingly modest, due to the hostile reaction of the authorities. Since they did not see any hope for bringing about this change, and since they did not wish to appear as desirous of harming the status of Amman, the centre of government of Transjordan, the Palestinians contented themselves, in general, with the demand that Jerusalem be proclaimed the second capital, so that foreign envoys would present their credentials there, as was done in Israeli Jerusalem.[65] For all that, clear hints were made that Jerusalem ought to become the sole capital of Jordan. For example, the newspaperman, Yousef Hana, said the presenting of credentials in Jerusalem would not be logical as long as Amman remained the official capital: 'And how can we demand of our opponents to acknowledge a fact which we ourselves were the first to deny and which we continue to deny?'[66]

In the face of these demands, the authorities limited themselves to a single session of the government in Jerusalem, and – as a result of pressure from representatives – to a single convening of Parliament in that city.[67]

When the demand to turn Jerusalem into a second capital also failed, the Palestinians retreated and began demanding that the city become the spiritual centre.[68] This demand, too, was not acted upon at the time;[69] so they began demanding regular sessions of Parliament in Jerusalem.[70]

When even this demand was not met, they started insisting on raising the administrative status of Jerusalem, by altering its status from that of a 'mutasarifiah' to that of 'muhafaza', in common with Amman. The authorities agreed to this demand, and Jerusalem was raised to the rank of a muhafaza in 1955.[71]

Only later, in 1960, did the authorities begin to accept the slogans of

'Jerusalem the spiritual capital', and 'Jerusalem the second capital'. This acceptance came about as a result of outside pressures that threatened the standing of Jordan on the West Bank. In fact, these proclamations were not accompanied by any action, and therefore these steps had no real effect on the relations between the authorities and the Palestinians.

### JERUSALEM AS AN ISSUE IN ALL-PALESTINE DEMANDS

The special status of Jerusalem, the residue heritage of the past and its being the centre of activity for both sides of the Jordan – all these combined to turn the demands to strengthen her, into an all-Palestine issue, in contrast to the demands of the other areas, which remained solely local demands.

Jerusalem became a symbol for the Palestinians, and the all-Palestinian demands concerning Jerusalem – in addition to the basic demand to turn the city into the capital – became a familiar subject, and the press, most of which appeared in Jerusalem, never tired of stressing these points.

The most striking and comprehensive expression is the memorandum sent by fourteen representatives (out of a total of twenty) of the West Bank to the Prime Minister, Abu al-Huda, in 1952. This memorandum was not published in Jordan, where only a casual note about it appeared. It was published in full in a Lebanese paper, and there is no doubt as to its authenticity. According to its signatories, the memorandum expressed the demands of the inhabitants of the Western Bank.

The demands concerning Jerusalem were as follows:

(a) The preservation of the moral and material status of Jerusalem by setting up branch offices in the city of the various ministries, which would have extensive authority to enable them to solve all the problems of the inhabitants of the Western Bank.

(b) The establishment of a special bureau for the encouragement of tourism, having its centre in Jerusalem.

(c) The execution of government projects and the erection of special government buildings, which would calm the population and renew their confidence.

(d) The strengthening of the municipality of Jerusalem, in order to improve the city and preserve its historic sites.

The memorandum demanded that Jerusalem be the administrative centre of the whole of the Western Bank and explicitly declared a lack of confidence in the authorities. It also made clear that the authorities had neglected the city and not taken care to develop it.

The timing of the memorandum does not seem to have been accidental. It was written in an interim period of government, after the assassination of Abdullah and just before Talal's abdication, when it was becoming clear that he would not continue for long as King. Serious apprehensions were rife among the Palestinians concerning the attitude of the government towards them in the future. This is why they presented these well-defined demands. Nor is it conceivable that such a memorandum could have been written at a time of a stable government, for the authorities would have prevented it and the representatives would not have dared to take such an action.

No less significant is the fact that the authorities on their part acknowledged *de facto* that Jerusalem represented the Western Bank, and they recognized Jerusalem's status as representative of all Palestine. This expressed itself at times of crisis, especially in relations with other Arab states.

In the days of tension with the Arab states – in 1959 and in 1960 – when the 'Palestine Entity' was being mooted by Iraq, Egypt and the Higher Arab Committee, and which was intended to strike out at Jordan's control of the Western Bank, the Jordanian authorities did not hesitate to stress that Jerusalem was the centre and the symbol of the Western Bank. Their reaction was to organize demonstrations in Jerusalem and to convene meetings of the government, as well as of the House of Representatives, there in order to come out with declarations, objecting to the 'Palestine Entity plan'. The Prime Minister, Majali, explicitly declared on the same occasion: 'Jerusalem is the heart of Palestine'. When King Husayn finally set up his palace in Jerusalem, in 1963, the first meeting that was held there was with the dignitaries of the West Bank.

This recognition by the authorities of Jerusalem as the centre of the Western Bank, further strengthened the image of Jerusalem as a symbol in the eyes of the Palestinians. This was enhanced further when the Palestine Liberation Organization under Shuqayri established, in 1964, its headquarters in Jerusalem.

THE JORDANIAN AUTHORITIES AND JERUSALEM IN ABDULLAH'S DAY

The annexation of Cis-Jordan created serious problems for the Jordanian authorities. Apart from having to deal with the problems of the economy and of security, Jordan also had to develop a complex government machinery, and to build up Amman as the capital of a state with three times the population of pre-1948 Jordan.

Possibly, if Amman had already been firmly established as the political centre, the absorption of Cis-Jordan would have been easier. The question and the possibility of Jerusalem's becoming the capital would have never arisen, and a single centre would have unified both banks. But as it happened, in 1948, Jordan had to build up its capital, Amman, while simultaneously annexing the West Bank. Jerusalem at times thus overshadowed Amman and created an opposite pole of attraction. The authorities were interested in Amman being the capital and went to great lengths to develop that town. Therefore they could not afford to impart a political status to Jerusalem, for this would have been at the expense of Amman and would have increased Palestinian separatism.

There was a notable difference between the attitude of the authorities towards Jerusalem in the days of Abdullah and later. Abdullah's attitude towards Jerusalem during the Mandate influenced his later attitude. After 1948 he treated the city like a second capital. He decreed that Friday prayers be held there permanently. These prayers have great political significance in the Islamic world. In order to be present at these prayers, Abdullah would spend Thursday nights in Jerusalem. He used to extol the sanctity and importance of Jerusalem to Islam and in the addition to his memoirs, written in 1951, he devoted a whole chapter to 'The praises of Jerusalem'. Abdullah paid his homage to Jerusalem in many ways. An important gesture was the appointment of the Inspector of the Mosque of Omar and Keeper of the Holy Places, with the rank of a cabinet Minister, who was to represent the King in the city. He moreover appointed former Jerusalem mayors to this post: Raghib el-Nashashibi and then Dr Husayn Fakhri al-Khalidi. The appointment of Abdullah al-Tall as governor of Jerusalem should also be regarded as a gesture of Abdullah's, for al-Tall had been popular with the inhabitants since the war of 1948.

Abdullah's assassination on July 20, 1951 symbolized in a tragic fashion the failure of his policy concerning the Palestinians in general and concerning Jerusalem in particular Understandable and striking is the fact that Abdullah was not buried next to his father's tomb in Jerusalem. Abdullah's assassination marred the relations between the authorities and Jerusalem, and marked the beginning of a new period.

### AFTER ABDULLAH

The attitude of the Jordanian government towards the city underwent a radical change. Moreover, the assassination increased the authorities' apprehensions about Palestinian subversiveness; a plan to take over the government was suspected. And since Jerusalem served also as a symbol of Palestinian aspirations, they treated the city with utmost severity.

The military forces ran riot in the city after the assassination and caused a rift in the relations between the population and the authorities.

Talal, who was deposed on August 11, 1952, had not had time to lay down a definite policy concerning Jerusalem. In the inter-regnum a marked regression occurred in the attitude of the authority to the city. On August 13 Dr Khalidi resigned his post as the supervisor of the holy sites, 'due to the refusal of the government to recognize the authority invested in him by King Abdullah'.[72] In the wake of his resignation this high post was abolished and the function was transferred to the govęror of Jerusalem.

Husayn, whose reign began on May 2, 1953, was standing at his grand-father's side when the murder occurred, and barely escaped death himself. He described the murder as 'the profoundest influence on my life',[73] and therefore, undoubtedly, remained hostile to the city. The evidence shows that he did not pray in al-Aqsa on Friday until 27.1.1960. On June 26, 1963, did the Jordan newspapers report, with emphasis, the fact that Husayn had visited the Mosque and had inspected the repairs that were being carried out there. But even on this occasion he did not pray there.[74]

The main difference between Abdullah's attitude and that of his successors, lay in the fact that Abdullah's actions concerning Jerusalem sprang from his own initiative, while his successors acted only under pressure from outside and at times of internal crises which threatened the unity of the kingdom.

The government was convened in Jerusalem in 1953 in protest against the transfer of the Israeli Foreign Ministry to Jerusalem, and this was only done under pressure of public opinion demanding counteraction. After pressure by members of the parliament a parliamentary session was also held in Jerusalem.[75]

Reacting to plans for a 'Palestine Entity', brought forward by Iraq, Egypt and the Higher Arab Committee, and which aimed to undermine Jordan's position on the West Bank, both the government and parliament were convened in Jerusalem in 1953 and in 1960.[76]

The many promises which were made concerning the city, most of which were never kept, prove the insincerity of the authorities. Some of the promises were implemented only after much delay. Husayn himself promised as far back as 1954, that he would reside part of the time in Jerusalem,[77] and repeated this promise several times, but only at the end of 1963 did a royal palace begin to be built in Beit-Hanina, a northern suburb of Jerusalem.[78]

The government, too, made many promises. Promises were made, even as far back as 1953, that government sessions would be held regularly in Jerusalem[79] and that a Government House would be erected there.[80] Occasionally it would be declared that a sum had been allocated in the budget, but no work was carried out. It should be remembered that the promise of 1953 was made under pressure of the reaction to the transfer of the Israeli Foreign Ministry.[81]

The fact that various gestures were made by the authorities on behalf of Jerusalem under pressure of crises or tensions, is also shown in a different sphere; that of the appointment of Jerusalemites as members of the government. This was particularly striking after the dismissal of the Nabulsi government in April 1957. Dr Husayn Fakhri al-Khalidi, the Jerusalemite, was then appointed Prime Minister, while Dr Amin Majaj, who had been Deputy Mayor of Jerusalem, was made a minister at the same time. This was the only time when a Palestinian was appointed Prime Minister. A similar case occurred when 'Arif al-'Arif was appointed Minister in the government of Haza' al-Majali in 1955, which attempted to make Jordan join the Baghdad Pact. At that time 'Arif al-'Arif was Mayor of Jerusalem.

During this whole period, government offices were being transferred to Amman and the status of the heads of the departments which remained in Jerusalem continued to deteriorate. This can be seen from the resignation in 1954 of the Deputy Minister for the Interior, who resided in Jerusalem; the office was then abolished; from the transfer in mid-1955 of the Religious Court of Appeal; from the removal – at the beginning of 1956 – of the Deputy Director-General of the Ministry of Welfare, whose residence had been in Jerusalem, and, finally, the transfer of the Office of the Council for Development from Jerusalem.[82]

The authorities took stringent measures whenever there were clashes in Jerusalem, and the Army that was called upon to restore order caused much bloodshed. As was mentioned above, the main clashes were as follows: in June 1951, after the assassination of Abdullah; the riots which took place after Nabulsi's dismissal, and the riots in the wake of the proclamation of the Egyptian-Syrian-Iraqi Unification Plan, in April 1963.

The harsh measures which took on the aspect of repression by an alien government, cancelled the effect of occasional gestures of goodwill. Now and again, even after Abdullah's death, the trace of an attempt to enhance the position of Jerusalem would appear. It may be assumed, that in this fashion the authorities attempted to isolate Jerusalem from the political instabilities between the two banks of the Jordan, in the hope that in the long run they would thus avoid turning the city into a symbol of Palestinian separatism and into a focus of opposition to the government.

This was brought about by stressing the religious importance of Jerusalem;[83] fostering the story of the deliverance of Jerusalem by the soldiers of the Jordanian army, in 1948; and – after 1960 – by brandishing the slogan that Jerusalem was the spiritual (and second) capital of Jordan[84] and, finally, by concentrating the festivities of 'Id al-Nahda, commemorating the Arab revolt, in Jerusalem around the tomb of Husayn ibn 'Ali.[85] This attempt, however, of enhancing Jerusalem's importance was not carried out consequentially, and was obviously not wholehearted.

One may assume that the authorities understood well that the demands made in the name of Jerusalem were actually a front for Palestinian demands, in general, for greater influence in the state. Therefore the authorities did not see much use in giving in to the demands in respect to Jerusalem, since this was not the way to get at the root of the problem of the relations of the Transjordanians and the Palestinians.

NOTES

1. At the end of the Mandate there were the following consulates in Jerusalem: Sa'udi; Syrian, Egyptian; Iraqi and Lebanese.

2. Kirkbride, 160; Bernadotte, 112; Kimche, 130. The change in the attitude to Jerusalem stands out when one compares the Takmila written in January 1951, which has a whole chapter in praise of Jerusalem (88–90) preceding the chapter in praise of Mecca and Medina, with Mudhakkirat, which was written in 1945. The latter is mostly in praise of the Hejaz, and does not praise Jerusalem at all.

3. Shim'oni, 282.

4. Enc. Britannica, ed. 1949, vol. 22, p. 1411.

5. Survey, 157, 159.

6. Shim'oni, 202–203; Abidi, 24–26.

7. Majali, 53–54.

8. Glubb, 62–66.

9. Majali, 64.

10. Glubb, 62.

11. Glubb, 118.

12. Glubb, 103–113.

13. In an interview in 1969.

14. Tall, 100–102.

15. Tall, 102.

16. Interviews with Jerusalemites in 1967.

17. About the clashes in Jerusalem, apart from Jordanian papers of the time, Hutchison 20–29; 55–59; Glubb, 332–334; Burns, 53.

18. *e.g.* in *Falastin*, 3.11.54, an article against rumours aimed at sowing fear and confusion among Jerusalemites, as though the city were in peril. Tall concludes his book (605) with the warning to all those responsible in the Arab nation and the Moslems, that danger was threatening Jerusalem. 'In this one should not depend upon the rulers of Jordan and a plan ought to be mapped out, to save Jerusalem from the slaves of the British in Jordan.' The former Mufti sent a memorandum to the government of Jordan, expressing the hope that they would preserve the status of Jerusalem and prevent the city from becoming Jewish, *Hawadith*, 14.7.52, quoted in *New East*, 13, 36.

19. Goren, 59; *New East*, 22, 134.

20. On 4.6.61.

21. On 17–26.11.52.

22. On 6–10.9.56.

23. Tall, 399–404.

24. *e.g.:* in 1953 representatives from the Arab states, Kuwait, North Africa, Indonesia, Pakistan, Iran, Caucasus, Turkestan, etc. took part in the congress. (*Difa'*, 10.12.53.)

25. Egypt decided to open a consulate in the middle of 1954 (*Falastin* 11.6.54). Sa'udia at the beginning of 1955 (*Falastin*, 22.1.55) and Iraq at the beginning of 1956 (*Difa'*, 22.3.56).

26. Concerning the financing of the riots in Jerusalem in December 1955 by the Sa'udi consul, see Glubb, 400. About the expulsion of the Egyptian consul: *Falastin*, 30.3.58; of the vice-consul, *Ahram*, 7.6.58.

27. Dearden, 191–192; *Falastin*, 27.4.54; *Difa'*, 27.7.54; *Difa'*, 29.6.56.

28. *Sarih*, 21.5.55.

29. *Falastin*, 30.6.63.

30. Goren, 158–159; Dearden, 80–81; Glubb, 292; Schwadran, 286; Eliav, 270–272; concerning the stand of Jordan, Pollak, 440–456; UN, 8.12.50.

31. Tall, 374.

32. *Mishmar*, 18.9.50, quoted in *New East*, 3, 215.

33. The Christian representative from Ramallah, Khulusi al-Khayri, objected to the meeting of Parliament in Jerusalem in 1953. The representative from Nablus, Qadri Tuqan, answered him, that this was not a question of 'to internationalize or not' (*Falastin*, 29.7.63).

From a letter from Yusuf al-Bendaq to his father Isa, who was the mayor of Bethlehem, it became clear that Yusuf supported the internationalization of Jerusalem and was in communication with circles in the Vatican (*Jihad*, 3.4.58). The letter was published by the Jordan government in order to censure the man who had fled from Jordan and who had attacked the régime.

34. Tall, 399.

35. The Islamic Conference in Jerusalem wrote, in its memorandum to the Pope on the eve of the latter's visit to Jerusalem, that rumours were being spread, connecting his visit with internationalization of Jerusalem (*Falastin*, 7.1.64).

36. *Falastin*, 11.2.50.

37. *e.g. Falastin*, Feb. 63. In this year, due to the tension, special stress was laid on the transfer of the Governor of Jerusalem.

38. See note 24. In 1960, Husayn was also present (*Manar*, 15.1.60).

39. McFadden, 19, 41–42.

40. UN 1286/a, 13–14; Dearden, 170; *Jihad*, 19.7.54; *Difa'*, 228.54; *Jihad*, 12.9.54; *Falastin*, 1.6.63; Sidham calls Jerusalem 'the capital of the Arab refugees'.

41. *Difa'*, 25.7.49; *Falastin*, 18.11.50, 12.12.50, 13.12.50; *Hayat*, 2.8.52; *Falastin*, 20.6.53; *Difa'*, 5.11.53; *Falastin*, 5.12.54; *Falastin*, 16.4.60, 10.1.63.

42. Concerning Tall and his activities, see memoirs; also Glubb, pp. 255–257; *New East*, 1, 61, 1, 216–218; Vatikiotis, 99–108.

43. Tall, 374, 367, 373, 374.

44. Tall, 372, 378.

45. *e.g. Difa'*, 5.11.54; *Falastin*, 20.11.52; 21.11.54; 11.12.54; 16.4.60.

46. *Hayat*, 2.8.52; *Difa'*, 7.12.54; 9.1.57.

47. *Falastin*, 2.12.50; 19.5.53. A demand was also made for an increase in the number of representatives from Jerusalem (*Falastin*, 27.12.53).

48. *Falastin*, 22.10.54; *Difa'*, 5.11.54; *Falastin*, 10.1.53.

49. *Falastin*, 1.6.63 – a review of municipal developments by the Mayor.

50. Tall, 372, 367, 375–8, 437–466, 581 and 605.

51. Concerning Abdullah's assassination, see *Falastin*, 21.7.51; Kirkbride, 164–167; Husayn, 1–9; for the trial which uncovers many details, see *Falastin* and *Difa'*, 19.8.51–29.8.51.

52. *New East*, 5, 38.

53. *Difa'*, 22–23.12.55.

54. *Difa'*, 29.12.55.

55. *Manar*, 16.4.61.

56. *Falastin*, 21.7.51; *Misri*, 21.7.51; *Ahram*, 23.7.51; *Misri*, 24.7.51.

57. *Ahram*, 12.8.51.

58. *Difa'*, 23.8.51.

59. *Falastin* and *Difa'*, 18–22.12.55; Glubb, 400; Burns, 127–128.

60. *Difa'*, 28.4.57.

61. *Falastin*, 13.1.63 and 11.4.63.

62. *Hayat*, 28.4.64.

63. Dearden expresses a different point of view. She suggests, 141, that many Palestinians were not interested in the transfer of the capital to Jerusalem, since they strove for a degree of autonomy for the West Bank; this being the case, they were not interested in having the centre of government transferred to the West Bank. This opinion does not stand up to critical analysis. The author obviously did not make use of source-material from the newspapers. It may even be that the authorities with whom she discussed the matters at great length supplied her with false information.

64. *Falastin*, 12.11.54.

65. *Falastin*, 12.11.54; *Difa'*, 22.2.56 and 9.1.57; *Falastin*, 22.11.61.

66. *Difa'*, 5.11.54.

67. *Falastin*, 28.7.53.

68. The Prime Minister, Samir al Rifa'i, declared that according to the law there could not be two capitals. The representative, Kamal Ariqat, answered that it was possible to alter the law (*Difa'*, 22.2.56).

69. The Prime Minister, Samir al Rifa'i, evaded the issue when he answered that Jerusalem was the spiritual capital of all the Moslems and Arabs (*Difa'*, 22.2.56).

70. *Difa'*, 9.1.57.

71. *Difa'*, 25.11.54 and 9.3.55. Hasan al-Khatib, a Transjordanian, was appointed to this office.

72. *Falastin*, 14.8.52.

73. Husayn, 1.

74. *Falastin*, 26.6.63. The item appeared on page one in a frame, with no mention of his praying. Interesting to note that the Beirut paper *Hayat* wrote also that Husayn prayed, for the reporter did not imagine that Husayn would visit al-Aqsa without praying.

75. *Falastin*, 28.7.53.

76. *Falastin*, 21.8.59 and 20.1.60.

77. *Falastin*, 31.10.54.

78. It may be assumed that the palace was built outside Jerusalem for security reasons and perhaps because of the King's personal attitude.

79. *Falastin*, 28.7.53. On the same occasion a promise was also made that a central branch office would be opened for each Ministry.

80. *Falastin*, 21.1.60.

81. The promises were made during al-Mulqi's Liberal government.

82. *Falastin*, 5.12.54; 29.7.55 and 23.4.56; *Difa'*, 17.4.60.

83. *e.g.* the Prime Minister, Bahjat al-Talhuni, *Falastin*, 19.12.61.

84. *e.g.* King Husayn and the Prime Minister, Bahjat al-Talhuni, *Falastin*, 20.1.60; and al-Talhuni, *Falastin*, 19.12.61.

85. *e.g. Falastin*, 61.1.63 and 25.12.63.

## REFERENCES

*Arabic Newspapers*
*al-Ahram* – Cairo.
*al-Bilad* – Jerusalem.
*al-Difa'* – Jerusalem.
*Falastin* – Jerusalem.
*al-Hawadith* – Beirut.
*al-Hayat* – Beirut.
*al-Jihad* – Jerusalem.
*al-Manar* – Jerusalem.
*al-Misri* – Cairo.
*al-Sarih* – Jerusalem.


*Books and Articles*
'Abdullah, King, 1945, *Mudhakkirati* (My Memoirs), Amman.
'Abdullah, King, 1951, *al-Takmilah* (My Memoirs Completed), Amman.
Abidi, A. H. H., 1965, *Jordan: A Political Study*, New York.
al-'Arif, 'Arif, 1967, *Tarikh al-Haram al-Sharif* (The History of The Dome of the Rock), Jerusalem.
'Alluba, Muhammad 'Ali, 1954, *Falastin wa-Jaratuha* (Palestine & Its Neighbours), Cairo.
Aruri, Naseer H., 1965, *Jordan: A Study in Political Development 1921–1965*, University Microfilms, Ann Arbor.
Bernadotte, Folke, 1951, *To Jerusalem*, London.
Buhl, F., 1924, 'al-Quds', in *Encyclopedia of Islam*, Leiden, pp. 1094–1104.
Burns, E., 1962, *Between Arab and Israeli*, London.
Dearden, Ann, 1958, *Jordan*, London.
Eliav, P., 1953, *Medinot 'Arav Ba-'atzeret Um* (The Arab Countries in the General Assembly of the UN) *Hamizrah Hehadash*, Vol. IV, pp. 264–277.
Esco, 1947, *Palestine, A Study of Jewish, Arab and British Policies*, Esco Foundation, New Haven.
Glubb, J. B., 1957, *A Soldier with the Arabs*, London.
Goitein, S. D., 1966, 'The Sanctity of Jerusalem and Palestine in Early Islam', in *Studies in Islamic History and Institutions*, Leiden, pp. 135–148.
Goren, A., 1954, *Haligah Ha'aravit* (The Arab League), Tel-Aviv.
Hirshberg, H. Z., 1949, 'Meqomah shel Yerushalaym Ba'olam Hamuslemi' (Jerusalem in the Islamic World), in *Jerusalem*, pp. 55–60.
Hutchison, E. H., 1956, *Violent Truce*, New York.
Hussein, King of Jordan, 1962, *Uneasy Lies the Head*, London.
Kimche, John & David, 1960, *Both Sides of the Hill*, London.
Kirkbride, A. S., 1956, *A Crackle of Thorns*, London.
MacFadden, T. J., 1953, *Daily Journalism in the Arab States*, Columbus.
al-Majali, Haza', 1960, *Mudhakkirati* (My Memoirs).
al-Mufti, Haj Amin al-Husayni', 1954, *Haqa'iq 'an qadiyat Falastin* (Truths about the Palestine Problem), Cairo.
*Mawkab al-Shuhada*, 1961?, (Procession of Martyrs).
Parkes, J., 1950, *The Story of Jerusalem*, London.
Pollak, G., 1957, *Jerusalem & the Protection of the Holy Places*, London.
*Report of the Commission on the Palestine Disturbances in August 1929* Cmd. 3550, London 1930 (Shaw Report).

276

Shwadran, B., 1959, *Jordan, A State of Tension*, New York.

Shimoni, Y., 1947, *'Arveye Eretz Yisrael* (The Arabs of Palestine), Tel-Aviv.

Shimoni, Y., 1962, 'Ha'aravim Liqrat Milhemet Yesrael-Arav' (The Arabs and the Israel-Arab War), *Hamizrah Hehadash* No. 47, pp. 189–211.

Sidham, Edward, 1961, *Mushkilat al-laji'in al-'arab* (The Arab Refugee Problem), Cairo.

Sofer, N., 1955, Hishtalvuta Shel Hagada Ham'aravit Bemamlechet Yarden (The Integration of Arab Palestine in the Jordan Kingdom), *Hamizrah Hehadash* No. 24, pp. 189–196.

*A Survey of Palestine*, 1946, Jerusalem.

al-Tall, Abdullah, 1959, *Karithat Falastin: Mudhakkirat* (The Palestine Catastrophe: Memoirs), Cairo.

UN General Assembly, Ad Hoc Committee 74th Meeting, 8.12.50, 471–473.

UN, 1950, *Question of an International Régime for the Jerusalem Areas, Special Report of the Trusteeship Council, Supplement No. a (A/1286)*.

Vatikiotis, P. J., 1957, *Politics & the Military in Jordan 1921–1957*, London.

# Revisions to Professor Brenner's article, pp.114-142

In fact the decision to establish the *Haganah* was taken at the *Ahdut-HaAvodah* conference in Kinneret in 1920 and not in 1929 as stated by me (p.114). The *Haganah* split into the *National Haganah* (or *Haganah B.)* and the general *Haganah* in 1931. In 1937 the *National Haganah* became the *Irgun*.

The leader of the 'Stern Gang', Mr Friedman-Yellin, has since changed his name to Yalin-Mor, and his name, even then, ought to have been spelt Friedman-*Yalin* and not Yellin the way I did (pp. 118–121, 128, 137, 142). Mr Ysernitsky also changed his name to Shamir, and he is now the Speaker of the Israeli Parliament (pp. 120–121, 137, 142). Dr Sheib has altered his name to Dr Eldad (pp. 120, 142). Dr Sneh has died (pp. 128, 142). Mr Galili is now a strong supporter of Israeli land annexation policies (pp. 128, 142). Mr Begin has become the Prime Minister of the State of Israel (pp. 128, 142). Mr Shertok, also deceased, had changed his name to Sharett and was for long Israel's Foreign Minister, and for a while also Prime Minister (pp. 131, 142).

Concerning my conclusions about the assassination of Count Folke Bernadotte, I must confess that my confidence has been somewhat shaken by recent statements on Israeli television and radio made by Dr Eldad (Sheib) and Mr Nadel (reported in *HaOlam HaZeh,* 9.8.1978). They claim that the decision to assassinate Folke Bernadotte was taken by all members of the 'Fighters for the Freedom of Israel' leadership. Mr Friedman-Yellin, i.e. Yalin-Mor, who is now actively engaged in favour of the establishment of an independent Palestinian Arab state in the occupied territories, has to the best of my knowledge not yet publicly denied these allegations. But then he is not in the habit of either confirming or denying any of Dr Eldad's statements. The rank-and-file of the F.F.I. were, however, at no time informed of the organisation's responsibility for this deed. The identity of the *Homeland Front* which had claimed responsibility for the deed was never established. The present implication of Yalin-Mor in this affair may well have something to do with Dr Eldad and Mr Nadel's strong opposition to Mr Yalin-Mor's current pro-Palestinian engagement (p. 137).

My statement that following the hanging of the two British sergeants by the *Irgun,* no more hangings took place in Palestine (p. 138), also needs modification. It ought to read 'Mandatory' Palestine; because Eichman was hanged in Israel, and several Arabs were hanged between 1948 and 1967 under Jordanian rule in Palestine.

*Supplementary bibliography*

The most important sources of information about the Fighters for the Freedom of Israel which have to be added to the original bibliography are the two large volumes of documentation *Lohamey Herut Israel Fighters for the Freedom of Israel: Collected Works*, Volume 1, 1959, and Volume II, 1960, Tel-Aviv (Hebrew). Another important source is Nathan Yalin-Mor, *The Fighters for the Freedom of Israel*, Jerusalem 1974 (Hebrew) and its abridged French translation *Israel, Israel . . . .Histoire du Groupe Stern 1940–1948*, Paris 1978.

The Poems of Avraham Stern have been published under this name in Tel-Aviv, 1964 (Hebrew).

Baruch Nadel published a book, *The Murder of Bernadotte*, Tel-Aviv 1968 (Hebrew). Eli published a memoir, *Recruited for Life*, Israel 1969 (Hebrew) and Zwi Tal a memoir, *Nearim BaMachtereth*, Haifa 1977 (Hebrew).
Galila Ron-Feder published a book about Stern, *Ha Mored*, Tel-Aviv 1973 (Hebrew).

The events leading up to the assassination of Lord Moyne were reviewed in the Israeli weekly *HaOlam HaZeh* 25.6.1975 (1973). The splitting up of the *Haganah* and the *Irgun* was discussed in *HaOlam HaZeh* 7.9.1977 (2088), and *Open Season* was discussed in a series of articles following a meeting of the people concerned with this (Dr Sneh, Mr Begin, Mr Riftin, Mrs Cohen, Mr Landau, Mr Shamir, Mr Livneh and Mr Yalin-Mor) in the Hebrew daily *Maariv*, April 1966. A good general description of terrorism in Palestine on the eve of the establishment of the State of Israel can be found (in English) in J. Bowyer Bell's book *Terror out of Zion*, London and New York 1977.

———————————

Y. S. Brenner